LETTERS

FROM THE

UNITED STATES, CUBA AND CANADA.

BY THE

HON. AMELIA M. MURRAY.

TWO VOLUMES COMPLETE IN ONE.

NEW YORK:

G. P. PUTNAM & COMPANY, 321 BROADWAY,

OPPOSITE PEARL STREET.

1856.

John F. Trow,
Printer and Stereotyper, Nos. 377 & 379 Broadway,
Corner of White street.

PREFACE.

The writer of these letters did not cross the Atlantic to make a book. She has no wish to enter into controversy, or to be supposed a partisan; but facts can never injure truth, on whichever side it may lie; and statements made with fidelity and accuracy ought to be welcome. To shrink from their perusal is to exclude (in the present case) one means of knowing the condition and probable future of that race for whom a deep interest is felt by the British public, as well as by the writer of these pages, however different her convictions may be from the opinions commonly maintained.

Should anything here written excite bitter feelings, or cause individual pain, the error must not be thought intentional.

A. M. M.

CONTENTS.

LETTER XXVI.

LETTER XXVII.

LETTER XXVIII.

LETTER XXIX.

LETTER XXX.

LETTER I.

THE VOYAGE TO HALIFAX.

On Board the Canada,
Banks of Newfoundland, *July* 29, 1854.

My Dear Friends,—

A week ago, on the 22nd, we left the Mersey at 11 o'clock, A. M.; but this is the first moment that head, hands, and eyes have been willing to work together for the purpose of writing. Captain Stone says he may put letters into a bag at Halifax, and that we are likely to arrive there on Monday night or Tuesday morning, so I will try to have this ready.

Good, kind Mr. and Mrs. Rathbone had exhausted every possible thought for my present and future comfort; and Mr. Rathbone crowned all by conveying me to the steamer in the *Jackal* mail tender at the last moment, that I might not spend a single unnecessary hour on board.

The sun shone cheerily, the lively breeze was but just sufficient to give a gay jaunty air to flags and sails, and no sensation, either sad or nervous, affected me, to mar the pleasant scene. I found my two companions already in the ship, and my case of plants happily established behind the wheel-house, where the steersman sits comfortably sheltered, and almost hidden from view.

I arranged my cushions, cloaks, and books on the deck, so as to make me a back of the mizen-mast, and in the persuasion that I was about to pass a most agreeable and intellectual afternoon, I

1*

sat down to enjoy myself, with Mrs. F—— by my side. I had often heard of the Bell buoy, but no very particular idea had ever been suggested by its name. In the reality, however, there was something very solemn and affecting—its deep-measured musical sound booming over the sea. It called up the first saddening thought that had yet crossed my imagination—the thought, that for how many gallant ships that had gone forth, hopeful and cheerful as our own, had it tolled a knell.

The wind freshened, the motion deepened, and in less than an hour my companion was compelled to desert me. I endeavoured to preserve a stout opinion of my own good sailorship, and opened a book, but as that demanded too much attention, I changed it for the *Illustrated London News*, of which I accomplished one column, and then tried a nap. Thus I maintained my position till about three o'clock, when no resolution would longer avail, and I was forced to call for help. I almost threw myself into the arms of the stewardess, who still asserts that I am an excellent sailor; I am willing to believe her, as I never arrived at the conclusion of most great sufferers, that it would be a mercy to throw me overboard; and on Monday I created quite a sensation among the stewards in the saloon, by appearing ready dressed for breakfast soon after seven o'clock, oblivious of the fact that eight o'clock soon becomes seven in crossing the Atlantic. However, no harm was done. I sat down, and found myself able to read through the *Illustrated News*, which had become incomprehensible to me at the second page on Saturday; and though that was the extent of my literary efforts for twenty-four hours, I hailed it as a symptom of convalescence. My friends on board were still *hors de combat*, and did not revive to an enjoyment of existence until two days later. On Tuesday, Hugh Miller's *Schools and Schoolmasters* became a source of great pleasure to me; and to-day I can write as well as read without inconvenience. There are not more than three or four English among our fellow-passengers. Canadians, Germans, French, but chiefly Americans, make up a hundred guests, entertained in the chief saloon by our captain. Not more than twenty of these are women. There are seventy-four second-class passengers besides. All are kind, sociable and gentlemanly. Three of the men were formerly known to my friend, Mrs. F——, and I am becoming well acquainted with them. It is very agreeable, as well as useful, to have some gentlemen in the party from whom we can ask and receive kind offices without scruple; and when these are bestowed by men of cultivated minds and Christian courtesy, improvement as well as pleasure must be the result of the voyage.

Sunday, July 30.—Such a lovely morning. Air enough, sun enough, sea enough. But I missed seeing three whales, and also a sight of the *Asia* steamer on her way to Liverpool, by my doubts as to the propriety of making my appearance on deck soon after five in the morning, as I did yesterday. Captain Stone, however, promised to send a messenger to my cabin door on future occasions of the same kind.

We had two magnificent sunsets on the passage—one last night and one on Thursday. I had never till now beheld the sun go down without a cloud or speck of land in sight. It was very striking. A young silvery moon stood just above us, and the scene reminded me of Turner's picture, 'The Old Téméraire.'

It seems we passed Newfoundland early in the morning, and I would have 'turned out' to see it, had I known in time. Yesterday we were on the Banks, and saw one schooner drawing up cod-fish out of the water. Some fog attended our passage over these Banks, which are so called because soundings can be made over them, while the main sea is unfathomable.

Health is now restored to the passengers. A cheerful tone of feeling pervades the saloon, where we all resort to read, write, play at chess, or whist; converse in groups or pairs, or take a sound nap in the midst of noise and bustle.

In our whole society, I do not find one person acquainted with the vegetable world, except as regards the edible individuals belonging to it. One poor lady was distressed yesterday at the apparent failure of her endeavour to cultivate, and revive a little plant of Mimulus moschatus, by sending it to the ice-house. I rescued the poor thing from the frozen regions, cut off its perished shoots, and begged its owner to give it a sunny berth with a tumbler placed over it to save the yet surviving roots from the sea-spray; but life was too far gone to recover it.

I was fortunate before leaving England, accidentally entering a bookseller's shop in Leamington, to find two interesting new publications, Hugh Miller's *Schools and Schoolmasters*, and Murchison's *Siluria.* They not only interest me deeply, but afford pleasant reading to my associates.

July 31.—The sun set in a bank of clouds, and we have had some wind and rain in the night; finding my berth close, I was on deck very early. The Captain of an American merchant ship showed me a Mother Cary's chicken which was flying just above the water near us. He gave a decided opinion that the best manner of combating sea-sickness is by determined exertion, and by getting up as soon as possible after the first attack. He says the first effort is equally great whether it is made the second day or the twentieth; he has known people keep their bed eighteen days, and suffer just as much at the end of that time in their attempts to sit upright as they could have done seventeen days sooner; so that the earlier the battle is begun the sooner it is over. This morning there is more sea than we have yet had, and I bear it well. It is expected that we may reach Halifax late this afternoon, perhaps not till eight or nine o'clock in the evening. I shall be sorry if the hour will not allow us to land; but I am told that it is a custom among the inhabitants to light up their houses when the arrival of the steamer is known, and that will be a pretty sight. In case I should not be able to add to this letter, I will conclude it now.

Yours affectionately,

A. M. M.

LETTER II.

BOSTON.

On Board the Canada.
August 1, 1854.

My dear Friends,—

My letter was put into the ship bag before we arrived in the fine Bay of Halifax, about nine o'clock last evening. An hour earlier we could have seen the town and distant country to greater advantage; but it would have been ungrateful indeed to require more, when we were already blessed by so much. An off-shore wind, soft and balmy; the sea like an inland lake, reflecting, as in a golden mirror, each little boat; brilliant paths of light, derived from moon or lighthouse, or shore lamp; a full round red sun had sunk behind the town and bay, but he left behind him an hour's twilight of crimson and gold, which had also vanished before our ship touched the Nova Scotian shore. We made a party for walking about Halifax by moonlight. The streets appear to consist of rather irregular, low houses, built chiefly of long thin boards, called 'clap-boards,' with shingle roofs. I am told these houses are painted bright colours, but it was too dark to see this. We stumbled along the dimly lighted streets, and at last took our way up a steep one, which led to the Battery Hill. From thence we had a fine moonlight view of the town and bay. We also saw the supports of the electric telegraph, and passed by-two chapels, and some trees of a kind there was not sufficient light to recognize, but my companions thought they were the Button wood (*Plata-*

nus). There was music in some of the houses—universally Scotch airs—'Johnny Cope,' 'Annie Laurie,' &c., &c. As a Scotchwoman, I felt sure of a welcome, if I had wished to intrude upon the performers. We returned to the *Canada* before she fired her guns to announce our approaching departure. The echo of these guns was the loudest and finest I ever heard, reverberating like thunderclaps all down the coast. We steamed forth about eleven o'clock, Jupiter in the east, and the whole sky bright with the brightest stars, and meteors could be seen frequently striking across the heavens. About twelve we were asleep in our berths, and I slept late; but it is a beautiful morning, so that we can walk the deck and admire the still sea and the coming shore. Our last dinner was all conviviality and merriment, everybody complimented everybody, and particularly the captain; and most of us agree it will be useless to go to bed again, certainly not to sleep, so impatient are we for the first sight of Boston, which is expected to be visible at sunrise.

August 3.—I think the Bay of Boston must be as wide as that extending from the island of Portland to the Start, in England. Nearing the harbor, I expected to see trees, but the low downs and numerous islands which surround it, though green, are bare of anything but houses. It is the finest harbour I have yet seen, and I should imagine might be made as impregnable as Cronstadt, if as many batteries were planted upon its numerous islands—*one* only, defends the entrance. I now feel as if everything round me belonged to some of the Leicester-square life-like Panoramas; my voyage seems a dream, and facts *un*real. Once in the harbour, if blinded and turned twice round, it would be difficult to say at which point we became embayed, and surrounded by the islands and capes—vessels sailing about, or at anchor, in every direction. Owing to our quick voyage, the *Niagara* (sister of *Canada*), which leaves at twelve to-day, for Liverpool, had not vacated her berth; therefore our captain was obliged to lay-to, and await her departure. We arrived about nine o'clock, and the Custom-house appeared to ignore our presence for some time; in fact, I suppose they would rather not have us upon their hands till they get rid of the other two Cunard steamers, the *Niagara* and the *Alps;* and it was an hour or two before a Tug came to take luggage and passengers ashore. This was not objectionable to me, because it gave me time enough to look about; but it was trying to Mrs. F——, who had brothers and sisters waiting to receive her, after five years' absence. The first thing which charmed me on landing was the cleanliness of the wharves, and the complete absence of sea or harbour odours. No sensation reminded one of departed miseries; in this Boston has a great advantage over Dover and Folkestone, where one is made sensible (in some degree at all times, and specially at low tide) of a commingling of mud, gas, and sewers, which is certainly not consoling for the past, or promising for the future. The Custom-house officers were civil and obliging, bothering us as little as possible; but the large number of passengers coming and going, and an avalanche of boxes and packages, made it impossible, even for Americans, to 'go ahead;' and so we had to wait for three mortal hours in the chairs they set for us, under a tolerably cool shed.

Mrs. F——'s brother, Mr. C——, then procured a carriage, and cart for our baggage, and I was taken to the Tremont Hotel, in their way to his house in Chestnut Street. I found a pleasant drawing-room for the occupation of ladies, and bedrooms for self and maid, and a kind fellow-passenger to take charge of me at the table-d'hôte. I found excellent cucumbers, boiled maize, undressed tomatoes, baked fish, and lobsters—pleasant cool diet to a person suddenly plunged into a heat beyond our most extreme dog-days. The first luxury I welcomed with gratitude was the abundance of ice—a jug of ice water placed even in my bedroom—on the table of the ladies' saloon, and everywhere at meals. After dinner, Mr. D—— was so obliging as to procure tickets for a garden, five or six miles off, belonging to Mr. Cushing, and also for Auburn Cemetery. Mr. Cushing's flower garden and houses are considered the finest in New England; but they were not beyond a third-rate or fifth-rate in our old country. The fruit-houses seemed in good order—the flower-houses not more than tolerable; I saw no plants that were not old acquaintances of mine in most of our gardens, with the exception of one, a creeping annual or biennial, which had been allowed to ramble over the flower-beds; the gardener (a young Irishman) could not tell the name of it. Its foliage and buds looked like a soft woolly convolvulus, the flowers double, each separate one, when plucked, in size and form like a flaccid pink Soapwort. The gardener told me of two pretty wild plants which had particularly struck him in the neighbourhood; from his description one might be a Saracenia, the other some species of Ornithogalon. I asked Captain Stone's hospitality for my precious Ward's case of plants on board the *Canada* till I can make the acquaintance of Dr. Gray, to whom I wish to consign them. They have flourished since their emigration, as all plants in hermetically sealed cases do flourish.

My American friend, after our visit to the garden, conveyed me to Mount Auburn Cemetery, that last resting-place for humanity, an example of what I hope, some day, to see copied in the neighbourhood of London. In feeling and taste it is really perfect. No crowding up in disgusting heaps like our own churchyards. Shade, elegance, and that stillness so soothing to the grief, the recollections, and the hearts of surviving friends—a place interesting to strangers, and not disagreeable even to the young and gay. The burying-ground of each family is as nearly as possible alike in size, all fenced off by strong but neat and pretty iron railings, with small gates; over the front of every entrance, simple surnames and Christian names belonging to first purchasers, with dates, all in iron; each family is permitted to place monuments and tombs within its own enclosure. I do not know if there is any check which may stop the exercise of atrociously bad taste; but by some means or other this must be effected, for all the tombs are simple and inoffensive, and some of the monuments beautiful. I was surprised to see that a few were protected by glass, particularly one pretty recumbent statue of a child. Nearly all the erections are pure white marble; generally low obelisks or slabs. I saw not one objectionable in feeling or in taste, and no pompous fulsome epitaphs. '*Implora Pace*' might have been inscribed over the entrance of this cemetery, without causing any revulsion of sentiment within its precincts; in this matter, certainly, the mother land may well take some hints from her child's example. As we drove away a man offered a bunch of water-lilies for sale (or rather buds which are to open to-morrow). My companion gave me three. He tells me they have long-shaped, sweet white blossoms; and the stems are very long. I saw no leaves; but it is certainly not our Thames white water-lily; this one is Nymphæa odorata. Last night the closed buds looked too firmly shut for me to see them soon open, but even before sunshine has touched them, at eight o'clock this morning, they are wide awake. I see no difference between them and ours, except that the petals are longer and more pointed, but they have a much more pleasant scent. Our drive was through a thickly-inhabited suburb, going by Brookline and returning by Cambridge and Harvard College; one country house and villa succeeding another. The architecture and elevations, and green external blinds, make them much resemble houses around Frankfort; but apparently they have arisen so fast, that there has not been time enough to ornament the gardens with flowers; a rather rough lawn, with a few shrubs, chiefly Arbor vitæ and Pinus, perhaps a tree Hibiscus here and there, was most commonly all. The general aspect of Boston, with the exception of a few of the principal houses, say, 'We have been in such a hurry, we must finish by-and-by.' But I don't dislike the appearance of the unhewn grey stone, a granite of which some of them are built. When of brick, in this neighbourhood, the colour is more pink and less glaring than ours. Soon after my return to the hotel, Miss C—— came and brought a sister, sister-in-law, and a nephew to see me; and afterwards Mr. D—— introduced Mr. and Mrs. Mills (the latter a daughter of a benevolent agriculturist, Mr. Colman, who died in England); on her return home, she kindly sent me a beautiful nosegay, and this morning Mr. D——, before his departure for New York, left me two more letters of introduction for Nahant, where I think of going this afternoon, as I find Mr.

and Mrs. Longfellow are there, and I much wish to see them; besides which, this town is like a bakery, it is so hot. I shall probably visit Mr. and Mrs. B——, at Newport, in a day or two. The cholera is said to be raging at Montreal and Quebec, so I shall not hurry myself to get there; and I shall wish rather to linger among the valleys and hills of the Connecticut River, after leaving Newport: then I am to visit the White Mountains; and my present idea is to reach Washington by the opening of Congress in December, and afterwards travel southward to Virginia, Louisiana, Florida, and perhaps Cuba. If I accomplish this tour successfully, I imagine it would be pleasant to follow the spring of 1855, northwards; chiefly for the sake of botanical researches, and then to return to Boston in June or July, when I may spend my remaining three months either in this town or its neighbourhood. Of course, my plan may be modified or changed, but it offers a prospect of much interest and amusement. Sir Charles Grey, the late governor of Jamaica, who joined our ship's company at Halifax, and is now in this house, complains of the frigidity of winter, even in the southern parts of the States, and strongly recommends me to take shelter in Florida, where he says I shall find warmth and amusement for a few weeks; but probably, after so many years passed in tropical climes, his constitution is more sensitive to cold than mine.

Boston, August 4.—A delightful day yesterday. Too tired to write my letter, and get to breakfast, much before ten o'clock. I was not dressed when Mr. Mills sent up his card. He said he would call later; and while I breakfasted, Mrs. F——'s brother, Mr. C. C——, came to me, both offering services; then came Mr. F——, Miss C——, and F——. I received a very kind farewell note from a friend (who left Boston for New York at six o'clock), with some letters and notes of introduction. My first immediate object being Dr. Gray and the Botanical Garden at Cambridge, Mr. Dwight (a former acquaintance in London), and Mr. R. C. C—— accompanied me there. My expectations were not at all disappointed: I met with a hearty welcome, and all the information, and enthusiasm for plants, I desired to find. With the intention of returning to dinner here at two o'clock, I found it more than half-past before I thought of leaving the Garden, and I then made an appointment to meet my Ward's case of plants at Dr. Gray's house by nine o'clock this morning. Upon looking over the lists, nearly all the plants I have brought are new to him; Weigelia rosea and Deutzia scabra he has, so they will belong to Mrs. F——. I learnt much botanically, and have promises of aid; the trees in this Garden interested me deeply —so many are quite new to me. One or two of them I am sure would do at Abbotsbury, particularly the beautiful Virgilia lutea. I saw such pretty mallows,—in short, I felt as if transported to the Fairyland of Flowers. Newport this week is out of the question, for Dr. Gray has proposed botanizing over part of this country with me; so we are going to have a walk to-morrow, and we are to go to Nahant, and perhaps I shall stay there a few days. I am told I shall find good sketching, and Mr. and Mrs. Longfellow and Professor Agassiz are there. We returned to the Tremont Hotel, and afterwards Mr. D—— took me to call at Mr. Elliot's, Mr. Ticknor's and Mr. Abbott Lawrence's, and then showed me the Athenæum (the finest architectural building in Boston), where there are public reading-rooms, a good library and some tolerable pictures, particularly two unfinished heads of Washington and his wife, by Stewart. I admire Alston's portraits, but not much his landscapes; perhaps those I have seen were not his best. There is a statue of Washington in the entrance which looks like a French caricature, the head thrown back in a forced ungraceful way; but there is one on the opposite side, of a well-looking man—celebrated here but unknown to me, so I have forgotten his name,—an evidently truthful resemblance; it sits in an easy contemplative attitude, with an expression of countenance so very like the venerable Mrs. Fletcher, of Grasmere, that I could fancy him her father. Our dinner-hour was long past at the Tremont Hotel, but I got something from a long printed bill of fare, which is struck off each day, and some refreshing lemonade. I remember reading somewhere, that English people, who are used to good servants, must make up their minds to be indifferently waited on in America, but at present here I should rather complain of being too much attended to. The waiters seem innumerable, and at least two are constantly on the look-out to find out the requirements of a guest. I mentioned three times this morning that, having been supplied with tea and rolls, and broiled salmon and broiled mackerel, I required nothing more, but still an attendant was always at my elbow in two minutes after I had civilly dismissed him; and as board, and I believe all payments, must be included in the five dollars a day for self and maid, their attentions are not individual affairs. C. F—— came at seven o'clock to conduct me to his aunt's family tea. I found his mother in the midst of brothers, sisters, nephews and nieces, in a room with a verandah, vine-embowered, and the bunches of grapes hanging thickly above it,—a cheerful, pleasant party of young and old, we remained together till past eleven o'clock, when my host, Mr. E. C——, and his sisters walked back with me, about half a mile, to my hotel. The air was pleasantly warm and balmy; only one individual crossed our path, but I heard the persevering cricket grating away from many an Althæa frutex, which forms the principal ornament of the tiny gardens before most of the houses.

Saturday, August 4.—Here am I—I don't know where! for I am writing the first thing in the morning, and such was my interest and pre-occupation and delight at the wholly unexpected beauty of this place last night, that I did not ask its name. Imagine scenery more like Mount Edgecumbe than anything else I ever saw or heard of in Great Britain; only with few ships on the sea. Pines and cypresses, and shrubs of the (to me) rarest description, growing down to the very margin of the picturesque jagged shore, with grey and red porphyry rocks starting up on all sides, even from the very door of Mr. L——'s charming cottage, —Cherokee-roses and honeysuckles on the verandah; various plants and shrubs, and even blackberries new to me, one with a delicious fruit, something between blackberry, mulberry and raspberry in flavor (*Rubus villosus*, high blackberry), rambling over the grey boulders, and in front a sea studded by islands.

In the evening there was a glowing sunset on the land side, Jupiter, amidst the eastern constellations, shining over the bright calm sea; imagine also the air just freshened by a shower, and you may form some idea of the enjoyments I had in a moonlight walk with Dr. and Mrs. Gray last night. But I must try and give some rational account of how and why I find myself somewhere near Beverley, in the United States, instead of at Nahant. This place is called Glencove, and the one adjoining, where Mr. L——'s son lives, is Burnside. I find it difficult to write, and even to dress, the view from my bed-room window is so attractive. The pleasure ground below, upon a rough hill, which descends rapidly to the sea, is sprinkled over by apparently upheaved granitic boulders, interspersed with Pinus rigida, Junipers, a large shrubby white-leafed honeysuckle, fine fruiting rubuses, roses, and various kinds of wild flowers new to me; the shore, with occasional dark masses of volcanic strata bursting through the rocks; a bay dotted by islands, some with buildings on them, and one having a tall lighthouse; ships and little boats sailing about in all directions; a long promontory stretching to the south between this place and Nahant; the weather warm enough to have windows wide open all night, and yet not the least oppressive; with all this to distract, you may wonder that I do get dressed soon after seven—the breakfast hour of my hospitable entertainers.

I must go back to the time when R—— and I left Boston yesterday morning. We drove to Dr. Gray's soon after nine o'clock, my purpose being to open the Ward's case of plants with him, and then to proceed to the hotel at Nahant to stay a day or two. I found Mrs. Gray, who was absent yesterday, had kindly come home to meet me. She and her husband, whose acquaintance was my first wish in America, and whose scientific knowledge can only be exceeded by his kindness, had prepared a pleasant surprise for me by arranging with her father and Mrs. L—— for my reception here. They proposed my accompanying them, after he had facilitated my trip to Nahant, to visit Mr. and Mrs. Longfellow, and to make the acquaintance of Mr.

D——'s brother and sister-in-law, to whom he had given me a letter of introduction. He drove back to Boston, and I made my first American railway journey for a few miles only, as far as Lynn. I found the long gallery carriages comfortable and airy, the communication from one part of the train to the other complete and easy, and although passing across the streets and roads without tunnels or barriers is rather alarming, yet, as the engines have a large bell, and great boards are placed all across with notices to look out, and not cross while the bell is heard, I suppose that individual caution may avoid a smash; but sad accidents do sometimes happen. Two young ladies driving in an open carriage near this place, last year, being interested in their own conversation, were thrown off their guard, when a train came upon them. One was killed on the spot, and the other never recovered the shock.

I found a gigantic ugly hotel at Nahant marring the beauty of its situation: it is a great boarding-house brimming over with company. I was received by Mrs. C. D——, who engaged Dr. Gray and me to dine with her at the public table, at four o'clock, and directed us to Mr. Longfellow's residence. We had passed the cottage, about a mile off, in our drive from Lynn; so we got into the carriage which brought us, and, in pouring rain, retraced our way. We were cordially received by Mr. Longfellow, though Mrs. Longfellow had not received a preparatory note, which had been forwarded, immediately upon our landing at Boston, to their house at Cambridge. After a short stay, he was so kind as to walk with me; and in a heavy rain he held an umbrella over my book, while I made a sketch of the rocks and bay. I thought several times, with alarm, how I should answer to the world if I were the cause of Mr. Longfellow catching his death! particularly as he would go on in wet clothes to dine with us at the hotel; but he assured me a brother was there who would let him take measures of prevention, and I was too happy to make a sketch honoured by such company and conversation. So it was done in spite of rain as heavy as one of our heaviest thunder-showers in England, and I did not lament that my thin muslin dress was fairly soaked. But on reaching the hotel, Mrs. D——'s Welsh nurse (a Glamorganshire woman from near Cowbridge, who knew about all my friends there, and in consequence gave me sea weeds she had preserved) afforded me the means of becoming tolerably dry before dinner. This is the largest hotel I ever saw. When quite finished it will accommodate five hundred guests. It belongs to the same proprietor as Tremont House in Boston. I did not inquire the dimensions of the dinner-saloon, but I imagine that three of the size of the Kursaal dining-room at Homburg might be contained in it. I sat between Mrs. C. D—— and a gentleman to whom she introduced me: Mr. Longfellow joined us after dinner. I was happy to see his coat was changed, a fact which, in some measure, relieved my mind of the fear that I might be answerable for his death. If Dr. Gray had not so obligingly prepared the way for my escape to a residence more accordant with my tastes and pursuits, I doubt whether even the vicinity of friends could have reconciled me to a stay of more than one night at Nahant, though Mr. and Mrs. R. W—— (he an old acquaintance in England) sent me a kind offer of the use of their sitting-room and carriage; but a few hours was enough just to glimpse at the humours of the place, where I suppose a large number of the busy and the industrious come to enjoy relaxation and idleness. I ought to add that I was introduced to Chowder, a most praiseworthy preparation, enabling you to eat soup and fish at one time.

The rain had now subsided into a thick fog. Dr. Gray and I got into the Carry-all I had kept waiting to take us back to the railway station; and in half an hour we arrived at a picturesque valley surrounded by rich woods and tumbled-about sienitic rocks. Here Mrs. L.——'s carriage (driven by a man who had lived with the late Lord Camden) met us, and in a few minutes we reached Glencove. Its rare beauty was an unexpected surprise, for Dr. Gray had only promised me a quiet botanizing nook. His father and mother-in-law, with Mrs. Gray, received me with great kindness Mr. L.——is in the legal profession. A few years ago, when seeking repose and rest from over work, he accidentally stumbled upon this place, purchased it from the farmer to whom it belonged, and built his comfortable cottage, and one adjoining it for his eldest son, who is at present travelling in Europe with an invalid brother, having left a wife and three nice children at home. Mrs. Gray is staying with her, as well as a lady, who promises to induce her husband, a sculptor and an artist, in Boston, to come here. Besides a little boy and girl in this house, Mr. L—— has a large family of grand-children, belonging to another married daughter, near at hand. Another of my acquaintances at home, Mr. F——D——, lives within a short walk. After my arrival here, the weather was so obliging as to clear up, and I had a delightful scramble to the Eagle rock, where I yesterday made a sketch, for I am now filling up my letter on the 7th. Saturday, was a day of enjoyment. We breakfasted soon after seven o'clock. Perfect weather; not too hot; so that after wandering about the grounds, Dr. and Mrs. Gray, and Mrs. L——, took me a drive to see two lakes (or ponds as they call them here). Essex Pond is an almost exact counterpart of the Lake at Long-leat, only surrounded by more extensive forests, and with others larger, in its neighbourhood. I sketched it, and afterwards Hamilton Lake from a distance, for we spent so much time in botanical researches, that we could not attempt to go farther. I gathered about forty plants quite new to me, and was particularly pleased to find the Pontederia cordata, which we prize so much in the fountain at Abbotsbury, and the Rhexia virginica growing at the edge of the water, with quantities of the pretty little rare English plant Eriocaulon septangulare;—it is such a pleasure and advantage to have the company of a botanist like Dr. Gray to give me at once the names of plants new to me, instead of spending perhaps hours in seeking them out. Among the most beautiful of these new acquaintances was Spirea tomentosa, a pink shrub, Osmunda spectabilis, and Leucocarpus conyzoides, and I was much pleased with a sweet Gale, larger and handsomer than ours, and quite as odoriferous. But I must add a list of plants to this letter, for those who care about them—though certain friends of mine will only be bored by their long names. We got back just in time to go and dine at Burnside with Mrs. W. L.——. The view from her verandah and windows, looking accross the bay towards Marblehead and Salem, and over Mr. L.——'s garden, with a rocky cove below and the islands scattered about, was lovely beyond description. I have made a sketch which does not do it justice. Yesterday we went to church, about three miles' distance. The service was well conducted; the congregation large; no signs of poverty; the people looking well-to-do, and even rich in appearance. The edifice very plain: all grey inside; behind the reading-desk and pulpit a large globe, painted in fresco, with clouds around, appearing as if being dispersed by the sun rising behind—emblematic of course, and pleasingly executed: the roof went up into a large kind of open tower, finished at the top by a simple large white flower; blinds upon each window outside; a good organ; the singing well conducted; the hymns pretty. The minister preached, not extemporarily, from the text, 'We must all appear before the judgment-seat of Christ.'

After dinner, Dr. Gray and Mrs. L—— took me to walk in a wild wood, chiefly of hemlock spruce and Weymouth pines; both are more beautiful here than they are in England; and the bold massy sienitic rocks, many of them covered by various-coloured lichens, among which were Tripe de Roche and Umbellicaria vellea, with its graceful black wreaths; the ground was tinted by Reindeer moss, with its soft bluish grey; which with the bright scarlet berries of Comus Canadensis, dark-leaved Pyrolas, Gaultherias, Linnæ borealis, twining in amongst them with white pipes of Monotropa uniflora peeping up from under rare ferns, and elegant Vaccineas, formed a foreground which, for softness and variety of colouring, exceeded aught I ever saw even in Scotland. In the forest we met a son-in-law of Mr. L——'s, Mr. J——, botanizing with three boys, the youngest not more than seven, yet all appeared to take an eager and intelligent interest in the pursuit, and each was loaded with a splendid bouquet, from which they showed me a pretty new Asclepias (*incarnata*). Having now three strong arms to carry us through difficulties, Mrs. L—— and I got down a steep descent in the wood, and in a little opening below, we gathered Onoclea sensibilis, Osmunda spectabilis, and Veronica scutellata. I must finish this abruptly, as Mr. L—— tells us our letters must go now, to be ready for to-morrow's post to England. Mrs. B——'s communication of August 3d, that she would send to meet me on Saturday last, has only just arrived. I now propose to go to her at Newport on Thursday. Lord Elgin also writes that the accounts of the prevalence of cholera are exaggerated, and proposes to receive me at Spencer Wood, near Quebec. I think of going from Newport, through the Valley of the Connecticut, to the White Mountains, and thence by Lake Champlain to Montreal; but I shall probably send off another letter from Newport.

Yours affectionately,

A. M. M.

The sketching here is very interesting.

August 9.

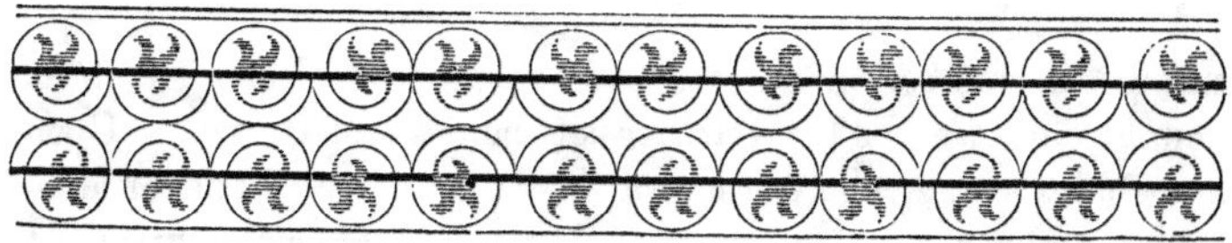

LETTER III.

NEIGHBOURHOOD OF WENHAM LAKE.

GLENCOVE, *August* 10.

MY DEAR FRIENDS,—

I am rather tormented by what are here called mosquitoes, but they are not a bit worse than our gnats and midges and harvest-bugs; indeed, I doubt whether I could have frequented woods and bogs in England for as long together as the time I have passed these last few days in the forest, and by the sea and lakes here, without being more devoured; and as to really venomous reptiles, I have not stumbled upon one: indeed, I have seen nothing disagreeable belonging to the animal world, and only one little dead snake, not much larger than our slow-worm, and, I am told, harmless. I hear of humming-birds occasionally on the honeysuckles, but it has not been my good fortune to see one; indeed, I have observed very few birds. There were two or three yellow linnets, like canary birds, in the Botanic Garden, and I heard one little warbler in the morning from my window, but he sings very sparingly. The railroad is audible at times. I can hardly believe we are so near to the business side of life, from the quiet tranquillity immediately around; though we can see towns on the distant shore, and vessels of all kinds on the sea.

Soon after breakfast this morning, Mr. L—— took up Mrs. W. L—— and me, driven by Mr. E——, to see Wenham Lake (or pond). It is a fine sheet of water, clear, and pure looking, about four miles round the banks; easy of access, and at each end are a number of wooden ice-houses; a railroad has been brought close up, for the purpose of easy transportation. Upon the pebbles at the edge of the water, we found two little opaque-looking, oblong eggs, supposed to belong to a small turtle. I sketched the lake, but found few flowers, though, on our way home, we gathered Solidago Canadensis. After dinner Mr. and Mrs. L—— took me to call upon their daughter, Mrs. J——, and upon Mr. and Mrs. D——, who have houses about a mile on the shore towards Beverley, but I think not quite so prettily situated as this cottage. In the evening, I wrote letters. We breakfasted at seven o'clock, as Mr. L—— went early into Boston. Sketched out of doors, after paying a visit to Mrs. W. L——, who accompanied me with her cousins, Mrs. G—— and Mrs. L——; and Dr. Gray returned to dinner: afterwards, Mrs. L—— drove with me to Mr. M——'s, to see Mrs. F—— and Miss C——. Quite a surprise to me to find them so near. It is such a clear night, with a bright moon lighting up the islands. Three lighthouses are visible from these windows—Baker's Island, Boston, and Marblehead; the last only a revolving light.

I forgot to mention that Mr. S. C—— gave me a very curious animal production, a kind of elegant little vase, about two or three inches across, the colour and substance of fine grey cloth, edged in scalloped plaits, which were very gracefully formed out of sand and an adhesive substance. It is supposed to be the work of some kind of cockle by the sea-shore, for the purpose of catching and confining its usual food. Much care will be necessary to carry this fragile curiosity safely to England; and I am doubtful how to preserve my two little turtle's eggs; they are too solid to be blown, and I propose to varnish them, which, perhaps, will prevent their destruction. Mr. Forbes (the gentleman who so nobly distinguished himself during our Irish famine, by undertaking to freight a ship with provisions and carry her across the Atlantic) dined here. He considers himself to have some descent from or connexion with our Murrays in Scotland, and we are quite ready to acknowledge the relationship.

Thursday, August 10.—Mr. L—— provided two Carry-alls

to convey a pic-nic party to see Eagle Head, a fine porphyry bluff about seven miles distant. Mrs. W. L—— took out her fine good-humoured baby-girl, not seven months old, and she seemed to enjoy the expedition as much as any of us. In our way we passed through a bright, white, and clean-looking upholstery manufacturing town, called Manchester, the strongest contrast to our black, dirty-looking Manchester possible. The factory young men looked like smart London tradespeople, and the women were equally well dressed. I have only seen one ragged-looking body in these parts, and that was in Boston. He was supposed to be a recently imported Irishman. This part of the country looks rather sterile and unproductive, in an agricultural point of view; more thickly sown with picturesque rocks than corn, and therefore at first it seems a miracle how the population can make themselves so comfortable, and their general appearance to be that of people well to do in the world; but they have plenty of employment in various handicrafts. Between this place and Beverley, and towards Wenham, there are numberless tidy-looking small shoe-workshops—many shoes are made all through the neighbourhood; these workshops are distinct from the residences of the shoemakers, who reside in houses all made of wood, but of a comfortable size. One sees no very small cottages. I have met two or three people who say they have come over from England to make a little money, and mean to return there.

The views all around Eagle Head are fine; numerous indentations and islands on this coast make it so picturesque. We lunched on water-melon and cakes; and, after spending two or three hours very pleasantly, returned home. Our party consisted of Mr. and Mrs. W. L——, Dr. and Mrs. Gray, Mrs. G——, Mrs. L——'s brother, Mr. E——, two young girls, and the baby. Mr. L—— was taken away by the unexpected arrival of a party of workmen for the construction of a ram, which he was obliged to superintend. After dinner Mr. W. L—— proposed a row on the sea by moonlight; all the ladies except myself were afraid of the undertaking. The tide being low, we were obliged to be drawn into the water by a horse upon a low truck, and the difficulty of sticking to it when the horse made his first effort to drag the machine out of deep sand was considerable. We returned safely, however, without paying any other penalty for the experiment than getting rather wet.

Friday, 10*th*.—After breakfast, Mr. L—— walked with me to Sunny Bank. I sketched, before leaving, this pretty place. Mr. L—— showed me the difference between common maize and sweet corn. The latter appears to be only more delicate than the former. It is very good, when the corn is young, served up simply boiled, to be eaten with butter and salt. By the four o'clock train I left Glencove with Mrs. G——, Mr. and Mrs. L—— seeing us off. It was more like parting from old friends than from the acquaintances of a week; I had found myself so pleasantly at home among them. We reached Boston about six o'clock, when I was introduced to Mr. G——, who met us at the station; and Mrs. G—— took me home with her to Ashburton Place; I found a nice house, belonging to her mother, with every comfort; and in the evening Mr. and Mrs. G—— took me to call on Mr. and Mrs. Abbott Lawrence, where we passed a pleasant hour, talking over English matters. Next morning early, I went with R—— to Tremont House, to unpack my baggage and arrange it for future use. From ignorance of hotel customs in this country, I had left my trunks with the hotel authorities; and they charged me during my absence as if my boxes had eaten and drank, so that my bill was more than forty dollars, though I remained so short a time in the house, and only had two small bedrooms there; but payments are made for rooms, not for board or attendance; and whether an individual person or an individual box, eats or not, the same money is paid. Mr. G—— took me to his studio, to see an interesting design for sculpture. The subject was a shepherd boy: he is supposed to have carried off a young eaglet, and to be attacked by the mother bird. She has alighted upon the shoulder of the lad, who, borne down in a stooping posture, seizing one wing of his assailant, grasps in his right hand a knife, with which he is prepared to defend himself. This idea is expressed with great force. I did not admire

Chantry's statue of Washington at the State House; it is wanting in character. The one at the Athenæum is better; but neither of them satisfy the imagination as much as Stewart's unfinished heads of Washington and his wife in the Picture Gallery. Among the sculpture there are several busts by native artists, which would, I think, be considered fine in Europe. There was a bas-relief by an elder brother of Mr. Greenough, now dead, a sketch of which I fancy to have seen somewhere in England. At the house of his sister I saw another work by the same artist; two children—the one as an angel leading the awakened soul of the other, with an inscription below; very pretty.

Mr. B—— had advised me to start by the four o'clock train for Providence to take the Newport steamer; I was agreeably surprised by the pleasure of Mr. G——'s escort and company the whole way: he was so obliging as to make the discovery that he too had some friends to visit, and this added much to the ease and the interest of my journey, which was longer than I expected —three or four hours by rail, and at least twenty-five miles up an arm of the sea to Rhode Island. It was dark before we reached Newport, but I found Mrs. B——'s eldest son and Mr. B—— awaiting our arrival: they conveyed me in a carriage about two miles to their villa, which, as it has no name, I shall call Ocean Cliff. The sea view has only some small islands to break the expanse of water; so, if it were possible, one might see as far as the South Pole. The high ground between this place and Newport is studded by villas; fine rocks, which look like limestone, edge the points and bays of the shore, and just below, black coal-looking bluffs crop out into the waves: last evening I walked to look at them, but I understand there is no fear that the smoking chimneys of steam-engines, or the black produce of the earth, will ever mar the beauties of this shore. The next morning after my arrival, young Mr. B—— drove me out in what is here called a wagon, a four-wheeled kind of dog-cart, with very high light wheels (wheels very general round this country, but such as I have only seen attached to velocipedes in England), drawn by a spirited little horse, having the same good quality which I also observed in the larger one belonging to Mr. L——, that of standing patiently when left to himself; in this respect horses are better trained here than with us. When we were wandering about for an hour or two, the carriage could be safely left, with the reins only slightly attached to some gate or paling, and the horse, though powerful and spirited, never seemed to have an idea of walking off. I asked the English groom how this was taught, but received no other explanation than that they were trained to it; and a great convenience it is. One sees butchers' carts in London standing unguarded at houses, but I never found that carriages could be safely left, particularly with the temptations of green fields and trees in every direction. We drove by Newport to the bathing sands, where gentlemen take charge of ladies in the surf: it was to me a very singular and amusing scene—numerous carriages, drawn up before a semicircle of small bathing-houses, containing gaily dressed occupants, who had taken their marine walk, or were waiting for the ladies, young and old, still frolicking about among the waves, children dancing in and out, gentlemen handling about their pretty partners as if they were dancing water quadrilles, and heads, young and old, with streaming hair dipping in and out: it was very droll, very lively, and I daresay very amusing to all engaged. No accident has ever occurred here, for the bay is protected by capes on each side, and the water is shallow for some distance out. A white flag is raised during the hours appropriated to ladies, and it is succeeded by a red one, later in the day, when gentlemen take possession of the shore on their own account. The scene resembled that on a race-course in England. I made a slight sketch from the hill above: it was unique in its way, for I believe there are few places, even in America, where the sea would be safe for such an experiment: and even here the aid of strong arms is at times very necessary to save ladies from being knocked over by the waves. There was considerable surf to-day, but, from the numbers who breasted it, I suppose the courage necessary for the undertaking is not so great as it appears to me. I should look on a long while before I could try this kind of experiment.

Sunday, August 13.—I went to the Episcopal Church, which was built during the English occupation here; Berkeley, Bishop of Cloyne, presented a good organ. The service was well read: our Liturgy, with only an occasional change, which I thought an improvement. The sermon, preached by a Mr. Cook, good in matter and in manner, and ending at the right moment—not spun out so as to weaken its effect: as it was neither commonplace nor dry, I did not think whether it lasted for twenty minutes or for fifty minutes, and I really do not know what its duration may have been. The subject was Christ's command to 'follow him,' and the moral deduced was, that the experiment of obedience, if fairly tried, will never fail to convince the sceptic, and to strengthen the believer. Dinner was at three o'clock; afterwards, Mr. G—— joined us in a walk to the shore. Tea was ready when we returned; a beautiful moonlight, starlight night. Mr. Lawrence, an English artist, walked in; his crayon portraits are much liked here, and with good reason; they are true, pleasing, and spirited. I much admired a sketch of Rogers, done just before Mr. Lawrence came from England last spring.

I see nothing like timber upon this island. Mrs. B—— showed me a little bit of primeval forest yesterday; it appeared to consist of hickory and sassafras, low, thick, and scrubby; but the English are accused of having destroyed nearly all the natural wood during the revolutionary period. The Gulf Stream touches this shore, which makes a mild and genial climate, though I am told that sharp winters here destroy myrtles and pomegranates, which flourish upon our south-western coast, while a warmer summer sun ripens fruits that fail with us. I must, however, try to introduce an excellent vegetable into England, which is called here by the name of Okra. I have not yet seen the flower expanded, but the plant looks like some kind of Hibiscus, with a long green fruit, which makes a delicious ingredient in soups; it is softer and more gelatinous than asparagus, and when young and tender is cut in slices: it is an annual, and perhaps will not ripen seed with us, but is surely better worth raising in hot-houses than French beans. I will get some good seed by and by; this and the Rubus villosus would both be good introductions; there is a high variety of the latter, which might, I think, be cultivated in our warmer gardens, like raspberries; the fruit is in size and colour between the blackberry and mulberry, and I think much better than the first, and much more certain than the last, though the flavour may not be quite so high as that of a really good mulberry. I am surprised that it has never yet been cultivated in England. At six o'clock this morning, a thick fog, which ended in rain and a fine day.

There are people this side the Atlantic who, as new acquaintances, are very pleasant. This morning I have been introduced to Mrs. and Miss B——; they sympathize about flowers and stones, which is rare in this country; and they are not the least stiff or cold. When people are cultivated and warm-hearted, I soon forget and forgive their habits of making all our vowels double, and even the nasal tone of some among them. There is a genuine characteristic frankness here which is very pleasant. There is no reason why we should treat our fellow-beings that happen to be new acquaintances, with less kindness than dogs or horses. I am afraid this is a fault in our national character. I believe we are honest and sincere, and that is better than mere surface politeness; but we lose so much time in our cautious civilities, that in some cases life is half expended before we dare exchange mere acquaintanceship for a warmer feeling. The Americans, who are a go-ahead people in all their concerns, appear to me to carry their hearts in their hands; this is very pleasant to a stranger coming suddenly among them; and it is difficult for me to 'realize' that it is only fourteen days to-morrow since I landed on these shores, so many homes and hearts upon it have already been opened to me. Perhaps I shall find a difference in other places, and I may have been particularly fortunate in my first acquaintances. There is certainly great beauty and refinement of feature among the mass of the people, but it is accompanied by a fragility of look which raises painful feelings. As far as I can judge at present, this is owing partly to hereditary causes, partly to actual habits. The excitement and anxieties of business life in a new country probably entail constitutional delicacy upon the children of parents so eagerly occupied, and the sedentary city education and pursuits of the young of the last and present generation, unfavourable to out-of-door interests and amusements, do not harden, and strengthen the nerves and muscles. I am already tempted to controvert the assertion of American ladies, that their generally delicate health is to be attributed to climate. They may have severer winters and warmer summers than ours, but these are accompanied by the advantages of less damp, and of brighter sunshine. I have not had an hour too warm for exercise during any part of the day, for though the sun is brighter, it does not always beam so furiously as with us. The climate of Massachusetts seems to me a charming one, and I believe another generation will discover its merits, because I entertain hopes that the children now growing up will acquire more hardy habits. The evil I am speaking of cannot be remedied in a day; and I find American ladies are at this moment so little informed with regard to natural productions, and so unfitted for country pursuits, that their ignorance of these matters is at once the evidence and the cause of their lack of physical strength.

Newport, *August* 15.—I was introduced to about thirty new faces yesterday. Among them the Governor of New York. A pleasant acquaintance; he gave me much geological information, and promises to forward my seeing Albany, &c., to advantage. I took a walk on the shore just below this garden, and was much interested, as well as a good deal puzzled. My little geological knowledge is quite at fault; sand and quartz rocks, coal and limestone, and they say granite beyond; this seems to me a jumble. I suppose it will be reduced to order by and bye. After dinner Mrs. B—— took me a distant drive, up the island, to call on Dr. and Mrs. Howe: the doctor's name and benevolent deeds have long been familiar to me. We found also, visiting them, a nephew of the late Dr. Tinkerman,* and Mr. and Mrs. Carlton,† descendants of Lord Baltimore. Dr. Howe has bought a cottage in a pictu-

* Tuckerman?—*Am. Ed.* † Calvert?—*Am. Ed.*

resque valley, about a mile from the sea-shore, and is busy making walks and opening out views; his children will benefit in health and tastes. The sun set before we could tear ourselves away, and so we got home in the dark, and broke an engagement to drink tea out; but Mrs. and Miss B—— came here instead, and we had a pleasant evening. Miss B—— will come soon after eight to-morrow morning, to take me to the rocks; she is the only active young lady I have met with!

August 16.—After an early breakfast, Miss B—— took me to Newport, to get an American trunk to pack parcels; and in coming back we went to see the pretty view from Mrs. B——'s house, and after carrying home our purchase, we drove to Mrs. C——'s villa, which is built close to a shore of fine granite rocks. Several lady visitors were with Mrs. B—— before I came away. Soon after one o'clock I called for Mr. G——, who accompanied me on board the steamer, where I had the pleasure of meeting Dr. and Mrs. Howe. The Doctor went on with us to Boston. Dr. Gray came to Ashburton Place, and promises to go with me to-morrow, as far as Lake Winnipiseogee, ('Spirit of the Waters,') which I am to see on my way to the White Mountains; from thence my proposed route to Canada is by Burlington and Lake George. Although so much is said about cholera, Lord Elgin mentions that there is great exaggeration. Rain is prophesied to-night, and it would be better to have wet before my next journey, to lay the dust. There has only been one showery day since my arrival in America, a fortnight to-day; it seems more like two months than two weeks—so many new ideas have been crowded into the time. The *Canada* sails to-morrow. I have had no news from England later than the morning I left Liverpool; and probably my letters have gone to the care of Lord Elgin. No time for more to-night.

Yours affectionately,

A. M. M.

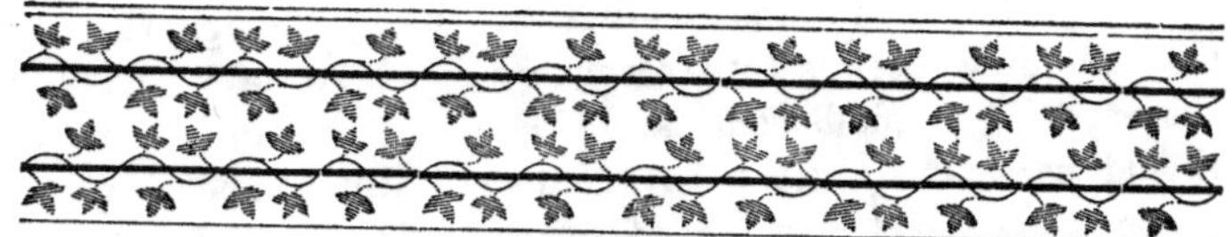

LETTER IV.

SLAVERY QUESTION.

Boston,
Wednesday, August 16.

My dear Friends,—

My last letter will go by the *Canada* this morning, if possible (as the train by which we travel towards the White Mountains does not start till afternoon). I shall try to see Captain Stone before he sails. Mrs. G—— is gone to Sunny Bank, so I miss her here; her sister received me, Mrs. L—— being confined to her room by illness. I am told that after leaving these Northern States, I shall find the country, and the people, and the habits, much less English; here the shade of difference is very slight—certainly not greater than a difference of institutions necessitates. A supply of excellent water is so abundant in Boston (derived, I am told, from Lake Cochituate, forty miles distant,) that by six o'clock in the morning I see the servants belonging to houses watering the pavement before the doors with a long hose, as we should water our gardens; and the house-maids, with those clean, convenient, light-looking Shaker brooms, sweeping away the dust. I do not know any one of our towns (not even Bath) which exceeds this in purity and neatness; and, as there is a great deal of cholera abroad, in coming through the streets the other day, I found them perfumed with hot vinegar. I was told a carriage full of that fumigated liquid had been driven smoking through the streets. There are deaths every day here, and some at Newport; but it is not believed to be contagious at present, only carrying off the profligate and the debilitated. I hear, though, that tho deaths at New York last week, among a population of five hundred thousand only, equalled our usual bills of mortality in London. I should particularly dread any epidemic falling upon a people which, as a general rule, looked so over-worked, and fragile, and thin as these Northern Americans. Dr. Howe says it is climate; as yet I am incredulous upon this point. My friend, Mr. L——, confessed he was almost in his grave when, eight years ago, he bought his pretty place. Now, with the revivifying influence of his farm and garden (although he does not entirely give up his legal duties), he looks as strong and healthy as any sexagenarian upon our side of the Atlantic. I should like to transplant all the sick dyspeptic men and women of New York and Boston into gardens and fields, before I will admit that this pleasant climate is to blame. I am rather inclined to assert that mental excitement, and money-making, and sedentary employments are the real criminals, and that something is due to the laws of inheritance even in this unentailing country. Till my introduction to the Governor of New York, I did not know that each State has a Governor. Governor Seymour lives at Albany. Some of these Governors are only elected for two years, and this gentleman does credit to popular choice.

What is likely to be the effect of the Nebraska Bill upon the Slavery question? Some intelligent men appear to think it is as much a political catch as some of those divisions in our House of Commons which are rendered nugatory by after divisions; and that it has roused the feelings of the enlightened and liberals, who consider the question as one merely of time, a disease requiring only the treatment of wise and not too hasty physicians,—perhaps this apparently retrograde step will ultimately hasten the desired change. One kind person, who is a planter, told me he has no other wish than to see his black children able to use the gift of themselves, which few deny to be their right, if they can use it; but, like our Colonies, they must become men in experience and intelligence before they can take care of themselves, and I am already inclined to hope that the 'Legrees' are as much exceptional beings, as idle and profligate landholders among ourselves. In saying this, I know you will not think me upholding Slavery; Christianity will and must subdue it—not by teaching us to vilify and persecute those less fortunate of our brethren who have had the curse of human possessions entailed upon them—but by enlightening the darkened, and instructing the ignorant; and even (if that should be necessary) making such property valueless in a commercial point of view. No individual selfishness, and no political intrigues, can prevent the wished-for consummation; and I firmly believe there are few, very few, even in the South, who will not hail with joy the moment of emancipation—a movement at present delayed by doubts and fears. This is my first view of a vexed question; I may alter it—I may change it altogether; but in the meanwhile, such as it is, I give it.

Yours affectionately,

A. M. M.

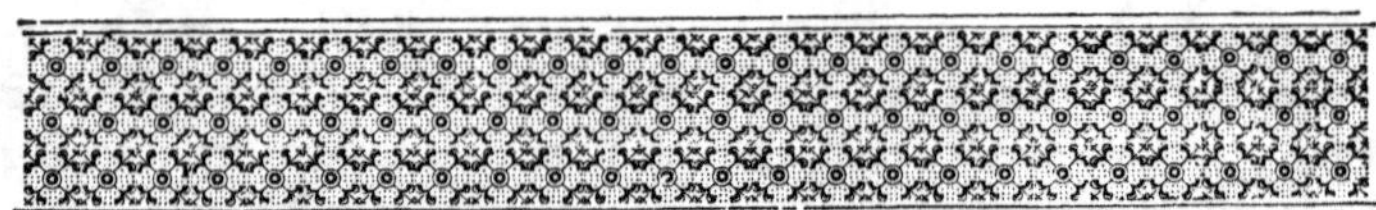

LETTER V.

THE WHITE MOUNTAINS TOUR.

ALTON BAY, NEW HAMPSHIRE,
August 17.

MY DEAR FRIENDS,—

Owing to a mistake about the railroad hour, I am here, instead of at the most frequented end of Lake Winnipiseogee, in what is considered a wild village; but this simple little hotel called Winnipiseogee House is clean, and much more comfortable than any out-of-the-way Scotch inns I ever was at; and it is well to see here a specimen of the wonderful industry of this people—railroads down to the very water. I forgot to mention that before we left Boston, Dr. Gray took me to see Faneuil Hall (Huguenot name), built, as a public gift to the town of Boston in old times, by a merchant. It is the place where the first public meeting was held during the Revolution; and there is a large picture of Webster speaking in Congress upon the Nullification question. It is well painted for its purpose, and the portraits are considered like. I afterwards made a sketch of the oldest house in Boston, now a shop, the date 1683. Rather before two o'clock we left in the railway cars for Winnipiseogee. The line goes through a country much resembling English park scenery; glades and woods and single trees, sugar maples, red maples, hemlock spruce, Weymouth pines, black, white, and red oak, with creeping juniper, and occasionally wild vines, which associate ideas of high cultivation with the landscape in an English mind, from such things not being indigenous in our country. We passed through towns and villages called Charlestown, Somerville, Edgware, Malden, Melrose, Reading, Andover, Haverhill, Newton, Kingston, Exeter, Newmarket, Durham, Dover, Berwick, Portland, Rochester, New Durham, and Alton, and these following, as I have written them, to the utter confusion of English geography. Among them were some Indian names, much more beautiful and appropriate to this country. Swampscot, Cochego, Scournamagowie (how like Scournalapich, in Ross-shire), Agawam, &c., &c. At Dover, after passing the Miramachi river, we changed cars, and entered a branch railroad for Alton Bay. This was very slow, as it stopped at several stations for mercantile purposes; and though we left at five, we did not arrive till after eight o'clock, having been more than three hours going about twenty-five miles; but the route was pretty: sometimes cut through a drift of sand, containing boulders of granite, with large plates of mica, it occasionally reminded me of the forest of Fontainebleau, but without fine timber, this forest being all young; no trees looked older than thirty or forty years. We had a hospitable welcome; clean rooms and beds, charges moderate. Here, for the first time, I see hand-lamps in which a mixture of camphene and alchohol is used; it burns clearly, and gives a pleasant light. This camphene is chiefly manufactured from turpentine collected in the pine woods of North Carolina.

August 18.—Before breakfast, I sketched the lake, &c., from my window. A large quantity of wood lay about in all directions, for the purpose of supplying the car engines and lake steamers with fuel, wood only being used: the railroad carriages are never called by any other name than cars; they are more like movable galleries; in some respects I prefer them to carriages; they are more airy, and the seats, holding two all down each side of the centre, are roomy and comfortable. A cord runs along the middle of the roof, by which the driver may be communicated with; it is out of the reach of children: there is a conductor, who walks backwards and forwards between the long cars, which I imagine convey from sixty to eighty passengers in each; these are occasionally refreshed by an Aquarius, walking with his little fountain of iced water, distributing it liberally at the cost of the Company. Even this small and not very much frequented place has not only a railroad which takes one down nearly to the landing-place, but also a branch off it, to convey wood. Certainly, Americans are very purpose-like and industrious, and I have as yet met with nothing but what has been polite, with the exception of the unintentional rudeness of two or three country people here, who established themselves at the window listening to our conversation, and asking for my sketch-books; but it was in the simplicity of their hearts; they meant no ill, and were only doing as they would be done by. Here I was sorry to part with Dr. Gray, who kindly came so far to put me in the way of American travel; but he first drove me in a 'wagon' about two miles' distance, to see an extensive view of the lake, which must be from seventy to eighty miles round, with deep indentations, and numerous islands thickly clothed by wood; which, not being of a size to pay for transport, is left undisturbed. I did not observe any of them to be inhabited.

I am rather pleased that our mistake about the train from Boston caused us to come here instead of to a place called the Weir; as from hence I shall go the whole length of the lake, instead of only about twelve miles to Centre Harbour, the point from which I am to visit the White Mountains. In going up the hill I saw a fine paper birch. Those trees are numerous here, and Dr. Gray took off some sheets for me to draw upon: it is prettily shaded, and easily takes either pencil or colour; being both tough and soft, it comes off in layers. I can easily imagine how the Indians make canoes and all sorts of things of it; the tree is handsome, with larger leaves than ours has, and a still whiter stem. I found, too, the high blackberry, a handsome shrub; and a witch hazel, different from ours. Upon a beautiful spot overlooking the lake, we came to a house, deserted by its inhabitants about a year ago. The doors and windows were still perfectly good, and of a size far beyond a cottager's abode in England. In a week I could have made it comfortable enough to live in. A boy told us the owners had built one larger, and in a more sheltered situation. The first steamer had departed just as we returned, and it was four o'clock when Dr. Gray entered the train, to return to Boston. R—— and I went on board a very comfortable, clean boat called the *Dover*. There were not many people on board. One American gentleman, who had been in England, Scotland, Ireland, and apparently all over the world, came and talked to me, and then presented his card before landing at Wolfsborough. At first the lake reminded me of some of ours, but it soon widened out so as to be on a grander scale; and, with its numerous islands and mountain background, I thought it exceedingly beautiful. It was twilight before we landed at Centre Harbour, the sun having made a glorious setting. We found a very comfortable hotel here.

August 19.—Early this morning, I went with Mr. and Mrs. T—— and a party, in a kind of *char-à-banc*, which held nine, to Red Hill, so called from the brilliant color of the foliage late in the year. I refused to drive up the ascent, and therefore paused at a small farm to draw. The family consisted of a grandmother and several sons, with a married daughter and children. The old woman was very obliging; she let me taste a cheese she was making, and gave me a seat at the door, where there was a beautiful view. The daughter soon came down stairs; she looked delicate, as almost all American women do; and I was amused at the simplicity with which she informed me she should like to take a pattern of my gown, as it was exactly what she wanted; so I gave her leave to get her paper and scissors for the purpose, and she accepted my permission quite as a matter of course. This evening I saw seven or eight cows driven by the owner, who occupied a gig. He was a respectable looking man, with a good horse, which he drove, *ad libitum*, first on one side the road, and then over the turf or into the ditch on the other side!

After considering different routes, I am inclined to go by Conway to-morrow to the Notch, instead of Plymouth. I got a yellow Geradia to-day, on the Red Hill; it is a beautiful plant; perhaps it is Geradia quercifolia.

August 20.—*Centre Harbour.*—Last night I made acquaintance with a brother and sister of a gentleman who came over in the *Canada;* we determined to go on together by the Conway House route to the White Mountains in a kind of *char-à-banc* we are to hire for the purpose, instead of proceeding by coach to the Weir (another place on this lake), and there taking the road for Plymouth. We arrived at the Conway House before three o'clock, having been long in making the journey of thirty miles, owing to a very hilly road, nearly all the way through deep sand. The drive was hot and dusty, but very beautiful, through woods and by lakes; one called Long Pond, another Six-Mile Pond, &c I could have supposed myself in Scotland, in the neighbourhood of Loch Awe, or the Garry Lochs, had it not been for the paper birch, sugar maples, &c., &c., and the undergrowth of shrub oak —a very pretty shrub, which I have not before seen. There were no horses to take us on, after our dinner at Horace Fabian's house, therefore, we must make up our minds to go very early to-morrow (Sunday), so as to get to Crauford House, at the Notch, White Mountains, by one o'clock.

We left Conway this morning, August 20th, at six o'clock, in a very comfortable open carriage, with three horses; such a beautiful drive! The country resembles Braemar, near Invercauld, but is still finer, as the mountains are higher and the foliage is more varied. We passed the Willow-house, out of which an unfortunate family of nine persons fled, a few years ago, to avoid a slip in the mountains. The house was untouched, and these poor people were buried alive by the falling stones a short distance from it. We arrived at the hotel in good time; I found some acquaintances there, and was induced to accompany them in a *char-à-banc*, drawn by six horses, to the summit of Mount Willard. Having once embarked in the undertaking, I was ashamed to insist upon being let off; but the ascent was really a tremendous one for any vehicle whatever; and how we ever got safely up and down again, is a marvel to me. This house is full of people, but all is comfortably arranged. I like one American plan, of paying for inn accommodation; no bill of items is ever given. The payment is at the rate of three or four dollars a-day, and there is an end of it. This saves much trouble and time. Dining is not cheap at those hotels; but those who keep them for the convenience of travellers must have a certain sum; and what does it signify whether this is charged for wax candles or for bread and butter?

August 21.—A party went off this morning by eight o'clock to ascend Mount Washington on horseback, and perhaps to spend the night there; but I resisted all temptation to join it, having quite enough to amuse and occupy me below. Another beautiful day—beautiful for us, but not for the poor farmers, who feel the present drought. Most of the streams and waterfalls are dry; but we are ready to compound for some loss of picturesque effect for the sake of the charming weather. Yesterday I ate sweet potatoes at dinner; they taste very like chestnuts. Such things are not grown here, but come from the South. I find extreme civility and attention from all the waiters and attendants in the White Mountain hotels. On the whole, my impression of the American people has been hitherto far more agreeable than I expected. One gentleman, at Centre House, held forth upon the backwardness of England, and about her institutions having been stationary for the last two hundred years. I asked him whether he had ever visited the country, and upon his allowing he had not, I advised him to defer making up his opinion until he had had a fair opportunity of judging. I do not think his notions were sympathized with by those who were around us. The everlasting rocking-chairs among the ladies make me quite dizzy, and give me a sea-sick feeling: and the custom raises an idea of want of rational occupation, without even the doubtful satisfaction of a '*dolce far niente.*' The broad English farmer-like pronunciation is also unpleasant to English ears; but good-humour and the laws of kindness have prevailed wherever I have yet been, united to a higher general intelligence than among the majority of our population. The difference between us appears to be that our higher classes have more principle, elegance, and refinement; the women more energy and activity, and the men more athletic amusements; while our middle and lower classes are less highly educated, perhaps rather more narrow minded, and physically, work harder; although, in some respects, I think the Americans wear themselves out sooner, particularly those occupied in manufactures or mercantile affairs. The race and the appearance of horses is an example which runs through everything here. There are none so perfect as our most perfect; but the animals generally go better, and are better fed than second or third-rate horses in England. I had a pleasant walk with Mr. T——, who was very kind in helping me over difficulties, and patient in waiting while I drew, or hunted for plants. I found Trilliums in seed, and the roots of some kind of Epiphyte, and a beautiful little creeping evergreen (*Chiogenes*) on the rotten trunks of trees; many other forms were new to my eyes. The party who went up the mountain have returned, excepting one lady and some gentlemen, who determined to pass the night in a little hotel there, to see the sun rise. All were much fatigued, and a storm of wind and a foggy morning disappointed those who had adventured an uncomfortable night.

August 23.—My acquaintances invited me to join a party of ten in an open *char-à-banc* to go on to the Profile House, about twenty-five miles, at Franconia. We started as soon as Mrs. P—— came down from Mount Washington, about three o'clock. The drive was beautiful, just our Highlands upon rather a greater scale as to forests and torrents; with mountains about the height of those around Braemar. Smoke rose in all directions from the burning trees. We passed close to one of considerable size, which was on fire at the bottom, with flames creeping up the trunk and peeping out of holes. It was dark before we reached the Profile House, an hotel built, as usual in this country, upon a very large scale; the saloon or drawing-room I should imagine at least thirty-eight feet square, and the dining-room sixty feet long. There are probably eighty travellers accommodated here at this moment. Streams of visitors usually succeed each other for about three months; but during the rest of the year few people come to this mountainous district. After breakfast to-day, our party set off in the *char-à-banc* with four horses, to see the waterfalls and the Valley of the Flume; passing by the mountain Profile and lake. A legend is attached to the latter, which says, that all who rise early enough may see the old man of the mountain take his bath in the lake. The scenery round the Flume House is so fine, that I mean to remove there, five miles from hence, to-morrow; and I shall join an American acquaintance, Miss F——, who has been much in England, and who likes drawing and rambling as much as I do. I shall be the more willing to exchange my quarters, as the friends I have travelled with from Lake Winnipiseogee return to their homes at Boston to-morrow. This afternoon we rowed upon the Echo Lake, and heard all its reverberations of horns, and cannon, and voices, which are very clear and distinct. It is a 'pond' of no great size, but deep—very deep. Before tea I walked to Profile Lake to finish a sketch, and look for flowers. I found a very sweet and pretty yellow Utricularia, quite new to me, growing at the edge of the water; and I also picked a copper-coloured cotton-grass to-day, near the Flume House, besides a beautiful little creeping plant in the woods. To-night, the forest is on fire upon a mountain just above this house; the sight is grand, but rather terrific. These fires are believed to arise from carelessness, or, perhaps, occasionally from some spirit of wanton mischief. They can only be extinguished by heavy rain; and now the underwood is so very dry, much damage may be done. I suppose the flames we have been watching may be at two miles' distance; but if the wind should rise and drive them down towards this hotel, I should be alarmed for its safety; being erected entirely of wood, sparks falling upon it would be very dangerous. For some days past we have observed these forest fires in many directions. Sometimes they are intentional, to make clearings, but in general they are regretted; and I feel grieved at the destruction of the beautiful trees and underwood which thirty years' growth cannot replace.

As the weather continues so enjoyable for mountain exercises, I propose to remain at the Flume till Monday next; then, probably, we shall take the railroad, ten miles from thence, and visit

Lake George, if I hear that Mr. T—— is there; or else I may go by Montreal to Quebec, putting off the Falls of Niagara until after my return, as I am told that brilliant autumn tints will add to the picturesque effect, and if possible increase the splendour of Niagara. This evening a German gentleman played on the piano in the large room, with the usual taste and musical knowledge of his country, and some young ladies and gentlemen waltzed quietly and gracefully. All the travellers I fall in with are civil and obliging. I have not had as yet the least reason to complain of want of attention from either master or servants. I am told I may be less fortunate as we travel further west or south; but hitherto none of my own little preparations or conveniences against travelling difficulties have been in requisition; the only thing I miss is good household bread. There seems to be no such article in use; nothing but new soft rolls and biscuits, and buckwheat cakes, which are so like our pancakes, that I mistook them for something of that kind. So much for eatables. As to drinkables, I have hardly observed any one gentleman or lady take any other beverage than iced-water, milk, or tea. It is said that all classes of men make great use of brandy, but I have not seen any of it drunk; and as to smoking, it is not more general here than in England. It is not made half as disagreeable as in Germany.

Yours affectionately,

A. M. M.

P. S.—This letter will be conveyed to Boston to-morrow morning. I have not any time to read over what I have written, therefore repetitions are probable. I have little chance of hearing from England till I reach Canada, and the month since I left it appears four times as long, from having already seen so many new faces and fresh places. Very little public news has reached me, and I feel anxious about the Baltic fleet, particularly as I hear that cases of cholera have occurred on board the *St. Jean d'Acre.*

LETTER VI.

PLEASANT RAMBLES.

FLUME HOUSE, WHITE MOUNTAINS, NEW HAMPSHIRE, U. S. *August* 25.

MY DEAR FRIENDS,—

I came here yesterday from the Profile House, in one of the usual *char-à-bancs ;* some friends went the other way on their return home, but I found all my new *compagnons de voyage* obliging and agreeable. As the distance was only five or six miles, I requested to be left to sketch rocks and a waterfall by the roadside, about half of that distance, where the mountain-torrent has worn the granite into a singular bowl. After trying almost fruitlessly to give some idea of the place, I enjoyed a pleasant walk through the still and tranquil forest, with a sense of the most perfect security. No fear of Indian tomahawk, or wild or uncivil or riotous human beings; not a reptile of any kind to prevent me from going into the bush and bog after flowers; even bears are now hardly ever seen in these woods, though it is said that one has made its way to a patch of corn near this house. I think there is no positive proof that some tamer animal was not the marauder. When I reached this hotel, I found R—— comfortably settled, and my things in a pleasant room with a verandah, looking upon an extensive view on two sides. I have both windows wide open all night, without feeling any draught, though I sleep between them; and yet I have felt no heat so oppressive as that of a warm summer's day in England.

August 26.—Yesterday, I much enjoyed the fine scenery. A

lady who has passed some time in England went out to draw with me; and after dinner, Dr.—— and Mrs. B——, both kind and pleasant people, accompanied us in another ramble. What is called 'the Flume' is very fine; and the water being so low, there is no difficulty in walking up the bed of the torrent. Enormous tables of granite rock, apparently without a flaw for twenty yards together, bed the stream in an easy ascent to a rocky gorge, where an immense boulder, almost circular, hangs suspended overhead, jammed in between two cliffs. How fine it must be, when the water roars down this chasm! though a drought now enables us to see the channel more completely; and at another point called the Dell, a steep descent brings one down to a pool of twenty or thirty feet in depth, clear as crystal; here, a rude boat has been established by an old man and his wife, with their son; for this little emerald-coloured mountain 'tarn' is of sufficient size to paddle about in it.

The larger drawing-room in this hotel, is fitted up with every comfort, and there is an excellent piano. The evening party was large, perhaps from forty to fifty; an elephant well manufactured out of two bipeds walked in to amuse the children; one of the house-attendants played quadrilles very fairly on the violin; two sets were made up for dancing; some young ladies also sang in tune and very sweetly together. Attached to both this house and the Notch, there are bowling-alleys under cover, where ladies and gentlemen can take exercise and amusement in wet weather. On the whole, I doubt whether in England as large and heterogeneous a society accidentally gathered together, would conduct itself with so much good humour and propriety as that which I find here. All converse without introduction, yet I have seen nothing like forwardness or vulgarity of manner: though there is a *degree* of restraint and stiffness, I find myself much more at home than I should be in any hotel, either on the Continent of Europe or in the British Isles—it is more like the freedom of a very large country-house in England. This peculiarity of American manners I have never heard mentioned—and it is certainly a striking one. I hear the gong going its rounds to awaken the sleeping, as we breakfast at seven o'clock, and at as early as six a gong is sounded; the same custom prevailed at the Profile House, which belongs to the person who has this hotel also. I go to bed at nine or soon after, and get up with the light.

August 26.—We had rain yesterday, the first which has fallen in this mountain region for three months; and it gave me an opportunity of seeing how a wet day is got through here. After breakfast, there was a great deal of agreeable music, to which the whole company listened with enjoyment; two or three young ladies and one gentleman sang duets and trios and lively songs very well. Afterwards, a large party adjourned to the house appropriated to bowling: there are three alleys, and slides for the return of balls; the game was played with sides: it is a good exercise. After joining in one game, I left them, the weather having rather improved, and went out with my umbrella and sketch-book,—as I was anxious to see a view overlooking the house. I got drenched, but succeeded in my wishes, and after dressing, I went down stairs to a comfortable wood-fire in one of the smaller parlours. Before tea there was some needlework going on, a whist-table (but no one plays for money here), and a young lady played nursery songs at the piano, six little children belonging to different visitors joining their voices in the choruses, one as young as four, but all were in tune, and seemed to enjoy it much. After tea, there was again music and dancing, and I played a rubber of whist with two gentlemen and a lady till bedtime. One of the gentlemen had lent me a Boston paper containing the last news from Europe, by which it appears that the Island of Aland and the Crimea are both under attack. Some of the people here are Southerners, and two families have black nurses.

These mountains attract visitors from all parts of the Union, and I have no doubt the summer meetings—either here, at Newport, Nahant, Saratoga, or the Virginia Springs—tend much to promote acquaintanceship and good feeling among the different States, which vary so much in their internal laws and regulations. Bigamy is severely punished in nearly all, while polygamy has been hitherto not only permitted but encouraged among the Mormons. Yet I am told that the Mormon delegate to Congress is thought a sensible and intelligent man, though he has seven wives! but it seems to be hoped that much time will not elapse before the immorality and absurdities introduced by Smith and Young, and hitherto enforced upon their deluded followers, will be cast off. At present their polity is a kind of spiritual despotism; yet it is generally admitted that their community is orderly and very industrious; though as no man can leave his property to his children or relations, it falls to the church upon his death, and the accumulation of such riches must strengthen the power of the priestly Mormons, and enable them to keep their people in subjection for a considerable time to come. I do not yet understand how this accumulation of property is to be applied.

August 27.—There is a chapel here, which is used if any clergyman who is travelling can do duty; but that not being the case to-day, service was not read. No church is within an accessible number of miles. After dinner, two or three families, consisting of seventeen individuals, went away for the purpose of sleeping to-night at Plymouth, twenty-five miles distant, to catch a railroad there early to-morrow, or, as it is here expressed, 'to meet the cars.' Nearly all the travellers and inmates gathered at the door to see the party off, and to wish them good-bye, although many had met here for the first time in their lives. Greater cordiality and kindness of feeling was evinced on this occasion than I ever saw before among people so new to each other. But I am told that in hotels in and near great towns, there is little of that frankness and cordiality which have so pleasingly impressed me at the White Mountains.

The weather was again fine to-day, and in the afternoon I walked alone up the Flume. It is the bed of a torrent which comes down a very picturesque defile: now, while the water is low, one can walk along the wide, smooth, granite tabular rocks, which during the winter are covered by the foaming waters. I never saw such huge masses of granite before: it is very white and large grained; and as I saw no mica, I suppose it may be sienite. When I returned home, some of the people had got what they called a hedgehog, just caught in the woods; I did not see it very near, but as it was the size of a small pig, I concluded it must have been some species of porcupine.

August 28.—This morning Miss F—— and I got to the top of Pemmewhasset, a mountain above this house, from which there is a charming view up and down the valley of the Saca. The ascent was gradual and easy, but we did not reach the Hotel again till long after dinner-time; and though we met a party going up on horseback, we did not regret having trusted to our own feet, which is much pleasanter than riding, and enables one to look after plants, besides which, I feel more safe, and by sitting down frequently to rest, the fatigue is not very much greater than on horseback. After our return, the weather cleared sufficiently for me to see an extensive view of the valley from my window, which has hitherto been hid by smoke and clouds; and I made a sketch from the verandah. The coach brought many more visitors, among them a Mr. and Mrs. C——, from the South, who will go on with me to-morrow as far as Plymouth, and I am by and by to try if I can visit them at Appalachicola, in Florida.

August 29.—I proceed this morning after breakfast, at eight o'clock, for Burlington, going round by Plymouth instead of Lyttleton, to avoid returning ten miles by the same route which brought me here; and I thus see the Saco valley, which I am told is beautiful.

August 30.—*Wells River, New Hampshire.*—This is so pretty a place, that I determined to stop here at three o'clock yesterday, and go on to-morrow by the eleven o'clock cars, which will reach Burlington by five. I have a letter to the Bishop of Vermont, who lives within a mile or two of that place; it is on Lake Champlain. The weather is again perfect. I spent all yesterday evening walking about and sketching. The people here vie with one another in kindness and civility, yet I have been troubled with nothing unpleasantly obtrusive. From the Flume House we came hither in a coach, with six active horses well driven in hand. It carried eighteen passengers, nine inside and nine outside. The road, through deep sand, runs nearly the whole way by the River Saco, the same we passed at Conway. I am told it flows into the sea somewhere near Portland, and that this valley is not that of Merrimac, but Saco. The Merrimac river is the outpouring of Lake Winnipiseogee. We had observed it flowing by Dover, &c., as we came from Boston; it is a handsome river. Mr. and Mrs. C——, from the South, and six other ladies, all agreeable people, were my companions in the coach to Plymouth. We dined there; they took the cars for Boston, and R—— and I for this place. A smaller and a larger river unite here; the Indian name of one is Ammonoosuc. I hope I may find out the translation of it, for these Indian names have always some beautiful meaning. The two railroad stations are almost close together: one is called Woodsville, and another Wells River *dépôt*—the word used in America. The hills around, well wooded, but with openings and rocks enough to be picturesque, are tossed about in every direction. All this country is called granitic on Marcou's geological map; but we passed through a cutting yesterday which looked more like something Silurian; it might have been a mica schist of some kind. The breakfast hour here is half-past six; and before I start for Burlington by the eleven o'clock cars, Mr. Wild, the master of this Wells House Hotel (he was born and brought up in the White Mountains, between the Notch and Profile Houses), offers to show me the rapids of the Connecticut River.

August 31.—*Burlington.*—I had a pleasant, though hot and dusty journey here yesterday. Notwithstanding the frequent changing of cars, which occurs sometimes four or five times in a distance of about 120 miles, I prefer the American mode of travelling in long cars, to that upon our railroads. I have as yet seen no great carelessness, except that of crossing the roads with no other warning than large boards overhead, on each side with a notice to 'Look out for the Engine,' in large letters—(about Boston '*while the bell rings*' is added); and it is the duty of the fireman, or the conductor, before and after passing every crossway, to ring a large bell, which swings above his head; but from Plymouth here, I have heard none of these bells. The long cars, which on an average carry sixty each, are comfortable; you may turn two seats so as to face each other; and tnough they are intended to accommodate two or three each, R—— and I, by taking possession in time, have always been left to ourselves; and even if you have a dirty or disagreeable neighbour, it is not half so bad at any time as the Rhine steam-boats—for no smoking is allowed in these cars. They are very airy, and have comfortable seats. There is a sense of security, too, in the greater width and solidity, and the power of ready communication with every part of the train. I may change my opinion, but hitherto I have found travelling in the American cars less fatiguing than in our railroad carriages.

I gained some information from Mr. Wild, in our walk to the rapids before leaving Wells River. R—— and I set off with him about half-past nine o'clock. When we got to the descent through thick forest down to the river, she was obliged to give up the attempt, having got some flowers for me, and too much in her hands for the scrambling necessary. Between the drought and the fir-choppings, it was so slippery that even Mr. Wild fell two or three times in giving me assistance; and I was often obliged to take to my hands and knees, from not being able to keep upon my feet; however, I got down to the edge of the river. The Connecticut widens out here, looking almost like a lake, and then rushes through such a narrow gorge between rocks, that an active hunter might leap his horse from one side to the other. In winter, it must be a fine rush; at present, the river is so low that it can get through the passage quietly enough. I find that three rivers meet at this point. I thought there were only two. I suppose, therefore, 'Three Rivers,' which I found marked upon a map I have, is the right name of the place.

We returned only just in time for the eleven o'clock train; and as there is no other for Burlington, to have missed this one would have been inconvenient. I never had such a beautiful drive as that through the whole country to Lake Champlain. As far as White River junction, it follows the Connecticut for fifty miles, and then the White River. The scenery may be compared alternately to that of the Tay, the Tweed, and the Tamar, but still finer than all; with gardens, ornamental trees, relieved by maples now getting their scarlet liveries, foregrounds of maize and brilliant orange pumpkins, and every now and then a column of white smoke rising from the forest fires. These Vermont Mountains are not higher than those around Blair and Invercauld, so that they never rise into the gigantic peaks of the Swiss Alps; but they are very lovely.

On reaching Burlington, though nearly dark, the master of the hotel provided me with a safe little carriage to drive out to the Bishop of Vermont's, about two miles' distance. I found him with his family, and received an obliging invitation to spend the next day with them. There is not much to be seen at Burlington. I have heard of its beauty, but, with the exception of the lake, it seems a sandy, uninteresting place,—the lake itself looking like a sea; and it would take seven or eight hours to steam rapidly down it. I find myself in a comfortable, large hotel, well provided in all respects. At ten o'clock, I walked with R—— out to the Bishop's. I did not see a great many flowers on our way, owing to the vegetation being so burned up; but I found fine trees of the black oak, covered with acorns with large bumpy cups: the 'pigeon grass' (so called here), and a pretty little vetch. I made a sketch of the lake, and of Burlington, from the Bishop's verandah—a fine eagle soaring about as an accessory to the view; and, after an early dinner, we walked down to a beautiful little rocky bathing bay, where the children disport themselves in the water without the least fear or danger. Growing among sand and rocks, a pretty Iris in seed. Whether unknown in England or not, I cannot tell; but in going through a rocky copse, I gathered a fern, and several things new to my eyes; and on the shore I picked up some fresh-water shells. I understand there are rattlesnakes in one or two spots in this neighbourhood, but it seems they have so large a bump of 'locality,' that they remain as constant to particular spots as flowers to their habitats. So that, unless one goes to visit them, there is no danger of making their acquaintance; therefore I shall always inquire their whereabouts. I did not take my leave till near eight o'clock at night.

September 2.—*Quebec, Spencer Wood.*—As I left Burlington in the steamer, to take the cars at Roches Point, by four o'clock in the morning, arrived at Montreal by eleven, and left for Quebec at seven in the evening, I had no time for writing, yesterday. Dr. L——, the professor and a clergyman, was so obliging as to take me a pleasant drive round the heights, from whence we had a fine view of the St. Lawrence River and the neighbourhood. I visited the Roman Catholic church and the Museum, where I saw some stuffed specimens of the wild beasts which are now becoming extinct in the woods of this part of Canada. I saw also a specimen of a small owl which is peculiar to these parts.

Before seven o'clock we went on board the steamer, which was very full of passengers for Quebec. Among them a party of squaws and Indian boys from some tract bordering upon this great river: they had a large assortment of neat and showy handiworks in beads for sale—gentlemen's travelling caps, bags, slippers, and watch-cases, and seemed to be very shrewd and cautious in carrying on their bargains, though I could not make them understand either French or English. I do not know when they '*absquatulated*' (to use a Far West expression), but as we stopped several times during the night, and I did not see them afterwards, I suppose they landed somewhere. We did not undress. As some individuals of our large party in the ladies' cabin were talking or moving about at all times during the night, we could only get snatches of sleep in our berths; and I thought this night's voyage so tiresome and tedious, that with the first dawn of light I went on deck; but owing to the great width of the river, and the steamer keeping in mid-channel, we were not close enough to either shore to make her progress interesting. I think the St. Lawrence is nearly as wide as Ullswater is long, and it is difficult to realize that we are traversing a river instead of crossing a lake. I saw very little shipping till we arrived at Quebec—a few lumber schooners, at anchor here and there, but nothing sailing; very different this from the liveliness of the sea around Beverley and Salem.

The population of Quebec and Montreal, upon a first inspection, does not look so well-to-do, and thriving as that of Boston and some other American cities; this may be partly owing to the prevalence of Roman Catholics here, just as one finds it in Europe. Where that persuasion has the ascendency, the people are either stationary or retrograde; and in Quebec, there are more churches and more beggars than in any other place I have yet seen on this side the Atlantic. Indeed, I never met a beggar in Boston—not even among the Irish; and ladies have told me they could not find a poor family on whom to exercise their benevolent feelings. We arrived at this place by breakfast time: it has a thoroughly English appearance, with a splendid view of the St. Lawrence from the windows.

Lord Elgin tells me this is the day for the letters to go, so I must conclude hastily; and, as there is rain, I shall probably do little more to-day than stay in-doors and rest myself.

Yours affectionately,

A. M. M.

LETTER VII.

QUEBEC.

Spencer Wood, Quebec,
Sept. 2, 1854.

My Dear Friends,

I suspect that the end of the letter which I sent off yesterday, just after my arrival, was dated the 3d instead of the 1st: my notions about days and dates are rather confused, from having been very little in bed since Wednesday night. I find now that my letter written a week ago from Wells River, to fix the day of my coming here, never reached Lord Elgin: the American post-office does not appear to be as exact or as well-regulated as ours. I hope you receive all my packets? I think this will be the fifth or sixth letter I have sent off. I generally write about one a fortnight—but not a line from you yet, or from any one in England, excepting a letter I have got from Mr. S——, dated August 2nd; but despatches from home are expected to-day, and I hope to get something. This morning, at seven o'clock, it is still thick and rainy—I cannot even see the St. Lawrence from my window; and all day yesterday we had a large coal fire. September is considered the last of the summer months in Canada; and with the leaves still green, the weather looks and feels, at present, very like a mild November in England.

This is a large house, with a good conservatory, and handsome reception-rooms, though they are considered low for their size.

The fields and turf look as green as in England—the first bit of fresh-looking grass I have seen these three weeks. At Montreal there was not the least appearance of verdure, and very few trees, even immediately about the town, though the villas and the hills are well wooded. I found that place prettier than I expected; but it must be an uninteresting residence, as there appears to be but one drive around the hill at the back. A bridge on the tubular principle, which will be the largest in the world, is begun; it is to unite the town with the railroad over the St. Lawrence; I was told that 1600 workmen are already employed in its construction. It is the undertaking of an English company, and may vie with our Crystal Palace in the enterprise and skill it will call forth.

Lord Elgin is much occupied just now by the opening of the new Canadian Parliament, on the 6th; and of course the party spirit, and agitation, and jealousy which the reform and enlargement of that body have excited is unbounded. Every one wants to do and to be everything; and though to an impartial stranger it is a difficult matter to comprehend what these people would be at, yet it is interesting to observe the efforts of a young nation to make use of a newly acquired power. It resembles the first attempts of an infant to exercise its legs—eager, awkward, and almost alarming, though necessary and salutary to gain habit, future strength, and experience; but as patience and temper are required from a good nurse when her child begins to walk alone; so even the calmness and placability of Lord Elgin is likely to be severely tried by his wayward children here—they may even quarrel with their own bread-and-butter to begin with.

Sept. 3.—*Monday.*—I had a day of repose yesterday. The gentlemen went off early to their official duties, and I was very glad to rest myself, and gather up my thoughts a little. We dined at seven, and I went early to bed. This morning an English mail arrived, and we got letters. Cholera seems worse in England than I had any idea of; that complaint has abated here. In the afternoon, Lord Elgin drove me in his phaeton to the Cathedral at Quebec—a large respectable building, with a good organ, remarkably well played, and the singing led by the pleasing voices of young Quebec ladies and gentlemen. After church we walked on the platform overlooking the St. Lawrence, where there is an extensive and beautiful view. Before going home we called to inquire after a sick young lady at Sir H. C——'s, and saw another fine view of Quebec, with its mountains and river; we walked back from thence two miles to Spencer Wood. The Sunday amusement of young men here seems to be driving about little gigs, or wagons as they are called, in the most reckless and furious way possible; it seemed to me as if they would knock down even their Governor-General without the least compunction, if he happened to be in their way!

September 5.—I did not write yesterday, In the morning I was absorbed by a file of English newspapers down to the eighteenth of last month. Alas! social questions seem to be still made of secondary importance by the war. Not a word about the erring children, so I conclude nothing has been done to save them from deeper crime. A young man of twenty, at Dartmoor, has made a most furious and savage attempt on the life of one of the keepers. Ten years ago that man was a child—who but the Parent State is to blame that he is now a murderer?

September 6.—In the afternoon of yesterday, I spent three hours botanizing. There are some interesting plants in a wood not far distant, particularly some ferns, worth transplanting into our English gardens. The Governor-General opened the Parliament to-day; but as he leaves them to choose their Speaker, preparatory to his speech being delivered to-morrow, I put off going till then. I went to call upon a lady to whom I had a letter of introduction: she lives for the present (while out of town) at a cottage within a walk of this place, where I found a garden with some interesting plants of this country, and one of the most venerable-looking paper birch trees I have yet seen, for they have generally been straight and of no great size; this has many arms branching to the ground. Mrs. M—— told me that only yesterday a humming-bird came to the creeper near her window. I did not know they were found so far north; and I have not yet been so fortunate as to see one.

A Mr. Sicotte has been elected Speaker, upon the principle (as far as I can understand it) by which the Americans most usually elect their Presidents. Neither party being able to secure the election of their own man, they unite in voting for an individual not popular with either; so that in practice a popular election makes an unpopular choice—what a paradox! Each individual voter saying to himself, 'If I am not to have my *own* man, no one else shall have *his* man;' and so nobody's man is the man chosen—is not this an odd practice? A very stormy night—thunder and lightning, and rain—very cold, too. How lucky we have been that the bad weather has kept off till now, when, in a comfortable house with a bright fire, we can rest; and, enjoying the retrospect of past sunshine, look forward to an Indian summer for Niagara.

September 7.—Another cold and gloomy-looking morning, so I wrote letters, hoping for sunshine by three o'clock, when we were to go to Quebec to hear the Governor-General make his speech to the Canadian Parliament. The weather cleared up in the middle of the day; Captain H—— drove me into the town, and Colonel I—— placed me with Mrs. and Miss I—— in the gallery of the concert-room, where the Canadian Parliament has assembled since their own houses were burned. The whole place was crammed, and in the gallery were nearly as many ladies as gentlemen; the assembly showing the most breathless interest. Behind the throne there is a reporters' gallery; before it a table and chairs for judges, of whom Mr. Bowen is the oldest in the Queen's dominions. On each side were rows of double desks, covered with crimson, two members sitting at each; and as they choose their own seats, and retain them, a man can have his particular friend by him during the session—an advantage, particularly in this country. The ceremony is much like that in England. Guns are fired when the Governor arrives. He read the speech well and most distinctly, first in English, and then in French, the House of Deputies standing at the Bar. I thought

Lord Elgin was well received, an air of great respect pervading, and I heard applause as he went out. His great ability, united as it is with firmness, and the most straightforward character possible, has been of infinite value to this rising country; although party feeling and the tempers of a few disappointed spirits, aided by an ill-written and abusive Press, in some measure dim the brilliancy of his career; or rather misrepresent it at this moment.

September 8.—At twelve o'clock last night, I returned from Quebec, after sitting almost nine hours, watching the proceedings of the House of Deputies with so much interest that, for the time, I was neither hungry nor tired. The order of the day—an Address upon the Governor-General's speech; but this was not brought forward at all during my stay, so what happened after twelve o'clock remains to be seen; but it appeared to me the business they had in hand was enough to occupy them during the whole of their first sitting. A *Rouge* member took precedence, by a motion to the effect that a certain Timothy Brodeur, a unanimously returned member for the district of Bagot, having illegally acted as returning officer after his election, and thus returned himself—the said Timothy Brodeur was illegally seated; and the motion therefore went on to summon Timothy the returning officer to the Bar of the House, to be questioned as to whether he was Timothy Brodeur, Esq., who was elected member for Bagot, or not. This motion was opposed by the lawyers attached to the Government; first, because they knew nothing about the case; secondly, because they affirmed it was an act of tyranny to oblige the said Timothy to give evidence against himself, without any previous notice; and, thirdly, because Timothy Brodeur the member not being proved legally to be Timothy the returning officer, it would be a breach of Parliamentary privilege to order a member to the Bar without first proving him to be the person required. Both sides of the House, however, admitted there was but one Timothy; and it seemed to me, upon a simple, unlearned view of the case, that there was a great deal of quibbling and special pleading; so that I, as an unprejudiced observer, should have voted with the Opposition against the Ministry; and I imagine Mr. Hincks, the prime minister, was not very well satisfied with the grounds upon which his colleagues were battling, for he kept out of the way as much as possible, and took no part in the long debate which followed. There were several divisions, in all of which the Ministry were beat by a majority of twenty-four or twenty-five; apparently, the question was not if Timothy should be questioned at all, but whether he should have time to answer whether he was the real Simon Pure, or not? And the fight seemed to be about the words 'immediately,' or 'to-morrow,' or 'next day.' I imagine that in England the whole affair would have been referred to a Committee of Privileges, and not have been allowed to stand in the way of the Address upon the Queen's Speech; but there appears such a determination in the majority to turn out the present Ministry, that perhaps it prefers to show its strength upon this question (which does not touch upon the Governor-General's speech at all, and who does not even know the circumstances which gave rise to it), than upon the Address itself. But of course this is only my conjecture, founded on the difficulty, that any truly patriotic Canadian could grumble at the speech delivered from the Throne on Wednesday last. It was more than half-past ten o'clock before Timothy was fairly brought to the Bar of the House. First, the Serjeant-at-Arms was sent to summon him; but Timothy only shook his head and remained unmoved, (having the whole evening heard the complaints and borne the attacks against himself in the most silent and imperturbable manner.) Then the House felt its dignity insulted, and another motion was carried, to the effect that the Speaker should make out his warrant for the arrest of the contumacious Timothy; and lastly, the Serjeant-at-Arms, removing the mace from the table, walked up with it to the contumacious member, who then followed quietly to the Bar, and stood there looking simple and innocent as a lamb—a gentle-looking old man, unable, I suspect, to speak English; perhaps he only half understood the business, after all. He admitted that he was Timothy Brodeur, Esq., the member, and also Timothy Brodeur, the returning officer; and that he was to be paid twenty pounds for executing the latter office in his own favour; but he said the money had never been paid to him. After this I came away, leaving Mr. Brodeur in the midst of his questioning; and as the Opposition hinted at two other cases of the same kind they meant to bring forward, it was hardly possible the Answer to the address could be debated this morning, so I hope to hear it still.

The use of the two languages, at the pleasure of the different members alternately and indifferently, had a curious effect to me. Sometimes a member, after speaking in French, was asked to repeat in English what he had said in French, and *vice versâ.* It seems that many of the new members understand only one language, and this must complicate affairs considerably. The manner in which divisions are taken is good in a small assembly, but it would occupy too much time in our House of Commons. The Noes stand up, and a clerk calls over their names to be written down at the table, and then the same process is gone through with the Ayes. This is advantageous for a stranger, as it identifies each member.

September 9.—Another cold showery day, and I preferred walking into Quebec to going in a carriage, having had no exercise yesterday. I called on Mrs. Mountain, the wife of the Bishop of Quebec, who sat by me at dinner here on Wednesday; and then Captain H—— took me from Judge Bowen's into the House of Deputies. There was great excitement, for the news had become generally spread that the Ministers had resigned, and that Sir Allen M'Nab was forming a new Government. This was confirmed, immediately after the House met, by Mr. Hincks himself, who moved that the orders of the day should be postponed till Monday, in consequence of the resignation of the Ministers; and then spoke for some time. He gave a sketch of all that had occurred during his tenure of office which bore upon the state of parties; alluded slightly to the numerous measures for the improvement of the people and the prosperity of Canada which had been originated and carried out during the six years he had administered public affairs; spoke feelingly of the base attacks which had been levelled at his character; and of the desertion of some former adherents who had played a base and double-dealing game, differing from the open and honest opposition which had characterized the conduct of other men whose motives he respected. Mackenzie, that little Celtic-looking deputy who was one of the leaders of the rebellion, had removed from his own seat, and placed himself in an arm-chair so as to be nearly opposite to Mr. Hincks: he took the opportunity of uttering a loud 'Hear, hear,' upon some observation, when the speaker, immediately looking him full in the face, broke forth into a very powerful, animated, and sarcastic exposure of the bitter animosity with which Mackenzie had pursued him, showing that he (Mackenzie) uttered by various means, and through numerous channels, the most false and libellous accusations, and then had ended by becoming his opponent at the election; 'but,' continued Mr. Hincks, 'if I have had personal enemies, they have been more than counterbalanced by devoted friends. I had the satisfaction of polling more than three hundred votes when my adversary could only muster twenty-three; and also of being returned for another place, without having asked for one suffrage from the electors.' It was generally thought that the retiring minister erred only in a too modest appreciation of the services of his administration. He merely said that the statute-book would show what had been effected during the time he had been employed in the service of his country, without even pointing out that he received his office when the people were discontented and adverse to the rule of England; and that he gives it up, leaving them rapidly progressing, happy and loyal, with railroads opening and opened in all directions; the most magnificent bridge in the world in progress, to connect the opposite shores of the St. Lawrence; matters which have long been the cause of disunion and irritation permanently and irrevocably put to rest; and the revenues of the two divisions of Canada trebled in amount. Deeds, not words. Mr. Hincks may not have said all he might have said for his own glorification, or even for the reputation of the Governor-General; but he has left his office, having completed and carried out measures for which the Canadians will have reason to bless the rule of Lord Elgin as long as their country has a name; and, before one winter has passed over it, I am inclined to believe they will be sensible of the benefits which their late minister has been instrumental in securing to them, and who, upon looking round their House of Assembly, stands almost as superior to his detractors as Sir R. Peel once rose above those who believed themselves equal to attacking him. The House adjourned till Monday, immediately Mr. Hincks resumed his seat; and then numerous members—even Cochon and others who had been in Opposition—rushed forward to offer their hands: it was quite an interesting scene, and I observed tears on the cheeks of many.

I walked back to Spencer Wood over the Plains of Abraham, passing Wolfe's Hotel, and other memorials of by-gone events. The weather was cold and threatening; we want sunshine much; but I reached home without rain enough to annoy me. Part of the way I walked over boarded paths, which are very common about the towns instead of flagstone pavement. They are much less fatiguing, but more expensive than pavement, as frequent renewal is necessary. I have not yet attempted any sketches here. In the first place, the air has been cold, and the distances too hazy; and then I have also been occupied by the interest of the present state of affairs. I have been very fortunate in arriving just at a crisis which is quite exciting, and of course these circumstances enable me to study and to understand the state of parties and the feelings of the people here, better than I could do under the usual routine. Colonel C——, who was a former Secretary to the Governor, is here. He married a Canadian lady, and lives wholly among the French Canadians. He tells me they are a most amiable people, quite free from bigotry of a proselyting kind; that priests constantly visit at his house, but there never has been the least attempt to disturb his Protestant convictions, or to evince any irritation upon the subject. He has kindly invited me to visit his place of residence, near Montreal, when I leave this: and I shall like much to profit by what may be my only opportunity of becoming acquainted with the manners and habits of Lower Canada, which I believe are in many respects very different from those of the Upper Province.

It seems that poor Monsieur Timothy Brodeur, the cause of all the disputes and excitement in the Parliament the day before yesterday, is a deputy from Mr. C——'s neighbourhood; that his error has been wholly owing to want of knowledge. He was made to come forward rather against his own inclination, and has sacrificed his tastes and his domestic enjoyments to get into this hot water—poor man! Of course he is very much annoyed. It seems that most of the business of his return was conducted by another officer, but he unwittingly signed the paper himself, not being aware of the consequence, and the matter was taken up by another French Canadian, who, being a *Rouge*, wished, I suppose, to spite his quieter countryman; but one thing is certain, that Timothy Brodeur is not likely to attach himself to the Rouges after this business. He is an acquaintance of the new Speaker, Monsieur Sicotte, who was proposed by the Rouge party. By the by, he seems a gentlemanly, quiet man, who conducts the business pleasantly, and who, I should imagine, will be very generally liked by the members, though he seems to have been a man little known till he happened to be brought forward on this occasion.

If this day is fine, I shall make interest with the gardener, and get him to accompany me with his spade to a wood near, to dig up some ferns, and then I will pack up the roots and send them straight to England from hence, which I think may give them a better chance of existence than going all round by Boston.

Lord Elgin is going to have a dinner-party this evening, when the twelve retiring ministers will be present. I shall have the luck of seeing the two Cabinets all together upon two different days—the Outs and the Ins. This will be a fine opportunity for speculation. No one yet knows the names of the men likely to be put together by Sir Allan M'Nab, who may be considered the Lord Derby of Canada; and he will have a similar difficulty as the one which beset the English Conservatives—for no minister can stand here who attempts to preserve the Clergy Reserves: whether right or wrong, the people are almost unanimous in condemning them. So, as Lord Derby was obliged to confirm free-trade in opposition to the principles of his life, so Sir Allan M'Nab must sacrifice the Clergy Reserves in opposition to his. He must select a mixed Cabinet, as his own party is otherwise too weak to stand, and nobody seems to know whether he will seek for assistance from the Rouges or the Whigs; but, as extremes generally meet, perhaps he will prefer the ultra Radicals, with whom he has voted to turn out the last Government, rather than ally himself with those who have been more provoking, because their opinions were not so antagonistic to his own as those of the Rouges. So it is in politics as well as in religion. I observe some people are more tolerant of Jews and Mahometans, than they are of Christians who may differ only a shade from themselves—just as family quarrels are the most bitter quarrels of all. One comfort is, the people here have not any ground left now upon which they can fight to any very mischievous degree; and this happy agreement they certainly owe, in a great measure, to Lord Elgin. As well as I can guess, the present change may be attributed to a longing for office in some individuals, and a craving for variety in others. People get tired of the best thing if they have it always, provided there is any possibility of getting something else instead; and this is one of the many advantages of our hereditary monarchy—the complete prevention of change for the sake of change. As to the purity of election and national choice, I have already discovered that neither the one nor the other is attained by American institutions, although as a whole, for a new country, they work very well; and I should not imagine that the United States would be more prosperous under any other form of government than the one they possess; still, many people assert there is now more positive individual liberty in Canada than among the Americans. Of this I have, as yet, had no fair means of judging. As the post for England goes to-day, I must leave the solution of the ministerial crisis here for the next mail, and let this go as it is.

Yours affectionately,

A. M. M.

The English mail has just arrived, and not one letter for me! I shall probably stay here ten days longer, and it is best that every thing should be directed the same until after the 1st of October, when my friends must address to New York; till then, Lord Elgin will know best where my letters can be sent. The sun has at last appeared, and I am going this afternoon to see the Falls of Montmorenci. I can leave this packet at the office at Quebec in my way. I will number my letters from this time, which will enable you to tell whether they reach England as regularly as I send them.

LETTER VIII.

QUEBEC.

SPENCER WOOD, QUEBEC,
September 11, 1854.

MY DEAR FRIENDS,—

After sending off my last letter on Saturday, Lord Elgin's carriage took me into Quebec; and from thence Capt. H—— drove me to see the falls of Montmorenci. I once heard a waterfall in the Isle of Man compared to Montmorenci; but if there is any likeness, it is only that of a dwarf to a giant. The river Montmorenci pours down, almost suddenly, more than two hundred feet—a height greater than Niagara. It is received by the magnificent St. Lawrence, and the views ten miles up it, to Quebec, and almost as far down, to Cape Tourmente, are very fine. The drive home was beautiful. Owing to a custom here of roofing churches and houses with tin plates, the city of Quebec looked in the sunset, as if gemmed with diamonds. We had a bright, frosty-looking sun, with the air as cold as in November, in England. All the ex-ministers dined here to-day. During the evening I was told of another place, called Three Rivers, between this and Montreal, where some beautiful scenery is accessible. By stopping there one day in my way back, I should break the fatiguing monotony of another night voyage.

Sunday, Sept. 10.—We went to morning service at Quebec; very cold drive; a sharp north-easterly wind. In the afternoon we walked to the Protestant Cemetery upon the next point above this place—a beautiful situation. We passed two handsome new churches, almost finished, within a quarter of a mile of each other; one Roman Catholic, the other Protestant. They were Gothic, built of the pleasing coloured grey stone of the country. Though the great mass of the population around and in Quebec are Roman Catholics, one does not hear of religious disputes; since Gavazzi excited an uproar at Montreal, I believe nothing of that kind has occurred.

I went to call upon a Canadian lady, near eighty years of age, who understands the botany of this country better than any one I have met with. In earlier years, during the time of a former Lady Dalhousie, Mrs. M—— acquired this taste from her, and she is quite pleased to have it revived. She took me to Quebec, and at three o'clock I went to see the Canadian Parliament assemble. Sir Allan M'Nab was announced as the new minister; having formed his Government upon coalition principles, he has taken in all the old ministers but three; changing his policy upon the Clergy Reserves, &c., &c., from deference to the general voice of this country. Sir Allan is perfectly aware that no Government can stand which refuses to adjust the Clergy Reserves. It is supposed that there are not now ten votes in the House willing to support them. So it seems the new Government comes in, only to carry out the views of their predecessors; a strong proof that this change is only made for the sake of something fresh. Of course the new ministers could not take part in the debates, as they must be re-elected. Mr. Hincks made a frank and clear statement, in refutation of accusations which have been freely circulated during the last few days to the effect that he had recommended his successor, and sold his party to him. At the same time he expressed his intention of supporting the new administration, as long as they were willing to carry out good measures. I remained in the House till it was time to return to dinner at Spencer Wood; the speeches were generally dull, excepting those of a few, whose disappointment and anger, at the result of the changes, created some excitement. One speaker actually maintained that any attack out of doors upon the character of a prime minister, was sufficient to render him unfit to continue in office, because such attacks weakened the confidence of the people, and agitated the country;—so, according to this doctrine, a leader is to be always at the mercy of the mendacious scandal-mongers of a community!—a most extraordinary political axiom. Capt. H—— drove me and Mr. C—— home; it was a cold, frosty night, but not quite so sharp as yesterday, when Dahlias and potatoes were cut down; but I console myself by hoping this may be all the winter I shall get, if I proceed toward the South in December. It strikes me as singular that the weather should be so cold, while the leaves are still upon the trees, for I see none fallen, and only here and there a branch of foliage turning red and yellow.

September 12.—Yesterday, a lady took me to visit at a very pretty place, called here Carouge, a corruption of Cap-rouge, on the banks of the St. Lawrence, where the river Carouge falls into it. The view from the windows reminded of Colonel Harcourt's, near Ryde. I gathered acorns off two or three oaks there, differing from ours; one with the mid-rib of the leaf red; and, ultimately, I hope to collect all the American species. In a wood near the house, some Indians had erected a wigwam, oblong in form, and not very picturesque; it was lined throughout with birch bark. The drive from Spencer Wood to Cap-rouge along the banks of the river is very beautiful; the villas between the road and the banks belong principally to merchants engaged in the lumber trade, for the edge of the river all the way to Quebec is covered by rafts of timber, and numerous vessels are ready to convey it to England.

September 13.—I spent the morning with my old friend at Ash Cottage. She gave me many specimens of the early-blowing flowers, of which I can now only find the leaves, among them the Mocassin. We afterward drove along a beautiful river-coast road, and went through St. Foy. In the evening there was a ball here, attended by many pretty young Canadian ladies, who were dressed in good taste, and danced well; their general appearance and manners were beyond what is to be commonly met with at country town balls in England. I made the acquaintance of a Mr. Cameron, who lives near Lake Huron, and who promises that his daughter shall introduce me to the plants of that vicinity.

September 14.—Lord Elgin took me to the great Agricultural and Industrial Exhibition of Quebec, held in a fine situation overlooking the river. I saw some interesting things; one useful little instrument, not much larger than a hoe, a kind of earth-boring screw, with which you can dig to the depth of two or three feet in as many minutes. There were a few minerals, and some very pure-looking gold, found about sixty miles from hence; but unfortunately these things were placed so much in the dark, that it was difficult to see them. An address was presented to the Governor-General, which, though unexpected on his part, he replied to, in a speech made with great promptness and facility. An early dinner, with champagne, was prepared by the committee for him and the gentlemen assembled. A farmer from London, Upper Canada, made a very purpose-like and fluent speech, and gave a general invitation to an agricultural show which is to take place in his town on the 26th instant. The sheep were scanty and poor at this exhibition. I did not much admire the pigs, though some were thought good; but there was a fine show of Ayrshire cattle, and very good cart-horses; no Durham cattle, which are not thought to suit this country; but the London gentleman said they were popular in his part of the world. I was disappointed in the flower-tent; what they had of flowers and fruits having been almost destroyed the night before last, when a storm of wind blew down the tent upon them. Rain kept off during the show, but a wet evening followed. One amusing part of the scene was the different fire-brigades with their engines, competing for prizes, given according to the height to which they could eject the water. This part of the affair was very entertaining to a large majority of the crowd. A great number of people from various districts were present.

I spent the afternoon at the house of a very pleasant kind family, and went to the House of Deputies before eight o'clock, hoping to hear the conclusion of an adjourned debate upon the

Address. I found the members engaged in conversation upon the motion of Mackenzie, the former rebel. He is a singularly wild-looking little man, with red hair, waspish and fractious in manner —one of that kind of people who would not sit down content under the government of an angel. He has evidently talent and energy, but he seems intent only upon picking holes in other men's coats. He spends the money of the colonists with great profusion, for one purpose—printing returns from which he hopes to cull something which may damage somebody. He moved last night for the returns of all names of individual shareholders in banks, railroads, or companies of any description! Some members opposed this, as wasteful of the public money, and useless to the public business; only likely to minister to a prying, morbid curiosity about the affairs of private persons, and to be the means of annoying individuals who might not like their investments to be made a topic of gossiping conversation. Mr. Mackenzie ended by adjourning his motion. Upon the order of the day for going on with the debate about the Address, Dr. Rolph got up and made what seemed to me a very pompous and unfounded attack upon the Governor-General for having, upon his own judgment, selected Sir A. M'Nab to form the new ministry. Dr. Rolph maintained that it was a breach of the Constitution for the Crown to send for any man to organize a new government without the advice of a minister; that if the late Premier did not tender his advice on this occasion, it was his duty to have done so; that if he did not tender his advice, it was the constitutional duty of the Governor-General to have taken that of this person, or that person (and here Dr. Rolph gave the names of several gentlemen, whom he seemed to consider more fit for the Premiership than Sir Allan), and he ended by saying, if none of these would do, 'You, Mr. Speaker, ought to have been sent for.' I thought all this very extraordinary, and contrary to the English modes of procedure; and so it appeared did the assembly. I was surprised to hear afterwards that Dr. Rolph had been considered one of the most gifted, powerful, and dangerous of demagogues, till the Governor-General, by trying him in office, showed how little talent he really possessed. I did not get away till nearly midnight, and the House adjourned directly afterwards.

September 15.—I had intended to have crossed over to the opposite shore of the St. Lawrence, to see falls called the Chaudière, but the weather looked gloomy and unfavourable, and having other things to do, I put off that expedition: and this was fortunate, as I should have otherwise missed Mr. F——, whose energetic devotion to the cause of the emigrants from England made me desirous to know him: he came out a steerage passenger in the *Cleopatra*—a sacrifice of comfort he has before made, with a view of ascertaining practically the treatment of emigrants. He is again going west, for information which may assist the cause he has espoused; and if I had not been so fortunate as to see him this morning, he would have left Quebec. I drove in with Lord B—— and Mr. F—— to the Government Office, and introduced the latter to Mr. O——, who gave him an invitation from Lord Elgin to dine at Spencer Wood. The afternoon turned out very fine, and I had a delightful botanical excursion across the river to Point Levi: upon rocks, and along the edge of the water, I found one of the only two Primulas of America, the rare Hedysarum boreale, Primula Mistassinica, Lobelia Kalmii, Gentiana saponaria, &c., &c., all beautiful plants and quite new to me. This locality was pointed out to me by Mr. Shephard, the enthusiastic and intelligent Scotch seedsman of Montreal. Without a hint I should never have found the Primula, as it is, of course, not in flower now. I made two sketches—one of Quebec, which looks well from this place, and another of the island of Orleans, with Cape Tourmente and the mountains behind the Falls of Montmorenci; these can only be seen fom the opposite side of the river. Point Levi is a rambling Canadian village, where the inhabitants are all Roman Catholics, and speak little English. The place looks untidy and backward in civilization. The contrast is great between Point Levi and hamlets in the United States: everything looks new and hasty there, but all is at the same time neat, and significant of present and future prosperity. I found an odd-looking conglomerate rock along part of the road here. A clumsy dirty little steamer performs the part of ferry-boat between the opposite shores; it is the worst thing of the kind I have seen this side the Atlantic.

S ptember 17.—Yesterday an accident occurred, which might have been attended with more serious consequences: the horse of one of the gentlemen here fell, whilst cantering, and rolled upon him; but, with the exception of an injury to the shoulder, which obliged him to go into barrack, at Quebec, for medical treatment, no bad consequences ensued. I drove Mrs. M—— in Lord Elgin's phaeton into the town. We found the wind not quite so cold. In the evening there was a very large dinner-party, including the whole Legislative Council. A Scotch gentleman from Perth, one of the senators, acquainted with members of our family in former years, invited me to visit him at Bytown, on the Ottawa River, about one hundred and twenty miles from Montreal, and as I hear much of the beauty of that flood of water, I am going from hence on Thursday, taking advantage of the first day's opening of the new railroad, which will spare me another stupid night voyage down the St. Lawrence. I shall see a new country, too, and do the journey to Montreal in a shorter time, which makes it worth my while to give up Three Rivers and the Falls of the Herwaniack, and also to leave this a day or two sooner than I intended, as the cars will not be available to the public in general till about a week later, and then this expedition will be only for directors, one of whom promises to take us. By the bye, there was a very curious meteoric light on September 13th, the night of the ball here, which attracted the notice of all those who came. It was, I suppose, a kind of Aurora borealis, a broad path of shining white light, extending east and west from each horizon: when I saw it, there was no flickering; it had the appearance of a beautifully defined straight-edged zone, bright as a moonlit cloud, and about as wide as the apparent distance between the two constellations Lyra and Aquila. It remained a long time visible, considerably more than an hour; but I am not sure of its exact duration. I never saw anything like it before, nor had any one else among all who saw it here. It was not like any Aurora borealis I have before seen, because it appeared so stationary, and its direction was not at all northwards.

September 18.—Bishop Mountain preached yesterday; and after church I went with Lord Elgin to visit a Canadian lady of great age. She remembers the Duke of Kent here, and Lord Dorchester, who was four times Governor-General. She looked like one of the old Flemish pictures, with her thick black dress and simple thick white cap, with grey locks escaping at intervals from beneath it; very lively and energetic, though unable to leave her room. She was delighted with the gift of a bouquet from the Governor-General, in honor of her natal day. She spoke entirely in French; expressed the most lively sentiments of loyalty towards the Queen; and looks to me as if she may live to number one hundred years. Her countenance bore the stamp of cleverness and of great originality. Colonel I—— took me to inquire after Captain H——, who is going on well; and I then saw the fine strong citadel, from which there are splendid views of Quebec and the St. Lawrence. Colonel S—— embarks his regiment for England next week, and is so obliging as to take charge of a box of plants and ferns, which I hope may get there in life. Some of them, though indigenous here, I have never seen in our gardens, and being hardy, these will be valuable additions. I have found seeds of an Onobrychis, I think, of which it is probable specimens have not yet been seen in England. It is pretty enough to be a nice addition to our hardy plants, if I should be successful in introducing it. To-day we are going on an expedition to Lake St. Charles, about fifteen miles from Quebec. I am told it is well worth seeing. We left Spencer Wood before noon. The day turned out wet, but it was little more than drizzling rain; and as there is a merry party of young people, no weather damps their enjoyment. I first saw the Falls of Lorette, and upon the rocks there found a beautiful and rare fern (*Allosorus gracilis*): then, while the rest of the party preceded us, Mr. K—— was so obliging as to take me to visit a hamlet of civilized Indians, one of the Huron tribes. We missed seeing the chief, who was at his farm, but his squaw received us in her neat house, as comfortably furnished as any belonging to our best farmers. She told us her husband's mother was of French origin, but that she was pure Indian. Her age must be about seventy. She has decidedly the features of a squaw, but she is extremely intelligent, and speaks good Canadian French. This chief has only one son, but that son has six children. We bought little boxes, baskets, and pin-cushions, all made out of birch bark by Mrs. Paul and her husband; some of them very prettily embroidered.

The people of this village wear a kind of half Indian costume; the men, generally, very bright scarlet caps. They are Roman Catholics; and a woman showed us their little chapel, which possesses a miraculous wooden Virgin, which was supposed to have escaped burning, when everything round it, in a former locality, was destroyed by fire. This place, better built, and more clean and orderly, than most European villages, at once sets at rest the question, whether Indians can be induced to give up a nomadic life. From Lorette to Lake St. Charles, the road was but indifferent. At the house of a habitant farmer we found our pic-nic party assembled. There was an attempt to embark in canoes upon the lake, which was abandoned because it rained too heavily. The rest of the party returned for shelter, but I made a sketch from under an umbrella, and discovered two or three more plants—another pretty fern, at present quite unknown to me. Upon reaching the house, I found a merry round game going on. We then had an excellent dinner; and afterwards, to avoid a bad road in the dark, we all got into the carriages, and returned as far as Lorette, where there is a small hotel: two fiddlers, both of Indian blood, played quadrilles and waltzes in excellent time; ten or twelve couples were made up, and people were so well content with this amusement, that we did not get back to Quebec much before midnight.

September 19.—Rain as heavy as that of the heaviest thunder-storm in England, from six to nine; and, when I set out to walk at noon, expecting a temperature cold as November, I found shawls and wraps quite in the way; it was like a warm June morning; such a rapid change I hardly ever remember, even in our changeable climate. I went to sketch a fine view of Quebec and the St. Lawrence, as far as Cape Tourmente, from the citadel: it was very windy, and even the shelter of one of the great guns was hardly enough to enable me to keep my paper from being blown away. Afterwards I drove to see a pretty place and nice garden belonging to Dr. Douglas, at Beaufort, near Quebec. Mrs. Douglas received me very kindly, but I was sorry to miss the doctor, who went yesterday to the Chaudière. There is a very well conducted and comfortable-looking public lunatic asylum, in which Dr. Douglas takes great interest, adjoining his grounds, which are extensive, and laid out with great taste. I returned to dine with Mr. and Mrs. K—— at Quebec, intending to go to the Parliament House to hear the Address discussed; but as the debate appeared likely to linger on during the night, and we had a pleasant party and agreeable house, I remained all the evening where I was.

September 20.—A stormy night, and the weather again bitterly cold. I went into Quebec upon hearing that the Assembly had sat all night, and were still discussing the amendment on the Address, which, after all, was only to substitute the word 'secularization' for 'adjustment.' I was fortunate in getting to the House about half-past two o'clock, before the adjournment; so I was present at the finale, when there was a great majority for the Ministers, and it was agreed, without a division, that the address should be carried up to-morrow by the whole House, which should adjourn till four o'clock, Thursday.

September 21.—Colonel Tulloch, the Government Commissioner for settling and looking after the military pensioners who have had grants of land in Canada, dined here. He has been very successful in improving their condition, and land is not—as it used to be—a misfortune, rather than a blessing, to the pensioned soldier. This improvement is partly owing to Colonel Tulloch's plan of making the grant to consist of three or four acres instead of one hundred, as was formerly the case, when the occupant, unfit to clear and bring into cultivation so large a portion, was ruined by it. Now, the smaller allotments are cultivated garden fashion;

and one individual made fifty pounds last year from his three acres, principally by growing vegetables for the Toronto market. In case of the death of an occupant, his widow is left in possession on condition that she re-marries with no one but a soldier; and no widow has ever yet (Colonel Tulloch declares) remained two months without a husband. Such is the anxiety for a housewife, that men of fifty marry widows fifteen years older than themselves, rather than remain bachelors. What a chance for antiquated spinsters wishing to change their state!

Four of the gentlemen who dined here yesterday sang Negro and Canadian boat songs in the evening, all in good time and tune; they are very pretty airs. The 71st Regiment embarks for England on Saturday, much regretted here. I think this is the most variable climate I ever visited. Last night it was bitterly cold; this morning the sun shines, and every thing again looks summerish, while yesterday, no wraps could enable me to stand for ten minutes at the citadel to finish my sketch; but I am told this month is not usually so cold; there have been many icebergs seen lately near the coast, and that is supposed to be the reason of the unusual frigidity we feel here. I miss the furs which were left behind at Boston, supposed to be useless encumbrances at this time of year; but it is to be hoped that, after my return to Montreal, I shall find myself again in a warmer climate. There is certainly more difference between the temperature of the two places than the distance would lead one to expect: here, the grass has been extremely verdant this summer, while at Montreal every blade was burnt up; and I saw nothing green whatever, except the trees. I am afraid my hopes of going back by rail are illusory. Sir Cusack Rowney was here yesterday, and he seems to consider the line wholly impassable at present, and likely to remain so till the 16th of next month; so, instead of going by cars to-day, I must delay till Saturday, and then reconcile myself to the steam-boat passage down the St. Lawrence; now, I shall not have time to stop at Three Rivers.

September 22.—Yesterday I was present at the Roman Catholic Archbishop's palace, to see the assemblage of the clergy of that persuasion, for the laying the first stone of a college. There were seven bishops, besides the archbishop, all benevolent-looking men. There does not seem to be much religious bigotry with that Church here—or at any rate it keeps out of sight—and the present Governor-General does all in his power to maintain peace and charity among the differing Churches. He made a most eloquent and facile speech in French, although wholly unprepared. He alluded to the vast progress in the material world; to the marvels of electricity and of steam, by the agency of which the inhabitants of remote settlements are brought into connection, and railroads convey the luxuries of civilization to the backwoods of Canada and the solitary dwellings of the Far West. He then reminded the assemblage of differing Christians that the spiritual empire of religion and morality could only be made to keep pace with material progress through the cordial union of Protestant and Catholic, in the great work of educating the young, and guiding the mature, by the lights of piety and truth. The observers and listeners of each Church appeared interested and pleased, and I trust something was effected on this occasion towards allaying and appeasing their differences. I went to make my sketch from the citadel, and afterwards returned to the Government House, to get a peep through an open door of the ceremony of taking up an Address by the whole Canadian House of Commons. It was much the same as in England. The Roman Catholic bishops afterwards presented a loyal address to Lord Elgin. I drove Mrs. K—— to her father's house on the St. Foy road, and went to take leave of Mrs. Montazambert, in my way back to Spencer Wood. There was a party of twelve at dinner—several ladies.

September 23.—Yesterday I went a long expedition with Col. I——, to see the Falls of the Chaudière. We crossed the ferry at Point Levi, and the drive of about ten miles on the other side of the St. Lawrence, nearly following the line of the new railway to Montreal, is very beautiful: the St. Lawrence on the right, streams and rivers occasionally flowing into it; and rough cliffs, and woods, and hamlets, all along the left hand. The rocks in some places were shaded with soft grey, yellow, and brown; and all was pleasant but the road, which proved difficult, rough, and sometimes dangerous; more than usually so (I was told,) owing to the railroad operations; but the old French Canadian, and his little black horse, which drew our *calèche*, did not seem at all put out, by what in England would have been thought impracticable, even though the way was evidently not well known to him, and he took us three or four miles above the Falls to a railroad bridge over the Chaudière, so that we were obliged to retrace our steps; and this, with the intricacy of the place itself, when we got there, wasted some time. The body of water which comes down is more considerable than that of Montmorenci, and the spray was too wetting for us to do more than take a glimpse of the Fall from above. I believe we ought to have been on the other side, but there was not time to remedy this mistake, and the view we did get was fine. We scrambled through a thick forest, and came out, through bog and brake, some way from the place where we had left the carriage; so Col. I—— walked back for it, and I went on to get a sketch of the Chaudière, where it joins the St. Lawrence. The sun was setting before we got to the shore, nearly opposite Spencer Wood, and if we had again taken the roundabout way, by Point Levi, we might have missed the last ferry, besides incurring the chance of breaking down before getting there; but we were fortunate in finding a hospitable lumber-merchant and his wife, who welcomed us to their warm and comfortable fire-side, and sent us at once across the river in their little boat. We landed at a wharf, about two miles from Spencer House, and got home before eight o'clock, so that I had time to get some dinner and rest, before dressing for a ball, given by Lord Elgin, as a farewell to the officers of the departing 71st Regiment, which is to embark to-morrow for England (Sept. 23d). The dance was very lively and brilliant, and was kept up till past three o'clock this morning. The Canadian ladies certainly amuse themselves more easily and pleasantly than we do; they are more like the French, in their enjoyment of passing moments, and are generally pretty, natural, and well dressed; so that I have found their acquaintance agreeable. The Governor-General went in state to-day, to give his assent to the Reciprocity Bill; and that glorious measure is now all settled, happily for both countries. There was a very large dinner-party here, almost entirely composed of Deputies and their Speaker; and we all went to bed considerably tired with the fatigues of the last week. I had intended to have departed by this afternoon's steamer for Montreal, but since that arrangement was made, Lord Elgin has decided upon going himself to Upper Canada, on Monday, and the railroad Directors have therefore made a great exertion for the purpose of conveying him along the new line, so I shall benefit by being of his party as far as Montreal; and thus, after all, escape that odious night voyage down the river; besides which, I shall have an agreeable drive through a beautiful country by daylight, and do the journey in eight hours instead of twelve.

I will write again from the next place, which will probably be Major C——'s, St. Heliers, near Montreal. No letters for me again! This is very disappointing.

Your affectionate,

A. M. M.

I shall get no letters now for three weeks, as my tour in Upper Canada will take at least that time; and anything which comes here must be forwarded to Albany, care of the Governor of New York.

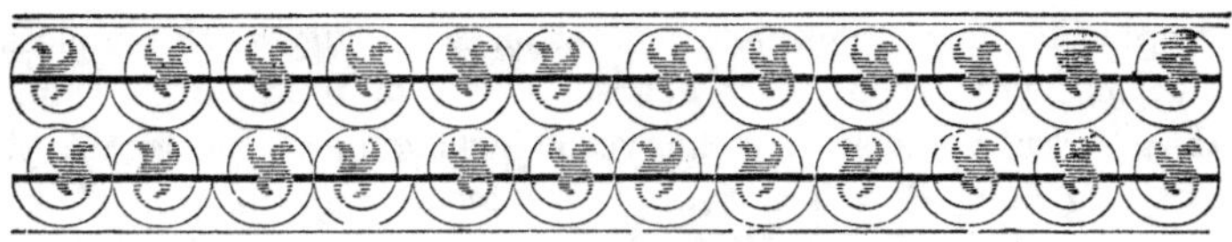

LETTER IX.

MONTREAL.

MONTREAL, *September* 27.

MY DEAR FRIENDS,—

By seven o'clock yesterday morning, Lord Elgin and his suite were ready for embarkation in a rowing boat which was to cross the St. Lawrence from the Cove beneath Spencer Wood. The weather proved favourable, less cold, and, though rather damp, not rainy. Quebec looked fine in the misty atmosphere, the citadel looming above it, and much shipping upon the river below. I felt sorry to leave that beautiful place, but we had an agreeable passage across; and a little boy, the son of Mr. K——, only ten years old, sang Canadian boat songs with great spirit. On the opposite shore we found Sir Cusack and Lady Rowney, and the chief conductors and engineers of the Great Trunk Railroad, waiting with a car. They gave us a plentiful lunch on our way to Richmond, where we joined the original line. That place and Melbourne are on each side of the St. Francis River, both prettily situated. This single line from Quebec is in so unfinished a state, that as yet there are no fences, and it required some skill and caution to avoid smashing the cattle which had strayed upon the way. We were often suddenly brought-up for this reason; and once the coupling of the engine broke, from the unsettled state of the trams, and we saw the machine running off from us without its followings; however, no harm ensued, we caught our horse again, and it went on so rapidly as to complete our journey in about seven hours. Opposite Montreal we found the *Beaver*, a powerful steam-vessel belonging to the company, awaiting Lord Elgin's arrival. She took us up (in spite of the stream running like a mill race) to the site of the works for the stupendous tubular bridge which is in progress. The Governor-General laid a first stone for the second pier, in the bed of the St. Lawrence. We were then rowed across a rapid to the first, which is already a mass of most beautiful solid masonry, strong enough to resist even the winter ice and floods of this gigantic river. A trowel was given to me, and I was invited to put in the mortar for a corner-stone of twelve tons weight, which we then saw lowered into its place; to remain, as far as human eyes can judge, as long as the world lasts. The material used is a hard black-looking limestone (and I heard of organic remains being sparingly dispersed in it)—probably Silurian. After much cheering for the Queen and the Governor-General, and the future Victoria Bridge, we steamed up the river again, and landed Lord Elgin at the Lake Champlain railroad station, Albany, being his best route for London, Upper Canada, where he goes to attend an agricultural meeting. My Canadian acquaintance, Mr. K——, brought me here to his sister's house, which I find a pretty villa, rather out of the town, with an extensive garden overlooking Montreal and the St. Lawrence.

September 28.—I went yesterday to seek out all my baggage, which came up by the steamer, as it could not readily be carried over chasms in the railway. After visiting Lady R——, and the intelligent seedsman Shepherd, at whose house I saw some very good drawings executed by his daughter (both flowers and figures), I returned to Mrs. J——'s, and after lunch she and Mr. J——, with the other gentlemen, took me a drive to see the cemetery, which is being established upon a finely-wooded hill, about three miles from Montreal. We drove back by the light of a brilliant young moon, which promises well for my three weeks' tour in Upper Canada. This morning I spent in the town of Montreal, making some arrangements, and re-packing my baggage, so as to forward every thing which I do not require for Upper Canada, to await my arrival at Albany. At three o'clock, Mr. J—— took me to the Ferry Wharf, where we found Major C——, whose place I had engaged to visit. After crossing the river, we had about twenty-five miles of railroad to his newly-built house, St. Hilaire, on the Richelieu,—a river as wide as the Thames at Battersea. A sweeping curve brought us up to the station, after going over a bridge. We had passed by the farms and holdings of habitants attached to another seigneurie, before reaching that of Major C——; but all these small farms are monotonous, bare-looking strips of land, without a twig of shelter upon them. The forests have been mercilessly extirpated, and these people have left themselves denuded of wood, and with land worn out by their short-sighted policy of squeezing all they can out of it, and giving nothing in return. This valley was once rich and productive. The good example of Major C——, and the advantages of the railroad, may in time induce these inoffensive but ignorant people to cultivate instead of racking their land; at present, I should hardly have supposed they could draw from it even a scanty subsistence. These seigneuries are of great extent in square acres; but the ground having been let on from father to son, at a rent almost nominal (about twopence an acre), any arrangement that will change a system so antiquated as their manner of farming, must be a good one for both landlord and tenant. Some kind of adjustment like that which was recommended in the speech of the Governor-General, will probably be made by the Legislature this session. Major C—— has built a pretty Elizabethan house, which it is to be hoped will serve as a model for an improved style of architecture in this land of ugly edifices; it is backed by the fine river Richelieu, and about three miles in front are the well wooded and picturesque mountains of Belleisle, which belong to his seigneurie; they stand alone, in the flat district. There is the Mount of St. John, probably of volcanic origin, but looking like a peaked barrow, about seven miles' distance; but otherwise the country is level as far as Montreal: and from the summit of Major C——'s hill the view is most extensive on every side, embracing four rivers and four lakes—the St. Lawrence, Ottawa, Richelieu, and Yamasee rivers; Lake Champlain, that of the Two Mountains, Lake Richelieu, and Lake Chambly.

September 29.—Major and Mrs. C—— took me after breakfast to walk about the mountain, and to see the hotel he is building, in a very pretty situation, upon the lower part of it. I found some interesting plants, and made sketches—one of a small lake in the bosom of the mountain, which is believed to fill up an extinct crater. Basaltic and other igneous rocks scattered about, are evidences of the nature of these hills; and one feels grateful to an outbreak which has so beautified the landscape. Excellent apples grow in the numerous orchards at the base of Belleisle, and here the people make a good deal of cider, besides manufacturing maple sugar in quantities during the month of April. I saw no flowers about the plank-houses, and their absence throws an air of desolation over the hamlets; but it must be remembered that their inhabitants have a winter so long and tedious, that during the short summer the time of the men, and of the women also, is so occupied by necessary agricultural and domestic labours, that they have none to bestow upon floriculture. Driving home I saw many little wooden troughs under the trees in the forest; I thought at first that they were for pigs to feed from, but they are receptacles for the maple sugar. Young trees produce the whitest and purest syrup; and a frosty night, followed by a bright sunshiny day, is the only weather which induces a good flow of sap. I do not see why we could not make maple sugar in England, unless it is that the sun is not sufficiently powerful during our spring. I saw a large closet at St. Hilaire, filled with cakes of varying purity; they looked very like a coarse brown soap. In the house, Major C—— has his office for the seigneurie—resembling the magistrate's room of an English country gentleman; and Mrs. C—— has her room for the reception of the poor who are sick or sorry, where she affords them aid and advice. She is much beloved among them, but never gives money. This place will be very pretty when finished, and as complete and comfortable as the residence of an English Squire. It is brick, with stone ornaments; and the interior is fitted up with carved oak, appropriate to the Gothic style of the building. After spending a pleasant day, I took the cars at three o'clock, and returned to my friend's house at Montreal by eight in the evening.

September 30.—*Silver Heights, Banks of the Ottawa.*—I left Montreal to embark in a steamer at La Chine, whither we went by the railroad—a beautiful drive. I was surprised to find the Ottawa another lake-like river, extending in both directions, and looking as if the banks of the St. Lawrence could never contain its waters, while there is much greater beauty and variety on its own shores. The first part of our voyage of thirty miles was a splendid one: we reached Carillon about three o'clock; there I found a note from Mr. and Mrs. F——: and Captain W——, with his two daughters, drove me to this place. It is now twenty-five years since he became a settler. At that time the undertaking of building and clearing must have been a fearful one; but they have now a fine farm and an enjoyable home, to which steam and electricity already add the comforts of society, and afford a rapid communication with the world; but when Captain and Mrs. W., as a young couple, sat down in the bush, what a store of patience and energy must have been required to endure and to conquer the difficulties of their situation! As we proceeded, there were some Indian villages at intervals on the river banks: priests landed occasionally from our boat; and once I saw two comfortably clothed squaws, with long cloaks, and baskets of wood at their backs, get into a canoe at the edge of the water; but wigwams and tomahawks seem almost out of date hereabouts.

October 1.—We left Silver Heights yesterday; Captain W—— kindly drove me in his wagon to Grenville, that I might be spared ten miles of a rough coach; for the rapids here prevent any navigation of the river between Grenville and Carillon. As we were rather too soon for embarkation, I walked on the banks of the Ottawa, and picked up some curious-looking fossils out of the clay slate. It was about five o'clock when the boat reached

Petite Nation. A finely-wooded shore extended all the way, but no striking features in the landscape. As we disembarked from the steamer, I saw a squaw with her papoose wrapped in her blanket. She did not seem to comprehend a word of French or English, and soon paddled away in a canoe with her husband, who was dressed like the other peasants, and I should hardly have recognized him as an Indian. People speak of the 'extermination' of the savages; but I should rather say that the race is being amalgamated and absorbed in that of civilized men. It is said here that the priests rule the Roman Catholic Indians with a rod of iron; that they do not permit them to accumulate property, but that the Church keeps a hold over their means; and that, in consequence of the despotic rule of ecclesiastics at Claire Point (an Indian settlement we passed yesterday), the people are fast emigrating to Bytown; but still it appears to me that Roman Catholicism is best adapted for civilizing the Indians. The latter place derives its name from a Captain By, who was the Government Superintendent of the Rideau Canal, which extends from this part of the country to Kingston. The city is in future to be called Ottawa. M. Papineau received me very kindly at Petite Nation. It is not more than five or six years since he was his own architect, and built the pretty stone house he now inhabits with his family, after he gave up political life. This has been a wet day; but I am fortunate in being detained in a place where I can benefit by the conversation of an agreeable and well-informed host. Speaking about the proposed arrangement of the seigneuries, M. Papineau fears that the preponderance of Upper Canada in the Legislature may lead to an unjust solution of that question. It is proposed to make the seigneurs sell their reserved lands, he says. Where a man has purchased a seigneurie at a price which has never been remunerative, expecting one day to make a fair interest for his money, it would be injustice to enforce a sale, just as the approach of civilization is giving value to the purchase; but even if the Canadian representatives are regardless of the rights of individuals, I cannot believe that any English Governor-General, much less the present one, would give his sanction to any act of spoliation.

October 2.—A very pleasing and intelligent young curé drank tea here last night. He told me that there is an Indian encampment squatted down on the other side of the river, and I shall hope to go and see it.

After breakfast, Monsieur Papineau took R—— and me across the river to visit the Indians and their wigwams, so it seems they are not quite extirpated from this part of the country. These people belong to the tribe of Alloconquins, once so powerful along the shores of the Ottawa. They were designated as the '*great nation*,' and were generally fierce and warlike; but upon the ground now occupied by the seigneurie of M. Papineau, the French, upon their first visit, found a peaceable and gentle settlement of natives, whom they designated as 'La Petite Nation;' hence, the present name of the place. With these inoffensive savages the strangers fraternized, and in consequence, their fiercer brethren of the Indians raised the war-whoop, poured down in numbers, and with fire and tomahawk destroyed the Petite Nation, and murdered nearly all their white guests. Upon this occurrence, the French Government gave up any attempt to settle on these shores, and refused permission to individuals to do so. It was not till after the English conquest of Canada that the Ottawa river became by degrees the residence of Europeans. There were only a few wigwams at the place where we landed; we spoke to an old woman and her two daughters, who were making boxes of birch bark; and to a young and rather pretty squaw, with her baby and her husband, who was busy preparing the skin of an elk for mocassins. They all spoke French a little; and being acquainted with M. Papineau, they did not shun conversation. The woman was the same who, when I spoke to her on the other side of the river, shook her head, and pretended not to understand me; and this, it seems, is a common habit if they are addressed by strangers. All the Indians I have yet seen are warmly and comfortably clad; a blanket or dark cloak being their outer covering, and they have good strong shoes and stock-ings. M. Papineau says, the accusations I heard made against the priests at Point Clare are unjust: that they only use their influence to prevent the savages from destroying themselves by 'Firewater;' and that the evil inclined complain bitterly of this check, and go off elsewhere to indulge those drinking propensities which will be the ultimate ruin of the race. After seeing the encampment, we landed on the small island of Vagit; there I found interesting plants and river shells, and made a sketch of M. Papineau's pretty Scotch-looking house, with its two towers and high roof. The wind freshened, so that we were soon obliged to hasten to the shore again, and returned in time for the two o'clock family dinner; after which, Monsieur and Madame Papineau, with the lady's sister and sister-in-law, took me to see a very handsome and well-built family chapel, and mausoleum, in the grounds. The style is solid simple Gothic, with a low belfry, like the Welsh churches. The interior has a beautiful roof, flying timbers; and one or two stained glass windows, over the door and over the altar, give all the light that is admitted. Each side is filled up by large plain black slabs of marble, upon one of which will one day be inscribed the names of those who then stood around me. I liked this little burying-place better than anything of the kind I have before seen.

October 3.—A very wet day, the wind blowing and the rain raining. When it does rain on this side of the Atlantic, the down-pour is more continued and violent than with us; but then there are very seldom three wet days in succession.

October 4.—After breakfast this morning, Madame Papineau took me to walk in the forest, which, like that behind Mr. Loring's house near Beverley, is interspersed with fine rocks of sienite. It is now rather too late for wild flowers in this part of the country; but I found some beautiful ferns, and the first snake I have seen in America glided away from our path; it was long and slender, black, marked with vivid green, and it was not disagreeably near to us. Pretty little ground squirrels ran about among the rocks; they are less agile than ours, and want the bushy tail, but they are beautifully striped; I also saw a black-and-white species of woodpecker, and a partridge, though birds are generally scarce. The afternoon proved very wet, but M. Papineau kindly accompanied me to the little wharf, to wait for the steamer to Ottawa city. We sat for a considerable time in the parlour of the French Canadian auberge, as bad weather had made the vessel rather later than usual; and we were almost drenched, whilst only walking over the small wooden pier to the boat, where it was not without a feeling of regret that I took leave of my courteous host, who with his family had made me so kindly welcome to his forest-home. The evening soon closed in, and I was vexed to pass up another fine river in the dark. Monsieur Papineau had speeded my departure in the rain, and Mr. M—— came with his carriage to meet me under the same disagreeable circumstances.

Wednesday, October 5.—The moon was hid by clouds, and rain poured down as fast when we left the boat as when we got into it, almost wet through by having waited five minutes on the shore; but the sun shines out this bright frosty morn. Having heard much of the scenery round Ottawa, I was at first disappointed at the bare look of the place itself; for, excepting a small tract of forest left near this house, the axe and saw have cleared away every tree around it; and the buildings straggle on, nearly all the same in form, though of varying material and size; some were built of wood, some of brick, and some of a coarse kind of granite, speckled by garnets. When the intermediate space shall be filled, (which is in a fair way of being accomplished, for buildings are rising up in all directions, and one very pretty Elizabethan house is erecting for a son-in-law of Mr. Mackay's, which will set the example of a more picturesque style of architecture)—a large city will stand at the confluence of the rivers Ottawa, Gatineau, and Rideau. The present town will then change its former ugly name for that of the Ottawa, the largest of these three fine rivers; on the banks of which it has sprinkled itself to the extent of about three miles, reaching to a handsome suspension bridge, which crosses the torrent very near the spot where it tumbles down a ledge of rocks packed over one another in tabular masses. These falls are very grand, second only to Niagara. At one place the stream, after tumbling over, enters a large circular hole, and vanishes beneath in a whirlpool. Each side the river, slides of water have been formed, down which the rafts rush so furiously, that though the men upon them look perfectly cool and unconcerned, I should not much like to be in their company. What a turmoil of waters there must be at other times, since now that they are considered very low, the rush I see is so magnificent! I suppose it is well to visit these falls before Niagara, but it is worth while to cross the Atlantic for these alone. About thirty years ago, the gentleman, at whose house I am now staying, was at these rapids late in the evening, with a lady now of my acquaintance, and upon her expressing a wish to stand upon a tabular rock which divides one of the larger falls from the caldron below, he carried her across upon a drift plank at the edge of the torrent. It was only by the same way that they could return; and Mr. M—— allows that at the moment he repented his daring, for one inch on either side would have been fatal to both. However, the lady preserved her composure, and he his courage, and so they repassed in safety; but he afterwards confessed to his wife, that he shuddered upon looking at the place by daylight—for it was by the light of the moon this feat was performed. Last year, a raft containing nine men was wrecked just above the falls. Thousands of spectators crowded the banks, and by means of ropes, the poor fellows were rescued; but one was dragged so far through the torrent, that he was brought senseless to the shore.

Friday, 6th—This morning, one of the young Mr. M——s drove me about eight miles up the shores of the Gatineau (in some places over a corduroy road, in which the holes were deep enough to have smashed an English carriage), to see some falls upon that river, which, if not finer than the Chaudière or the Ottawa, are still more strikingly situated: a series of falls and rapids two miles in length, backed by hills of untrodden forest, and as yet unencumbered by saw-mills and water-slides, can be seen from the ascent above. It is certainly the most beautiful view I have visited in this fine country. There is also a lake near; but time was wanting to reach the spot; and I believe few people, except trappers and raftsmen, have as yet penetrated farther up this river. The post this day has brought us news of the successful landing of the army near Sebastopol. I may possibly hear no more till we get to Niagara. Montreal papers describe Lord Elgin's progress through Upper Canada, where he seems to have been extremely well received; met by loyal addresses at every place, and answering them by impromptu political, social, and agricultural speeches, which read as well as if they had been carefully prepared. I have waited long here, vainly hoping to be overtaken by a missing trunk, in which are all my books, paper for plants, and other things of every day requirement: it was left behind at Montreal, entirely owing to the intended care which every body evinces for our interests, so that we find it the most difficult matter possible to take care of ourselves. Parcels are taken from our hands, boxes carried off or retained, baskets and tin cases put aside, and we never know whether the luggage is right or wrong, either in the United States or in Canada, because every gentleman takes it into his charge. American ladies are so accustomed to be watched and waited upon, that an independent Englishwoman is quite in despair at being treated as if she could not take care of her own concerns. I never mislaid and lost so many things in the travels of my whole life, as have been dropped or left behind since R——and I landed on this side the Atlantic. We never know when our baggage is accompanying us, or when it is lagging behind; but usually every thing turns up again in due time. We must leave this place at seven o'clock to-morrow, by the Rideau Canal for Prescott, or we may not be able to proceed before the middle of the week; and though I give up seeing Lake Huron, ten days will be required to go by Belville, Coburg, Toronto, and Hamilton, before we shall reach Niagara. The season is now getting late, and I much fear the great beauty of the foliage will have passed before I reach the falls. Some trees have already lost their leaves—a change which has occurred rather earlier than usual, owing to the storms of the first few days of this month.

Opposite the window at which I am writing, I now see crimson maples, orange birch, and scarlet oaks, interspersed with dark furs and bright green beech, and silver stems glistening here and there, making this corner of a primeval forest in itself a picture. Some of the charred black stumps, too, are always to be seen here and there standing up; at times they look like black points, or like gigantic figures among the trees. I sympathize now more than ever with poor Mrs. Moodie. 'Life in the bush' must indeed be a hard life for any civilized woman to go through. With all the aid that capital and strong arms can give, clearing is slow work, and one sees land that has been years in cultivation, still covered over at intervals by great black stumps, which look as if they might yet keep possession of the ground for the next twenty years. It is impossible to grub them up without such an outlay of time and trouble as is out of the question; and they have already been charred and girdled till their durability has been the more confirmed; so between rocks, and bogs, and timber, it takes a weary time before the poor settlers can grow more than a sprinkling of potatoes; and I am now fully convinced of the wisdom of Colonel Tulloch's plan, of giving only very small portions of land to pensioners, that an old soldier may be prevented from attempting a hopeless amount of exertion, which wastes his strength without repaying him in food. Still this country is a fine field for capital and talent. Young engineers make their fortunes rapidly. The overlooker of a mill receives one pound a day; a good foreman or clerk five or six hundred pounds per annum; and any tolerable workman may earn his dollar or two each day—more than some of our naval or military officers receive. With a small capital and a good recommendation, any active young man must prosper in Canada; but industry and temperance are just as necessary here as elsewhere; and those who fancy they may make money without earning it are worse off in America than in England.

Sunday Night, October 28—*Ottawa.*—I went to an Episcopal church here this morning; there was a large congregation. The service very respectably conducted; a small barrel organ accompanied voices in good tune. Protestants and Roman Catholics are about equal in numbers here, and there are chapels of various denominations. One or two convents of Grey Nuns, and some Jesuits, have made this place their head-quarters. It is a healthy situation, and no cholera has made its appearance, though it has prevailed much at Montreal. Hull, on the other side the suspension bridge, was settled before Bytown; it will eventually be a mere suburb belonging to Ottawa city. The population here is a mixture of Scotch, Irish, French Canadians, and Upper Canadians, with a few Germans and Americans. Bytown is in Upper Canada—Hull, in lower; so the Ottawa divides the two provinces. I will leave this letter to go from hence, as we start by the early steamboat to-morrow for Prescott, and this is probably the best locality from which to ensure the transmission of a packet for England—so I close in haste.

Yours affectionately,

A. M. M.

OTTAWA CITY, ON THE OTTAWA, UPPER CANADA,
October 8, 1854.

LETTER X.

LAKE ONTARIO.

COBOURG, LAKE ONTARIO,
October 12, 1854.

MY DEAR FRIENDS,—

I write now from another hospitable villa, on the borders of this inland sea. I heard the sound of waves on the shore last night, as on a calm summer evening at Brighton. There has not been one minute in which I could put pen to paper since we left Bytown, now Ottawa city. During this journey I have come to the conclusion, that there is no dependence to be placed upon the hours or the distances named to a traveller in Canada or the United States; you may be informed as to the usual hour for the departure of a steamer, and yet she sets forth half an hour before, or she may arrive at a point whence to start again at five minutes' warning, two hours after she was expected. When we embarked (with all Mr. M——'s experience) we reached the Rideau Canal ten minutes too late for the vessel, which went off sooner than was expected; but as there were four locks to be passed here (thirty-seven ultimately) we drove off to catch her at some convenient point, but at the distance of two miles she came up to us, having already been left behind. The only misfortune was, that as she could not come close to the shore, we had to reach her by means of a raft, which happened to be moored at the edge of the water; both R—— and I got soused over our ankles. We were all day in wet things, the stove not being powerful enough to dry us. However, the excitement and interest of travelling are so conducive to health, that we caught no cold, though, in addition to wet feet, we had a rainy afternoon, and the vessel was so small and close, that I preferred staying on deck under an umbrella to the shelter of a crowded cabin. It was consoling that the edges of the canal afforded some picturesque views. We passed one fall, and when we got into the wide calm stream of the river itself, its banks were interesting. Here I first saw true swamps—wastes of water, with occasional cedars, stumps, and reeds; blasted or sickly-looking trees and shrubs appearing at intervals above the surface. To my surprise, among the submerged vegetation I saw now and then log-cabins, with the heads of women and children peeping out of the doors or windows—not Indians, but Europeans. What beings can they be who choose to inhabit such places in a country where there is certainly no lack of dry locations! These spots looked like the personifications of ague and yellow fever; but sometimes the banks of the Rideau are embellished (like all American rivers at this season of the year) with thickets of scarlet and gold, each beautiful form and shape dressed in the most gorgeous colours possible to imagine. I suppose it is the hotter sun and sudden night frosts which tint the foliage with hues of a brilliancy unknown to us, though I suspect we have not exactly the same trees, with the exception of a few in our gardens. The sugar maple, the soft maple, and the scarlet and white oak, are the chief pigments for coloring American forests. I should like, as an experiment, to plant enough of these together in England to see if they would dress themselves as becomingly on our side of the Atlantic: the Virginian creeper does so; and then we could shade them with copper beech, which would make the picture still more beautiful.

The *Prince Albert* steamer is little worthy of its royal designation, for it is the smallest and dirtiest vessel I have seen in Canada, excepting, perhaps, that wretched ferry-boat at Point Levi; but the railroads are superseding canals, and already there is not traffic enough to pay any company for good accommodation. I

found on board an agreeable lady from Norfolk, who has settled with a brother in this country near Ottawa. She regrets I did not visit the pretty place of her relative, about six miles above the Falls at the suspension bridge. This lady had an excellent English maid, who was made so happy by meeting with mine, that as mistresses and maids suited equally well, we agreed to fall in with each other (if possible) again at Hamilton, in order to visit Niagara together. I disembarked at Brookville, with a host of German emigrants, all of whom being unable to speak either English or French, they were under the guidance of a conductor, who appeared careful of his charge. But there were not carts or carriages enough to convey these poor people, with their great boxes and their bedding; and when we got to the railroad-station at Kemp Town, three miles' distance, the train was delayed more than two hours, until the emigrant party could be brought up; so instead of our reaching Prescott early enough to cross over to the hotel at Ogdensburg, on the American side the St. Lawrence, before sunset, the ferry-boat did not put us and our baggage on shore till dark. Not a carriage or a cart was to be seen upon the landing-place, and we thought ourselves in a desperate fix. However, a good-natured woman, who had also crossed over, and who was acquainted with the locality, set off with R——, while I stayed in charge of the baggage. They returned with an old Irishman, driving his small cart. He was very civil, and succeeded in guiding our little party across a rotten plank bridge, and then took us safely through the dark and rather difficult streets to a comfortable hotel. Canada, and this bank of the St. Lawrence, will now advance rapidly under happier circumstances; but hitherto it has evidently been kept back and misgoverned, materially as well as morally; and in consequence, everything on each side the water is twenty years behind other American shores—hotels, conveyances, cultivation, habits. During our detention in the railway cars at Kemp Town, I listened with interest to a long political conversation among some Upper Canadian gentlemen. They spoke of Lord Elgin's late visit to this part of the country, and they said that it was a well-merited triumphal progress, for in their opinion, he had proved himself the most honest and able Governor that had ever ruled them; and that his giving up the reins must be a matter of regret to all reasonable Canadians. But (they remarked) he has so ordered the Government that it must now be our own fault if evils are not rectified, and if our country is otherwise than prosperous; for we have now a truly free and constitutional executive, whilst till within these last ten years our freedom has been a fiction. Only time and patience are now required, that we may learn how to use our power of self-government to the best advantage. They spoke of the probability that the seat of government would eventually be fixed either at Ottawa or Toronto.

There is a proposal now before the Legislature for erecting a Parliament house, and all buildings necessary for the executive, at the former place. But in spite of the rapidity with which everything is done in America, it must require many years to prepare the necessary accommodation at Ottawa, though the growth of Canada, and its central situation, may ultimately point to that place as the best capital of the country. The city has several hills which would admit of strong fortifications. Three fine rivers afford the advantage of immense water power, and there are railroads in progress, which will be the means of rapid communication in every direction. It has good limestone, excellent clay for brick-making, and virgin forests, extending hundreds of miles towards Hudson's Bay, with an active and energetic population of about sixteen thousand, carrying on thriving woollen manufactories, and gigantic saw-mills. The terminus of the Rideau Canal is surrounded by fine scenery: I can hardly imagine a place more likely to become the site of a great and thriving city.

Neither Quebec, nor Montreal, nor Toronto, offers all these desiderata, though the latter place, in ten years, has increased its population ninety-five per cent. I can imagine a vast empire, embracing New Brunswick and Nova Scotia, having for its capital 'Ottawa,' and with its ports upon the sea-coast and the St. Lawrence, becoming one day a power equal to the United States;

these two great nations, each encouraging a wholesome rivalry in the arts of peace and good government, content to be agreeable and hospitable neighbours, without envying or coveting each other's possessions, but setting an example to Europe of Anglo-Saxon perseverance and industry. This may be no more than a pleasant dream; it may be that nations will never be convinced that there is a more noble game than that of cutting throats and robbing fellow-creatures. Still, I have better hopes from civilization and progress; those who live twenty years longer, will, perhaps, be convinced such hopes are not fallacious; in the meanwhile there is no harm in hoping the best. I might have written this in no very good humour with things as they are, for our journey to Cobourg was the least agreeable of any journey I have yet made on this side the Atlantic.

Being told we must be ready to meet the *Lord Elgin* steamer at Prescott, by seven o'clock, Wednesday morning, we crossed over exactly at that hour; but it was half-past nine before the boat arrived, so for more than two hours we had to stand waiting on the wharf; luckily the sun shone, and it was not very cold. When the steamer took us on board we passed successfully through the Thousand Islands, and beautiful they are: of every possible form, and in size from an acre to several miles, they lie glowing and gleaming upon the blue waters, making the most singular labyrinth in the world. Of course we could not see the half of them. Arrived at Kingston, we changed our steamer for that called the *Bay of Quinte*. Upon one of the smallest islands a solitary man has resided in a tiny cabin for years; he seldom looks at, or is seen by, the passing vessels. He raises no flowers; apparently he has not even a potato ground in cultivation. What can he do? I saw nothing like a canoe; and it does not seem that he even visits the opposite shores. A fine moonlit evening succeeded our brilliant morning; about eleven o'clock at night we hove-to to take in wood from an island of considerable extent, belonging to Lord Mount-Cashel, which, I was informed, is in the market: it is extremely fertile, and has a village with a church belonging to it.* By midnight we reached Belville—another dreary Canadian town, where, if it had not been for the captain's assistance, we should have again been without a vehicle; he was so obliging as to get a small waggon of his own, with a quiet horse, which I was able to drive; and thus we reached a small hotel, from whence we were told a good coach would start at four o'clock in the morning for Cobourg; but no beds were to be had; we got a sitting-room with only a hard sofa, and a few harder chairs, so I was not unwilling to start at the appointed hour. Till near three the house was in an uproar with the noise made by smoking and drinking customers; it was six before the coach (which turned out the roughest covered waggon I ever travelled in) came to the door; and then, without any breakfast, except a cup of miserable tea and a few biscuits, procured at a stopping place by the way, we were jumbled over very bad roads, forty-five instead of thirty-five miles to Cobourg,† glad to turn out of our uncomfortable vehicle about five o'clock. We found some difficulty in procuring beds at the hotels, owing to an agricultural meeting that day, and a steeple-chase which was ridden yesterday; but I had letters which procured us the hospitable reception I have found in this house; and a delightful expedition to the Rice Lake yesterday; which was a compensation for the unpleasant journey from Belville. Mrs. H—— kindly took a drive of fourteen miles, to show me that charming lake village, which has only been settled about eight years. A half-pay colonel was the first who bought part of the Rice Lake shore, where we visited him. Another pleasing family soon became his neighbours, and now there is a thriving village, with its hotel and church, in the most beautiful situation possible. This lake may be about as large as, or larger than, Windermere. Indians still live upon its shores; one of their villages is nearly opposite, and a fine bridge for the Peterborough railway extends three miles over the middle

* Here we had entered in the Bay of Quinte, so called from a Frenchman who first navigated it.

† About twenty miles on the Belville side of Cobourg we first saw Lake Ontario, and almost coasted it to the latter place.

of the lake. We crossed the Trent River, which flows from it, upon a bridge some miles farther, on the Belville road; the country from thence is highly cultivated. We passed fields of turnips, and orchards loaded with apples, between Cobourg and Colburn; but twenty miles from Belville the land looks poor and dreary, and very little cleared from stumps and fallen timber. Cobourg itself is a clean, regularly built small town, with three pretty good hotels, and many shops well supplied. A steamboat will take us to Toronto at night; it is about sixty miles' distance on Lake Ontario.

October 14.—I slept on board the *Maple-leaf* last night, although we reached Toronto before eleven o'clock; but there were comfortable 'state-rooms,' and I had found so much inconvenience from landing at night in strange places, that I was glad to accede to the Captain's proposition for our sleeping in the vessel. He greatly relieved my mind by an assurance that the unhappy *Arctic* was not sunk by collision with the *Cleopatra*, which must have been hundreds of miles distant, but that it was a French propeller with which she came in contact. It does seem an extraordinary recklessness which causes these dreadful occurrences, when railroad whistles would guard against them. Why are they not attached to every vessel? They are universally used upon the American lakes, and the captains tell me they can be heard at ten miles' distance; yet we submit to the risk of our vessels running one another down, rather than make use of this reasonable precaution, just as we retain our separate railroad carriages, at the risk of being burned, or murdered, or doubled up, rather than travel in long cars, or have a line of communication through the small ones. I heard the other day that one of the public carriages used on this side the Atlantic costs £750, but as that holds from sixty to eighty passengers, I imagine it is less expensive than our compartments which hold six or eight; and in the larger ones we have the advantage of ready communication, and I think more air with less dust. We left Cobourg about one o'clock, and it was a pleasant voyage along this sea-like lake to Toronto. This large town is so English in habits and appearance, that I can hardly believe myself visiting the capital of Upper Canada. We are in a comfortable hotel, kept by Mrs. Ellah, who came from Plymouth, and was originally housekeeper to Lord Seaton. She is very happy to see English customers, and we feel at home in her house. It was a wet morning when we landed; but in the afternoon I drove to see the cemetery, which in Canada, as in all the towns in America, appears to be placed on one of the most picturesque spots in the neighbourhood. That at Toronto is called Bon-vale. A stream runs through the pretty dell which forms part of the enclosure, and this, with the hills above, forms the burying-ground. It is about two miles from the town, and is also named St. James's Cemetery. Here I found (in seed) a smaller Anemone than that which grew at the spot appropriated for the same purpose at Hull, overlooking the great Falls of the Ottawa—the only two localities in which I have found Anemones.

October 15.—Fine early, but like a cold March day in England. The north-westerly wind was high, having much the sharpness of our easterly breezes. This hotel is a large square red-brick building, in what is called Front-street, facing the bay. A railroad runs between it and the water, which here looks like a river not much wider than the St. Lawrence, the indentation from the lake is so deep. I see nothing like a mountain in the neighbourhood, or even at any distance from Toronto; and the forests by which the town is backed are at too great a distance. The country for some miles round is flat, well cleared, and in good cultivation; but, with the exception of the little dell I visited yesterday, there is no other attraction of scenery than the ocean-like waters of Ontario; but the streets are wide and well laid out. When polished a little, Toronto will be a noble city, though Ottawa may hereafter vie with it as one of the capitals of Canada.

October 16.—The cathedral here is a pretty new church, in style, early perpendicular. It was built by a young architect from England, of the name of Cumberland, and is very creditable to his taste. The eastern termination is an apse rather than a chancel. I thought the windows particularly good, and they will be beautiful when a little painted glass is introduced, with a due regard to harmonious colouring; this happily must be done in small compartments, as the glass is already thus arranged: it is almost entirely in patterns formed by triangles, with a small cross in the centre of each circular termination; but these triangular panes are so varied in size and shape (although there are few much larger than the old diamond pane), that a pretty light design is the result of these different combinations; the lead which divides and unites them is very small and light. A service was performed, half-an-hour longer and half-an-hour later than any at Quebec; so that I did not think it so well arranged here as there, where it was conducted with equal attention to the ordinary routine, but without tedium. Yesterday was bitterly cold, so that I heaped on every wrap in my possession; and if this is only a foretaste of a Canadian winter, I feel happy at the idea of escaping from it; for, though every one tells me about the delights of sleighing in clear, bright, frosty weather, that does not sound tempting to me. This morning I saw the new University, and at the Parliament-house Professor Hincks showed me his commencement of a museum of natural history, already containing some very interesting specimens.

October 17.—I left Toronto at two o'clock yesterday by the *Highlander*. Having been assured that we should reach Hamilton in daylight, I was weak enough to be again deluded by uncertain or false information; but the steamer stopped so often at various towns and settlements (among them Port Credit and a pretty little place called Oakville), that it was quite dark before we arrived; and if it had not been for the kindness of my friend Miss C—— and her nephew, who came down to the wharf with their carriage to take charge of me, I should have put up with any accommodation on board, rather than have run the risk of another landing like those at Ogdensburg and Belville,—not only disagreeable, but, as it appears to me, really dangerous; for on these wharves there is nothing to protect strangers from walking over the edge into the water; and a few weeks ago, at Cobourg, a poor young woman, carrying her infant (although she had her husband with her) stepped off the side, and was drowned, with the child, before any assistance could be afforded her. I was hospitably received at the house of Mr. B——, and passed an agreeable evening.

October 18.—When I came down to breakfast yesterday, I was told the reason of all the bell-ringing and firing I heard last night; having been so accustomed to noise, I went to sleep without any idea that news had arrived, after I went to bed, about a great victory over the Russians, and the taking of Sebastopol. This came by telegraph from New York; and about midnight the Mayor and inhabitants assembled, amid cheers for the Queen and groans for the Czar, to fire a salute of twenty-one guns; and no place in England could evince more joy and loyal feeling than the town of Hamilton, at the west end of Lake Ontario. I understand there were equal rejoicings at Toronto, where a large bonfire was added, to mark the event; but some touch of sorrow for the unhappy victims of the Russian Emperor's ambition among his people, and anxiety about our own gallant friends, makes us rejoice with trembling. It is impossible not to dread the details, while we are thankful for the results.

Yesterday, I was taken a beautiful drive of sixteen miles to Ancaster, an older settlement than this. We first went up what is here called the mountain—a cliff-like hill, supposed to have once been bounded by a vast sheet of water, which covered this whole country; so that the northern shore of the St. Lawence, up to Quebec, was then also another limit. In our way back to Hamilton, we came by a fine Macadamized road, descending gradually, in a manner which reminded me of Haldon hill, in Devonshire; beautifully wooded park-like ground, gullies, and ravines, on our right hand, terminated by a high mountainous ridge, along the side of which the London railroad is carried, passing by the settlement of Dundas, which has already a population of about five thousand, which has located itself in a pretty valley between the hills. Passing along this district, I could imagine myself in a well-cultivated, picturesque part of England, if the superabundance of timber and the 'snake fences' (containing more wood upon fifty acres than we should use to fence five hundred in the old country) did not speak plainly of American forests. Before the lapse of ten years, Hamilton, following the promise of most Canadian towns, will be a large city. It has already spread itself out some miles, and building is going on in every direction. This morning Miss C—— promises to take a drive of fifty miles with me, to find out a family (settled at a place called Milton), about whom I am interested.

October 19.—I succeeded in discovering the M—— family, and we were fully repaid for a long drive, by the joyous gratitude with which our visit was received. We found Milton to be a thriving small town on the banks of part of the Sixteenth River (why this name, we could not make out). An annual show of cattle and agricultural produce made the place like a fair, and numbers of very respectable-looking farmers were walking and driving about. We found two daughters of Mr. M——; one of them wife of the principal hotel keeper, the other married to a well informed, gentlemanly young man, the doctor of the place, who has good connections in England. We dined with them, and afterwards walked three miles with her father, to his own farm. We found Mrs. M—— knitting, seated by a glorious log fire, and everything around told of the comforts and contentment of a good English farm-house. These farms are divided into what are called lots; each lot is one hundred acres. Mr. M—— purchased a lot and a half. These farms are much better cleared from trees and stumps than the land through which we passed from the Rideau canal to Belville; and this part of Canada is altogether much more advanced than the lower division.

We got back to Hamilton by dark, without any difficulty. Next day, Mr. B—— drove me to the suspension bridge, over the canal, near Dundum Castle, the residence of Sir A. M'Nab; though a pretty situation, it is placed between the lake and a marsh, on which account it is considered very unhealthy. We visited the cemetery enclosing the ground where the British troops were entrenched before the battle of Stony Creek. By the cars which start at three o'clock, Miss C—— and Mr. S—— promise to go with me to Niagara.

October 20.—*Niagara.*—We had a fine afternoon for our journey to this beautiful place, and soon after leaving the railroad cars, I got my first view of the Falls. I had not a feeling of disappointment; they are quite as magnificent as any imagination need desire. I was told that the Falls of Montmorenci had the advantage of some feet in height; but it would be as reasonable to compare the Thames with the St. Lawrence, as the Falls of Montmorenci with Niagara! I was up before six this morning, to see the sun rise; it appeared above the horizon, between the village of Niagara and the American Fall, rather behind both: a fine red sun, promising good weather, I settled in my own mind, I would try to make a drawing to-morrow at the same hour, with the salmon-coloured sky in contrast with the white waters. This first day it was impossible to draw; I could only look; for some hours we walked about; I wandered into the wood behind the Table Rock, or rather where the Table Rock once was; for it has now nearly fallen into the boiling waters beneath. There I gathered two of those beautiful flowers I first found at Point Levi—Lobelia Kalmii and Gentiana Saponaria; and down close to the brink of the river, above the Falls, Mr. S—— and I picked up three or four kinds of shells; one very small bivalve, differing from any I found in the Rideau. After dinner we took a carriage, and went over that marvellous suspension bridge, below the Falls, connecting the two shores, already open for traffic beneath, but not yet finished for the railroad cars to pass over above. I felt rather glad; it was awful enough now to pass, looking down hundreds of feet upon the racing torrent below. I I do not think I could endure being in a carriage upon this bridge, with a railroad train rushing over my head, yet it is constituted for, and believed capable of supporting all together. The engineer is a German. This is only a little less wonderful than the Montreal tubular construction. Many people still doubt the success of both, and consider it beyond the power of humanity to pass, as proposed, over the chasm of Niagara, or to combat the waters and ice of the St. Lawrence. Time will show. My courage was again tried in traversing the wooden bridges which are built over the rapids between Niagara city and Goat Island. That place also, was quite different from what either my imagination, or drawings had led me to suppose. I expected to see an uninhabited, rocky, woody, small island, dividing the two grand Falls; but it contains fifty acres, the greater part a grove of fine trees, and upon one side there are houses and gardens, with a productive orchard. Upon the other shore it appears as if island, and trees, and people, must all tumble down the Falls together; indeed between rapids and torrents, it is a marvel that Goat Island exists. I must spend a day in trying to draw here, though without a hope that paper and pencil can give any real idea of the truth. The news to-day is, that the accounts of the fall of Sebastopol are false, and that we have been rejoicing without reason. Terrible fighting is still going on, and already ninety British officers have fallen. Alas!

October 21.—I covered myself with wraps, and put a blanket round my feet, so as to be able to endure a sunrise from the verandah long enough to draw yesterday. It rose red and clear, and almost cloudless, and afforded the colouring I wished for. Mr. and Mrs. B—— obligingly called in their carriage, to show us the whirlpool, where the river suddenly turns below the suspension bridge; we went also to the rapids beyond and above the Falls. Everything here is on a larger scale than I expected, though I ought by this time to be prepared for all. When I looked down upon the whirlpool, and saw the carcase of a wretched horse (which had, we suppose, been accidentally hurried down the Falls) twirling round about, and up and down, in appearance like a small wooden Dutch toy, I was in some degree made sensible of height and distance; a house too, on the rocky, wooded point opposite, was no more than a speck, so that, by comparison, I brought my ideas to something like fact.

The English are accused of being a grasping nation in requiring fees for sights, but nothing I ever met with equals the charges for the contemplation of Nature here. The possessor of Goat Island makes one thousand pounds a year of those strangers or visitors who land on its shores; but this day we were actually charged one shilling each for only going into the wood, from whence a good view of the whirlpool can be obtained! As ground is becoming of great value in this neighbourhood, it may be necessary to require payment for keeping any part of it free from the desecration of taverns and saw-mills; but a more moderate fee would answer better to the proprietors, and not act as a prohibition to a large class who have not many spare shillings in their pockets; penny postage proves that small charges answer better than large ones. This has been another beautiful day, and I trust we shall be favoured by such weather during our stay among this most magnificent, most lovely, and most interesting of all scenery. Yesterday was pleasantly warm, and if the sun shines out for a day or two longer, we shall be as fortunate in temperature as possible, for earlier in the year the heat and the mosquitoes are trying; now we have no reason to complain of either, and the great stream of visitors being over, we are here just at the right time for enjoyment; and I must remain some days, for there is no end to the beauties of Niagara—it ought to be visited for weeks instead of days; besides the great variety of views and objects on all sides,—the ever-changing appearance of the Falls, spray sometimes going up from the centre in columns and graceful curves, now half concealing, now lessening, now enlarging—rainbows starting across, and above and below—waters, snow-like, surge-like—aquamarine, emerald, sapphire, swelling, eddying, foaming! It is certainly worth crossing the Atlantic for Niagara alone. I have come to an end of my paper, and this shall go.

Yours affectionately,

A. M. M.

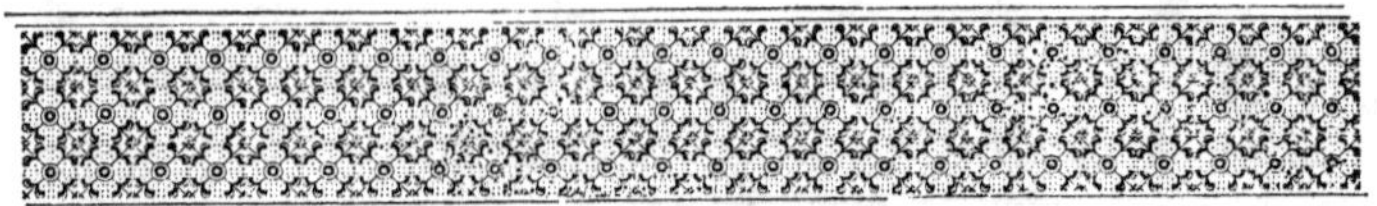

LETTER XI.

NIAGARA.

NIAGARA, *October* 23, 1854.

MY DEAR FRIENDS,—

Upon Goat Island yesterday, I parted with the two agreeable friends who have added to my enjoyment here by sharing it. I spent the whole afternoon that side the water, having passed to and fro by the ferry, and mounted by the rail and endless chain, at the very edge of the American Falls. Both these operations are awful, though perfectly safe; and it required some determination upon my part to be reconciled to profit by them, though they put one across the river in half the time required to go round by the suspension bridge. I tried to give some idea of the two cataracts on paper, which, at any rate, will be recollections for myself. I suppose it is not possible to impress their grandeur upon the minds of others by any representations. For the first time, I felt rather angry at the impertinent kind of curiosity evinced by passers-by while I was drawing, because they did not seem to care the least about disturbing or annoying strangers busily engaged. A well-dressed woman said, in a rude way, 'Pray what are you making there? You are a Canadian, I guess?' I replied, 'I am making nothing; I am trying to draw.' 'Oh, you are—how do you do it?—where do you come from?' I felt provoked, and said, 'I am sure you are an American.' 'Well, how do you know that?' 'Because you ask so many questions, a Canadian would be more civil.' This answer was effectual, and she turned away. Since my stay here, I have observed more of unpleasant manners, as I have read of them in books, than fell in my way during my tour from Boston in August; and, certainly, among the secondary classes, I see little of the marked attention supposed to be shown to ladies in the States. Last night in the ladies' saloon here, two gentlemen kept possession of the most comfortable arm-chairs all the evening, and when Miss C—— and I entered the room, round which was a circle of strangers from various localities, not one among them rose to offer us seats, so we walked out again up and down a corridor till some of these people *absquatulated.* This might be accidental, but I do not think it could have occurred in the old country. It seems to me that the Americans mistake rudeness for republicanism, and incivility for independence. Nationally, I mean, for of course there is polished society, as I have been perfectly ready to admit. Yesterday, a lady from one of the Southern States remarked, that we 'English still owed America a grudge for what was past.' I could not help assuring her she was mistaken, for that neither man, woman, nor child in the British Isles now troubled themselves about the war of American Independence, except to think their ancestors unwise for having fought about it. The day before yesterday, I was busy making a little sketch from the verandah, when I felt a hand familiarly laid upon my shoulder. Of course I supposed it was a lady with whom I had some acquaintance, but when a strange voice asked a question, I turned round: it was with no small degree of astonishment that I found the liberty was taken by a perfect stranger, a young lady, apparently about twenty, who had been one of the last arrivals. She did not seem the least daunted by the expression of surprise which must have passed over my face, but went on questioning me with the coolest manner imaginable! The Indians and their squaws have the manners of gentlemen and ladies, and it does seem curious that even individuals, among a people who are so anxious to assume the names of gentility, should remain so wholly ignorant of the manners which are supposed to indicate a superior station and a refined education. I do not the least quarrel with the simplicity of the Bush, and the poor woman who took possession of the pattern of my gown, and the men who claimed a right to my sketch-book, were most welcome; but the mixture of assumption of high breeding with inattention to the common rules of politeness, not even that natural feeling of regard which a common Anglo-Saxon blood originates, can make one excuse. Indeed, I think our relationship makes it more galling, for a parent is always observant of the errors of her children, and it is perhaps in some degree the fault of the mother country when her descendants are unpolished. She may well be proud of the energy and perseverance of her large American family: it is to be hoped that some day their young people may add graces from the old country to the agility of the new, and that they will not be ashamed of cultivating the virtue of filial affection, which at present they seem to conclude would be a feeling derogatory to their rising dignity. At this juncture it is difficult to believe that parts of the Democratic Union actually sympathize with Despotic Russia rather than with Free England! I do not believe this to be the case with the flower of the land, or with the really superior and enlightened of her sons; but I fear many would sympathize in a wish I heard heartily expressed by one of them, 'That the old country might get well sold, and thoroughly whipped during the present war!' No details have yet arrived of the Alma battle, excepting that there has been sad loss of life. The first news was probably falsehood, spread by the Russians, with the view of creating dissatisfaction when the real facts became known; but what must be the weakness of a despot who can resort to such expedients to bolster himself up—conduct more like the futile struggles of a maniac, than the efforts of a powerful Sovereign. Before going to Albany, I intend to visit the neighbourhood of Sandwich, and of Detroit and Cleveland; and to do this, we must again pass through Hamilton and return to Niagara; but, as I shall have no other opportunity, I must take advantage of this last week in October, go from hence to-morrow, and return for one night to this house on my way into the States. It is satisfactory that a good reason exists for seeing Niagara once again.

October 24.—A beautiful day, with a bright young moon in the evening. I was out alone from morning till dusk. While sitting sketching on the hill, an old Irishwoman accosted me, but with a very different tone and manner from those people I met with yesterday. 'Ah, ma'am,' she said, 'you are from the ould country; and sure you are making a plan of the glorious waters.' 'How do you know I am from the old country?' 'An' sure then, an' don't I know English ladies at once; they're so busy, an' they don't dress as fine as our folks.' I found she had been twenty-five years in Canada; that she has eight sons and daughters, a good husband, cows and horses, a thriving farm here, and one hundred acres of land at Toronto, and now, she said, she no longer fretted to go back once more to Ireland, because 'Isn't the dear ould father dead at last; and he one hundred and eight years of age, and never had a doctor till the last hour, and was able to keep his church, two miles' distance, till he was laid on his bed a-dying.' She told me she had given her children a good education, and 'that her daughters were not dressy, nor her sons drinkers.' It is singular that these Irish people are so different in their habits away from their own land. There is an electric telegraph in communication with all the lines from this place in the house. Mr. Shears, the master, conducts it; he sent a message to Sandwich for me last night, and one for a military officer to Quebec; and we had both replies in half an hour. This hotel belongs to a company: it is by far the most pleasantly situated at Niagara; those on the other side of the water have no views of the cataract. The vibration caused throughout this building by the falling waters makes every door and window shake; but it is not enough to disturb the rest of a traveler, and one soon gets accustomed to it. Besides the main hotel, there are several small separate houses behind, which can be taken for the summer or for short periods, by families who prefer a more domestic life. I can hardly imagine pleasanter summer residences.

October 26.—*Detroit, National Hotel.*—Again I had the misfortune of travelling last night for three hours in the dark—thus losing the prettiest of the scenery between this place and Niagara. The first part of the railroad line from Hamilton runs through monotonous forests, only occasionally broken by clearings and rising towns. We passed through the township of Dundas, and by Paris, Prince Town, London, &c., and crossed over the River Thames, which is but a small stream even comparing it with our Thames; but for America it is little more than a brooklet, at least that part I saw. As far as I could judge by the bright starlight, for about twenty miles from this place the road is carried along a fine terrace overlooking the country towards Lake Erie, and as we approached Detroit, Lakes Erie and St. Clair looked beautiful, with shores dotted by lights from the towns of Windsor and Detroit. They were so numerous that it appeared like an illumination. Our journey was less pleasant than any I have yet made, owing to the crowded state of the railroad cars; though the train was a long one, some passengers were actually obliged to stand the whole distance. This crowd was owing to the numerous emigrants who are coming up the country; and several little children wailed and fretted all the afternoon, evidently tired and exhausted by continued travelling. However, the people were good-humoured and patient; I heard no cross words, saw no ill-natured scrambling; every one appeared to make the best of things as they were; and though we were near two hours after our time, there was nothing like a grumble. The station-master was so civil as to take me across the water, as he recommended this hotel as more comfortable than those on the Canada side. We passed over in a few minutes in such a magnificent steamer (where people from the railroad cars found a comfortable meal ready prepared in the saloon) that it was only like walking through a good house. Ormolu lamps, mirrors, and sofas—it was difficult to realize the fact that we have been journeying through the backwoods of Canada. I am surprised to find Detroit already a city of forty thousand inhabitants, and one of the finest I have yet seen on this side of the Atlantic. A large open space in the centre will some of these days be a magnificent square. There are a number of churches, chiefly with spires. The streets are wide, some of them planted with avenues of trees. The town contains two very large hotels, besides many smaller ones. The one I inhabit has a dining-room one hundred and twenty feet in length, capable of containing four rows of tables in the width, a ladies' saloon, and other rooms in proportion; and I am told the Biddle House is equally commodious. Almost all these places have lanterns in the roof. After breakfast, the master took me up to the one here, from which the view astonished me. I have heard there is no place in the world from which you can see five miles in every direction, except from the top of the highest mountains, but this place belies that assertion: it is a perfect panorama, and as there are no hills in this part of the country, one sees in every direction from ten to twenty, and possibly thirty miles. On one side Lake St. Clair, with the beautiful River Detroit connecting it and the Lake Erie (about twenty miles distant). The town runs along the banks of the river, Windsor and Sandwich, both in Canada, on the other shore. Numbers of vessels are passing and repassing, and there is an uninterrupted water communication through all these fine lakes and rivers, two thousand miles, to the Gulf of St. Lawrence. What an empire this will be when all its resources are developed! And they are developing with great rapidity; for of all the towns I saw in passing from Niagara yesterday, not one was in existence twenty years ago.

October 27.—Yesterday afternoon Mrs. P—— came to call, and kindly brought me at once to this place, Park Farm, in Sandwich. We crossed the river without moving from the carriage, and arrived at the house in time to take a walk. Colonel P—— has not gone upon the usual plan in this part of the world —that of rooting up the forest, without any idea of leaving ornamental timber; and his place is beautified by woods, at proper intervals, while the cultivation of the land is that of an English farm. The Colonel tells me there is fine shooting all about here—deer, within ten miles. Yesterday, he and his son brought in as many snipes, woodcocks, and a small kind of quail, as they chose to shoot.

October 28.—A dreadful accident occurred very early yesterday morning, near Chatham, about fifteen miles from Detroit; upon the same railroad by which we came from Niagara. Some trucks, filled with gravel, were proceeding at the rate of sixteen miles an hour, actually in front of the express train, going at the rate of forty. Of course there was a collision; three or four of the first cars were smashed; and it is believed that sixty or seventy persons are killed; exact particulars have not yet reached us; but this seems one of the most fatal of all the railroad catastrophes, and caused entirely by carelessness. There was a dense fog at the time it occurred; but surely the gravel-trucks had no business in the way of the coming train. I am surprised at the large number of blacks and coloured people hereabouts; nearly all the lowest population appears to consist of them; they are idle, and very insolent in manner. I met with an English clergyman on board the Lake Ontario steamer, who was on his way to this country, with the intention of making an effort to civilize and educate the negroes who have settled here. He told me there are at least twenty thousand, chiefly runaway slaves, in Upper Canada. One of the evils consequent upon Southern slavery, is the ignorant and miserable set of coloured people who throw themselves into Canada. Colonel P—— told me yesterday he was brought out home from Windsor, by a black driver, who told him he had 'run away from his good, kind massa,' years ago; and that though he was free, and able to get his own livelihood, he had never ceased to repent his folly. The black should be educated for freedom, or he is not the happier. If mere children, sent into the world unfit to guide themselves, negroes suffer more by freedom than by servitude; and I must regret that the well-meant enthusiasm of the Abolitionists has been without judgment. Dr. Howe, Mr. Dillon, and others devoted to the real welfare of the black race, all are of opinion that in their case, as in many others, ill-judging friends have proved worse than enemies; and, without having been among the planters, my observation in the States, of the majority of free blacks, already leads me to the same conclusion. It is not a question between the wickedness of a system of human bondage and the duty of shaking it off, but one as to the wisdom of getting rid of an evil, without making use of common sense in the manner of curing it. Colonel and Mrs. P—— took me a drive yesterday afternoon along the shore of the Detroit (which is rather a strait, twenty miles long, connecting the Lakes St. Clair and Erie, than a river). It looks, in some places, from five to seven miles wide; and there is no more stream than that movement which is occasioned by a slight difference of level between the two waters. Some fishermen were fishing for white fish, and a kind of fresh-water herring. The nets were taken out in boats, as in England; but, when the ends were to be drawn in, the rope was fastened to a windlass, and a horse trotting round and round, soon brought the net on shore—a saving of both time and labour. I saw a curious kind of fish-lizard brought out; it was about two feet in length from the end of the tail to its round, cat-like snout; it crawled along the ground on its short legs and tortoise-like feet, and was altogether a disgusting-looking beast. The fishermen said its bite was very poisonous, and it had the yellowish brown lurid look which seems to appertain to venomous reptiles; but Dr. Kirtland says it is perfectly harmless. We induced them to throw it back into the water, where it probably exercises some virtues not to be guessed when it is seen out of its natural element. I found many little fresh-water shells on the shore, and one mussel, with a wing appendage almost like that of a rostellaria. A sunset more lovely than any I have before seen; it promised fine weather—a happy promise for me, as I find myself again obliged to take part of my voyage to Cleveland by night. No steamer leaves Detroit earlier than four o'clock to-day; but I shall have daylight for the river, so I must be reconciled to being in darkness on Lake Erie, with the consolation of a moon, now some days old. Such quantities of apples here, rotting on the ground for want of hands to gather them. The negroes will not take that trouble, even for pay; and, in spite of the great emigration, labour is much wanted: people are in distress for both out-of-door and in-door servants. I walked with Mrs. P—— down to the river: many black and mulatto children were playing about near some small log-houses, close to a marsh, on its shore; one clean-looking intelligent girl, about seven, helped to look for shells, and then asked me to visit her mother, who, she said, was sick in a hut close by. I followed the child, and found her mother in bed, quite alone, with the exception of a tiny black babe, only two hours old, by her side. She received me cordially; conversed in a cheerful, intelligent manner, and said she was brought by a lady from Maryland to this place, twenty years ago, when only seventeen years of age; this kind mistress gave her freedom, and she married a husband of her own colour, who works in the boats. I said, 'Are you glad to be free?'—'Oh, am I not? it is only the ignorant and the lazy ones who do not care to be free; but then they be most so.' She has three girls alive, besides her baby-boy, whose arrival makes her very happy, because she has lost three boys. Everything around this woman spoke of tidy and cleanly habits; a little Bible well bound was on the table close to her bed, and other comforts evinced education and order beyond the usual negro habits.

I afterwards visited the hut of an old negro washerwoman, who lived alone, and seemed a kind, industrious old soul. In the other houses of the black people, I was told I should find nothing but dressy, saucy, idle folk. We were in Detroit to meet the steamer at four o'clock; then it was discovered she would not start till night, and after spending many tiresome hours, waiting and expecting, the *Ocean* did not get under way till near midnight; and when on board I found out I might have set off by nine o'clock this beautiful morning, if I had gone by a boat to Sandusky, whence a railroad would have carried me to Cleveland before dusk, and I should have steamed up the Detroit River, with a bright sun over my head, instead of traversing it when even the early moonlight was over. *En revanche*, I had a fine sunrise on Lake Erie. I have now passed one night on the St. Lawrence, one on Lake Ontario, and the last on Lake Erie, besides two or three landings in the dark; and this obscure mode of travelling is so usual on this side the Atlantic, that it requires some perseverance and energy, really to acquire knowledge about localities in America. To-morrow I shall set forth by rail to Buffalo—in daylight I hope; so that only the last part of my journey will be in the dark, and I shall reach Niagara by moonlight. These late slaughtering railroad accidents are enough, I should think, to counteract the American and Canadian predilection for night travelling. But it does appear as if these active people would rather sacrifice their lives than lose an hour of their time while they do live. 'Dollars and time, time and dollars,' should be the motto on this side the Atlantic. Cleveland is another pretty place, with streets as wide as those of Detroit, and a growing population of forty thousand. New churches here also starting up in every direction. Religion has certainly her due place in the hearts of the inhabitants, though the worship of Mammon may here, as elsewhere, compete with a better faith.

October 30.—Here I am still at Cleveland, in spite of my resolution to return to Niagara this evening: but it was quite impossible to resist the temptations offered by the kindness of Dr. and Mrs. Kirtland, and we slept last night at their house, five miles from hence. His garden was the first I have ever seen since that at Cambridge, which offered many objects of interest. Besides other plants new to me, I gathered berries of a singular colour, greenish blue, from an Ampelosis, with briony-like leaves. Dr. Kirtland has paid great attention to the improvement of fruits, particularly cherries, and he is a most scientific naturalist; his birds, stuffed and arranged by himself, excel those of Waterton; and the manner in which his entomological specimens are preserved is quite unique and admirable; they are in frames, with glass behind and before, so that they can be observed on all sides, and when held up to the light, while, being rendered impervious to air and unassailable to insects, they are indestructible. I am promised a specimen case, which will be an invaluable example to collectors and museums in Europe. Dr. Kirtland was also so obliging as to give me numerous shells from the fresh waters of this district, which differ from those I found on the Ottawa and on the shore of Lake Champlain; and this morning he took me a

6

walk through the forests, where I found a great deal of the pretty Cornus florida, and seeds of a Geradia, differing from that growing near Lake Winnipiseogee. The oak most common here, is called the grey oak: there is another with chestnut-shaped leaves and a long acorn, and one with deeply cut, small, shining leaves. The Sassafras and three or four species of poplar also grow in this forest, but no evergreens; and none are to be seen between a place called Paynesville and Detroit, unless in gardens; no firs, no cedars, no Lignum vitæ (which grows so beautifully on the banks of the Ottawa and the Gatineau, and again at Niagara); but the variety of trees and shrubs is greater here than in the neighbourhood of Sandwich, where the forests are principally beech, and the white and scarlet oak, with tamarisks in the swamps. The orchards at this place are very productive: peaches, cherries, and excellent apples. Among the last, the true golden pippin and nonpareil. Dr. Kirtland is famed for his cultivation of fruit.

This evening I have been much interested, having for the first time read the details of the sad, though successful battle of Alma; but our heroes have not died in vain—they died as missionaries of truth and civilization. Those English and French soldiers who have fallen side by side at the battle of Alma, have sealed with their blood a lasting alliance between their respective nations; and thousands of serfs will go to school in England, and there learn that they are men. I came back to sleep at the Weddell Hotel, where the accommodation is excellent, and we hope to ascertain exactly the hour when a railroad train starts for Niagara *viâ* Buffalo, to-morrow morning. One comfort is, the time of the cars cannot be so difficult to discover as that of the steamer *Ocean*, at Detroit, where we walked up and down the wharves for more than two hours, without being able to find out, from any man, woman, or child, where the great steamer had hid herself! People in these rising cities are all too busy to know anything that does not concern their immediate objects.

November 1.—*Niagara.*—To-day we go to Canandaigua, having safely returned last night to this place.

November 2.—Owing to the impossibility of getting correct information, I was sent across country, and we were all day on the American shore of the Falls. At half-past seven in the evening the cars did start, but before eight we were brought to a stand-still; for the engine and the two first carriages ran off the line, owing to some miscreant having removed a rail. No person was injured, but for six mortal hours we were kept waiting until trains came up each way, so as to allow of an exchange of passengers and luggage; and it was seven in the morning before the cars which received us at the place of stopping reached Canandaigua. The lake there is not so picturesque as most of those I have seen; but there is a nice small town, and the house from which I write is the most comfortable and best appointed of any I have yet seen in the United States. Ithaca will be our next halting-place; it is upon the Cayuga Lake.

November 5.—*Cayuga Lake, Ithaca.*—In our way to this place, yesterday, we came by rail to Cayuga Bridge, and there awaited the steamboat *Forest City*, to carry us forty miles down the lake to Ithaca. During the three hours of our detention, I took a walk, made a sketch of the place from a spot about a mile and a half off, and found a plane tree, which appears to me to differ from both the oriental and occidental, though rather more like the latter. It is here called button tree, from its hanging, round seed-vessels. I gathered some of the latter nearly ripe, and also a leaf. Upon the weeping elms it is interesting to see the little nest of the hanging Oriole, which thus builds out of the reach of danger from terrestrial enemies—boy, beast, or reptile. Whether they have winged assailants I do not know. A wind from the north yesterday was very cold, and on board the steam-boat I was obliged to confine myself to the cabin; the shores of these lakes are pretty, and we touched at a village called Aurora, a very rural-looking spot. I saw many nice-looking houses, with a better show of flowers and of well-kept gardens than is common in America; and as we advanced towards Ithaca, rocks and pic-tnresque gullies became frequent; the country hilly and broken. A railroad, carried to the end of the long pier, received us on our landing, and took the passengers to Ithaca, a mile beyond, where

I found Mr. G—— had obligingly brought his carriage to take me to his home. Sunday: a bright sunshiny morning, like a fine November day in England. The leaves here have nearly all fallen, and it is time to give up touring in the Northern States; but, as I understand the election for the Governorship of New York takes place on Tuesday, and that on that day Governor Seymour will either be re-elected or supplanted, I shall remain here to-morrow, and sleep at Syracuse on Tuesday, se as not to pay my visit at Albany until the election day is over.

Ithaca,, November 6.—Snow and ice; bitter cold north-east wind, so that though Mrs. G—— kindly drove me out to make a sketch of the place, we were both too cold to fulfil our intentions of visiting some of the waterfalls in the neighbourhood· I could only view one of the most considerable from a distance. It has a height of between two and three hundred feet, and must be fine when water is abundant. From the great depth of these falls, the stream now looks only like white gauze spread over the rocks, and it disappears in foam. A gentleman told me that the derivation of the word *Ravine* is *Ravel*, from the waters being ravelled out as they tumble down.

Syracuse, November 7.—We came fifty miles round yesterday, through the Valley of the Susquehanna, to avoid retracing our way by Lake Cayuga. A new railroad was opened only last month, from a place called Binghampton (about thirty miles from Ithaca) to Syracuse. Oswego was our first stopping place; the inconvenience of choosing an indirect route being, that we have to change cars twice. Two gentlemen, to whom I was introduced before leaving Ithaca, Mr. Cox and Mr. Parker, reside at Oswego. A fine example of engineering is displayed in getting the cars up the steep hills, by forward and retrogressive movements, with a switch at one point; so that the pretty 'Forest City,' Ithaca, is seen at various distances several times during the first five miles of the ascent; but no chains are used. The country has a wintry appearance—snow upon the hills, and even a little by the wayside. We passed through part of the picturesque Valley of the Susquehanna, following that river close upon its banks some way. There I saw timber-trees of the hemlock spruce; and at a large town called Homer, five churches, each of considerable size, all in a row, without any intervening houses. No time or room for more.

Yours affectionately,

A. M. M.

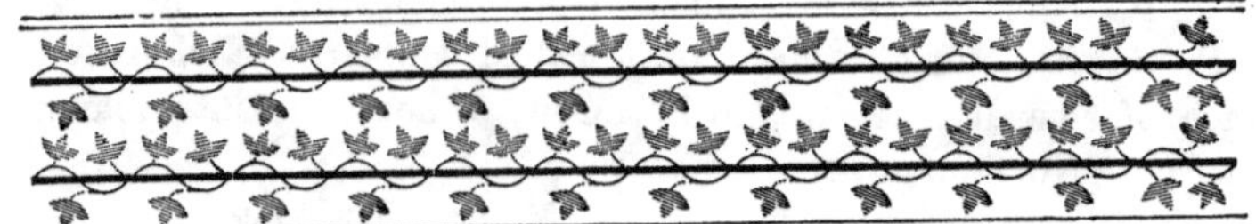

LETTER XII.

ALBANY.

ALBANY, NEW YORK,
Nov. 8.

MY DEAR FRIENDS,—

A snowy morning at Syracuse made it impossible to see anything of that town, or its salt-works; the valuable briny springs there so cheapen one great necessary of life, that I am told, twenty miles off, a large barrel of salt may be purchased for a dollar. The ladies' saloon at the hotel where I slept, exhibited that usual absence of occupation which I have remarked at all such places—rocking-chairs, lounges, and *ennui!* One young lady took something like a small tract in her hand, and in a few minutes was asleep on a sofa—this at half-past ten in the morning. When a gentleman came in, and asked for her—'Oh!' said another lady, her companion, 'she's asleep; but she'll wake up by dinner time.' And this information was not given the least in a satirical tone. We left Syracuse by the eleven o'clock train during a thick snow-storm; but at noon sunshine broke out. We passed through a fine country by Rome, Utica, and Schenectady, skirting the river at the latter place. At Little Falls such abundance of rocks! I longed to stop for a botanical scramble among them. Perhaps next June, when the weather is more favourable for a visit to Utica and Trenton, I may be again at this place. By five o'clock our train reached Albany,—a pleasant, rapid journey of ninety miles, during which the cars slided safely and pleasantly along. No troublesome companions—but some pretty young ladies behind me appeared to think themselves privileged to laugh and talk louder than any one else, because they were better dressed; and a gentleman in front evidently considered it the bounden duty of an American citizen to be bearish. In the hope of softening his temper, I offered him the morning paper; he took it without the smallest acknowledgment, and, when done with it, put it down without even returning it. Whether he discovered we were 'British,' and an anti-English feeling possessed him, I don't know; but still there was a spice of kindness lying under his sulky manner, for when a poor old woman and a girl entered the car, he removed his valise, and gave them his seat.

While stopping at one of the stations, a tall handsome Indian girl, with some bead-work in her hand, entered the car; she wore a picturesque dress, with a black hat and feather, and silently presenting her wares without importunity, she glided on. The noisy and reckless, or ungainly, sulky manner of those around contrasted unfavourably with the subdued, unobtrusive, graceful dignity of the squaw. Nature's gentlemen and gentlewomen, the Indians have a true courtesy and a simple politeness, which might be advantageously copied by those who are their superiors in knowledge and power.

The Governor of New York, to whom I was introduced at Newport, met us at Albany station, and I am now at his house. In the midst of a severe contest with two opponents (an election, for which the votes amount to 500,000), he preserves a manner of calm indifference which his friends do not emulate. I confess myself deeply interested in the result—not so much for Mr. Seymour's sake (because with his love of country pursuits, and his freedom from weak ambition, I really believe his personal happiness will rather be increased than diminished by a return to private life); but because I believe the welfare of this large population to be well cared for while the power is in his hands. In England we have but little idea of the influence exercised by the local Governors in the Union. Governor Seymour has the un limited power of pardoning criminals, and is also Commander-in-Chief of the Army and Navy of this 'Empire State.' He holds his office for two years only, unless re-elected at the end of that time. In some of the States, the Governor's tenure is four years; and Wright, of Indiana, has now been its head nearly eight years. They are, to all intents and purposes, constitutional sovereigns for the time being; and seeing a man of Horatio Seymour's benevolence, judgment, and ability placed in this situation, I shall regret if popular caprice replaces him by an inferior statesman. One of the candidates is a 'Know-nothing,' and he has only party support. I have no acquaintance with Mr. Clark, the man who runs Seymour hard; if he succeeds, his success will be owing to an amiable, though I suspect a mistaken public feeling—about the introduction of the Maine prohibitory liquor law. Governor Seymour has fearlessly and honestly withheld his assent to the introduction of that law into this State. Upon all other points, he is popular; but an extreme and (with some) a religious feeling, moves the popular opinion, and Clark is a 'no liquor man.' None can have a more sincere horror of intemperance than myself; but there is a use as well as an abuse of all things; and I doubt the wisdom of guiding a people to the wise use of a useful article, by prohibiting it altogether.

Albany, Nov. 10.—I went to a wedding last night: very differently arranged from an English marriage, but interesting. A pleasing, well-attired young bride of twenty—the bridegroom twenty-six. They stood side by side, at one end of a well-filled room, while a Presbyterian minister addressed a suitable but short exhortation to them. He then gave the ring to be placed upon the bride's finger, telling her to wear it as a pledge of her husband's affection, and as a reminder of her own duties; and after his blessing upon them both, the ceremony was concluded. It took place at eight o'clock, in the presence of from two to three hundred friends. The young wife remained awhile in her place to receive the kisses of her relations, and the congratulations of all. I was introduced; and she thanked me prettily for my presence, and offered her cheek. Her dress was just like our English brides, excepting that the white robe had a train. She looked calmly happy. The evening was closed by a plentiful standing supper—hot oyster soup, &c. In the morning I went to see hot-houses and greenhouses belonging to a relation of Mrs. Seymour, managed by a gardener who was under Sir Joseph Paxton. Mr. Morison does credit to his teacher: he has the best managed collection of plants I have seen this side of the Atlantic, and a Lycopodium quite new to me. The view from an elevation in Mr. Corning's garden is very extensive, overlooking Albany and Troy, with fine reaches of the Hudson; the Catskill mountains in the distance one way, and a range in the northern part of the State in the other. It is difficult to realize that in coming from Niagara here, I have traversed as much country as if I had journeyed from John O'Groat's House to London! I begin to think nothing of a distance of two hundred miles. This evening we spent some time in a Museum of Natural History, which is doubly interesting, from being entirely confined to the productions of this State; so that, my mind not being overwhelmed with variety, I was able to see, and to understand what I did see, to much greater advantage. The geology of New York is an epitome of that of the world, though it contains some details as well as numerous objects not known in Europe. Our chalk and oolite beds are wanting; but at some hundreds of miles distance green sand is to be seen, rich in fossils, scaphites, &c., three times the size of ours. In Minnesota, about seventeen hundred miles from hence (south-west of Lake Superior), exists a tract one hundred miles in extent, called by the Indians, *Mauvaise Terre*—'The bad country'—and well does it merit that appellation. It consists of clay mountains, placed side by side like huge ant-hills, wholly bare of vegetation —not from infertility, but because their component parts are so little coherent, that rain and torrents wash them clean of verdure, whenever it makes its appearance during a spell of dry weather. Fine specimens of animal remains—tortoises, turtles, &c., are found at the base of these clay hills. The curator of the Museum, Mr. Hubbard, has given me a very curious recent fish from Lake Champlain, deeply interesting as the only lingering denizen of those early periods of the world when fishes wore their bones externally instead of internally. This creature looks like an antediluvian, with his enamelled exterior and his bony tail. I think he must have been a hard morsel, even for the digestion of an ichthyosaurus. He is called here the gar alligator. Mr. Hurst, one of the naturalists belonging to this Museum, has invented a beautiful manner of preserving fish, reptiles, &c., so as to make spirits unnecessary, and greatly to facilitate the examination of them. But so much arsenic is requisite for the process, that his hands are excoriated, while his complexion is improved by its poisonous fumes. The Governor has kindly given me a trout, which is an admirable specimen of this ingenious mode of preparation.

Nov. 11.—For once, I enjoy a pouring wet day, as it gives me time to arrange a chaos of seeds, plants, shells, and stones, which I have collected during my rapid western tour, and to look over the fine Hortus Siccus, arranged by Dr. Torrey, in fifty volumes, for the Museum. As it is of course confined to the flora of New York, I have many specimens not included; but it enables me to determine some which have embarrassed me. I saw an alligator alive, and some curious little turtles and tortoises; the latter are common hereabouts, and I am promised a pet, in the shape of a small tortoise which has the faculty of shutting itself up like a box: it is a vegetarian, quite gentle, hardy, and long lived. If my favourite puss does not take umbrage at him, he will be a clean, innocent, happy favourite. The snapping tortoise is larger, and quite a savage beast. There was a live snake in a box, but I declined his acquaintance. I was surprised to see the wild turkey so much larger than the domesticated; his plumage, too, is finer—almost resembling that of a peacock.

I begin to feel quite excited by the ups and downs of the State election; for though all the votes were taken in one day (the 7th), the various towns and districts send their numbers dribbling in, so that though Governor Seymour has never been without a general majority, yet the whole is extremely fluctuating; and as yet his fate remains undecided. I had a long talk with him about the Slavery question, and was much impressed by his calm and statesmanlike views: he is as desirous as any man can be, to see slavery abolished; but he sensibly says, that, like most other things in connexion with the general welfare, it is to be considered with reference to political economy; and that in our enthusiastic headlong anxiety to do justice to the black race, we have surely (though quite unintentionally) delayed its freedom. This is, I believe, the opinion of Dr. Howe, and other enlightened philanthropists. Twenty-six years ago New York was a Slave State. How has the curse been shaken off? Not by stringent laws and ill-judged prohibitions, but by the introduction of free labour, which rendered that of bondage expensive and inconvenient—though it does not improve the condition. The wisest people say, that Slavery was on the point of extinguishing itself in the South, when, by rendering the supply piratical, the value of the article was so raised in the market, that it became a a profitable concern to grow slaves. As Governor Seymour graphically explains the matter:—'If the early settler wanted to buy beef, he must buy the whole ox—hide, horns, and tail; then comes a time when he can procure a quarter; and at last, as population increases, he can go to market and purchase a beef-steak, or any joint most pleasing to his taste. Now the same thing occurs in the case of labour, which, after all, is a marketable commodity. At first it may be necessary to take the whole man; then you can hire part of a man; and in due time you may be able to get so much of the time of a man as may just suit your purpose, without being burthened by his infancy or his old age.' Thus we, who have been seeking to check the institution of Slavery by violent means, have unintentionally been prolonging it; but time will repair this mistake, by rendering the possession of slaves an expensive mode of cultivation—that is, if cotton can be cultivated without it. Slavery existed and does exist in Africa, and in a more suffering and degraded form than that of the West Indies, or of the American Southern States. The slaves benefited by their change of servitude; that was a first step towards ultimate freedom; and if, when a sufficient number had been imported, their labour had been naturally rendered of less value by the introduction of others, Slavery would quickly have abolished itself; but anti-slavery laws checked the natural course of Providence: slave-labour increased, and the chain of the African was riveted by his intended emancipator. Another practical exemplification of an 'ill-judging friend being worse than an enemy.'

We dined out to-day—a pleasant dinner; the only peculiarity was the name of each intended occupant being placed on the table opposite every chair. Codfish appears to me more delicate here than upon our coasts; but in general I do not think American fish equal those of the English shores. I have now tasted white fish, black fish, masquelongi, and salmon. The masquelongi is a fresh-water fish, plentiful in the Rice Lake. It appears to me a superior kind of pike.

Sunday, Nov. 12.—We went to the church still served by Dr. Potter, the new Bishop of New York, who does not give up his duty till after his consecration. He is a kind and agreeable, as well as a good man; and I never heard our service with greater pleasure: it was so admirably arranged and read here, that I could not help contrasting it with the church at Toronto, where the service was conducted in a heavy, tedious way. Election returns still incomplete; the majority supposed to be for the present Governor; but no one can give certain information.

Albany, November 13.—One circumstance is to be observed of the American Episcopalian clergymen, and, as far as I have been able to remark, the same thing may be said of the Presbyterian,—that they all read well, without the nasal tone or the peculiar pronunciation of the North-eastern States. It is a pity that civilians, especially diplomatic men, do not imitate their clergy in this matter. I think the latter, as a body, superior to ours. Among those whose churches I have attended, two ministers, educated and ordained upon our side the Atlantic, both good men, were pompous and tedious in the reading-desk and pulpit. And we must confess that not many in England either read or preach in an attractive manner. On Saturday, the Governor took me to see an excellent Penitentiary belonging to this district. The house has been lately built after the plan of the superintendent, Mr. Pillsbury, a man who possesses the qualities of firmness, order, and benevolence in a high degree. The cells are arranged in a way differing from what I have hitherto seen. An oblong block of three or four storeys (the upper ones reached by exterior staircases and galleries, capable of accommodating 185 people) is placed within a large kind of hall admirably ventilated; every cell has an iron bedstead, and those of the women a chair. The large door of iron grating which closes each, is so constructed as to admit sufficient light and air. All are shut by the same mechanical process, managed by an iron bar, which runs the whole length of the block, and even if any one is by accident left unlocked, the door cannot be opened. About three hundred prisoners, male and female, are now confined here—all for short terms: those under long convictions are taken to other prisons. These people are sentenced for a period of about three months; many of them for a shorter time. We found the men at work in two large workshops, one entirely devoted to making cane-bottomed chairs, the other harness. All were busily engaged; not one lifted an eye or spoke a word. In the women's ward, there was more variety of employment; washing, ironing, mending, and cooking—but no speaking. One haggard looking crone of more than eighty years of age, here for the fourth time, looked the personification of incorrigibility. Some few men were at work in the grounds, which having to be newly laid out, afford much promise of occupation; and it has sometimes happened that emancipated prisoners have entreated for employment there. Mr. Pillsbury's success appears to be owing to his unflinching will and determined discipline; to the strict enforcement of cleanliness, and, above all, to the influence of love which this kind man brings to bear upon his prisoners, for his heart seems to be of the most tender mould. Yet I could wish that the tongues of these unfortunate ones might be a little loosed, just so much as is allowed by the Governor of the gaol at Munich without being followed by evil consequences. There, the prisoners are permitted to speak on matters connected with their labour, but if that liberty is abused, they are made to work alone. Upon the entrance of a prisoner here, he is told he must be industrious, never look up from his work, and keep silence, and that if he conforms to these rules, he will be well fed and kindly treated; he usually conforms immediately. The house has been erected, and all expenses of the establishment are defrayed, by the profits which accrue from the prisoners' labour.

Near Utica there has long been a white rock held as a sacred stone by the Indians. This veneration was owing to its being a kind of sienite unique in the district. As its situation was near a spot lately formed into a cemetery, Mr. Seymour proposed that this stone should be removed there to save it from destruction, and to show sympathy for Indian feelings. An agreement with them was made for that purpose; they also being allowed the liberty of interment in the grounds; and the stone may be seen now on a mound at the cemetery.

After the election of the present Governor, a chief came to Albany, to prefer some request to him. Being an Oneidan, he spoke of his tribe. Mr. Seymour kindly replying, said—'I also am an Oneidan, for my residence is at Utica.' The Indians designated the local Governors as their 'Father,' and the President as their 'Great Father.' But upon Mr. Seymour making this remark, the Chief quickly and gracefully changed the term of relationship. 'My Brother then is an Oneidan; he will feel for the wants of his Brethren.' Although the Indians may speak and understand English, and when not conducting a diplomatic interview will converse in our language, yet in formal intercourse with the Governors or Governments, they will only carry it on through an interpreter, bearing in mind the view of preserving their dignity and nationality. I believe they are now very kindly and considerately treated by the United States. Their religion is a pure Theism; and some of those we call the Pagan Indians are, alas! superior in Christian conduct to the converted; for the latter practise the vices of cheating and drunkenness, while the former are simple, pure, and sober, until contaminated by the white man. They believe in a great creating, superintending Spirit, who rewards the good and punishes the evil in a future life; and they have public meetings for prayer and thanksgiving. One is called the 'Feast of Strawberries,' when they assemble to offer up thanks to the Great Giver of all good for the returning crop of that berry; and there are other periods of general thanksgiving for a sufficiency of game and for the fruits of the earth. Thus they acknowledge the unity, omnipresence, and omniscience of the Deity; the freewill, responsibility, and immortality of man; and these truths being known and assented to by the American Indians, Christianity is received and accepted by them without much difficulty, as a further dispensation and message from the Universal Father.

From the Governor of New York I have inquired and learned the meaning of party terms which have before puzzled me—such as Adamantines, Hard-shells, Soft-shells, Loco-focos, Rick-burners, and Pollywogs. It seems these names are highly figurative—they have originated in casual expressions made use of by public speakers which have happened to hit the fancy of the hearers, so that they become cant terms. A Democrat in this country is synonymous with a Whig or Liberal in England, while he who is denominated Whig here, is really a Tory or Conservative. The latter party advocate prohibitions, and tariffs, and interference of the Central Government with local improvements; while the Democrats are free-traders, and promoters of self-government in each State. They say that railroads, and harbours, and bridges, and canals, can be formed and conducted at less expense and more advantageously on the spot, than when planned and directed by the Central Government from a distance of many hundred miles, where they are apt to degenerate into jobs. Upon some occasion, when the moderate Democrats were accused of yielding rather too much to the views of their opponents, a wag, during his address to a popular assembly, said: 'Now I think these politicians are blowing hot and cold; they are too much like crabs when in a state of transition between the soft and the hard shell. I am for the whole hog—I am a Hard-shell.' And another said,

'They are Pollywogs' (the Indian name for tadpoles). So with the Loco-focos, of which party the Barn-burners were an extreme. Now I understand the meaning of the following curious paragraph in one of the local papers some weeks ago: 'The organ of the Hard-shell Democrats says that orders have been sent from Washington, enjoining all persons holding office under the Central Government to keep away from the approaching Soft-shell Convention at Syracuse; for this reason it is anticipated the Barn-burners will have control of the convention, and pass anti-Nebraska resolutions.' The peculiar circumstances which gave origin to the Loco-foco and Barn-burner, are these; during an assemblage of Democrats, some who wished to disperse the meeting obtained command of the gas-pipes, with an intention of throwing darkness over the deliberations of the said 'convention;' but the Hard-shells, getting a hint of this plot, provided themselves with lucifer-matches and candles, and when the gas went out suddenly, they soon re-illuminated their proceedings. Hence they were called Loco-focos; and an ultra Loco-foco was taunted with the sobriquet of Barn-burner.

We dined yesterday at a very pretty and well-arranged house, belonging to Mr. and Mrs. Pompelly—an Italian name, which has been spoiled by the substitution of an English termination. The dinner was much like one in London, except that the hour was six instead of eight. I sat by an American Major-General, who has travelled much in Europe. From his countenance and manner, I should have supposed him Bavarian; but this city contains a great mixture of the varying national characteristics of Europe. In one quarter Germans are so numerous, that the signs and designations of the shops and eating-houses are in German. Many also of the respectable inhabitants there still speak Dutch; French is less common, but the American, Scotch, Irish, and English blood is mixed up in tolerably equal proportions, and in a short time all these heterogeneous elements will be happily amalgamated.

To-day I went to visit the library—a handsome and convenient building, well supplied with valuable and useful books; and afterwards the Governor introduced me to the studio of Palmer—a sculptor of evident taste and talent, who has hitherto depended upon the inspiration of his own mind, rather than upon the study of ancient art. Near a spot chiefly inhabited by Dutch settlers, I endeavoured to make a sketch of Albany with the distant mountains, and an extensive view of the Hudson River; but my fingers soon became so benumbed by cold, that I had not much success. The weather continues very like winter in England, but no decided snow here at present.

November 16.—Yesterday was nearly all passed in visiting, to return the civility of those who have called, or given me invitations. I entered a great many houses. The reception rooms are generally on the ground floor, handsomely fitted up, usually covered by English or French carpets, but extremely dark. They are commonly kept very warm by stoves, or rather furnaces, below. I only saw one open fireplace, in which the fuel was a kind of anthracite coal. The houses are good, almost always entered by a single flight of stone steps; from three to four rooms on a floor, but these rooms have a bare, unhomelike appearance to an English eye, from the absence of books, and work, and writing materials; they look as if in use only for company. We had an agreeable small dinner-party at home—the Bishop of New York; Mr. Hall, the palæontologist, and his wife; Mr. Johnson, a judge; and one or two more. It is believed that the re-election of the present Governor is secure. I rejoice in this, as an indication that good common sense, after all, prevails over an ill-regulated enthusiasm. The other day, a young man received his pardon from Mr. Seymour, after a short imprisonment. In such a case he usually sees the offender upon his liberation; and he gave this youth some friendly advice upon the danger of intemperate habits. The man looked surprised, and exclaimed: 'Why, sir, I had been told you were all for liquor, and you don't look like one who cares for it.' 'Remember,' was the reply, 'that no human law can make a man good. He must learn self-control, and be actuated by principle. If laws would have prevented you from getting into mischief, you would not have been sent to prison.'

One day is annually set apart by the custom of each State for a general thanksgiving. Here is an example of the form and manner in which this is done. The Governor for the time being selects a day, and then issues his Proclamation, which is published in all the papers :—

PROCLAMATION.

By Horatio Seymour, Governor of the State of New York.

An acknowledgment of our dependence upon God, and of our obligation to Him, is at all times the duty of a Christian People. But when the Almighty has again crowned the year with his goodness, and we are enjoying the gathered fruits of His bounty, it is eminently fitting that we should offer the sacrifice of praise and thanksgiving.

I therefore appoint Thursday, the 30th day of November, for this appropriate service; and invite the citizens of the State to assemble on that day in their respective places of worship, to present their acknowledgments to the Parent of the Universe for his multiplied mercies. And with our thanksgiving let us mingle prayers for a continuance of the numberless blessings we, as a people, enjoy, remembering that His wisdom alone can rightly direct, His power support, and His goodness give strength and security.

[L. S.] In witness whereof I have hereunto subscribed my name and affixed the private seal of the State, at the City of Albany, this 10th day of November, One Thousand Eight Hundred and Fifty-Four.

HORATIO SEYMOUR.

By the Governor. H. W. De Puy,
Private Secretary.

In driving down one of the streets here, my attention was attracted by the Manx Arms—the three legs—as a sign over a tailor's shop. I was sure the occupant must be a native of the Isle of Man, and on our return I requested to stop the carriage, that I might ask a question. Upon going into the house I found a man busily employed upon a coat. 'You are a Manxman, I am certain?' 'To be sure I am,' was the answer; 'but who are you?' The tailor and the tailor's wife and daughter were delighted to hear the name of Murray, and to find I had been at Jurby, about four miles from Bishop's Court, where the man was born: he has been nineteen years in America; he says he has got on pretty well, but that he works harder than he did at home. I was invited to tea, and though I could not accept the invitation, it gave me pleasure to see that my visit was fully appreciated. I have made a sketch of Bishop's Court, for this my friend, (Mr. Crow,) from memory; and as he maintains it to be the most beautiful place in the world, I think the remembrance will be valued.

Albany, November 17.—Mr. Seymour and his opponent are still running neck to neck, although we have several times supposed the affair settled; this election has been more fluctuating and longer about than any I ever heard of, not entirely owing to the great extent of territory concerned—for all the votes were taken at the different places in one day; but they have been very long coming in here. At New York, and I think I may say in all the enlightened cities, Seymour has an overwhelming majority, but the distant counties and towns vote for Myron Clark, and it is now believed they will elect him by a trifling majority. The numbers to-day are 132,264 for Seymour—131,111 for Clark; there are, however, a few more returns to come in, which may be in favour of the latter.

November 18.—We spent yesterday evening quietly, drinking tea with Mrs. S——'s sister, who lives nearly opposite: her interest and excitement at the present moment are naturally great, as a change of Governors will separate this family. Our weather to-day prómises to be clear and fine; we have had hardly anything but gloomy, wet, cold days since I arrived here ten days ago. Perhaps we shall go to New York this afternoon. I have heard of the arrival of my Virginian friend, Miss G——, from England, and I hope to meet her there. A mere child, named Eli Rheem, has performed an act of heroism worthy of more years and of noblest times. I have cut the details out of a trustworthy print—for this deed deserves te be celebrated as evincing a courage which throws that of warriors into the shade.

A NOBLE BOY.

RESCUE OF A PASSENGER TRAIN FROM CERTAIN DESTRUCTION.

We mentioned a few days since the burning of the Tunnel Bridge, on the Baltimore and Susquehanna Railroad, about five miles south of York, and since learn that the conflagration came very near being followed by one of the most terrible disasters that has lately occurred in railroad travel. It is supposed that the bridge took fire from the freight trains which passed about half-past seven o'clock in the morning, and the structure was totally enveloped in flames before it was discovered by the residents in the vicinity. At about nine o'clock the frame-work of the bridge fell through, and among the spectators, some twenty in number, was a little boy about twelve years of age, named Eli Rheem, who, remembering that the express train was then about due from York, started off at the top of his speed to endeavour to stop the train, which he knew must be close at hand. As soon as he reached the curve, about two hundred yards from the bridge, he observed the train coming at full speed, and fearing that he would be unable to stop them unless by the use of extraordinary means, the noble little fellow took his position on the track, and running towards the approaching train with his hands raised, caught the attention of the engineer, who immediately reversed his engine, and stopped within four hundred yards of impending destruction, the piers being some twenty feet from the rocky bed below, and the gap some sixty feet wide. Had the boy not placed himself on the track, he would doubtless have failed in his noble effort, as the engineers are so often cheated by mischievous boys on the route that they seldom pay any attention to them. Even when he stopped, he thought he had been cheated by a youngster with more daring than his associates, and was surprised to see the little flaxen-headed fellow stand his ground, and endeavouring to recover his lost breath, to answer his questions as to the cause of his interruption. We learned that the passengers, when they ascertained the cause of the stoppage of the train, and viewed the precipice over which they were near being dashed, liberally rewarded the boy for his presence of mind and daring, and that the Board of Directors, at their meeting yesterday, appropriated 100 dollars as an additional recompense. Eli Rheem, a boy but twelve years of age, was the only one of twenty persons present, most of them men, who had forethought sufficient for the occasion.—*Balt. American.*

The name of *Rheem* leads one to suppose that this gallant little fellow must be of Dutch origin; I shall be glad if England can claim the originating of his parentage. Alas! for the horrors of war contrasting with the peaceful triumph of this child! Our brave soldiers sacrificed, to sacrifice those who under different circumstances they would die to save! I dread looking at the English news. Every mail now brings sorrowful intelligence of the fall of some young man who, if not a relative of my own, is the darling of some house and home for which I feel an interest. What does not that Russian deserve? I trust he will some day be shut up as a madman, unfit to be trusted with a knife; and then perhaps his wretched serfs may learn that Christianity does not teach them war. To-day the Governor and Mrs. Seymour took me to see a community of Shakers, who live about ten miles from this place; they appear to be a harmless industrious set of people, a kind of Quaker Order of Monks and Nuns, who feed well, set a good example as to morality and neatness, and eschew as a crime everything approaching to beauty and elegance. We had some excellent bread and cheese, saw them make their useful brooms, and bought some of their delicate baskets, in the manufacture of which the line of beauty has unconsciously introduced itself. Kind Brother Frederick, the ruler of the establishment, showed us all over it. A Shaker village has one great advantage over all monastic communities—no vows are imposed, and the freedom of egress is perfectly unshackled. We drove through a high sandy district, with scattered woods of birch and yellow pine, the ground diversified by low hills, with extensive views of distant mountains and the Hudson River. In passing through Albany, I was shown some old Dutch houses, constructed of bricks which were actually brought here from Holland! Now, the great majority of buildings are of brick made on the spot. In this neighbourhood the usual snake fences, made with as large a quantity of timber as can be put into them, about six feet high, are beginning to be rare: the divisions consist of fences straight and regular; once it was considered a beauty to have as many fences as possible, now a contrary opinion prevails hereabouts. In new clearings, glaring white houses, with green or red blinds are still considered the best taste—naturally enough; for in the dark forest they were more visible, and spoke of comfort and civilization: now some taste for architecture is springiag up in cities and their environs. Mr. Seymour drove me in a light open carriage, universal in America:

it has wheels exceedingly high in proportion to the size of the body. These 'wagons' are certainly airy and slight, and consequently plunge into the hollows and holes of the tracks without risk. We had a bright sun, and as the wind was quiet I did not mind cold; but it was very cold.

November 19—*Sunday.*—I believe that my journey to New York is likely to be delayed yet for days. Some gentlemen who came in last night, say that the voting is so close, that although State officers are now busy in investigation, it will require another week before the result can be declared; and even then the present Governor, if he should lose, would really have a majority; because a large number of votes have been given with the initial H., instead of Horatio, which invalidates them. The Shakers, too, wish for him; but the silly people consider it against their principles to make use of their votes. I wonder whether you in England will feel any interest in this election for my American friend; or whether you will be vexed that so many pages of my paper are devoted to New York politics. This packet will probably be sent off before the knotty point is made straight, so either way you will not get the conclusion until another mail. Though interested, my mind is not at all decided as to whether I really wish the present Governor to be in for another year or not. I should not like him to be beat. Yet I think the good effects of his rule will tell upon his successor, who, I understand, is much his inferior in education and talent; and rest will be good for my friend, while he and Mrs. Seymour will be more at liberty to make our proposed forests excursions next year. I shall remain until the matter is settled; for as they kindly wish to be my guides in New York, should we go there whilst the decision is pending, Mr. Seymour's visit there will be ascribed to political motives, which would be unpleasant to him.

After the service this morning, the Bishop-elect of New York baptized two children, one about four, the other rather more than a year old; the ceremony took place at the Communion-rail under the pulpit—the water being blessed on the reading-desk. The father and mother with their eldest child, alone stood and knelt at the rail; the other attendants remained in pews. I like the custom of allowing parents to be sponsors for their own children. The service was much the same as ours. But as after being baptized, the youngest child was inclined to be loquacious, he was at once taken out of the church by the person who carried him in her arms. I observed no particular smartness of dress on this occasion, either for the children or their attendants.

The Governor has just proposed that Mrs. Seymour and I shall go together to New York to-morrow; and if business permits, he will follow in the course of a day or two. So we shall start by the eleven o'clock train, and go to the St. Nicholas Hotel. I shall probably not extend my stay at New York much beyond a week; and letters in future must be addressed to the care of Mr. Crampton, our minister at Washington. He is the most likely person to know my whereabouts; and he will, I daresay, forward communications from home during the winter, or as long as I remain in the Southern States.

Your affectionate

A. M. M.

LETTER XIII.

NEW YORK.

New York, *November* 25, 1854.

My dear Friends,—

After travelling 2685 miles, here we are at New York. Since our arrival, on the 19th, I have not had time to write more than a few lines, which went by yesterday's mail to my nieces. I had a pleasant journey by rail down the beautiful Hudson; for the greater part of the way the line actually runs through the water; as between the range of the Catskills on one side, and the rocky shore on the other, it was much easier to form a road on piles, where the water is not very deep, than to tunnel and batter a course for the trains through the rocks: at one spot where we did go through them, a red flag brought us up for a few minutes, owing to some of the boundary having fallen in the night. Mrs. Seymour, her niece, and some gentlemen, accompanied me from Albany: the Governor has now arrived also, but it was not in his power to come down on Monday. This Hotel of St. Nicholas is quite a palace; its only fault being that the gorgeous silk furniture, mirrors, and carpets, are rather in the extreme of magnificence; however, the rooms are comfortable. I have a hot and cold bath attached to my bedroom: and as I happened to be rather ill yesterday (for the first time since I crossed the Atlantic), I found the warm bath an excellent remedy, and one which, if it had not been so conveniently placed, I should probably have gone without. Tuesday last was spent in shopping and visits. On Wednesday the consecration of my friend Dr. Potter, the new Bishop of New York, took place; I saw much of him at Albany, still as yet his residence. The ceremony was one of much more importance than that upon like occasions in England. Twelve bishops and one hundred and sixty clergy attended, besides two hundred students of divinity. It was performed in a pretty new church called Trinity, Early Perpendicular in style; all the windows edged and surmounted with painted glass, which, though not of the most perfect design and colouring, is still far better than common. The music was good, and I observed no great difference from our consecration service, excepting that the new bishop is robed in front of the Communion-table, a custom which has always prevailed in America, but which, I think, detracted from the solemnity of the occasion. In the evening I was invited to meet all the bishops and a large number of the clergy. It was a pleasant party; and I recognized the Bishop of Vermont, who received me with kindness on Lake Champlain. The consecration deed of Dr. Potter, designed and beautifully illuminated by a young lady, was on a table of mediæval appearance. I was introduced to Bishop Fulford, who was absent during my visit to Montreal. He preached in the morning. Thursday, Mr. D——, one of my American friends on board the *Canada*, took me to see many places in the city, and from the steeple summit of Trinity Church I gained a good idea of New York, with its rivers, islands, and environs; the ground it is built upon is almost insular—perhaps three or four miles in width, and fourteen in length, Broadway nearly dividing it in half. This street is something between our Strand and Oxford-street, rather wider than the former, quite as full of traffic as either; but then we must bear in mind that this is the only great artery of New York. We drove in an omnibus through Broadway to what is considered the aristocratic quarter—for it must be remarked that people here are not at all less exclusive than in London—only the differences of rank and wealth are evinced by more minute and elaborate attention to dress, and to trifling conventionalities, than with us. I have been surprised to hear some men of business, but of wealth, assert that cultivation of the fine arts is a proof of national effeminacy! American ladies bestow those hours of leisure, which English women of the same class give to drawing, to the study of nature, and to mental cultivation, almost wholly on personal adornment. Although it must be admitted that owing to the bad training of their servants, ladies on this side the Atlantic are compelled to look closely into the details of domestic economy, yet it is odd that they are generally far less competent to the performance of every-day and sick-room duties than the daughters of our noblest houses in Great Britain; and so long as girls here devote a whole hour for every ten minutes allowed by us to the toilet, they have no right to make domestic affairs an excuse for want of general information. Of course there are brilliant exceptions; but I fear the national character of women in the United States more resembles that of self-indulgent Asiatics than of energetic Anglo-Saxons. And, as far as I can judge, their children are not being reared in better habits. Human nature is prone to extremes; and these facts explain why some individuals desirous of improvement, have fallen into a mistaken imitation of manly character instead of cultivating feminine duties. Yesterday we dined with Mr. and Mrs. Bancroft, at their house in 22nd-street. Not having the organ of 'Number,' I am rather plagued by having numeral streets, in addition to the customary numbering of doors; and 8th street west and 28th street east (No. 8, perhaps), make a terrible hubbub in my memory.—The 23rd of November was a very wet day, and I did not go out.—Saturday, November 25th, Mrs. Seymour took me so see Greenwood Cemetery, which is extensive, and beautifully situated on the heights of Brooklyn. But the general appearance of this place is injured by a custom of using upright white stone posts as boundaries for the several family burying-ing grounds. I have remarked this at all the cemeteries, excepting those of Boston and Toronto. Auburn Cemetery, belonging to the former city, is much the most agreeable and soothing place of interment, from its quiet and unassuming, as well as picturesque scenery. Glare and grief are antagonistic, and intrusive objects should not meet an eye still dim with tears; each spot of ground consecrated to family affection should be securely, but almost invisibly guarded from intrusion. Among the monuments in New York Cemetery, that which marks the burying-place of firemen is specially interesting. It is crowned by the statue of a noble spirit, who perished in his endeavour to rescue a child. In one hand he holds a speaking-trumpet; his other arm clasps the infant, as with a firm, but apparently hurried step, and upturned head, he endeavours to reach security and meets death. I accompanied a party to see the Governor review the militia regiments of New York. These, like the yeomanry of England, are volunteers; men (even in the ranks) of property and consideration. English, French, Dutch, Americans, Irish, Scotch, banded together as far as possible according to their several national feelings and peculiarities, but each individual merging his national loyalty in one common enthusiasm for the protection of the country he has permanently adopted;—meet upon a day which is here known by the name of 'Evacuation Day,' to make a grand demonstration of this unity of sentiment; and, although their troops were not so compact and well-drilled as regulars, yet as a body of five or six thousand men, not called out for more than three days in a year, they are much to be admired; and one regiment, all dressed in bluish grey, manœuvred with great precision.

I did not feel my own national *amour propre* the least wounded upon this occasion. We may now rejoice over the 'evacuation' with as hearty good will as the Americans themselves, and at the same time feel a rational degree of pride that old England sent forth, and originally nurtured, such promising citizens for the New World. Although the Governor of New York is Commander-in-chief, and a staff of officers in full regimentals surround him, he wears no uniform, but always appears the civil officer of the State. Mr. Seymour reviewed these troops in front of the City Hall, with as much tranquillity of manner and simple dignity as might have been evinced by any one of the most experienced of our public men. It is impossible to find more entire freedom from self-consciousness in any man, while the claims of duty and kindness are never put out of sight or omitted by him.

On Sunday I went to a chapel in Brooklyn to hear the brother of Mrs. Beecher Stowe preach to a very crowded congregation. His sermon was one of great eloquence and originality; in style and manner too familiar to suit English ideas: but it was eminently practical, and so much of truth and wisdom was to be culled out of a somewhat rugged and informal chain of argument, that no eye slumbered and no person's attention flagged during a very long discourse.

November 27.—This morning I breakfasted with Mr. and Mrs. B——, to meet several agreeable people, among them the preacher, Mr. H. W. Beecher. I liked his earnest, powerful mind; although upon the topics of slavery and prohibitory laws, I doubted his arguments. In the afternoon, the Governor, Mrs. Seymour, and I visited print-shops and galleries. He wished much to see Sir Edwin Landseer's picture of 'The Twins,' but it had been just packed up and sent off to Boston.

November 28.—We all breakfasted with Miss Lynch the poetess; we had there another pleasant party, and again Mr. Beecher, whose discussions with the Governor upon social subjects were very interesting. I forgot to mention the opera last night—Grisi and Mario: the latter sang to perfection; Grisi less rich and powerful in tone than I remember her formerly, but still wonderful. Mr. D—— took me to visit a gentlemanly and intelligent young man, by trade a coachmaker, who seems to have travelled and observed nature more than is common in this land of business; and in his possession I saw one of those curious eyeless fish from the Mammoth Cave of Kentucky. It is preserved in spirits, about the size and somewhat of the form of a fresh-water perch, about five inches long. I thought there was a faint mark on the spots where eyes usually are, but nothing more: and a small kind of cray-fish from the same locality was also deficient in visual organs. I shall probably go to that Cave, when I may procure specimens; and I shall try to get one preserved without spirits. The rest of my day was taken up by necessary social visits; but I saw various parts of the town.

Wednesday, November 29.—I went with the Governor to view all the Philanthropic and Penal establishments, which, much to the credit, the generosity, and the good feeling of New York State, have been founded and organized upon the two Islands of Randall and Blackwell. The East River pours down in rapid torrents on either side of these islands, so as to add security, as well as to contribute to the salubrity of these establishments. A four-oared boat took us off about seven miles from the city. We first landed upon Randall Island, where there is a very large Refuge just opened for delinquents; and there the great pauper establishments for children, and also an Emigrant's Home, are situated. Eight hundred happy-looking orderly boys marched about to the time of their own drums and fifes, forming a young regiment. They manœuvred with more precision, and dressed their lines more evenly, than the troops we saw reviewed on Friday. Their commander and drill sergeant was an *idiot* man about forty. He has the love and the strict obedience of his children, although upon every subject excepting military discipline his mind is a blank. It was pleasing to see the innocent enjoyment of this poor general and his young soldiers. One point of sympathy links them together; may they remain warriors of love rather than of contention—the teachers and the learners of Christian obedience and of religious duty. The girls (about six hundred) appeared to be equally well trained and cheerful in their several occupations. In no institution have I ever seen cleanliness and order more complete and perfect than in these. The quarter for emigrants also gave rise to feelings of satisfaction. It is open to all destitute strangers during any period not exceeding five years from their first arrival on these shores. Six hundred infants, upon an average, are yearly born within its precincts. We saw mothers and infants well nursed and cared for—occupation for the industrious, training for the idle; and all appeared quiet and contented in their temporary home. I heard of very little sickness—only five or six cases of cholera; but there are hospitals for children with chronic diseases—one ward full of whooping-cough patients, and another where a few were sick with feverish complaints, all thoroughly ventilated, and apparently all made as comfortable as circumstances would admit. On Blackwell Island we saw a large and excellent Asylum for the Insane, a Pauper House of Industry, and a Penal establishment—good in their several ways. On the two islands there is a population of ten thousand—children, women, and men—destitute, sick, or sinful. Nowhere can one find a spirit of more generous and enlightened charity than that evinced by these and the other philanthropic institutions of New York. A great variety of shipping and numerous steamers are constantly passing down the river on each side. The sight of these, manœuvring through its shoals and rapids, must be a constant source of amusement and interest to the island denizens. I saw a steamboat which whirled down with a marvellous rapidity, and numerous sailing-vessels were tacking backwards and forwards, preparing to pass through that 'Hell-gate' on the river where an English frigate was once wrecked. This appellation was derived from Dutch settlers. We again entered a boat, and crossed the rapid stream to a point where carriages soon conveyed our party back to the St. Nicholas Hotel in time to fulfil a dinner engagement. I had the pleasure of sitting by the poet Bryant, with his picturesque grey head and beard.

Thursday, November 30.—Thanksgiving-day; an annual festival, religious and social, commanded and celebrated by each State. But it was sad to me; for that morning brought accounts from the armies at Sebastopol, and tidings of the death of General S——, and others known to me, or dear to those I know. Still I cannot wish the place to be taken until our troops are strengthened by reinforcements.

Friday, December 1.—Dr. Torrey came after breakfast; he looked over my gathering of plants, and was much interested by the specimens of those got at Point Levi. The fern I found in wet meadows at Lake St. Charles, is Botrychium simplex. I find the Garadias are most of them parasitical upon other living plants, which makes the idea of introducing them into our English gardens nearly hopeless. Mr. D—— was so obliging as to guide me to some necessary calls. I made one attempt to find my own way through these puzzling streets, and it proved very unsuccessful. Saturday, at Professor Renwick's, 21, 5th Avenue —I came here to an early dinner, after parting with the Governor and Mrs. Seymour for a few days; they promise to meet me on Thursday, at the hotel, West Point. Monday: Mr. B—— has made an engagement for me to go to see Mr. and Mrs. G. S——, on the Hudson, where I shall meet Washington Irving, who lives near. Before leaving the St. Nicholas, I was annoyed by discovering that my four best coloured drawings of Niagara Falls had been abstracted from a portfolio, and other indifferent ones left. This looks as if the thief had an artistic judgment, which is not very common here. I have offered a reward, and done all possible for their restoration; the loss is irreparable to me: and it is a poor consolation that any one should have considered them valuable enough to be an object of theft! The Canada Falls, and the American Falls from Goat Island, the latter at sunrise and the former at sunset, were the subjects which seem to have attracted the notice and the cupidity of some one who took them away from the Governor's private room. This is the third robbery I have suffered since I came to America. Paint-brushes and pencils all stolen out of my bag at Montreal; cloaks and shawls carried off during the railway accident between Niagara and Canandaigua; and now my drawings! So many indifferent subjects cross the Atlantic, in hopes of finding prey here, that pickpocketing and petty thefts are common; indeed it is almost impossible to guard against them; and according to the doctrine of compensations, I must be content to put up with such trivial miseries, in the hope they may frank my life and limbs through the perils of extensive journeying by land and sea. Sunday, I went to Grace Church, a Gothic elevation designed by a son of Professor Renwick; the effect is much injured by all the windows being of painted glass, of vivid colours, ill arranged; there were some good bits, and erasure with a sponge would relieve these loaded panes and improve the general effect, even without any change in the coloured glass. As it is, the church is made too obscure, and good taste offended by red, blue, and yellow, interspersed without the smallest reference to harmony—that great requirement without which design is nothing in stained windows. I walked back to 5th Avenue in such heavy rain that no umbrella could avail to keep me dry, even for a short distance; and though my 'locality' bump carried me back in the right direction, yet on arriving at the place, I rang at a wrong door; for as there is a street at right angles to the house, I had never studied its exterior appearance, and therefore was at a loss to distinguish it from three other corners; till I walked up stairs and disturbed a strange gentleman, I did not find out my error. Mr. F——, the protector of emigrants, whom I met last at Spencer Wood, accompanied me yesterday to see the New York Institution for the Deaf and Dumb. I had only a short time for my visit, but it was sufficient to satisfy my mind of their excellent training; one of the masters is himself a deaf mute who was brought up in the school, and the wife of another was also a pupil; she is pretty and intelligent, but still remains only able to express herself by signs and writing.

I was introduced to the first class as an English lady who had crossed the Atlantic to see their country and its institutions; each young person wrote upon his or her slate a little address, varied in expression according to individual character and feeling. Gratification at my vist and respect for Britain were predominant; one or two made use of the expression 'proud' England, but erased it immediately upon my suggesting that 'old' England would be more appropriate. The superintendent, Mr. Peat, made a request that I would propose a subject upon which they could offer the conclusions of their own minds. I inquired 'Whether the motive of love, or that of emulation, was that by which the course of education could best be guided.' All but one preferred love; some because it was the great Christian rule; others because it was the most effective; and one, who at first was in favour of emulation, rubbed out the sentence with an air of repentance, when she read what she thought the better choice made by her associates. I found that neither Mr. F—— nor Mr. C—— were of my opinion respecting the best modes of eradicating slavery and drunkenness. I thought their reasons for passing the Maine law told against themselves; for instance—'that a large number of the population were in favour of it.' Is not this very fact a proof that if you leave improvement to take its own course, the misuse of stimulants will cure itself; and a proof, also, that intemperance is gradually lessening? For, some years ago, the people would not have favoured a sumptuary law working against their own liberty, for the purpose of encouraging sobriety. It is said the Maine law is acting advantageously in that State. Not a good argument, I think; because temporary success does not justify mistaken principles; besides which, I have reason to believe that the improvement is more on the surface than radical; that much more drinking is now done on the sly; and thus ill-informed though well-intentioned people have been offering a bonus to hypocrisy, while they thought they were discouraging intemperance. I find there are now laws enough in the State of New York to keep down liquor-shops, if they were executed: but no; it is too difficult to put in force laws against individual failings. Therefore such laws become a dead letter; and now they want to heap more prohibitions on the statute-book, to make up for not enforcing the first. They may as well fight the wind. Human nature was put into this world to learn self-control, and to gain experience; a man will never be the more virtuous for prohibitions, or the more strong-minded for being kept wholly away from temptation; he must learn to refuse the evil and choose the good, and, if he will not learn this by the inculcation of good principles, he will never become more strong in virtue by being kept out of the reach of evil. This is the principle of the public schools in England. The head masters of Eton, and perhaps of the other schools, have falsified it with regard to smoking; and what is the consequence? The boys consider it manly to brave punishment; and there are few among them to whom cigars are not growing to be a necessary indulgence;

besides which, they half smother themselves by putting their heads under water to disguise the smell; whereas, if the habit had been treated as ungentlemanly and suited only to the ale-house, without any positive prohibition, it would probably, like other fashions, have become obsolete.

December 4.—I went with Mr. and Mrs. B—— and Mr. O—— to a pretty cottage on the Hudson River, to visit Mr. and Mrs. G. S——: the country all white; so much snow that, for the first time, I was driven in a sleigh from the railway-station. I found a pleasant family, whose mode of life and arrangements were very much those of a small household in England. We paid a morning visit to Washington Irving: he is a much younger looking man than I expected to see; nothing of the petted or the spoilt favourite in his simple retiring manner: he was all, and more, than I expected; and I felt unalloyed pleasure in such an introduction. Bitter winds and snow continuing, I must give up any idea of West Point for the present, and be content with two or three days pleasantly and quietly spent. To-morrow I shall go to Tarry Town; and if the Governor and Mrs. Seymour do not meet me there, I shall fulfil my engagement to them by returning to Albany.

December 8.—I came on to Albany last night in cold snowy weather, and rejoined my friends, as they were unable to come to me. The journey was not pleasant, though the banks of the Hudson were still fine, even in their wintry dress. The steamer which brought us over the river from the railway station went crashing through the ice; and I was not sorry to find myself in State-street.

Friday, 8*th*.—Mrs. Seymour took me out in a sleigh to pay some visits; the coldest day I have ever felt.

Saturday, *December* 9.—We walked to the Senate-house and some other places. The streets very slippery; sleighs with their bells in all directions. Dined out. Better news from the East: reinforcements have reached our army. As it has already fought and conquered five to one, I cannot share the apprehensions of those who fear the allied troops will be beaten out of the Crimea.

The power of Russia was underrated, and for that we are punished.

December 10.—There has been a thaw, and snow is decreasing. The sleighs seem to go heavily; those with one horse are called cutters. It is only the machines drawn by two which are dignified by the name of sleighs. The Governor is busy winding up business, so as to place the affairs of the State in the hands of his successor, Myron Clark, by the 1st of January. I have not seen this gentleman; it does not seem that his talents are appreciated highly by individuals who have been voting for him because he belongs to their particular party, while Mr. Seymour appears to be liked by those who voted against him. I extract the following from a paper politically opposed:—

'Governor Seymour, in his late admirable address at the opening of the New House of Refuge, near New York, stated that 'during this last year he had been compelled to act upon *two thousand cases for pardon.* This duty is not only most arduous, but most perplexing and unpleasant. To exercise the pardoning power discreetly requires much labour and anxious thought; the entreaties of friends, of wives, parents, children, is often overwhelmingly painful; and he would be more than human who did not sometimes err in the exercise of this important prerogative. Our Governors have, however, seldom subjected themselves to just censure in the exercise of their power, and Governor Seymour as seldom as any of his predecessors. His decisions have almost uniformly been wise and humane: and if he has sometimes crushed the hopes of the unhappy relatives of the imprisoned, it has never been because he did not sympathize with them in their deep misfortune, but because he believed justice forbade the exercise of the clemency sought.'

When one considers the vast distances in this Union, and the size of its component parts, it is easy to understand how little a government of centralization can ever suit the wants of so large and heterogeneous an Empire. The State of New York alone is as large as all England, and it is evident that local governments such as California or Virginia, must have a much better idea of the genius and the requirements of their several countries than can be gained by the President and the Congress in session at Washington; so, for all local purposes, each State ought to govern itself, and that must have been the intention of the founders of the Union.

It is true that as yet police and postal arrangements are in their infancy, and to an English observer they appear but clumsily organized; but time will improve and consolidate these matters, and I should hope that a future generation will also consider the exercise of political rights as due rather to property, and the virtues of principle, independence, and freedom from selfish motives, than to the mere fact of an ignorant, profligate individual having lived, and perhaps misused, twenty-one years of life; so instead of the 'Know-nothing' proposition to take away the elective franchise from newly imported citizens (which would be invidious enough among a people who owe their success and prosperity to a mixture of races added to the Anglo-Saxon element), it appears common sense that the electors of Governors should be those who have some reasonable ideas of government, and some stake in the common prosperity. We this day heard a sermon embodying higher church assumption than even English Tractarianism; it strongly maintained infallibility for the Protestant Episcopal Church in Scriptural matters. The kind and good Bishop of New York was present; but his advocacy of Church claims is not that of Spiritual despotism; like Fénélon, Bishop Horatio Potter would lead home the peasant's cow; his Christian benevolence can never be moved or guided by a thought which could mar its charity.—The rain falls fast, and I hope to get south before snow and ice again encumber the roads and streets.

Monday, December 11.—Snow again, but the thaw proceeding. I sent my letter, containing the hair of the poor old woman whose son has become a Mormon, by a channel through which it may probably reach the Salt Lake. I think the possible future of that extraordinary community an interesting speculation. Strange that the off-scourings of European civilization should establish polygamy—a practice branded as felonious by every other State in the Union, a barbarism which even Turkey is gradually casting off! Does not this show the tendency of ignorance to return again to the habits of savage life, and also to go back to the government of a theocracy because they feel themselves incapable of self-government? Yet even the present condition and past history of this singular community is not without some elements of grandeur, and even of promise. Expelled by persecution and violence from the parent State, the Mormons earnestly and sagaciously employed themselves to build up a state for themselves. 'Driven from civilized life, they sought rest and a home in the wilderness and the desert.' Blinded as they are by superstition and fanaticism, they are still pioneers of civilization, and it is impossible not to admire the vigour and energy with which they accomplished their hegira. Sitting proudly at the foot of the Wahsach mountains, the City of the Salt Lake begins to fulfil the magnificent projects of its founders, and rolls it along an arid desert like the roses of Jericho (*Anastatica*), to find fresh soil and new homes in the desert. Their settlement only dates from '47: yet wide and well-watered streets and gardens, churches, school-houses, mills, and public buildings, now ornament a city laid out upon a plan capable of including half a million of inhabitants. Though the people and their institutions have departed widely and vilely from the laws of morality and Christianity, as the darkness of ignorance becomes enlightened, we must hope the influence of designing villains will be shaken off, and that of the better minded gain a reasonable influence over the deluded, but not evil-intentioned majority; so that, before very long, the slough which at present contaminates and defaces the body politic of the Mormonite community may be cast off.

Your affectionate

A. M. M.

LETTER XIV.

New York, *Dec.* 13, 1854.

My dear Friends,—

An American gentleman with whom I have become well acquainted, took charge of me yesterday from Albany. I left Mr. and Mrs. Seymour with regret, but they promise to come to Washington before I proceed farther south. On Saturday I again visited the great palæontologist, Mr. Hall. He gave me an interesting and instructive geological chart of his own arrangement, which, while it exemplifies only the geology of New York and the adjoining States, is, in fact, an epitome of that of the world; as from the primitive rocks, the strata follow in regular succession up to the cretaceous, tertiary, and alluvial, wanting only those beds of oolite and chalk which, though well known in England, are not to be seen here. In Mr. Hall's map, the principal fossils to be found in each formation are represented above it—a plan which considerably assists the tyro. The Governor of New York promises me some specimens of a new mineral lately found on the shores of Lake Superior, which has been named 'chloractolite,' from its bright starry lustre. It something resembles a dark green serpentine in colour, but the shining brilliant appearance it has will render it valuable for jewellery purposes. No specimens have yet been found much larger than a sixpence, and most I saw were not bigger than pearls. Mr. and Mrs. Hall came to Albany in the evening; he told us about his geological tour round Lake Superior and Michigan, and let me have reports by the United States' geologists Foster and Whitney, which include some very interesting sketches of the trap rock called the Monument on Isle Royal, and of the singular castle-shaped formations which border part of Lake Superior. I recollect that Banvard's Mississippi Panorama represented rocks beyond St. Louis of a castellated form. The light was more favourable this morning for seeing the Hudson River than when I went up it last. We left much snow at Albany; but upon approaching New York the ground was no longer white, and an afternoon clear and sunshiny concluded by a promising red sunset. We arrived at the St. Nicholas Hotel soon after five o'clock. Mrs. Elizabeth Blackwell came to see me in the evening. I had some conversation with Mr. Delevan, one of the conscientious promoters of the Maine Law, &c. I was not convinced by his arguments; I could not help thinking that he forgot the American principle of individual freedom: the same reasoning he made use of would hold good for every kind of interference with our neighbors when we disapprove their conduct. It is curious that the New England people, descendants of those Pilgrim Fathers who crossed the Atlantic to preserve their own freedom of opinion, have ever proved themselves intolerant as regards the spiritual liberty of others.

December 15.—I visited the Five Points yesterday, and my expectations were fully realized. No fine buildings, no clap-trap exhibitions of classification and order and philanthropic luxury. Mr. Pease's charity 'worketh by love.' The destitute, the friendless, the erring, there find aid, friendship, advice, and consolation; the poor 'have the Gospel preached to them,' and the sick and the sorrowful are healed, comforted, and bid to go in peace, as Christ would have bid them go.

December 16.—A return of visits occupied nearly the whole of yesterday, as I set out this morning by rail to Philadelphia. I went across the ferry to Brooklyn, to call upon Mr. and Mrs. S——'s (of Ottawa) youngest daughter, Mrs. C——, and I there met John Mackay, who told me that my wish is gratified by the name of Bytown being finally changed to that of Ottawa City.

The weather here is now damp and mild. I crossed the North River ferry at nine o'clock, to take the cars for Philadelphia. We passed through several towns, in a flat country, devoid of picturesque scenery for the first sixty miles. Then at last I could have believed myself on the western outskirts of the New Forest, substituting hemlock spruce and red cedars for the yews and hollies of England. As we approached the shores of the Delaware, the red cedars became so numerous that many of the fields were bordered with them; and from their regularity I suppose they must have been planted. I am glad to see some signs of planted trees in this State and that of New York; so some of these days these may be fine single trees. At present I have not met with anything I should call fine-spreading ornamental timber; and I see that it can only arise from new plantations; for the trees of the forest run up tall and slender, without tap roots, and they have such slight hold of the ground, that when thinned out or left standing alone, the first storm lays them prostrate. The Delaware is a fine river, and Philadelphia an extensive city; but there is an uninteresting sameness in its long streets of red brick houses, with glaring white window-shutters. Circumstances will not allow of my prolonging my stay beyond to-morrow. I observe no more evidence of Quakerism in this town than in any other.

Sunday, December 17.—A gloomy-looking, wintry day, though without snow, and the cold less extreme than at Albany. After a search of two hours yesterday afternoon, I found the residence of the Bishop of Pennsylvania, brother to the Bishop of New York. I was kindly received by Mrs. Potter, and spent the evening at her house; but the bishop is absent upon distant episcopal duty—much to my regret. I was taken to St. Andrew's church this morning, and heard a sermon devoid of hope and love—depravity, total depravity—gloom, misery, and despair—the light of the Gospel extinguished, and sin and Satin made despotic over this wretched world! The church was crammed; but I saw several people sleeping soundly through the preacher's denunciations, and few appeared to be edified. I have now heard the two extremes of preachers, high and low, each taking a one-sided view, and each maintaining a kind of infallibility for their own individual opinion under the shields of Church and Scripture—both equally dogmatic, and equally sure that every view except his own is erroneous. I drank tea with Mrs. Potter, and at nine o'clock Dr. R—— called to take me to see Mrs. R——, and her fine house and conservatories, gorgeous French satin furniture, and Gobelin tapestried chairs worthy of Windsor Castle. Both in furniture and dress, the majority of American ladies appear to be wholly regardless of expense.

Baltimore, December 19.—Before leaving Philadelphia yesterday, I made acquaintance with an agreeable physician, Dr. G——, who introduced me to our consul, Mr. Mathew. The consul knows friends of mine, and I was much obliged to him for some useful information. Although heavy snow fell the early part of the morning, as my departure was delayed till twelve o'clock, the weather cleared. I had a pleasant sunshiny journey of four hours to Baltimore, where I found few signs of snow. Mrs. W——, one of my pleasant acquaintances of the White Mountains, met me at this hotel, and took me to her home—snug, cheerful, and well (though not too finely) furnished. My friend showed me some shells, and evinced more interest in natural productions than I have found among ladies generally in this country. We passed over three rivers in our way here yesterday—the Delaware, the Gunpowder, and the Susquehanna; the last a magnificent water, and the same I saw as a smaller stream in my way from Ithaca to Syracuse. Baltimore is situated upon the Patapsco, which is here very broad, and more like an arm of the sea than a river.

December 20.—Mrs. W—— took me this morning to see Mount Hope, a lunatic asylum, managed by about twenty Sisters of Charity, who reside at a house in a very pretty situation, overlooking the city and neighbourhood. The sisters act under the direction of an excellent Protestant physician—Dr. Stokes. No bigotry upon either side mars Christian labour; love, cheerfulness, comfort, and industry alleviate and bless the inmates of Mount Hope. So much pains is taken to avoid even the appearance of coercion, that the window-frames, which are made of cast-iron of a particular construction, are opened a little way by the same movement at top and bottom; thus letting in sufficient air, without the possibility of the gap being wide enough for danger, so that patients are allowed to open them without risk. A library of suitable and amusing books, objects of natural history, music, handiworks, are all at the disposal of the inmates; and though some must be under restraint, it is a restraint of the kindest and gentlest description. We afterwards went to a bazaar of ladies' work, held for the benefit of a home for the aged in reduced circumstances. All denominations of religionists had united their endeavours; and although I observe much variety of opinion in religious matters, I think that Christians here do lay aside their differences when a common work is to be accomplished. I dined and spent the evening with Mr. and Mrs. W——.

December 21.—Yesterday, I saw two of the prettiest and best-appointed houses in this place; both fitted up in good taste, but without the extreme extravagance and ostentation I remarked in some of the residences of the Northern States. Here, for the first time, I see nothing but black servants—slaves, I believe; but their manner and countenances express contentment and cheerfulness; and certainly the relation of mistress and servant in the South has a more agreeable aspect than that of the same station in the Northern States, which is commonly characterized by complaints of annoyance upon one side, and a saucy indifference upon the other. The dinner-party at Mrs. W——'s was agreeable, and I met there several pretty Southern ladies: their voices and way of speaking struck me as more refined and graceful than those of the other States I have visited. Among some of them, too, I find more just views of England and English society—at least, among those of Baltimore; further on, I understand, there is universal prejudice, and an embittered tone of feeling, arising partly from family recollections of the severities practised by the English government and military, in the struggle for independence; and partly from the well-intentioned but ill-judged interference of the present English generation about the Slavery question. I reached Washington this afternoon—so much in the dark that I was unable to judge of the beauties of the Potomac, the shores of which river we must have skirted in our way.

December 22.—I dine to-day with the British minister, who has been so obliging as to show me the Capitol and Museum, where I saw many interesting but uncatalogued specimens in natural history. There is an Alligator Gar from Lake Pontchartrain, which, as far as it was possible to judge from distant inspection, is of a different kind from that specimen which I obtained from Lake Champlain, although certainly of the same family. An extraordinary-looking fish, two or three feet long, with a platypus-like snout (which seems made for scooping up mud or sand, as it extends half a foot over the mouth), was in the same case. There are sitting mummies from Central America with singularly short forearms; and an ornithorynchus from Australia, the claws of which have the property of inflicting venomous wounds. Part of the Capitol is a handsome building, but the glaring white with which the stone is painted mars its effect; and heavy ugly wings are in process of erection. I shall not see Congress in session until after Christmas. From a verandah out of the library, I gained a good view of the site of Washington and the Potomac river. The ground plan of wide alleys diverging from the Capitol is a fine one; if ever the present small, mean-looking brick houses should be replaced by a handsome public and domestic architecture, this city will be worthy to be called the Capital of the Union. But at present the population is less than that of Detroit, and the general appearance of the town is not half as handsome.

Saturday, December 23.—I was introduced to several gentlemen, members of the Legislative Houses, and of the high legal courts; and I find society here most agreeable. Dr. and Mrs. B——, White Mountain friends, called and took me to pay some visits. And in the evening, at eight o'clock, I was politely received by the President and Mrs. Pierce. I was at first shown into comfortable and handsomely furnished rooms, alone; but she soon joined me, and after a while, the President came in. He is a quiet-looking, pale, gentlemanly man; but both he and Mrs. P—— had a manner of subdued unostentatious sadness, so that during this visit I thought more and sympathized more with the bereaved parents, than with them as the President and President's wife of the United States of America. In about half an hour I took leave, and returned to this hotel in time for a light tea.

Sunday, December 24.—Rain having fallen last night, and frost having followed, the pavement of the streets is covered by sheets of ice, and it appears quite impossible to venture out. I heard a great many amusing stories to-day of Southern origin. There is certainly great attachment between the negroes and their masters (speaking generally), in spite of the facts detailed in *Uncle Tom*. One gentleman told me that he has a distant plantation, which he sometimes visits alone; at dinner-time he finds a table loaded with all kinds of delicacies, presents from the slaves. He remonstrated with an old Darkey who waited, upon the uselessness of dressing fowls, turkey, geese, ducks, ham, &c., for one person. 'No matter, massa. When massa comes, must have good dinner on table, whether massa eat it or not.' A negro had an unfortunate love for brandy, and though in other respects a good 'boy,' he was caught stealing his favourite drink. At seventy years of age, his master did not wish to punish him severely. So he appealed to Blackey's own conscience. 'Harry, you know you deserve correction; but with all your faults, you have a notion of justice. Now, if you think it right, you shall go unpunished; if *not*, you shall condemn yourself.' 'Well, massa, me ole man—me take ten lashes, and me hope be better.' And he went out, ordered his own punishment, and submitted to it without a murmur!

A Frenchman and his wife, settled in the South, a few miles from a town where the husband went in every morning for his employment: he procured a horse, and his wife made him an ornamented bridle, and smartened him up, and he was to ride backwards and forwards to avoid fatigue; in coming home one day, a rattle-snake lay in a threatening attitude in the path; the horse started, and, when pressed to pass, threw his master actually upon the reptile: he jumped up and ran one way, the rattlesnake making off the other, and he told his wife: 'Never saw a snake so dom-scared in all my life!' On Christmas-day I walked to church with a young lady, whose family reside within a few miles of this place; but they take up their residence in this house during the winter. I understand that the habit of hotel life is every year becoming more general in the States: this is partly encouraged by the troubles arising from servants; the older ladies get rid of house-keeping, and the young ladies are indulged with constant society; but to English tastes this mode of existence would be unbearable—continued noise, bustle, and excitement, no repose of mind, and no home duties. It is advantageous to a foreigner, who wishes to become acquainted with the people of the country; but I should suppose it must be ruinous to the manners and the domestic character of the higher class of young women; frivolity and indolence must be encouraged, for any regular plan of industrial occupation is a hopeless attempt in such places as these. I would rather take up my abode in any farm-house in England, than be condemned to fritter away my life in a great American hotel. Still, for me, as a stranger and a traveller, it is uncommonly pleasant; I find acquaintances from Cuba, California, all the Southern States; from each of the Northern—even some from Canada; naval men, who have visited Japan; politicians, judges, bishops, botanists, geologists, educationalists, philanthropists, abolitionists, slave-holders, voyages of discovery-men, and men who have been some of all these things at various periods of their lives, with a large number of ladies, all willing to converse, and vying in kindness and hospitality towards me, the only foreigner and stranger among them. All this makes me sometimes fear I may be inclined to over-value myself, and that before my return to England I may be puffed up by conceit and vanity: the best hope is, that I hardly have time to become inflated; for there is also much here to make one forget self. The Bishop of Pennsylvania, brother to my friend the Bishop of New York, arrived here from a tour in his diocese (which has the extent of all England), the day before yesterday, to superintend or take part in an Association for educational purposes, which holds its sessions (or conventions, as they are called here) at the Smithsonian Institution. Bishop Potter is so good as to allow of my accompanying him there, so that he unites instruction and attention to a stranger with his professional duties: it is impossible not to feel deeply the agreeable and useful influence of his truly Christian heart and powerful mind, so that I consider myself most fortunate in such an acquaintance.

December 28.—I spent nearly all day at the meeting of the Educational Association; much interesting information was elicited, particularly from Mr. Barnard, who having been to England for the purpose of comparing our institutions with those of the United States, showed himself well-informed and candid in his deductions. I was surprised to find that there are still 600,000 people in the United States, unable either to read or write; and that this ignorance is by no means confined to the emigrant population. I accompanied the bishop to a party at Mr. Corcoran's, where there are some pretty pictures, one of Moreland's, from which I remember seeing a print in my childhood. The educational meeting did not break up until Friday, the 29th, after proposing that the next meeting of the Association shall be held at New York, the end of August, 1855. The Bishop of Pennsylvania and other members left Washington in the afternoon of that day. Among the remarks made by Professor Henry and others, as to the results of early discipline and self-control upon the character of after-life; it was observed that no instance of unhappy, childish old age could be brought to mind, in which the cultivation of the intellect and the habits of varied study, alternating with healthy bodily exercise, were continued without intermission after sixty years of age, and had been regularly pursued in previous life. It is supposed that old people must be wedded to the opinions and customs of their youth; but this is the misfortune of those only who consider their notions fixed and their education and information complete: a man still seeking instruction at seventy will be as open to conviction and to change of opinion as he was at seventeen: it is the '*too-old-to-learn people*' who sink into dotage and depression. Another awful fact for the dissolute or the idle youth must be stated—that even when the check of public opinion and love of approbation induce self-control and moral conduct during the middle age, if there has not been laid in early life a foundation of principle and good habits, the consequences of early profligacy show themselves in a return to vicious acts, as mental power wanes with added years, and the hoary sinner goes to his grave in sin and misery—so the end of that man is worse than his beginning. It may be well for the young to hear this; for it was enunciated and agreed to as truth by a body of men whose knowledge and experience can hardly be gainsaid. This evening I was invited by Mrs. Fremont, in the absence of her husband, to see a series of daguerreotypes, brought by Colonel Fremont from the Rocky Mountains: though many had reference merely to a choice of country for railroads, they are on the whole very interesting; some rocks of the old red sandstone formation stood up from a plain, in form and appearance like gigantic Egyptian statues; these were in the Mormon district. On returning to Willard's, I found dancing going on very merrily in the ladies' room, four negroes—piano, hautboy, violin, and violoncello—playing in excellent tune, and with sufficient taste and time. The ladies were all in *demi-toilette;* but I do not see so generally the absurd flaunty style of attire so remarkable at New York.

Yours affectionately,

A. M. M.

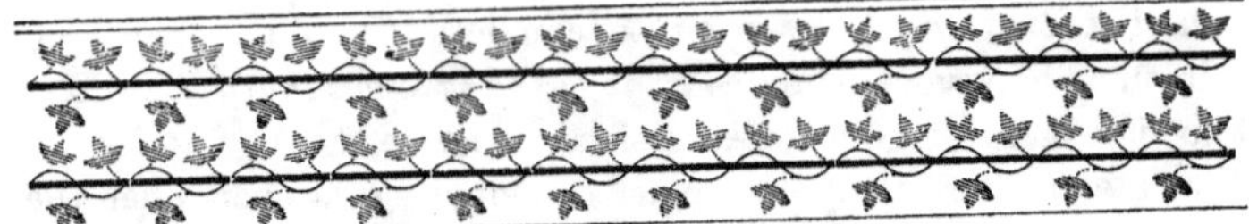

LETTER XV.

THE NEW YEAR.

WASHINGTON, *January* 1, 1855.

MY DEAR FRIENDS,

No former year of my life has begun so strangely as this! I think there is something beautiful in one feature of the American celebration of New Year's Day. It is made an opportunity for the oblivion of neglects, and for the forgiveness of social injuries. On this day, visits of kindness and congratulation are not confined to intimate friends, but every one who has a wish to be civil to his neighbour is cordially received by him or her. The ladies commonly stay at home to welcome their visitors, while gentlemen make a point of calling upon all their acquaintances, remaining at each house perhaps not more than five minutes; but still the call is accepted as one of cordiality and good-will. In many families, refreshments of an elegant kind are prepared and offered by the lady of the house; and from the President downwards, the population in all the towns and cities are intent upon the promotion of hospitality and kind feeling. Mr. Crampton took me into the diplomatic circle at the White House, where, being presented to most of the gentlemen, I actually shook hands with the Russian minister; and at this moment was not that the greatest homage I could offer to the peace-making duty of the day? We next visited Secretary Marcy's, where there was a reception, which, like that of the President, may be attended by everybody. As we were early, the party was small; but afterwards I went to Dr. B——'s, where for three hours I was present at an in-pouring of visitors, and I made the acquaintance of many interesting and agreeable people; among them a charming Lithuanian lady, the wife of a Polish gentleman of rank, nearly connected with Prince Czartoriski. Dancing and other amusements at the Hotel in the evening.

January 2.—Part of the morning was devoted to the School of Design, which is well directed by Mr. Whittaker, who was born an Englishman. A lady afterwards carried me to the State Paper Office, where I saw interesting documents; among them some private letters characteristic of the firm, purpose-like Washington; and a most touching original note, containing poor André's request for a soldier's death, instead of that of the gibbet. The calm, gentlemanly writing, without tremor and unmarked by haste—not an unnecessary stroke nor a useless word—takes one into the very heart of the man who wrote it. Washington was deeply moved, but gave no reply. After all he was right. Though poor André was the victim of that wretch Arnold (who lived only to die a hundred times over under the scorn of England and America), still he was taken in disguise; and since Washington felt that an example had become necessary, he was obliged to condemn André as the spy, not as the soldier. After our visit to the State department, I went by the request of Miss G—— and with her, to see a young lady, in the hope that, by joining my persuasions to Miss G——'s, we might induce her to assist some effort for training women, through an improved education, for teachers. In the evening, I accompanied another lady to hear Mr. Marsh's lecture on Constantinople and the Bosphorus. We met the President and Mrs. Pierce, who were on the platform at the Smithsonian Institute. The lecture was rather commonplace, but the large room was crowded by an intelligent and attentive audience. It is in form and arrangement one of the best lecture-rooms I ever saw. These last three

8

days the weather has been clear and pleasant, but not warmer than in England.

January 3.—Mr. Ingersoll took me to see Congress in session. I was fortunate in the moment accidentally chosen. After some time spent in hearing a rather confused and noisy debate, there were two good speeches in their several lines, one from a young man, the California member—clear, concise, fluent, and business-like; it was about a land commission: the other, from Mr. K——, of South Carolina—fervid, energetic, argumentative and eloquent. It must be borne in mind that the terms 'Whig' and 'Democrat' have different meanings here to those which they express in England. The American Democrat designates enlightened, consistent principles; the Whig, narrow-minded, bigoted, Republicanism. Mr. K——'s speech lasted one hour, without proving tedious or uninstructive. It is impossible in a few words to do justice either to his eloquence or his reasoning; but after making a rapid though comprehensive sketch of the present state of parties in this country, he affirmed, that in fact there never has been in the world, and never can be, more than two great parties—consisting, one of well-informed liberal men, the other of ignorant bigoted men; that new names and a new organization are only a sign that under old names one of the old parties has become effete. So, at the present moment, the Whigs have apparently disbanded, but in truth they have only reformed, to enlist and to march under the 'Know-nothing' banners. They have indeed assumed a most suitable and characteristic designation, one which might well have been selected by their opponents. Socialists in practice, they desire to arm labour against capital; Roman Catholics in principle, they would advocate bigotry in lieu of tolerance; arbitrary in government, they would enact white slavery while they profess to do away with black servitude. Falsifying the principles and tearing up the foundations of freedom, 'they are,' said the orator, 'mutes who would follow the funeral of the Republic.' Upon the whole, I was agreeably surprised with the good speaking and general appearance of Congress; because I had been told by almost every one since I came to America, that I should find a sad lack of talent and political honesty. Respecting the latter quality, of course I am not capable of judging; but there seems no lack of honest faces, and I find less assumption in manner than I expected. Mr. Ingersoll took me into the Speaker's private room, where we found Mr. Boyd alone, having been disengaged from the chair by a committee of the 'whole' (as it is called here), which enables the Speaker to place a substitute in his chair. In this room I saw the place where President Adams expired; it is marked by his bust. Upon my return home, finding Mr. C—— had called twice, I went to see him at his house, and we had an interesting conversation upon educational subjects. In the evening I dined with our minister, and sat beween Secretary Marcy and Mr. Cushing, the Attorney-General. There was a large party of gentlemen, and three ladies besides myself—Mrs. Marcy's sister (Mrs. French), Miss Marcy, and Mrs. Campbell, wife of the Solicitor-General. Upon returning to Willard's Hotel, I found the gallery and ladies' room crowded by visitors, and the mulatto band, as usual, in requisition. I was introduced to Mr. Kietl, the orator of the morning. There are 'Know-nothings' (even feminine ones) among the residents of this hotel. I can easily discover them by their crude, unintelligent style of conversation.

Thursday, January 4.—There was a great assemblage last night in the room underneath mine—a supper of gentlemen, for the celebration of some anniversary; a band of music, songs, speeches, and viciferous applause. Sleep being out of the question, I rose at two o'clock, and almost read through Lord Carlisle's *Diary in the Turkish Waters* before daylight. Of course I was gratified at finding our cousin of the *Retribution* so highly spoken of in it. This morning I was a good deal occupied in arranging a sitting in my own room, that Mrs. S—— (the only very talented American artist I have yet met with) might have the opportunity to make a drawing of an acquaintance of mine. In the library of the Capitol there is one of the most exquisite miniatures by this lady I ever saw. It almost resembled some of Thorburn's; but there is so little real appreciation of art in

Washington, that I found Mrs. S—— hardly able to procure employment, crowded as the city is with notabilities from all parts of the Union. Her slight sketches, as well as the more finished miniatures, are pretty, and her drawing correct; yet, excepting a little instruction from some English person when very young, she appears almost wholly self-taught. Lieutenant Maury was so obliging as to call; he gave me a tempting invitation to drink tea with his family at the Observatory, the first evening I see any chance of visible stars. In the afternoon, Mr. and Mrs. Ingersoll took me again to the Capitol. There had been an early adjournment of the Senate, and though Congress was sitting (it was not engaged in business which interested me), a large majority of members were occupied at their desks writing letters. This habit deteriorates much from the dignity and statesmanlike appearance of the House; and I remember observing the same thing, and making the same remark, in the Chamber of Deputies at Paris, Quebec, and in all the legislative assemblies in which the members, instead of being obliged to retire to the lobbies (as in our parliamentary houses) for letter-writing and private business, are accommodated with chairs and tables in the halls, where public affairs only should be transacted. Here members of Congress remain half their time, unconscious of what is going forward, absorbed in their individual interests, when they ought to be wholly given to those of the public—so that they look more like an assemblage of clerks than of statesmen. To-day I dined with the President, by the formal invitation of a week. The party consisted of about thirty-two. I sat between Mr. Broadhead and Mr. Ashley, two members of the Senate, who have passed some time in England. There were a good many ladies, but more gentlemen. The President and Mrs. Pierce sat opposite on each side the table; and I was near the former. The dinner was handsome, and well arranged in French fashion; flowers and fruit only on the table, and one dish at a time handed round. In the reception-room there were some splendid white camellias, covered by flowers which I think are larger here than any with us; great use is made of the fir-like Lycopodium and the elegant Steevia, in the composition of ornamental bouquets, some of which were placed at the disposal of the ladies. At half-past nine the party broke up, having met at six o'clock. Upon returning to the hotel, I spent the remainder of the evening in pleasant conversation—principally with Miss Cass; she and her father, General Cass, usually reside in this house during the winter. The society in the ladies' room is diversified, and by no means stiff. There are whist-tables, and occasionally dancing and music. I never saw any card-playing for money in the United States.

Saturday, January 6.—Mrs. Fremont called upon me yesterday morning; and from her brother-in-law Mr. Jones, I received a large long-shaped acorn, eatable like the Spanish chestnut. It was brought from a mountainous region in California. This and one black as ebony from the same country, I hope to send soon by a private hand to be planted in England. I have a pretty little sleeping tortoise also, the Picta; when Dr. and Mrs. Gray arrive, I shall ask them to carry it back to Boston to await my return there. I hope to have this, and a box tortoise from Albany, and a spotted one from Rhode Island, as live specimens of the tortoise families. I spent the chief part of the 5th of January in returning visits.

This morning, the 6th, I walked to the Smithsonian Institute, and got much information about objects of natural history from Professor Baird. Another foggy, damp day, quite as thick as any in London, barring the smoke. I have been reading two pamphlets giving opposite views upon the subject of the Smithsonian Institution. A controversy is going on here respecting the distribution of the fund left by our countryman to found an establishment at Washington 'For the Increase and Diffusion of Knowledge among Men.' It would be difficult to credit the fact, had I not the best authority for it, that the whole annual income, being thirty thousand dollars, a vote of Congress decided (appointing Regents to carry its decisions into effect), that 'a suitable building of sufficient size, with rooms and halls for reception and arrangement, upon a liberal scale, of objects of natural history, geological, mineralogical, and botanical, properly classed and arranged, with a chemical laboratory, lecture-rooms, &c., shall be organized;' and then assigned a sum not exceeding twenty-five thousand dollars for a library. If this were to be understood as appropriating five parts of the whole income to buying and collecting books, the absurdity of the first provisions would be evident; so the managers (as it appears to me sensibly enough) took advantage of the loop-hole afforded by the words 'not exceeding,' and have gone on, to the best of their ability, endeavouring to realize the apparent intentions of the founder and of Congress; and, as far as I can judge, in a reasonable and intelligent manner. Yet a party of men of some talent and ability are bent upon maintaining that a library, and a library only, was to be established. If Mr. Smithson had contemplated this narrow view, he could easily have stated it. I should imagine it was his intention, by 'A Central Institution for the Diffusion of Knowledge among Men,' to counteract the mercantile and Mammonite spirit which possesses the majority, and open the book of Nature to their comprehension: while by promoting healthier ideas upon education, the crude and absurd opinions too generally advanced and acted upon, will be amended and counteracted, and an improved and more practical female training will be encouraged. It will no longer be gravely enunciated at an educational convention—'That the stimulus which the human heart requires is wanting for women in the present age, and that society gives them nothing to aim at;' but if so, give them reasonable aims. Let them aim at duty, not notoriety. Let them keep within their appropriate sphere, cultivating sufficient moral courage to act within that sphere for the benefit of their fellow-creatures, and particularly for the advantage of their sex; disciplining and training their own minds to be the educated companions, not the rivals, of men. Let them be the heart-consolers, the binders-up of broken spirits, the 'sisters of the sisterless,' the presiding geniuses of the social circle. Is that not work enough for them to do? In this country, I hear that 'though it has no queen, *all the women are queens*.' I should rather call them playthings—dolls; things treated as if they were unfit or unwilling to help themselves or others: and while we in England have nearly cast aside arts of the toilet worthy only of dolls, I see here false brows, false bloom, false hair, false everything!—not always, but too frequently. Dress in America, as an almost general rule, is full of extravagance and artificiality; and while women show such a want of reliance upon their native powers of pleasing, their influence in society will be more nominal than real.

Monday, January 8.—This day I made my first appearance at a morning reception. Ladies here issue cards or notes, stating they are at home on particular days, when any acquaintances may visit them. This is a pleasant and rational mode of making calls, and appears to me worthy of adoption elsewhere. Mr. Ingersoll was so obliging as to take me to listen to arguments in the Supreme Legal Court, the only tribunal which is competent to settle questions which may arise between States. A counsel spoke so clearly and concisely upon a particular point of law, that he brought it within my comprehension; the case was, that of the boundary line to be drawn between Georgia and Florida. My friends Dr. and Mrs. Gray have arrived from Cambridge. I dined with them at Professor Henry's, and went to the Smithsonian Institute to hear the first of nine lectures on botany by Dr. Gray. Although the morning was fine and clear, rain came on at night; and since Lieutenant Maury's invitation to the Observatory, the weather has afforded no opportunity for its acceptance.

Tuesday, January 9.—Cloudy and damp. I went with an agreeable Cuban gentleman, Mr. ———, to a morning reception at Mrs. P——'s, and then he took me to see some pictures at the Capitol, which are to be disposed of by raffle. One, St. Thomas giving Charity (by a pupil of Murillo's, touched by the master), is an interesting picture; the others I did not admire. The absence of any positive news from England is very trying, and the details brought by the former mail most afflicting; still, however saddening, no English person can despair of the ultimate success of heroism and civilization against cruelty and barbarism.

I have become well acquainted with some pleasant intelligent Cuban families here, and their accounts make me feel it impossible not to wish that their fine island should be more free, misgoverned and pillaged as it is by its present masters; and not being very far from the American shores, I wish America could purchase it: the case would be analogous to that policy of Mr. Pitt, by which the Crown of England took possession of the little kingdom of Man; and with respect to which our family had only the choice of accepting a certain sum, or of having it seized by the law of the strongest. The mines alone in the last mentioned island now produce more than the interest of the money.

Wednesday, January 10.—Last night I attended an evening party, which included all the notabilities of Washington. It was much like a crowded assembly in London, except that I thought there was more amusement; because the Washington party consisted of a re-union of people who, though under the same government, reside thousands of miles apart. There I received invitations from the South and from the North, the East and the West, and fully mean to avail myself of some of them. I was given a very hospitable one, to visit a member of Congress who resides upon the Mississippi, not an impracticable distance from the falls of St. Anthony. Some of the invitations are to Mexico, Texas, and California; not forgetting the Salt Lake, in consequence of an introduction to the Mormon delegate—a gentlemanly, respectable-looking old man with a bald head. I did not inquire if he has twelve wives; but an amusing account has been given me with regard to the domestic arrangements of that strange people. It seems that when the first wife wants help in the household, she petitions her husband to take another spouse—a good cook or a dairywoman for instance, or a sempstress—so one wife is housekeeper, another has the cooking department, a third manages the nursery, and so forth; and as there is no small difficulty in getting good servants in the United States, this matrimonial plan ensures a more permanent and better ordered household than could be attained without it. I am informed that the domestic troubles of a wife in the United States are such that, unless she resides in the slave countries, she thinks it far more convenient to be first wife, with half-a-dozen subordinate ones, than to be sole darling with the disadvantages of saucy servants and the discomforts of bad dinners; so that, in fact, Republicanism, and an unnatural attempt at equality, has caused a return of the terrible evils of polygamy. What a curious result. I hope this strange custom will not spread over the Union!

January 11.—I spent three hours in Congress yesterday, hoping to hear Mr. C—— speak about the 'Know-nothings;' the House was taken up by a hot discussion upon the question of foreigners receiving immediate grants of land, with an understanding that the franchise will become theirs at the termination of five years, which is the present law. This of course bore upon the 'Know-nothing' ground, and it is sad to see how deeply a secret society, banded together upon exclusive, illiberal, and arbitrary principles, has taken root in the free soil of America. In conversation, it is easy to judge whether individuals are in their hearts favourable to such views; and every day makes me think the ramifications of the conspiracy have extended to a depth and a distance about which I was for a time incredulous. There is much reason to fear this irrational party may have power enough to carry the presidential chair: if so, I really think the 'mutes' may get their black trappings prepared to-morrow for the funeral of the Republic—a catastrophe prophesied by the member of South Carolina; and I fear those obsequies may not only be wept in sackcloth and ashes, but that they may be followed by a civil war. There seems a dearth of strong men in the Union—men capable of taking the lead, and sufficiently patriotic to sacrifice their own present personal interest to the public weal. I observe a sad spirit of corruption and of self-seeking among the younger men; and I also see that fear and doubt are shaking the spirits of the elder and wiser people. No one seems even to guess what will come out of the fermenting process which the commonest observer must see at work. The lees have risen to the surface; whether they will sink again to the bottom of the political chaldron without poisoning the life-blood of this world-wide community, is the question seldom uttered, but deeply seated in the minds of honest and thoughtful persons. I doubt whether this mental conflict here is not more alarming than the external and physical war the Allies have to wage against the barbarism of the North, inasmuch as open enmity is better than secret contention; the known foe can be met and conquered, but a concealed antagonist effects his mischief upon unconscious victims.

Yours affectionately,

A. M. M

LETTER XVI.

WASHINGTON.
January 12, 1855.

MY DEAR FRIENDS,—

I went yesterday, with Mrs. Seymour and Mrs. Cristobel de Madan, to hear the (almost single) Roman Catholic member, Mr. Chandler, speak in Congress, for the purpose of repudiating and denying the accusation brought against his co-religionists by Mr. Banks of Massachusetts (one of the advocates of the 'Know-nothing conspiracy), which asserted that they, the Roman Catholics, acknowledge a temporal jurisdiction in the Papacy. The House was at first occupied by a motion, made by some member from the South, for increasing the allowance to foreign ministers. He said, the salaries given are so meagre, that it is difficult to induce men of talent and experience to undertake missions, and therefore the affairs of the States (in Europe) are embroiled and mismanaged by a set of inferior diplomatists. I am not enough acquainted with the pulse of the American Congress to judge how this proposition was received; but the intense and respectful attention afforded to Mr. Chandler, I thought a good sign of generous and tolerant feeling; and this makes me hope that there is still freedom and impartiality enough in the Union to counteract the narrow and inconsistent opinions of Republican bigotry. Mr. Chandler's address was good, both in manner and matter: it was well worded, calm, logical and frank. He affirmed most solemnly, that so far from believing any right could be assumed by the Bishops of Rome touching upon political allegiance, he and all other good Catholics consider the spiritual rule, which they willingly admit, as quite distinct from the temporal: although history shows that temporal rule has been exercised by Roman pontiffs, it was not derived from the church itself, but from the Catholic princes of Europe, who chose to delegate undue power to the Popes of those times. 'And if,' said Mr. Chandler, 'the Bishops of Rome should now, or at any future time, invade the territory of this Republic, or of any other Protestant sovereignty, Roman Catholics would consider themselves bound by every principle, divine or human, to oppose and repel such an assumption of temporal power.' The Governor, Mrs. Seymour, and I, dined together at the house of Governor Hamilton Fish, Mr. Seymour's predecessor in the Government of New York State. I had a great deal of conversation with him, and with another old gentleman, upon the present state and future prospects of free slaves. They were both of opinion that some inherent difference of race is the cause that the black people die out and become extinct in one or two generations, after the attainment of freedom and of amalgamation with whites. This seems to be a universal law. Mr. Fish told me that, in his experience, it has worked so rapidly, that his family having about fifty years ago freed their negroes, though at the same time allowing them a claim for aid and future protection—letting them have the cottages and the ground to which they had been accustomed—still, under these advantageous circumstances, they had gradually dwindled away; and though Governor Fish considers the remnant almost as belonging to his own family, and they apply to him for advice and help upon all occasions, yet not above five or six individuals are existing, and no one of them younger than sixty. I accompanied some friends to the evening reception of Mrs. Marcy, which was well attended, although many other houses were also open for parties.

Friday, 12th.—A fine clear day. Mrs. Hamilton Fish took Mrs. Seymour and me a drive to the heights of Georgetown; and we also called on Mrs. Maury at the Observatory. It is in a beautiful situation, commanding the city of Washington, and also long reaches of the Potomac each way. Lieutenant Maury took us up to the roof of the building, and we are to have the pleasure of a visit to his observatory next week, if the stars will be favourable. I drank tea out with Mr. and Mrs. Seymour, and afterwards accompanied their party to the Presidential evening lev*ee* (as the word is here pronounced), to which all classes decently attired are admitted. We found two rooms crowded, but the company perfectly well conducted and orderly. In general aspect, I was reminded of an entertainment given by a London City Lord Mayor in the Guildhall. We returned to the hotel by eleven o'clock.

January 13.—I received a file of *Times* newspapers to the 23d of last month, and sat up nearly all night to read them. Sad and heart-breaking details; and in the paper of latest date, an article levelled against the Ministry and all the *employés* in the East, so bitter and vituperative in style, and so sweeping in accusation, that it tells more against the writers than in condemnation of those written against. In this house I have made the acquaintance of three distinguished Generals of the Republic—Scott, Cass, and Houston—all massive-looking, soldier-like men. After a fine morning the afternoon proved wet, so that I could not sketch or go to the Observatory; but Mrs. Fish was so kind as to take me out to pay visits. After dinner, there was an evening assembly and dancing for the young people. I was introduced to an interesting family, natives of New Orleans. They spoke English, but with some accent, their own tongue being French; but I much prefer our language a little broken to the broad and often nasal pronunciation of New England and New York. The Southern people have pleasing voices, and are much less provincial in their speech than those of the Northern States.

Sunday, *January* 14.—A blind minister preached yesterday at the Congress chapel. I should have heard him, but the service was earlier than I expected, so when I reached Professor Henry's Dr. and Mrs. Gray were gone. A cold clear day, but no signs of ice. Last night I saw a very interesting set of drawings of California and the Rocky Mountains, belonging to a gentleman who has been much in the Far West. He confirmed my deductions about the Mormonite domestic polity, having frequently conversed with the women of that State. The ladies are not shut up in idleness like those of Eastern harems, but live happily together, because they are too busy to quarrel. One woman told him—'We agree well: sister Dolly has the cows; sister Jenny, the children; sister Betty, the kitchen; and so on—all have plenty to do: and our husband is bound by law to support and take equal care of us; and then we are so *Hell-bent on Heaven!*' Is it not evident, slavery or polygamy is the product of an unnatural attempt after equality? I shall certainly return to England more strongly imbued with attachment to our orderly institutions. R—— has had offers of marriage in America; but she says, 'No, I will never marry here—not even if I could have the very President himself. Why, in England I may have my own station, and I'm content; but in America I should never know what I was.' I find many charming people, a great deal that is interesting, and much that is instructive, in the United States; but it appears to me that only the fear of starvation would induce an English man or woman to fix themselves for life in America. 'In whatever state of life you are, therewith to be content,' is a lesson which can hardly be learned this side the Atlantic.

January 16.—I walked up early yesterday to call upon Dr. and Mrs. B——; he and Mr. W—— brought me back, and Mrs. Fish was again so kind as to come and convey me to sketch on the Georgetown heights. And then she waited in the carriage while I paid a visit to the British Minister, who is confined to his house owing to the consequences of an accident. Mr. and Mrs. Seymour and I had a pleasant dinner at Mr. and Mrs. Taloe's, where we met General Scott, and the Mexican and French Minister, and *attaché*, Judge Drew, and other acquaintances. At this house is one of the prettiest Carlo Dolces I ever saw. It once belonged to the Duchess de Berri. On our return, Mr. Blake, the geologist, showed us beautifully crystallized and other specimens of Californian gold, and gave me some dust of Cuban iron pyrites as brilliant as diamonds.

January 17.—Directly after breakfast yesterday, I walked up to the Observatory, and spent two hours sketching from its roof. The views are fine every way, particularly up the Potomac towards that large aqueduct which carries a canal across to Georgetown. I saw Lieutenant Maury, and agreed with him that, as my travels must be pursued on the 18th as far as Richmond, Wednesday evening (stars or no stars) we must spend at the Observatory. I came home in time to dress for a wedding, when I found a pretty bride and a cheerful party; but according to custom in the reception-rooms of this country, they were so darkened that I should rather have supposed the assembly gathered together for a funeral than a wedding. I saw a great deal of beauty, although of one particular type. Proceeding towards the South, I find the manners soften as well as the voice, more frankness and cheerfulness; the rather stiff formality of the Northern States is replaced by ease, and at the same time the young people are merry without being boisterous, and no one objects to those games and amusements which the spirit of the puritanical times has handed down as crimes to be cast aside by their New England descendants. So oftentimes those good people are bored for want of innocent relaxation, and the elderly prefer staying by their own firesides to falling asleep in public for want of occupation. There is certainly an odd mixture of the 'go-ahead' and the indolent among our American cousins, which is exemplified in the saying, that such a man 'is running a sleepy race,' which means that his adherents are pushing him forward for election to some office, while the candidate himself remains in a state of somnolent indifference to the result. Mr. and Mrs. Seymour took me to a place which has been called Calametta, from its beautiful and sunny view of the Potomac, &c. We found it a pleasant, comfortable house, with bright-coloured peacocks walking about in the wood surrounding it. I dined at the Secretary of State's, with a large number of diplomatic gentlemen, and only four ladies besides myself. The French Minister sat by Mrs. Marcy, and I had Mr. Marcy on one side and the Spanish Minister on the other. The dinner could not be otherwise than agreeable. The Secretary is a remarkably frank, agreeable old man, and I was not afraid to joke him a little about his republican aversion to court dresses. I found out the whole secret afterwards. In his drawing-room there is an interesting picture, painted in the time of Louis XVI., of the King and Queen sitting in their circle, while some gay ladies of the Court crown Benjamin Franklin with a wreath of laurel. Franklin is uncontaminated by any attire more gay than his Quaker-like looking habiliments (though it seems he was occasionally seduced into a court dress, for a velvet one belonging to him is still preserved), and I *guess* the ladies around him were not without a little sly triumph of their own on the occasion which gave rise to the picture; but it is evident to me that scene was not one of a public reception, for no gentleman is present excepting the King. Secretary Marcy was (I think) sentimentally led astray in his crusade against European finery by this picture. I don't the least believe (an accusation I have heard here) that his motive was to curry favour with the American public, who may imagine an ugly coat and republicanism synonymous terms. He is a downright honest man, if ever I saw one; and with all his talents and knowledge of the American world, upon the subject of European dress, he was much more likely to err from simplicity than design. My neighbour on the other side could only express himself in French and Spanish, and as the Secretary confines himself to plain English as well as plain coats, the Spanish Minister is frequently obliged to have recourse to an interpreter, which, in a delicate diplomatic conference, he thinks is inconvenient.

I was introduced to the Dutch Minister, who speaks English like a native. The Prussian looked quiet and neutral; the French, anxious and incredulous. Mr. Crampton was prevented by his accident from joining the party, a circumstance generally regretted, for no one is more popular in the diplomatic circle. None of the second grade were present—only Ministers and their *attachés*. Mr. Marcy told me he could not receive the whole corps together, and therefore he takes the first rank with their belongings at one dinner, and others separate. Mr. and Mrs. Seymour, having dined elsewhere, came to take me home, and joined the party for a short time.

Richmond, Virginia, January 18.—I have just arrived at this place; but, before writing of our journey here, the conclusion of my stay at Washington must be told. Wednesday, I breakfasted with Dr. and Mrs. B——, my friends of the White Mountains. The Judge and Mrs. Maclean, and Mr. P——, a member of Congress, were of the party—it was very pleasant. Mrs. Maclean walked back with me as far as Professor Henry's, where I went to see Dr. and Mrs. Gray; and, before going home, I had to go to Mrs. S——, the artist. She has made a slight sketch of Longfellow for me. On my return to the hotel, I had much to do; separating wardrobe, books, and natural history accumulations, to be forwarded to Boston: my acquisitions increase like a rolling snow-ball; and from all the principal stopping-places during my travels, I send off packages to Mr. L——'s care. At Washington, bouquets are general in full costume; they are always made up by the gardeners, but hardly ever consist of any other flowers than Camellias, Canarinas, Heliotropes, Steevias, and violets, with the berries of Ardisia crenulata, and the feathery foliage of Lycopodium dendroides. I received two beautiful ones this afternoon from gentlemen; a sweet bunch of geranium and Neapolitan violets was given me by a young Cuban lady; and I had a white Camellia, also, from Miss Seymour. Mrs. Seymour dined at home with me, and at six o'clock Mrs. Fish called, to convey us to the Observatory, accompanied by Judge Drew and Mr. Miller. The stars shone brightly—the finest show of them I have yet seen in America. Lieutenant Maury took us up to the telescope directly on our arrival. We had a good view of a spangled bit of sky in Perseus, not visible to the naked eye. Sirius appeared like a tuft of blue, red, and gold feathers, waving in the heavens; Saturn's globe and ring perfectly clear and distinct; and the belt and five geometrical-looking stars of Orion very bright. After our eyes and minds were fatigued by these marvels, we went in to drink tea with Mrs. Maury, and then returned to town to attend Mr. Guthrie's reception, where I took leave of the Grays, the Quaker lady of Philadelphia, General Scott, Mr. Maury, and many others who have been kind to me at Washington. We returned home to the dancing party at Willard's, and found it crowded. I said good-bye to many friends there; and upon getting up at six next morning to depart, I found Mr. P—— and Mr. M——, both ready to see us safe on board the steamer; they accompanied us to the Potomac; it was quite dark, and their company was very cheering. A fine sunrise on the magnificent river, and after a very calm and successful passage of fifty-five miles, we found the railroad cars at Acquia Creek; the distance to Richmond was about seventy miles; weather continued bright, warm, and sunshiny. I felt the influence of a southern atmosphere, and the journey would have been pleasant if I had had pleasanter neighbours in the car; but just before me was a being who called himself the American Dwarf; he was about two feet high, with fin-like hands, and a head nearly as large as his contorted body: and, on my right a negro woman, in face resembling an ourang-outang, who gloried in a fancy straw bonnet, trimmed with white, with artificial roses surrounding her black muzzle. She became dreadfully sea, or rather rail-sick, and my window being open, although there was another on her side, she constantly leaned across me to take possession of mine; at last a gentlemanly-looking young man, who I conclude was her master, came to my rescue, and throwing open a window behind, he said a few words which made her keep to her own locality. This improved my immediate circumstances; but in a few minutes afterwards we were brought to a standstill, and looking out, saw a dreadful accident. Either from intoxication or insanity, a fine-looking young man, apparently not more than twenty-three, had placed himself on the rail just at a curve, so that the engineer had no time to pull up, though he did his best; the poor wretch was cut in two, and expired immediately. All the people evinced great feeling and kindness; the corpse of the poor stranger was taken up, and we proceeded. I found the Exchange a comfortable hotel, and the sister of Dr. Gibson of Baltimore, soon came to me with her married daughter; and they took me to their home, and I passed a pleasant evening, Mr. J—— being so kind as to walk back at night with me through the still and unfrequented streets. There was hardly a sound until that usual occurrence, a peal of fire bells, broke the quiet. I have never been in any town in the United States without hearing such alarms. At Richmond it is not uncommon to have two or three fires a night, and these fires are usually the work of incendiaries; wooden houses are so easily set in a blaze, that boys for mischief, and thieves for plunder, slily ignite them.

January 20.—I saw a great deal of this pretty town; if it had the castle and the ancient buildings of Edinburgh, it would resemble that city, the Powhatan River taking the place of the Forth. Mrs. J—— took us across the valley to sketch towards the east, and I made a drawing of the locality round Washington's monument, the various steeples, towers, &c., with the Capitol, a pleasing Grecian building, capping and overlooking the city, and the surrounding country. Under the centre of the dome, inside that building, I saw the best statue of Washington in the whole Union, by Houdier: it is said to be a good likeness, and, as a work of art, it is most interesting. I could not have believed that the stiff costume of that time could have been so idealized. The General stands in an easy attitude, leaning upon a bunch of fascines—the very buttons on his coat, and the high top-boots, &c. &c., are all indicated, and yet there is no lack of grace, no appearance of formality, in this very fine statue. Strange to say, an air of neglect and dilapidation is visible all round it; the interior of the building is sadly out of repair; the doors want paint, and all is dirty and quite unworthy of the best public building in the State of Virginia, the House of Legislature and of business. Perhaps a few years will dissipate financial difficulties, which have been brought on by an extravagant railway expenditure; it will, probably, repay the citizens in due time, and then they may be enabled to wipe off the disgrace of shabbiness which at present hangs over their proceedings.

Mrs. G—— called for a handsome agreeable lady, who accompanied us during the rest of our drive. They took me to the Cemetery, beautifully situated, and from thence I made a general sketch of Richmond, with its crowning Capitol, Powhatan River (undignified by the modern name of James), and a foreground of better trees than I had yet seen in America. In this place are many pretty hollies, with red berries like ours, but with leaves opaque instead of shining; and before going home we called at a nursery-ground, where there was nothing new to me, excepting a shrub which, though now leafless, has bunches of small lilac berries. The gentleman did not know what country it came from, or the tribe to which it belongs. Indeed, he told me, so little interest is shown for flowers in this part of the world, that since he came here from Scotland, he has rather lost than gained in botanical and floral acquirement. I declined an invitation to dine at three o'clock; such early hours at this time of year shorten the already shortened days. After returning to the hotel for the purpose of writing to Washington, I made my way alone across the river by a very long wooden bridge. On the other side I passed voluminous houses, which I was told were flour and cotton mills; beyond them the view of Richmond was fine. A brilliant sunset reminded me that there is little twilight here, and so I feared that I should hardly find my way in the dark to Mrs. G——'s, where tea awaited me. After some wanderings I reached her house before a very young moon had disappeared, and from thence I joined a small party at Mrs. M——'s.

January 21.—Our cars left Richmond at seven this morning, and the sun rose so red that I fear he promises rain. We reached Charlottesville soon after twelve, and passed through a very pretty country, which requires nothing but animal life and industry to make it charming. The absence of fencing to the railroads at once speaks of scanty flocks and herds; for, if these were not few and far between, the owners would insist upon precautionary measures. As it is, cows and sheep are occasionally killed by the trains; but when not more than fifty beasts can be seen in as many miles, the risk is not great. To-day we passed along a rolling* district, affording every promise of a grateful re-

* The common expression in America for an undulating country.

turn to energetic and industrious cultivation. Yet I saw ploughs worked by a single horse, which did little more than scratch the surface, and a rich soil beneath was only brought to light by the course of the railroad. Passing rapidly along, I observed much iron sand, excellent slate, volcanic rocks, gneiss, greenstone, quartz, plenty of water, a natural growth of oak and chestnut, and I have little doubt but that mineral riches are below. An English farmer who could bring free labour with him here might quickly make his fortune. The slave servants look generally well clothed, merry, and content; but of farm labour they have evidently but small knowledge; and a general population, either white or black, seems scanty. Upon arriving at the small town of Charlottesville, I was sorry to find that Mr. Stevenson, the former Minister to England, was absent from his house, a few miles distant. At the University, however, I was most kindly welcomed by the Professor and Mrs. Minor; he and Professor Maupin showed me the buildings, and an extensive view from the roof of the dome. This educational establishment was founded by Jefferson. It is ruled by nine trustees, who are newly appointed every four years by the incoming President of the United States; and it has this peculiarity—that the governing head of the institution is changed every two years. There is no professor of Natural History in any of its branches, and no teacher of Chemistry, either agricultural or medical; so that one cannot much wonder that ignorance respecting the soils and the mineral riches of this State should be evident, even to an unpractised eye. We slept at a clean and reasonable hotel; I walked up in a heavy shower of rain, through red mud (much like that of Torquay in Devonshire), to the college, for the purpose of taking leave, and got into the cars by twelve o'clock. After about fifty miles' journey, passing over mountains consisting of gneiss, greenstone, slaty rocks, and limestone, we reached Staunton by a wonderful line of road: the last part was engineered up, and ploughed like a deep furrow along the side of a mountain, to the very summit, and then down again to the plain below. The making of this line was ordered and superintended by the same

German engineer who planned and is erecting the suspension bridge from one shore of Niagara to the other, with a passage for railroad cars above the carriage road. From what I saw to-day, my faith in the success of that bridge is almost undoubting. We find the Virginian Hotel here comfortable, and the country we came through to-day must be very picturesque; but rain and fog prevented our seeing more than half a mile from the cars. Staunton is rather a pretty town: as we entered, I saw a handsome building for an asylum for the blind, and I was told there are several other large charitable establishments.

January 22.—Violent rain, storm, and wind during the night. We got up to proceed by the mail stage, which started at five o'clock, more punctually than is usual in America; and the bills here and at Charlottesville were fair and reasonable—not a third of what we have paid elsewhere. The charges have varied from two dollars to eight dollars a day: they are never more reasonable than in some parts of England, sometimes dearer than the hotels of London and Paris. With four horses, and only four persons in the coach, we did not reach Lexington till after one o'clock. At first, the master of the tavern made some difficulty about procuring us a carriage to go on seventeen miles to the Natural Bridge; but after a little demur, we got one so as to start by half-past two. Lexington is a small town, not very picturesque in itself, but standing in a plain with fine mountains all round at a few miles' distance—the nearest, a flat-topped massive-looking hill, is called by people here "The House." There are no Indians in all this part of the country, and even their beautiful names have been forgotten, and have given place to such Cockney appellations as James River, Louisa Court, Charlottesville, &c. &c. There are many signs of hard frost on the road, which was tolerable as far as Buchanan; planks were laid for that distance. When we turned off into the valley, about four miles from the rocky bridge, our carriage was much tried; the horses floundered along the brink of a precipice, our driver calling to us to throw our weight now upon one side, now on the other, to keep a balance. At one time within half a foot of deep water, where, in case of being overturned, we must have been drowed, if we had escaped being smashed in the fall; at another, with a descent of three hundred feet, without the smallest guard upon our right. But our Irish coachman was civil and expert; he assured me he would not have anything happen to us for fifty dollars, and happily, both traces breaking within a mile and a half of our destination, I scrambled out of the vehicle, rejoiced to find my feet once more, leaving R—— to take care of the vehicle, while the driver went back to pick up the scattered boxes. I made my way on, with the help of a bright young moon, to the first little hotel (there is another, near the Bridge). It was a rough place; but I was hospitably received, and the master's son, with a negro servant, set off to aid and guide the carriage through a track which had appeared to me in some places wholly impracticable for anything on wheels. However, fortunately, it was too dark for R—— to see danger, and the three men guided her on safely in about two hours, much to the relief of my mind. No other catastrophe occurred, excepting that some of my boxes, which had been shaken off, were considerably mauled, and I hardly felt this as a misfortune, in consideration of our own safety. The good people did their best to feed and warm us, but as their house is little prepared for winter visitors, and this night a frost occurred, seldom known in Virginia—in spite of a blazing wood fire, and a blanket hung up over our door, the water in the jugs and basins was frozen before daylight. However, I was glad to find, that by rising very early there would be time to see and sketch the wonderful Natural Bridge, and to reach the canal, two miles' distance, by ten o'clock. Most fortunately, the steamboat goes down tomorrow, otherwise we might have been detained till Thursday in Lynchburg.

January 24.—After all that has been said in praise of the Natural Bridge, I was not disappointed: the chasm over which it passes is narrower at the bottom than at the top: beginning at fifty feet, it gradually widens to near a hundred, and is about two hundred and ninety feet in height, while the way over the top may be about twenty or thirty in width, guarded by natural walls of rock, and covered by five feet of soil, made firm and bound together by trees and shrubbery. The small stream it crosses is called Cedar Creek, which, like all the rivers of this district, is as turbid and as muddy-looking as the Ouse, in Bedfordshire. The rich soils of these lands are borne down by all these waters, to fertilize neglected or worn-out farms in distant places. Looking at this bridge from a short distance, it has a magnificent appearance, and no one would guess Nature to have been her own architect. The arch is finely formed: over its centre the rock is chiselled into the appearance of a deep-set window, and on one side it seems as if supported by a gigantic buttress, backed by mountains, and set in a framework of verdure. Summer must render this bridge still more beautiful; but its grandeur can even now be well appreciated. I engaged our driver and carriage of last evening to take us to the place where the Lynchburg steamer calls—most fortunately—for no conveyance large enough for luggage could now have been hired. Fine mountainous and glorious forest views extend the whole way down the Powhatan. I was reminded of some parts of Germany; but the scenery of this river far exceeds that of the Rhine, though the water has not equal clearness or volume, and these mountains are not ornamented by ruined castles. Of the Rocky Bridge I often heard; but neither books nor travellers, familiar to me, have spoken of these forty miles of scenery passed through by a canal, which sometimes travels by one shore, then takes to the river, and once crosses over it to the other side. We passed at least twenty locks, going easily and plsasantly; our speed averaged about four miles an hour—quite fast enough, for I had time to sketch and to enjoy the beautiful scenery, instead of being steamed along too rapidly for either pleasure. A warm sun befriended us, and, though the air was rather cold, it was clear and still, so that with an occasional visit to the cabin to warm my hands, I was able to sit all day on deck; and this passage proved one of the most agreeable and least tedious of all I have had, though it occupied nine hours. Some of the valleys traversing this mountain region are suspected to be rich in minerals and precious stones, which is very probable. From signs I observed on the blue ridge which we mounted by the railroad, greenstone passes into limestone; mica, slate, and granite frequently appear, though I am not enough of a geologist to be able to mark and describe their exact locations. Beautifully white gypsum was placed in heaps by the river-side where we first embarked on board the canal boat, but no one could tell me from whence; I saw star-looking dark spots, as large as a shilling, in one mass, having almost the appearance of fossils, though I conclude they must have been some modification of talc. There was no time to get any knocked off; and, as people here consider attention to stones or flowers a very childish proceeding, it is difficult to gain their attention to such objects. About half-way down the river there is a large manufactory of cement made from a limestone which contains iron and aluminous matter. This is burned, then powdered, and put into barrels, which are sold for one dollar each. This is not the sole manufactory: there are other localities in the State of New York where it is made—towards the north, I suppose. This is the most firm and durable thing known for cementing stones together: it seems to become part and parcel of their very substance. An obliging gentleman on board procured me a specimen of the limestone in its natural state, and also before it is ground after burning.

Daylight had quite faded away before we landed here; the captain provided us with such an excellent dinner of turkey, roast beef, and cranberry tart, with common potatoes, sweet potatoes, fine celery, and glasses of sweet milk, that we were in no starving condition; and I recommend the *Links* canal-boat as one of the most pleasurable conveyances I ever entered, though it has no gorgeous saloon or even railed deck. The black cook, seeing me draw, came to beg 'missus would make his picture for his *ole wife,*' which undertaking was accomplished to our mutual content, Darkey having evidently no vanity to wound. I cannot always tell whether these black servants are free or slaves—probably the latter. They are merry, good-natured, and easy in their manner; familiar, but in a much pleasanter way than the helps of the Northern States, who mistake an impertinent manner for republicanism, and speak as if they thought themselves injured by serving you.

On my arrival at this, the 'Noble Hotel,' a black chambermaid took charge of us, and, though the bed-room felt warm, she insisted on lighting a fire, for fear 'missus should be cold.' 'Pray, missus, have fire; don't think of trouble, missus—don't mind trouble.' Some of these blacks are officiously anxious to oblige, and this without any motive of interest, as far as I can judge. We leave this place at half-past nine for Petersburg; stay there to-night, and next day go to Wilmington by steamboat, I believe, and then to Charleston on Friday or Saturday, I hope.

Petersburg, Wednesday Evening.—We left Lynchburg at nine this morning. As far as I can judge, it is a pretty place, and the views nearly all the way upon the railroad are fine. The country, Devonian in rocks and scenery; I could have fancied myself near Haldon Hill, it is so like the neighbourhood of Exeter, part of the way: the soil as red and the land equally rich-looking, but certainly not as well cultivated, or rendered as productive by good farming. At Petersburg we crossed the Appomattox river, which falls into the Powhatan twelve miles below that place. Petersburg is evidently a growing town. I suppose the numerous railroads which now traverse Virginia will quickly stir up the inhabitants, and make them aware that their State, as it is one of the most beautiful, has also capabilities which might render it the most rich and thriving. We came over the highest viaduct I ever crossed, one hundred and eighty feet! I was so terrified that I could not look out for giddiness: it is built on piles; the engineer who planned it and the bridges over the Powhatan at Lynchburg, was in the cars, and assured us of safety; but it was difficult to feel at ease during the transit. We reached this place before five, and I intend to leave it by the train at three o'clock to-morrow morning, for Wilmington.

Thursday, January 25.—We reached Wilmington by eight o'clock this evening, one hundred and sixty miles, nearly all the way through pine barrens, which are not barren of turpentine and tar; these products are extracted from the pitch pines. There are many large manufactories to procure them; the trees have the bark taken off about ten feet on one side, and vessels are placed to catch the turpentine. When this is exhausted, the trees are cut down, sawed into lengths, and placed in circles, with a fire in the centre, much in the way charcoal is made; but as the tar comes out it is made to run into pipes, and the wood when exhausted is covered over, and becomes charcoal. From Petersburg, the whole country consists of poor sands and clay, like part of Hampshire and the adjoining bit of Dorset. The sand during the greater part of the way is as white as that around Bournemouth. Not far from a place called Goldsborough, a colony of Irish appear to be comfortably settling themselves; what they cultivate I cannot judge, passing rapidly, at this time of year; they seemed healthy and well clothed; and I observed pigs of all ages, and several cows. It was a pleasant sight to see these poor people making the wilderness a springing well, and the barren land rich. I should like to bring all the 'Know Nothings' of the country to look at them. I am told this faction abounds in the South; it is evident there are men guiding this movement who ought to know better; but some are making political profit of the ignorance and mistaken patriotism of their weaker neighbours, and hope to attain power by such means. I am sorry to find a considerable party in the United States advocate openly the principle of 'doing evil that good may come,' as regards their own country; and Mr. Cushing, the Attorney-General of the States, informed me without circumlocution, speaking of the European war, that the Turks being *effete*, and a sea-board being necessary for the Russians, it was perfectly right and proper that the latter should devour the former. If it be possible for republicans to be in the pay of despotism, I should imagine this gentleman must be one of the favoured emissaries of the Emperor Nicholas. After passing through the rich, ill-cultivated Highlands of Virginia, it is curious to observe how much more is comparatively drawn from the unthankful soil we passed through to-day; half this care and industry bestowed upon the former would be returned tenfold. I observed some few Rhododendrons and Kalmias upon the blue ridge, as we descended by that wonderful railroad; and for fifty miles, as we approached this place, the undergrowth was rich in all those showy evergreens we call American. On the trees I saw bunches of an Epiphyte, growing like our mistletoe, and the long hair-like lichen, or parasitical plant, I have so often heard described as clothing the woods in the South; it covered and hung round many trees I saw in a swamp this afternoon. I am much amused with the 'Blackies,' who act as chambermaids everywhere now; they quite take possession of us, remain in the room *sans ceremonie*, and are officious and curious beyond belief. One watched me drawing to-night with great astonishment; she said she had 'never seen any one do that before; how can you make marks that look like places? You must have a clever head!' I begged for snuffers, a tallow candle having a long nose. 'Oh, I does that with my fingers; but I'll find you an old pair of scissors.' When we asked for some warm water, she thought the request very extraordinary, and burst into a hoarse laugh. They certainly are very unlike the white race; but everybody seems good-natured to them: they come into the cars and sit where they please. I see none of the white exclusiveness I had been taught to expect.

Yours affectionately,

A. M. M.

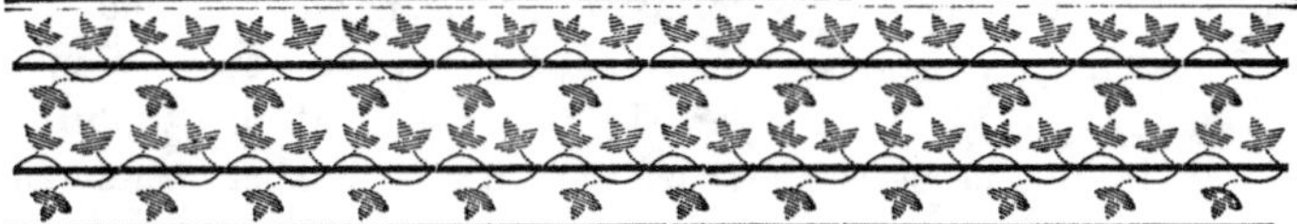

LETTER XVII.

CHARLESTON, *January* 7, 1855.

MY DEAR FRIENDS,—

The post for England went off to-day unexpectedly; I had only a few minutes' warning, and no time to look at my letter, so that I forget whether I wrote last from Petersburg; but as we reached Wilmington too late at night, and started too early to see anything of that place, I could not have said much about it. White sand and pine barrens made up the whole two hundred and sixty miles of yesterday's journey. It required twenty-two hours' railroad to accomplish that distance. Almost all the pitch pines are disfigured, and most probably will be killed, by the bark being stripped off, that the turpentine may drip from it into a small vessel placed on the ground. The forest looks as if it was planted with white posts; but this is occasionally relieved by thickets of Rhododendron, Kalmia, and Phyllerea, which must be splendid when flowering, in May; and about sixty miles from this place the pitch is superseded by the Pinus palustris. It is pretty to see the long tassel-like looking leaves streaming in the wind; but it makes a very transparent-looking forest, as the branches grow wide apart, and the bunches of foliage are also distant from each other. I begin to mark cotton plantations, and my compassionate feelings are rapidly changing sides. It appears to me our benevolent intentions in England have taken a mistaken direction, and that we should bestow our compassion on the masters instead of on the slaves. The former by no means enjoy the incubus with which circumstances have loaded them, and would be only too happy if they could supersede this black labour by white; but as to the negroes, they are the merriest, most contented set of people I ever saw; of course there are exceptions, but I am inclined to suspect that we have as much vice, and more suffering, than is caused here by the unfortunate institution of Slavery; and I very much doubt if freedom will ever make the black population, in the mass, anything more than a set of grown-up children. Even as to the matter of purchase and sale, it is disliked by masters; and I find compassion very much wasted upon the objects of it. An old lady died here lately, and her negroes were to be parted with; Mrs. S——, an acquaintance of mine, knew these blacks, and shed tears about their change of fate; but when they came to market, and she found all so gay and indifferent about it, she could not help feeling her sorrow was greatly thrown away. Mrs. Stowe's Topsy is a perfect illustration of Darkie's character, and many of the sad histories of which her book is made up may be true as isolated facts; but yet I feel sure that, as a whole, the story, however ingeniously worked up, is an unfair picture; a libel upon the slaveholders as a body. I very much doubt if a real Uncle Tom can often be found in the whole negro race; and if such a being is, or was, he is as great a rarity as a Shakspeare among whites. One particular want appears to me evident in negro minds and character: they have no consciousness of the fitness of things. I suffer now from the cold wintry weather here; and upon my begging Blackie for a better fire in my room, in the civilest, most anxious tone, he asked whether I would not like some iced water? (Knowing this to be a luxury in hot weather, he would never consider that it might be less acceptable in cold.) We have lately had black chambermaids in all hotels. They are perfectly good-natured, and officiously anxious to help us in all matters in which their assistance is not required. 'Let I do this, Missus,' and 'Let I do that,' when perhaps it is hard to induce them to do what is really wanted—to light the fire when we are cold, or to bring a little warm water when clean hands would be a luxury. They fairly take possession of us, and unless we lock them out, they stand to watch our proceedings, and curiously to inspect our things. 'Adeline,' at Lynchburg, saw my sketch of the black cook on board the *Links* canal-boat, at which she burst into a loud laugh, and exclaimed, 'He very like a monkey, missus—we very like monkies.' And she appeared delighted with her own wit—not at all hurt by the idea. A pretty Southern lady arrived at the hotel, with a fair infant in the arms of his black nurse. I came out from the tea-room rather sooner than was expected, and found all the Darkies that could get away assembled round the tiny massa, (they are very fond of children, and make capital nurses,—tender, watchful, playful, and yet, I think, firm; but they are firm only with children), jumping and screaming their delight. Upon seeing me an elderly man came forward, with a grin and a bow—'The black population are only enjoying themselves, missus.' I said I was glad they were happy, and left them to their happiness. At one of the railroad stations I watched a young and intelligent-looking black man, considerably beyond boyhood, perseveringly keeping up a kind of Highland trot over a number of small pitch barrels with all the zest of a white child from four to six years of age. I begin to doubt whether they ever grow mentally after twenty. They are precocious children, being so imitative; they soon ripen, come to a stand-still, and advance no farther. In this respect Uncle Tom is a myth, but Topsy a reality. I mean to go and see a sale of slaves; my wish is to judge the subject fairly in all its bearings, and this I may be trusted to do even by Abolitionists; for early prejudices and my national and acquired feelings are certainly opposed to slavery; but if countenances are 'a history as well as a prophecy,' the national expression of faces in the North as contrasted with those of the South tell a strange, and to me an unexpected story, as regards the greatest happiness principle of the greatest number! Of course, it must be borne in mind that no rules are without exception; but, oh, the haggard, anxious, melancholy, restless, sickly, hopeless faces I have seen in the Northern States—in the rail-cars, on the steam-boats, in the saloons, and particularly in the ladies' parlour. There is beauty of feature and complexion, with hardly any individuality of character. Nothing like simplicity, even among children after ten years of age—hot-house, forced impetuous beings, the *almighty dollars*, the incentive and only guide to activity and appreciation. Women care that their husbands should gain gold, that they may spend it in dress and ostentation; and the men like that their wives should appear as queens, whether they rule well, or ill, or at all; yet it is certain that I have made the acquaintance, and that I value the friendship, of superior women in the North, and if I should be thought to have expressed myself with too much severity, I appeal to their candour and judgment; and being American cousins they have the Anglo-Saxon love of Truth, and will not spurn her even in an unveiled form, or receive her ungraciously even when thus presented. I have reason to speak gratefully, and warmly do I feel, and anxiously do I venture these observations, which may seem even harsh and ungrateful. I do not yet know much of the Southern ladies; but from Washington to this place I have been struck by a general improvement of countenance and manner in the white race, and this in spite of the horrors which accompany the misuse of tobacco. If the gentlemen of this part of the country would only acquire habits of self-control and decency in this matter, they would indeed become the *Preux Chevaliers* of the United States, as their hills and valleys may prove the store-houses and gardens of the Union. May their sons and daughters look to these things, and increase in wealth, prosperity, virtue, and happiness!

In the railroad-cars the day before yesterday, when asking for information as to the name of a place, a youth sitting near offered to go and find it out for me; he had the air of a ruddy, healthy-looking Englishman, and I was struck by the frank, ingenuous manner with which he came forward: he stood by my seat, and afterwards conversed freely, yet without conceit or forwardness. I elicited that his parents are Bavarian, residing at no great distance from Munich; that at sixteen he came out to this country alone, as a traveller, in some business; that he loves his own people and his friends, and hopes, some day, to revisit them; but that it is probable the duties of his calling will detain him in America for years. I would stake my existence upon the honour and integrity of that boy; he will prove a fine example of the advantages of early collision and of self-reliance. I have heard the Lord's Prayer quoted as an argument for keeping boys out of the indurating process of early temptation. I cannot think that the words alluded to have any other sense than of an individual petition for strength to overcome. Every boy wrapped in what the canny Scotch wife calls the 'blue blanket,' may not prove vicious, but most of them 'sow their wild oats' between eighteen and twenty-five, instead of some years earlier; and those who do not, in ninety-nine cases out of a hundred become weak and undecided characters. It must be remembered that weakness comes nigh to wickedness, though it may not be (as the old proverb has it) worse than wickedness. The Professors at the Virginian University tell me they regret that Jefferson (its founder) placed it away from a town. I asked what their experience led them to think of home education for young men, and received the same answer as I have already from experienced heads of houses at Oxford and Cambridge: that all the care of a virtuous home will not make up for the life-training of the world, best given at an age when the temptations of vice have less strength, and its ugliness is more apparent than it will be some years later. I consider this subject as one of such overwhelming importance to the Christian and moral welfare of those concerned, that no scruples, either of affection or interest, shall induce me to conceal these opinions, or mask my own convictions.

Charleston, January 29.—A cold day yesterday, and wet all this morning. I have only made acquaintance with some friends of Mr. and Mrs. R——. They took me last night to what I should not have seen of my own accord in America, Waugh's Italia removed; it consists of beautiful panoramic views of all the finest sights and views in Italy. I never met with anything superior of the kind, and I hope they may some day be taken to England. This hotel is very good; much better ordered than

Willard's, at Washington; or even than the St. Nicholas at New York, in point of real comfort, although less gorgeously furnished than the latter. Of this city I have as yet seen nothing; but the streets and houses appear to be clean and well kept. Last night I heard parties of darkies singing, as they passed the windows, those negro melodies the airs of which have become familiar in England. Music, nursing, washing, and cooking are their peculiar talents, and cheerfulness their special virtue. After dinner to-day I had the first good orange I have tasted since I came South. It has surprised me to find that fruit is more scarce and dearer in Virginia and Carolina than with us. I am not to see orange trees till I reach Florida; and throughout the United States their fruit is much less plentiful than in England —perhaps at New Orleans I may find it otherwise. Sweet potatoes and turtle are both frequent at the dinner-table of this hotel. This evening one of my pleasant Washington acquaintances, Mr. P——, came to see me, and we are to go together to-morrow, to call on Mrs. H——. It has poured all the morning, so I have not been out.

This is a fine day; several ladies and gentlemen of this place called on me, and I received Mr. and Mrs. H——, who forestalled my intention, by coming to me. Professor and Mrs. Gibbs took me to make a sketch of the Ettewan and Yemassee Rivers from the Battery, at White Point. There I saw the first palmetto I ever yet met with in the open air; and, on my return to the hotel, a gentleman told me the *Isabel* steamer had just brought a cargo of oranges from Cuba. In one garden this morning, I saw a standard orange tree, with some fruit upon it, but it was supposed not to be sweet; and since that I have found several of the same, bearing only what we should call Seville oranges. The timber-trees of Magnolia grandiflora all about this place are fine, and must be beautiful in summer, but this severe winter renders vegetation very backward; and I see some of the live oaks (*Quercus virens*) rather cut by the cold. The Tillandsia usnoides (called everywhere here by the name of hanging moss), having the appearance, at a little distance, of our hair-like lichens, dresses most of the trees, but especially the live oak, with its graceful pendulous bunches, sometimes hanging a yard and a half long; the stem is not larger than a thread, set with small, rounded, frosted white leaves; the little sweet-scented, reddish, purplish flowers come out at the end of the rope-like stems which swing about in the breeze. They steep this Tillandsia in water, and use its black, hair-like fibres for stuffing mattresses and pillows; the seeds being light, are carried about by the wind, and stick and fructify in all the trees around; yet it seems difficult to cultivate, for I have never seen it in our English Epiphyte houses. The temperature of any greenhouse would suit its constitution, but I imagine it requires to be blown about; and a still atmosphere is probably uncongenial to the habits of this pretty waving plant. I have seen a live oak as large as any of our British oaks, having upon it as many tufts of Tillandsia as leaves; it does not appear to be injurious like the mistletoe, but adds to the beauty of its adopted parent without shortening the life of whatever sustaining tree may support it. I drank tea at Mrs. R——'s, and spent a pleasant evening with Mr. and Mrs. H——.

January 30.—Professor and Mrs. Gibbs called for me at eleven in the morning, and we had a delightful day in the open air, botanizing, &c. Dr. Gibbs knew every plant and seed. For the first time I found yarras and cactuses in the hedge-rows; ferns, such as Polypodium incanum, plentifully on ancient live oaks, Asplenium ebeneum, and Botrychium Virginiacum, in an English looking lane; the beautiful little Houstonia serpyllifolia and Mitchella repens, with scarlet twin berries; Prunus Carolinian; and the Jasmine-coloured Gelseminium sempervirens twining up it, and through the hedges of Ilex Cassine. I often feel in this country as if I had been removed to a new heavens and a new earth, and as if my enjoyments now are a foretaste of worlds where space and time will open out fresh delights, in a fuller comprehension of the mighty Creator and his mighty works.

At a pretty spot called Gibbs' Farm, belonging to some part of the Professor's family, we passed great part of the morning; in a small garden belonging to it, I gathered bundles of that beautiful paper Narcissus, so rare in England, and I knocked down what is here called a sour orange (*alias* bitter) from a fine bush thirty feet high. Then after making a sketch of that picturesque homestead, with its venerable oaks, the Tillandsia, imitating the white beard and silvery locks of age, Mrs. Gibbs placed at my feet a basket filled with oranges and bananas from Cuba, for lunch, and I made these a foreground for my drawing. We again got into the carriage and made our progress to Magnolia Cemetery. Owing to the usual recklessness of American habits, we had to cross a railroad which runs for some way along the side of the road; we had hardly passed over it a moment, when the train rushed by; there is not even a slight fence to divide the iron from the common track, and they say horses get used to the cars, and men to the necessary caution, so that after a little practice, few accidents occur; of course, cows and oxen and sheep are smashed now and then, but the Company pays, and that is all. I never cross these roads without a sensation of terror. Magnolia Cemetery is pretty; it has a chapel built like a country church in England; in style, simple perpendicular Gothic, with a light and elegant spire. The grounds are ornamented by a creek, which makes its way up from the Ettewan River, and its waters, even here, are rather salt. I sketched the entrance and chapel, and then a fine live oak, with Charleston and the Accabee River uniting itself to the ocean in the distance; a foreground of tombs, which are here well chosen in point of taste, and without those white boundary posts which I have mentioned as disfiguring Greenwood, Hamilton, and some of the other burying-grounds in Canada and the United States, which are otherwise so far in advance of the mother country in sentiment and beauty. Republicanism forgets itself in the concerns of the grave and of immortality. Strange that when all are really supposed equal, love and truth banishes the equality which is emblematical of pride, and cultivates only the freedom of virtue! There is more love of nature evinced in the cemeteries of America, than in the arrangements for the living; life is the myth, eternity the reality of existence; beautiful flowers are cultivated for the dead;

taste is pure, and feeling uncontaminated by dollars and cents. The monuments, tombs, and inscriptions are generally pathetic and interesting, free from the bombast and posthumous flattery too common in England. As the families are together in these last homes, usually the surname marks each entrance gate; within, one often sees a marble urn, or slab, marked with little more than 'our brother,' 'a dearly loved sister,' 'my wife,' 'little Addy,' 'our kind parents,' 'two precious babes,' &c., &c. These simple words attract the sympathy of strangers and awaken the tenderness of friends far more than eulogies. I never walk through these cemeteries without a sensation of pleasure derived from the consciousness of Christian brotherhood, rather than of sorrow from that of our common fate. Here I realize *more* that we shall all be made alive again, than that we shall all die. Till sunset we remained out; there was little temptation to return home for dinner; I was most willing to exchange it for tea; and afterwards my pleasant Washington friend called and took me to a little dancing party, at the house of one of his married daughters, where I saw young ladies more natural, and more gracefully and simply attired, than in the Northern States; both the tone of voice and the choice of words and pronunciation are much more like old England as one proceeds further south; the habits simpler and more unostentatious, and the dress of every-day wear is suitable and gentlewoman-like, instead of being, as in the North, unbecoming, stiff, and extravagant; the young women plastering their hair, and wearing silks fit for their grandmothers, and the middle-aged spending hours in repairing the ravages of time, by studious artificial contrivances, which, after all, make themselves evident to the most superficial observers.

January 31.—I spent a delightful day with Mrs. H——, who took me out to her cottage, four miles distant; there we provisionally planted the ferns and other treasures I took up on Tuesday. She will let them grow there until I am ready to receive them at Boston, next September, to be planted in my Ward's case. Belmont is a charming spot; it is (like the Southern ladies) not over dressed; it has the Ettewan on one side, and the forest on the other; slaves who are adopted children, and Irish labourers who have adopted a master and mistress. I begged to go into a negro cottage in the wood; the parents were out, and we found only a covey of tiny 'darkies,' from two years to eight—'very like monkeys,' as Adeline would have said. The negro race never sit down to a meal if they can possibly avoid doing so; they have always some sticks burning, and a kind of *pot au feu;* in one corner of the tolerably comfortable abode was a fishing net, and another net held an *omnium gatherum* of eatables: no great attention to cleanliness, but the appearance of everything out of doors was like that of a small farm in England—cows, chickens, &c., &c. I beg to think we anti-slavers and abolitionists are as much blinded by names as the republicans, who think they have shaken off an aristocracy, because they have got rid of dukes and duchesses, and lords and ladies. I must extract some observations from a work published here, which my short experience of a slave country induces me unhesitatingly to adopt as my own.

'Slavery may not be the best system of labour, but it is the best for the negro in this country. If it be true of the English soldier or sailor, that his condition has been ameliorated in the last fifty years, it is quite as true of the negro. Slavery is that system of labour which exchanges subsistence for work, which secures a life maintenance from the master to the slave, and gives a life labour from the slave to the master. Slavery is the negro system of labour: he is lazy and improvident; slavery makes him work, and ensures him a home, food, and clothing; it provides for sickness, infancy and old age; allows no tramping or skulking, and knows no pauperism. All cruelty is an abuse; does not belong to the institution; is contrary to law; may be punished, prevented, and removed. If slavery is subject to abuses, it has its compensations also; it establishes permanent, and therefore kind, relations between labour and capital. It does away with what Stuart Mill calls 'the widening and embittering feud between labour and capital.' It draws close the relation between master and servant; it is not an engagement for days, weeks, but for life. The most wretched feature in hireling labour is the isolated, miserable creature who has no home, no work, no food, and in whom no one is particularly interested. Slavery does for the negro what European schemers in vain attempt to do for the hireling. On every plantation the master is a poor-law commissioner, to provide food, clothing, medicine, houses, for his people. He is a police officer to prevent idleness, drunkenness, theft, or disorder; there is therefore no starvation among slaves, and comparatively few crimes. The poet tells us there are worse things in the world than hard labour; 'withouten that would come a heavier bale;' and so there are worse things for the negro than slavery in a Christian land. Archbishop Hughes, in his visit to Cuba, asked Africans if they wished to return to their native country; the answer was always, *No*. If the negro is happier here than in his own land, can we say that slavery is an evil to him? Slaves and masters do not quarrel with their circumstances; is it not hard that the stranger should interfere to make both discontented?

'All Christians believe that the affairs of this world are directed by God for wise and good purposes. The arrival of the negro in America makes no exception to that rule—his transportation was a rude method of emigration, the only practicable one in his case. Until this operation was interfered with and made piratical, it was not attended with the wretchedness often exhibited by the emigrant ship, even now, notwithstanding the passenger law. What the ultimate end of slavery may be we cannot presume to guess; but we can see much good already resulting—good to the negro in his improved condition—good to the country whose rich fields he has made productive in climates at first unfit for the white man—and good to the continent of Africa, as furnishing the only means of effectually civilizing its people. Whether Mr. Clarkson or Lord Carlisle approve of the mode in which it has pleased Providence to bring this about, the result will probably be the same. There has been malignant abuse lavished upon the slave-holders of America by writers in this country and in England; they consider abuses as its necessary condition, and a cruel master its fair representative. They have no knowledge of the thing abused; they substitute an ideal for a reality. They have shown as little regard for truth and common sense, as we should do if we were to gather up all the atrocities committed in Great Britain by husbands and wives, parents and children, masters and servants, and denounce these several relations in life in consequence of their abuses. If because of the evils incident to hireling labour, because there are heartless, grinding employers, and miserable, starved labourers, it should be proposed to abolish work for hire, it would be quite as logical as the argument for the abolition of slavery because there are suffering among slaves, and hard hearts among masters. The cruelty or suffering is no more a necessary part of our system than it is of the other. To attempt to establish the hiring plan with Africans is as wise as to endeavour to establish the constitutional government of England in Ashantee or Dahomey. Carlyle says that the world will not permit Cuffy to lie on his back and eat pumpkins forever, in a country intended by Providence to produce coffee, sugar, and spices for the use of all mankind; and that he must, one of these days, resume his work for Brother Jonathan, or some other master. The blacks in Hayti have only changed masters; they are the slaves of a black chief, as in Africa. Their pagan mummeries have been resumed; they are engaged in petty wars instead of peaceful labours. The Emperor has his standing army, and is as anxious as more important potentates to employ it in the legitimate business of cutting throats. The African cannot originate a civilization of his own; from the slave civilized and instructed by slavery can any regeneration of the African continent be alone looked for. We must believe that Christianity will at last be established in Africa, and carry there the improvement which always attends its steps. This is not to be accomplished suddenly by any compulsive movement, but slowly, and gradually—it is in this way only that Providence effects his great purposes. The black race always perishes if placed, as manumission would place it, in competition with the white. There is an obvious and irremovable dissimilarity between the white and black race. The number of blacks in Canada and in the Northern States is only kept up by the addition of freed or runaway slaves. In slavery they increase, as free they die out; therefore it is that the blacks in America cannot be made free for their own sakes, even if it were desirable they should be for their masters. Manumission would injure both.'

Alas! for distant Philanthropy! Whatever griefs and vices may be discovered in the Southern States, I fear their prototypes are to be discovered in London, in Paris, and even in New York. Let us take out the beam from our own eyes before we make ourselves so busy with the motes in those of our neighbour; and instead of abusing each other, let us assist in bearing one another's burdens, and the sorrows and faults of each will be lessened by division.

Friday, February 2.—Yesterday I saw much of interest in the Museum, had a pleasant dinner at Mrs. R——'s, and went to an evening party at Mrs. J. de R——'s. This day we embark for Savannah and Florida, to return the 15th, and to embark for Cuba the 19th. No time for more at present. Goodbye.

Yours affectionately,

A. M. M.

LETTER XVIII.

SAVANNAH, GEORGIA,
February 4, 1855.

MY DEAR FRIENDS,—

The *Calhoun* steamer left Charleston at four o'clock yesterday, and brought us here about three in the morning—a quiet and bright moonlight voyage. Mr. H——, to whose care I was recommended by my friend Mr. R——, of Liverpool, put me on board the vessel, and invited me to return to his house on the 15th, to take the *Isabel* for Cuba on the 19th. My last letter closed very hastily, as I had only just time to seal it before going on board. I do not know what you and our abolitionist friend F—— may think of my slavery conclusions. You will imagine that I have fallen under some evil influence; but really we in England know as little about the domestic arrangements of these Southerners as they do about our great landholders in England I have been several times assured that the present Duchess of Sutherland depopulated the Highlands for the sake of raising sheep there. They confuse dates and facts, and confound the present Duchess with the old Countess Duchess, whose energetic plans aided the starving Celts she caused to emigrate, and that outlay of money may perhaps now tend towards the improvement of the estates of the present Duke. I fell in with a personification of 'Rebecca' on board the *Calhoun* steamer. I was introduced when we embarked, and I felt myself attracted by her beautiful, melancholy face. When we got acquainted, she told me this singular story:—At thirteen, she had run away from doting friends with her present husband, who, being a Christian, was not acceptable to them, and they refused forgiveness. Some years after, when she was on a steamer with her husband and a young babe, she was induced to sing 'Sweet Home' on deck, in the dark. A voice not far off said, in a beseeching way, 'Again, lady—pray again.' A vague feeling crossed her that its tone was familiar, still she hesitated to obey the request, when a friend near exclaimed, 'Yes, do; it may be that the stranger is separated from those he loves.' She repeated the air, and no mōre was said. The next morning she saw her father in the vessel. She darted up towards him, but he turned his back upon her; and her courage failing her, she attempted no other appeal. Just after this he stopped the black nurse carrying her infant, took him in his arms, kissed his forehead, and said to a gentleman standing near, 'This is my grandson;' yet he forgave not; and some months afterwards he died without asking to see his daughter or her child again. She is now a fifteen years' happy wife, with eight children, and has at last been invited to visit her former home alone. Her husband insisted upon her accepting this invitation, though it excluded him, and to-morrow she will be received by slowly-forgiving relations. I could not but sympathize with her feelings.

Savannah seems a large town, with many pleasant squares, in one of which this (Pulaski) hotel is situated. It is so called in memory of a fine steamer of that name, which, before boilers were well regulated, blew up and engulfed members of almost all the principal families in this place. One family, consisting of thirteen, lost eleven individuals; only the father and one infant were left behind. In all the States of the Union I find complaints of poverty and public debt; so that while the Central Government of Washington boasts of a superabundance of money, the Empire as a whole is little less involved than Great Britain. I think this fact is not understood in Europe; and what is more, while the national debt seems not to clog prosperity in England, poverty makes itself very evident among the governments of the Federal States. Matters of public utility are at a standstill in their chief cities. It is very easy for President and Congress to have a surplus, as long as the Union remains at peace: taxes flow in, and there are few out-goings. In general, the local capitals are ill-paved, indifferently drained, and poorly lighted, and the public buildings are few and badly kept.

The air seems warmer here than at Charleston; but I caught cold on board the steamer, which confines me to the house for to-day, and not having taken off my clothes last night, I do not feel very excursive. The Bishop of Georgia (Elliott), with his lady and a gentleman and some ladies I knew in the North, have called upon me.

I find that the term 'Slave' is rarely made use of in the South. The blacks are called 'our servants,' or more commonly 'our people.' We must remember that when slaves are to be disposed of, people in this country do not consider they are literally buying *men*, but *services*, and what we hear of, are the abuses not the laws of the system. Should a master ill-treat a slave, the law protects the latter; and I am inclined to believe cases of such treatment are rare. If a slave violates the law, a judge sends to his master and says, This is your servant; if you do not punish him, I must. Of course, the culprit much prefers to be corrected by his own master, by whom all extenuating circumstances are understood and allowed for; and he is usually left in his hands.

As I have said before, the blacks are children of larger growth. They are tricky, idle, and dirty. An excellent English housekeeper, who has the management of this house, tells me that it is impossible for them to get on with the motives that would influence whites. She is very averse to reporting any of the darkies as requiring correction (*alias* a whipping); but without the power of doing so, they would be utterly unmanageable. As it is, one white servant would do the work of three blacks. 'Tom,' perhaps, has no other vocation than to light fires. I have been amused to watch the slow round-about way in which he performs the operation, never having all he wants at hand. This morning he brought no light; so before preparing to light the fire he takes my wax candle, lights it, and lets it stand burning uselessly. Then, after lighting the fire, he keeps the candle burning for half an hour in broad daylight, while he goes through various evolutions about the cinders and the dust, till he has settled it all to his satisfaction: and it is of no use to suggest any quicker mode of proceeding. I must repeat, over and over again, our ideas of negro character, and its capabilities, are little grounded upon truth.

We have cast aside the evidence of people who, with clear unbiassed judgment, have watched the African from his cradle to his grave, and taken the opinion and the advice of well-intentioned but hot-headed zealots, until we have damaged the cause of civilization, checked the progress of individuals of the black race, and at the same time done mischief to ourselves, and to fine islands and colonies which are now again tending towards barbarism. People of the Southern States might not be considered unprejudiced witnesses of the present condition and prospects of our West Indian Islands; but I know from other sources, and I appeal to Englishmen for the truth of my information. Barbadoes has already much deteriorated, and unless the power of landed acquisition by negroes receive some legal check (owing to the small disbursements necessary to their existence, and their giving no credit, with a deep laid intention of getting rid of white proprietors), the blacks will slowly but certainly gain possession of the island. The same process will follow in others; and when too late, the British nation will come to a conviction that it must either re-conquer its West Indian Islands, or permit them to amalgamate with the United States, which by that time will be too wise to permit them to remain free black republics. There is no doubt the blacks are susceptible of education and improvement, to a certain extent, under white influence. The darkies of Baltimore and Virginia are a shade higher in the scale of improvement than those of Georgia, from being more in approximation with whites in a mass; but you never can change the Ethiopian character, or wash white his skin. 'The pig will never grow into the lion.' Under good direction, it is a light-hearted, merry, unreflecting race, excitable and impulsive; but it has a sense of justice, and can be attached, and be made an honest, useful, and highly respectable servant, by judicious management and early training. A well-taught negro coachman drives admirably. They are apt at any mechanical employment. Some of them are very orderly, but put them out of a track to which they have been accustomed, and they rapidly lose themselves. A lady here has taken great pains with a negro boy born in her family. I was amused to see him standing behind her chair, with a tray under his arm, like a little black statue. He never forgets to come at a particular hour for her orders; but the teaching him to read is no small undertaking. He goes on the box of the carriage, and well performs any accustomed duty; but if you ask him to take a knife and dig up a plant, he looks utterly bewildered.

What are we doing? Instead of bringing away the African race, to return them in a generation or two, educated for the improvement and enlightenment of Africa, are we not *re-barbarizing* the Christian world by giving fair fields back again into savage hands? Negro Christians left to their own guidance fall sooner or later again into pagan habits. Inquire of the British consuls; ask the admirably devoted clergy and bishops of this land; take the convictions of any persons of experience and judgment who have lived among blacks. No discrepancies will be found in such opinions; but our people and our Governments of the last forty years have been led away by pre-conceived notions; they have listened only to well-intentioned, but weak religionists; and under a mistaken impression that they promoted freedom and Christianity, have they been giving encouragement to ultimate bondage and paganism. It appears that in this world God punishes weakness as well as wickedness. If we have intended virtuously as a nation, have we not acted weakly? Instead of being surprised that these slave proprietors feel themselves insulted and aggrieved by the manner in which English philanthropists have vilified and abused them, I am only astonished at the patience and gentleness with which they have endured our calumnies. They are just and kind towards us in spite of our faults, and for the sake of good intention, they forgive. It is said the 'Injurer never forgives;' let us beware how we realize that adage. Among a large class in the North I found a jealous and unkind spirit towards the old country; the reverse of this may be said of the South. I have observed a noble, generous, gentlemanly spirit in this part of the Union; I feel assured that if the Southern proprietors, as a class, had found reason to believe that the institution of Slavery was prejudicial either to the Christian or temporal interests of the blacks, they have chivalry enough in their composition to have cast aside mere motives of private interest; but they knew, and we did not know—that was the difference. They have a right to accuse us of ignorance and conceit, and they are more forbearing than we had any claim to expect. I will try not again to recur to this subject till I get to Cuba, but it meets me so at every turn here, it is difficult to refrain.

Savannah, February 6.—Yesterday, I had a pleasant breakfast with Mr. and Mrs. H——, to meet Dr. Elliott, as amiable and excellent as his friend and brother of Pennsylvania. He remained among his flock during the yellow fever, or rather plague, of the last autumn, the consoler and the nurse of old and young, and he escaped that pestilence all through a diocese as large as Great Britain. He is sincerely loved and truly valued, and amidst his onerous duties he neither scorns nor neglects the study of nature.

After breakfast, Miss T—— took me a delightful drive to the Cemetery of Buonaventura. We went part of the way through a forest, even now full of interest for the eye of a botanist. Rare pines, magnolias, Gelucinum sempervirens (here called Jessamine), fan palms, cactuses, live oaks, and palmetto trees, not, as in the Northern forests, set like pins in a pincushion, but sufficiently apart to allow for increasing size, with airy glades and a lovely undergrowth.

Buonaventura once belonged to a gentleman of old family here; he planted five avenues of live oaks verging to a centre, where stood his residence. That house was burned down; a decreased income obliged the family to part with their beautiful place, and it was bought by speculators, who are realizing large sums by turning it into a cemetery; it is a most appropriate spot for the purpose. The live oaks form arches equal to those of cathedrals; while the Tillandsia, weeping from every branch of every tree, unartificially sympathizes with mourners, and adds solemnity to the whole scene. Two palmettos standing near the entrance to the old house are magnificent specimens of that noble tree. I obtained some young seedlings from them, which I hope to carry safely across the Atlantic. We came home by a rice plantation and negro village, with its neat and comfortable houses; but in their interiors the people evince no ideas of tidiness or comfort. My negro woman at Sandwich had the only neat room I have as yet seen among them. I was assured by everyone on Saturday, that the *Seminole* steamer for Palatka would start at ten o'clock this morning; now I am told not till four in the afternoon. I hope this afternoon start will not turn out to be midnight, as at Detroit.

Darien, February 9.—Some days of adventure. It was midnight before the *Seminole* left Savannah for Palatka, owing to a necessity for repairs which the captain could not get executed—such is the slowness of negro work-people; but a brilliant moon made everything nearly as visible as day. I was tired, and after a while got into my berth without undressing—a precaution I had every reason to be glad of; for, about two-o'clock I was awakened by a terrible crash of timber on my side the vessel, only a few yards to the left of my head. I was sure a collision had occurred, and rushed out to ascertain whether the water was likely to rush in, the *Arctic* strongly in my imagination. I saw that a schooner had run directly into the paddle-box, just beyond my berth, and completely smashed that wheel. The man at the helm of the intruding vessel must have been asleep; suddenly awakened by the noise of our steamer, he steered his boat the wrong way, and before our pilot could do anything, she was plump into us. Had he only continued the course he was on, when asleep, we should have passed without damage; as it was, he broke his own bowsprit straight off, sprung his foremast, and crippled us thoroughly; so that all our captain could do was to cast anchor (fortunately within the bar of the Savannah River), and send off a boat instantly, eighteen miles to the town, for relief.

A tedious time we had of it till five o'clock, Wednesday, when a steamer came down, attached herself to our *well* side, and took the poor *Seminole* safely back to the wharf, from which she had started the day before. It was no use to give way to terror about proceeding in consequence of the singular accident which had occurred; I convinced myself we were not likely to meet with anything unpleasant again immediately; and, after all, feelings of thankfulness were those uppermost in my mind, that we had passed such a danger unscathed. I decided to set forth again by the *St. John* steamer, at eight o'clock next morning. Poor R—— could not get over the fright; and if there had been any back door to have run out of, for the first time I suspect she was almost inclined to desert; however, with a melancholy expression, she became resigned, and we returned to the Pulaski Hotel to sleep; for though Captain Postell was very kind, and offered us our berths on board, we were too much tired and exhausted not to seek quiet beds on shore. As in most bad cases there is compensation, so here good came out of evil. A common misfortune made me well acquainted with two agreeable and superior men, President Wheeler, of Burlington College, and Dr. Turner, of Savannah. They took charge of us as if we had been their sisters; smoothed every difficulty, and as it turned out, there being no hotel or place of reception at Darien, if we had succeeded in landing there the first night, we should have been thrown into an awkward situation. Now, Dr. Turner went on shore there to prepare accommodations; and he and the Professor took us to the house of a hospitable Mr. and Mrs. Smith, who gave us a comfortable bed in their nursery, evidently putting themselves to some temporary inconvenience to take in the strangers. This place, Darien, is where Gen. Oglethorpe entrenched himself during the war; it is singular in appearance, and must be pretty in summer. Now, from the absence of all bright green, and the grey tinge thrown over vegetation by the Tillandsia, it has a very original look. The houses are mostly scattered, built of a kind of oyster-shell compost, the usual material hereabouts; these oysters and mussels are thrown up in banks upon the shores of the Walaki (St. John's) River, and the brackish lakes, which here form a chain, sometimes communicating with the sea, sometimes joining the rivers, all the way from Savannah, upon this Georgian coast. It is a singular navigation; one moment we stole along between swamps of high grass, where it was not possible for the steamer to get through the narrow bends except by the assistance of a towing-boat; then we went out into the sea; then we came back into a wide river, but so shallow that we were frequently sticking fast in the mud; and at last, at night, we reached Darien. Fortunately a four-oared canoe-like boat, of Mr. Hamilton Cooper's, had come down from his plantation on the Altamaha, upon some business. Dr. Turner insured our being taken up with him; we met Mr. Cooper also by accident, and after a very pleasant row of about five miles, he brought us to his English-like house (as respects the interior) and interesting home, my first resident introduction to plantation life. A happy attached negro population surrounds this abode; I never saw servants in any old English family more comfortable, or more devoted; it is quite a relief to see anything so patriarchal, after the apparently uncomfortable relations of masters and servants in the Northern States. I should much prefer being a 'slave' here, to a grumbling saucy 'help' there; but everyone to their tastes. We left the river about a quarter of a mile from the house, and came up a narrow canal, between rice plantations, almost to the door; we passed two or three large flat boats, laden with rice; and Mr. Cooper took me to see the threshing machine which was at work in a barn; the women putting in the rice just as we do our grain; they were more comfortably dressed than our peasantry, and looked happier; otherwise (except the complexions) the scene was much of the same kind as that at a threshing-barn in England. It is in vain to intend keeping silence upon the one thought that must be uppermost in a mind accustomed from childhood to erroneous views upon the Slavery question;

and I may as well write on. I now see the great error we have committed is in assuming that the African race is equal in capacity with the European; and that under similar circumstances it is capable of equal moral and intellectual culture.

The history of Egypt, of Rome, of the English, French, and Spanish Colonies, and the experience of American slavery, prove the reverse. No separate African civilization has sprung up from centuries of contact. St. Domingo has relapsed into barbarism, except in the case of some of the towns. The other emancipated colonies, not excepting Jamaica, are retrograding fast in the face of a white population, and notwithstanding Government influence: in the United States, spite of more than a hundred years of white association, though they have been made rather superior to their brethren in Africa, in intellect and moral character, they remain, and ever will remain, inferior to the whites. I believe, and must not hesitate to confess my belief, the negro race is incapable of self-government; and I suspect its present condition in the United States is practically the best that the character of the negroes admits of. It is for their happiness and interest to remain in tutelage—at any rate for two or three generations. Is there any part of Africa, the West Indies, or South America, where three millions of negroes are to be found as comfortable, intelligent, and religious, or as happy, as in the Southern States? The most practical mode of improving a semi-barbarous race is to place it in the proportion of one to two in the midst of a civilized people. The system of slavery has been blamed for the ignorance and vices of the Africans: are they less ignorant or more virtuous where slavery does not exist? It has pleased Providence to make them barbarian, and as barbarian they must be governed, however Christian may be the principles and feelings of their masters. One of the mistakes we make is to attribute to a black the ideas and refined feelings of a white, and then we imagine his sufferings under circumstances of comparative degradation; but happily what would be intolerable to the refined and cultivated is easily borne by the obtuse and ignorant. 'God tempers the wind to the shorn lamb.' That evil must always exist under any system of almost irresponsible power is certain; and there are, of course, painful exceptions to the generally kind, parental, and just rule of Southern planters; but these are the exceptions. The duty of Slave States and slave-owners is, by law and practice, to limit arbitrary power. The condition of the race at present admits of no higher government, and the duty of all real philanthropists is to aid and support the masters in their efforts to ameliorate painful circumstances, by kind, liberal, and temperate suggestions of such correction as the system will admit of. As the Abolitionist is powerless, he should feel that 'moral suasion' is his only means of operating. If he means well by the slave, he will not create angry feelings in the master by inflammatory appeals to his people. I have heard individuals lauded for giving freedom to their slaves; my observations lead me to believe that such people have only cast off an onerous and painful responsibility. One of the most intelligent and independent black men I ever heard of, born free in Canada, said, 'I know enough to know that my race is not either happier or better for what is called freedom. I would myself rather have been born a slave!' He was asked why he did not go to Liberia. 'No,' he said, 'Republics are quite unfit for us—I will have nothing to do with them.'

Hopeton, February 12.—I went yesterday through a forest of Pinus palustris to a spot where it is Mr. Cooper's intention to build a house to be called Altama. It will be beautifully situated on the edge of a pine barren, a sloping thicket of live oaks, magnolias, and fan palms, on one side, ending in rice plantations, with distant forest and river views extending towards Darien. This place was once the site of an Indian village, and I picked up fragments of their pottery. But there are now none of the Aborigines left in the Southern States. General Jackson removed all westward. I have had some conversation with Mr. Hamilton Cooper about the monetary affairs of the States. He says my remarks respecting the local debts are just, as respects a few of the States and cities, but that generally they are trifling when compared with their means and resources. In 1853, the aggregate State debt was about fifty millions sterling—that of Georgia sixty-three thousand. Pennsylvania is the most indebted; but there the debt is not more than ten per cent. on the property of the State. Complaints of poverty at present are temporary, the result of reckless speculation. Evidences of wealth and prosperity in America must be sought for among the masses, not in public works of governmental origin; and the absence of appearance in State capitals must not be mistaken for State poverty. Money is laid out; but it is expended in magnificent hotels, in private residences, churches, schools, banks, railroads, &c. &c., in all objects ministering to individual enjoyment and to reproductive purposes. Corporate associations do all those things required for public convenience which are beyond individual ability, but public buildings and public works are generally put aside, or made a secondary consideration. I forgot to mention that there are from three to four hundred negroes on this estate. Mr. and Mrs. Cooper have no white servants; their family consists of six sons and two daughters. I should not like to inhabit a lonely part of Ireland, or even Scotland, surrounded only by three hundred Celts. I believe there is not a soldier or policeman nearer than Savannah, a distance of sixty miles. Surely this speaks volumes for the contentment of the slave population. When I think of the misery and barbarism of the peasantry of Kintail, and other parts of Scotland (putting aside that of Ireland), and look at the people here, it is hardly possible not to blush at the recollection of all the hard words I have heard applied to the slave-holder of the South. Why, the very pigsties of the negroes are better than some Celtic hovels I have seen. Mr. Cooper is under some difficulty about a negro family he took in trust to manumit from the produce of their own labor. The poor people are averse to being freed, and especially to being sent to Africa. It certainly seems a cruelty to force them to accept that which they consider no boon. I believe this is a dilemma by no means rare.

February 13.—Actually another white frost; every one says such cold is uncommon; I find the weather now, much like ours at this time of year, and I expect the Chamærops serrulata, and other plants which do not seem affected by the cold we have here now, will be quite hardy in the West of England. The red maple is in bloom; I have not ascertained the species yet, but it is quite new to me, and a very showy, elegant thing. Upon looking to Elliot's *Botany of South Carolina and Georgia*, I find this tree is Acer rubra; it has a smooth, clouded bark, and in damp, rich soils becomes a large tree; but near the sea, where salt forms a component part of the soil, it dwindles into a small shrub. I have been wandering about among the negro dwellings, seeing the ugly babes and still uglier old people; only one individual in bed in the hospital, and five or six in the male and female wards, cowering round the fires. Mr. Cooper tells me he once tried the capabilities of some of the most active among his people, by giving them the cultivation of fifty acres for themselves; the first season, under direction, the plantation cleared fifteen hundred dollars, which he took care to give them in silver, hoping that would excite their industry; the next year, left to their own management, the crop lessened one half; and the third season they let the land run to waste, so that it was useless to permit them to retain it. Yet these very same people will labour readily and pleasantly under good superintendence.

In warm weather alligators are frequently seen, but now they remain torpid in their watery or muddy dens. They are not able to pursue and catch live creatures on shore, although they like to bask in the sun; but if a young negro child, a calf, or a pig, lies down carelessly at the edge of the water, these American crocodiles use their tails to whisk such prey down where they can devour it at their leisure. A Southern lady told me that her son once brought home some alligator's eggs. She placed them upon a table; forty-eight hours afterwards, upon hearing a black girl scream, her mistress rushed down stairs: the warmth of the parlour had hatched three young alligators, two were running about the room, a third had been thrown out of the window, and in the fright of the moment, all were killed, to the grief of the boy, who would gladly have made them pets.

I have been out to sketch the house and plantation; the air is warm and genial—nothing to remind us of this morning's frost.

Yours affectionately,

A. M. M.

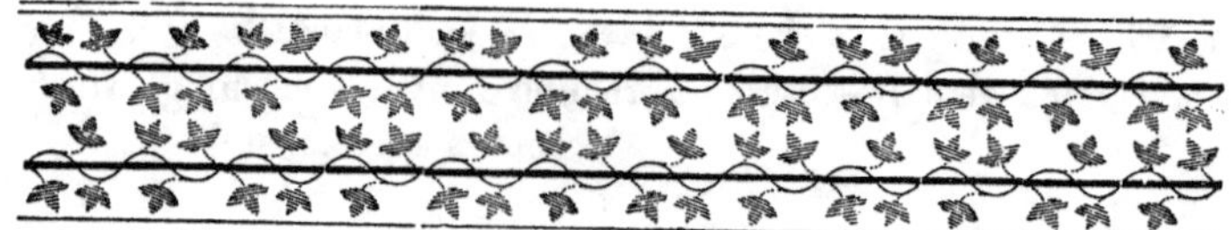

LETTER XIX.

HOPETON, ALTAMAHA RIVER, GEORGIA,
Wednesday, February 14, 1855.

MY DEAR FRIENDS,—

I hope my last letter arrived safely. Mr. Cooper sent down to Darien with it, so there is a good margin of time before the mail is closed for the 24th instant. After the sharp white frost of Monday, we had rain yesterday, and the folks here hope winter has at last taken his departure; there is a bright sun this morning, and I expect to see vegetation advance rapidly, when once it fairly starts for the summer. Only six days will be left for my Florida tour, and yet if I had been able to proceed sooner, the weather would not have been favourable. I may get to Palatka, Friday evening; in the next three days the orange-groves and Silver Springs must be accomplished, to leave one clear day for St. Augustine, where I should like to spend a week; but we must return to Savannah, so as to take the steamer which leaves for Charleston, the 24th. A glimpse of Florida is better than not seeing it at all; with that I must be content. I cannot find myself dull with this pleasant family; yesterday we did all sorts of things, just as I should have done among my own belongings in England. We cooked, and drew, and studied natural history. It has given me pleasure myself to pick up some interesting fresh-water and land shells in the rice ground; then I liked to hear all about the negro weddings; how the young ladies make the cake, &c., &c.; and I was amused by an account of one little

Topsy, who could not resist cents when they fell in her way; her mistress thought that by giving a few to her to take care of, she might be brought to some idea of mine and thine; but when the pence were asked for, they had vanished. With a sad face the child said, 'All gone; somebody *tiefed* from me.' Soon afterwards she said to one of the negro girls, 'Me very sorry, me could not help; me *tiefed* from myself.' It is not often the blacks of this country are dishonest, but they sometimes reason in this way: 'I belong to massa, all massa has belongs to me;' and there is some difficulty in preserving onions or fruits, because they are thought to be common property; they fish, and trap, and catch game; and if guns were allowed them, everything would be destroyed. The only security for fish and game is keeping the 'darkies' well employed; and such is their feeling towards their master, that in some cases where freshets have put his crops in danger, they have worked freely eighteen hours out of the twenty-four, for three weeks, to save them—more than they would have done for themselves in such a case. The thanks of Mr. Cooper, and a few little presents, make them quite happy: they are devoted servants, and miserable free people. This fact it is impossible to state too often or too decidedly. The Creator of men formed them for labor under guidance, and there is probably a providential intention of producing some good Christian men and women out of it in time. We have been blindly endeavouring to counteract this intention; we have thought ourselves wiser than our forefathers in all points, because we have advanced beyond them in others; and it has been the habit for us in England to believe ourselves more religious, and virtuous, and benevolent than these slaveholders; whereas, I fear there is a greater amount of irreligion and vice in one town of ours, or of the Northern States here, than in all the Southern States put together. When I watch the kindness, the patience, the consideration shown by white gentlemen and gentlewomen towards these 'darkies,' I could say to some anti-slavery people I have known, 'Go thou, and do likewise.' There is such a sense of security in this country, that doors and windows are as often left

10*

unfastened at night as not; and a slaveholder told me he had lived alone for eight years among his negroes, without once thinking it necessary to lock a door or bar a window.

February 15.—I spent two hours in the pine barrens and swamps yesterday, with some young friends, gathering seeds and taking up plants which I am going to send to England. However beautiful the flowers may be in May, this season is more advantageous to a gardener, because now roots can be moved with more safety. Mr. Cooper will go with me to Brunswick, where the *St. John* steamer calls, at three or four o'clock to-morrow morning, in her way to Palatka.

St. Augustine, *February* 19.—Brunswick is little more than the promise of a future town, but it is in a healthy situation, where there might be a fine park, at present there is only an hotel. Streets are marked out, and there are many pretty detached villas. Our way to it was over a deep sandy road, through the pine barren, and a continual undergrowth of that palm with a saw-like stem, and fan leaf (Chamærops serrulata), from the leaves of which pretty baskets are manufactured, and I imagine hats might be made equal to those of Leghorn; it grows all about this extensive white sand district, as thick as fern with us, and I think it would be hardy in the southwestern parts of England. As we approached Brunswick, fine specimens of the tree or cabbage palmetto were by the wayside; with difficulty we took up young ones for seedlings; some run so deep into the ground it is hard to move them. A very primitive kind of post-office may be observed in these forests; boxes without any lock nailed to a tree, into which, when a mail passes, letters are occasionally dropped.

The *St. John* steamer arrived soon after midnight, but the tide did not rise sufficiently for her to leave till near three in the morning, because she would not have been able to cross the bar of the St. John River. The following day proved bright and sunshiny, though cold for the climate; in the North the weather has continued severe, with deep snow. Before entering the bar at the mouth of the St. John (or Walaka) River, we had to cross the open sea for some miles. I saw palmettos, at least seventy or eighty feet high, upon the sandbanks as we entered the river; it is said their roots reach to the clay beneath, but they do not appear to require either rich or marshy land. The sand here is just like that at Bournemouth in Hampshire; but on this coast it extends over many hundred miles. I have seen nothing else all the way from Savannah; it has evidently been the bottom of the sea, and above it is a bed of shells, much resembling those of Hordwell Cliff, in England; and there is a tract of still more recent formation, between Brunswick and Hopeton, where the bones of the megatherium, &c. &c., are found in large quantities. A railroad is at present left in an unfinished state, as you approach Brunswick. Some of these days, if it is carried into the interior, that place will become of importance. We touched at a small village called Mayport, on the Walaka River; there the steamer grounded, and detained us for some hours, till the rise of the tide. I went on shore and picked up a curious little prickly fish, a plate bone of an alligator, and shells, among them some curiously-shaped oysters and delicate little pholases. We got off about four o'clock, and proceeded to Jacksonville; the sun set finely before we reached that place. This water resembles more a series of inland lakes than a river. We passed Magnolia and Picolata in the night, and reached Palatka about six in the morning. There I found it was not possible to get any conveyance to the Orange Springs before Monday, so I determined to return as far as Picolata in the steamer, and get across a pine barren to visit St. Augustine, as there will be time enough for me to be back at Palatka for the next mail. We had a delightful passage down again, through the still calm waters of the wide Walaka. Each shore fringed by live oaks, with occasional palmettos, and now and then an orange-grove—but oranges are very scarce, since a severe frost some years ago destroyed nearly all the trees. I have seen no fruit whatever, since the oranges and bananas imported to Charleston from Cuba. We got a rough carriage at Picolata; it was of a light description, and drawn by two large horses; but the deep white sand continued the whole eighteen miles to St. Augustine and it took us nearly five hours to get through it. I begin to see blossoms by the wayside; a pretty white Rubus, looking like a single rose, I never saw before, and a very large violet without scent, a pretty white Tussilago, or aster-looking plant, about three inches from the ground (*Chaptalia*), the white star-like Houstonia in bright patches, and the fragrant yellow Gelucinum, running among the bushes, and up nearly to the top of trees in occasional swamps; a tiny white violet below, with Andromedas, Gordonias, and Yucca filimentosa, now and then by the side of our track.

We crossed the branch of the St. Sebastian River, and a dismal-looking marsh near St. Augustine. Soon after my arrival, President Wheeler, of Burlington, and Mr. Myers took me to see the ancient Spanish fort, built of Cucino, a stone formed entirely of shell *debris*. This is a shell land; houses and walls made of shells, ground made of shells. I have got some recent ones—a fine large pholas, prima mactras, &c. &., but none I have seem to have the gorgeous colouring of those in the South. Two fine date trees stand in the garden of Mr. Myers's house. I do not know if these are remarkable specimens, but they have far exceeded my expectations; the regularly tiled bark, crowned by feathery foliage, more gigantic and noble-looking even than the Palmetto I admire so much, and the fruit (which hangs even now in wreaths between the leaves), when it has its golden purplish hue, must be beautiful.

I am disappointed to find that this place is not upon the main sea, but upon the St. Sebastian, which is rather a creek than a river. The streets are extremely narrow, and in general appearance the town is bare and dilapidated. Here, as well as at Brunswick, a railroad would soon be the means of improvement and ultimate prosperity; but I suppose there is not capital enough to construct one even over this flat country, with timber on every side easily turned into sleepers; only sixteen miles of rail would reach the St. John's (Walaka), but I do not hear of any proposition to make it.

Silver Spring, Florida, February 21.—At last I have got to this place, without regretting the trouble of coming two hundred and thirty miles from Savannah, although my journey has been a tedious and difficult one. Even with my superficial knowledge of geology, I find the features of this country very interesting; both at Ocala and here, there is a kind of chalk and greensand with the fossils belonging to a cretaceous formation, and the Silver Spring bursts forth just like many streams and springs in Dorsetshire, clear and bright as crystal; but I must go back to St. Augustine before I say more about this part of Florida. I got a kind of open vehicle with four horses, which in five hours took us to Picolata—there the Charleston steamer *Caroline*, which would take passengers on to Palatka, was expected; and we got shelter in a shed belonging to an Englishman, who acted as postmaster. It rained hard, but I took my umbrella, and walked out to look for plants in a wood near. Growing by a shed, I found a Solamen, new to me, which had been brought from the West; it was a shrub with white flowers and soft cottony leaves on, and growing under the trees. I gathered white blossoms of the beautiful little creeping Rubus I had before seen, like a small white rose; it resembled one much both in leaves and flowers. I also picked up seeds of the red maple, which also grows on the banks of the Altamaha, but then not forward enough.

The *Caroline* came about five o'clock; she was a swift boat, but less comfortable in point of accommodation than the *St. John*, as the ladies' cabin was below, and there was no pleasant place upon which to sit out upon deck. However, as the evening continued rainy, that did not signify. We reached Palatka about eight; and by nine next morning, a comfortable mail carriage with four horses took us in, bound, as I believed, for the Silver Spring, a place about seventy-six miles from hence. If I had known that we should not arrive there till after midnight, fifteen hours' travel, with one man driving four horses through a pine barren, which harbours wolves, bears, and panthers, my courage would have failed me. At last, when we reached our journey's end, I found myself not at the Silver Spring, but at a place called Ocala, which I had never before heard of; and I have since discovered that, owing to the abuse of power in this republican country, I was made to go six miles out of my way, because the postmaster, who has a small boarding-house near the Spring, was not a supporter of this President; so the democrats got the mail altered to Ocala, for the purpose of damaging Mr. Mann; and although there might be a practicable water-carriage by the Ochlawaha, straight from Palatka to the Silver Springs, where there is a perfect inland harbour for steamers, which ought to make that place a considerable one, with fair usage,—that harbour has been neglected or discouraged; so that cotton must be dragged the whole way we have come in bullock-wagons. Such an act of despotism could never have been perpetrated in monarchical England; after all, the most truly free country in the world.

At midnight, cold, wet, and dark, we at last reached Ocala. I fortunately had some tea with me; I begged some hot water, and a black girl brought in one hand an open iron pan, with the water escaping fast out of a hole; in the other, the remains of a china teapot without spout or handle.

'Missus, which shall I make it in?'

I said we had better put the tea into the one that had no hole in the bottom, and so we made something like tea. Next morning I was surprised to find some bits of greensand rock containing fossils, which first made me suppose there must be something like chalk in the neighbourhood. I asked where there had been digging, and Mrs. B——, sister to the landlord, who entered into the matter, proposed to walk with me to a spot, through the nearest hummock (or small wood), where there had been an abortive attempt to sink a well. She got a negro boy to guide us, and I found the spot; a shaft had been sunk to the depth of sixty feet, and there, sure enough, were fossils, Nummulites; pectens, &c., &c.

At first I was told it was not possible to get to Silver Spring. But at last, with some difficulty I procured two one-horse wagons, which took R—— and me to the little cottage hotel near the Silver Spring, from whence I now write; it is kept by the postmaster, Mr. Mann, who three or four years ago bought some land,

and settled here from Georgia. He and his good wife make us as much at home as they can by the side of their comfortable pine blaze, which is fire and candle in one; and with the aid of a feather bed and blankets, I did not suffer from cold in the night, although the roof was not wholly closed from the air, and light showed between the planked walls; frost outside. For twenty years such severe weather has not been known in these parts, and all still looks wintry.

I have been in a little boat upon the bright clear water, which in some places is forty feet deep, issuing freely, I suppose, out of the greensand rock below, which looks as if made out of solid aquamarine—every fish, and shell, and weed is perfectly visible. This silver stream flows a good sized river five miles, and then joins the Ochlawaha, which runs into the St. John's twenty miles above Palatka; and though it may be double the land distance from that place, the water carriage would be much pleasanter and more rapid than wading through about seventy miles of sandy, swampy pine barrens. I now find that a stage which passed ours on the road actually came straight by this place from Palatka, so I should have paid twelve dollars less, and we should have arrived here some time earlier, and not have had the difficulty of getting back again here, if it had suited the views or the interests of Palatka to let me know the Silver Spring was nearer than Ocala;—but I find, in this country, travellers must always be on their guard against false information, given from the selfish rivalry of parties or individuals; in this respect, America is worse than any part of the world I ever before visited. Mr. Robert Chambers was either much mistaken or grossly deceived when he published a letter asserting the absence of imposition at the hotels. For less real comfort, I have as yet been made to pay everywhere (with the one exception of Cleveland on Lake Erie) far more than in England; upon an average at about ten pounds a week for my maid and self, taking our meals at the public table, and without a private sitting-room. This exceeds anything I ever paid in any country in Europe; and there is neither appeal nor redress. Whether you dine out every day or not, no difference is made in your hotel expenses. It is true you may generally console yourself by the use of gorgeous mirrors, silk curtains, and splendid carpets; but few travellers wish for this kind of accommodation. Mr. Mann drove me yesterday to see the plantation of Mr. P——, a gentleman's place, where there is a really fine grove of orange trees; they are indigenous, some of them standing in a clearing, and others, as undergrowth in the forest, extending down to the river which flows from the Silver Spring. Some of these are thirty feet high, loaded with fruit of a kind called here the 'bitter-sweet;' they are good, if all the pulp is carefully taken out; but eaten without that operation they are as bitter as what we call Seville oranges. I saw several little green paroquets with yellow heads, the only kind of parrot common in Florida. Rattlesnakes are frequent, but they always get out of the way, if they can; wolves and panthers, too, are only dangerous to sheep and dogs. A gentleman hunting in this neighbourhood lately, on a mule, the animal trod upon a snake, which stung him so that he died in a few minutes; and some days ago, a tiger cat jumped out upon a negro, who drove it off by a stab with his knife; but the man's clothes were torn, and he was so terribly frightened that he could give no clear account of his assailant; these are the only casualties from wild beasts I have heard of, and I have seen nothing of the kind to alarm me. I have not even got a sight of an alligator yet, and the only remarkable birds I have observed, were a bald-headed eagle on the Altamaha River, and a very dim-coloured kite.

From the inquiries I have made, and my own observations, I suspect that the centre part of Florida was once an island, divided from the main land by a strait, which went across where a dismal swamp may now be seen; the sea, probably, extended from about St. Augustine to Savannah, across to Apalachicola; and from thence, towards Picolata and Alligator, the country begins to rise; then comes a volcanic and then the chalk district; and I understand there are higher limestone ridges further south, where the land falls down to the plains of the Everglades; a tribe of Seminole Indians (so called because they are runaways from the Creeks) still haunt those Everglades. The United States Government have military stations or posts to prevent them from coming further north; and some endeavours will be made to induce them to follow the other Indian nations westward. A chief once consented to such an arrangement, but his people refused to ratify it. The wood they call 'kindling' (*Pinus palustris*). Game, fish, and yams are so plentiful in the South, it is not to be wondered at that the poor savages are loth to emigrate to the cold north-west; but their fate is sealed; go they must, sooner or later, before the encroaching white man; however sad, there is no alternative. The Indian name of these springs is poetical and appropriate. 'Chatawa via wa—Chatawa via na wa' (Bright flowing river of silver silent waters). We have been living here, in Mr. Mann's open log-dwelling, with only him, Mrs. Mann, and their negroes, sharing pot-luck; R—— and I sitting by the blazing pinewood fire; little niggers at our feet; black 'boys and girls' of all ages coming in and out, and leaning and gossiping against the fire-place, whenever they 'minded.' Mr. Mann said, 'You see how it is; how much harder I and my poor wife work than these people; I would gladly give them all away for one good white servant; their food and clothing cost me more than I should have to pay for wages; and they are so wasteful. All my children are married. My old woman and I could be much more comfortable if we were not hampered by fifteen negroes. I should not like to sell them, or make them leave; it is a hard task we have; but it would be such a distress and ruin to the poor things, if we rid ourselves of them.'

Ocala, February 24.—In the afternoon of the day before yesterday, I returned to this place; symptoms of a chalky country the whole way. Before sunrise the next morning I was out. Upon going down stairs I found no fastening to the external door of this house; but a light chair was placed against it, which a child could have pushed aside. What an evidence of the security of property in this unguarded slave country, when locks and bolts are considered unnecessary. Before breakfast, I rambled two or three miles into a beautiful forest to the south-west, without the smallest fear of meeting anything more alarming than two or three black pigs, which are allowed to wander at will after roots and acorns; if rattlesnakes have finished their winter-nap, they are not up so early. Everything around was bright and tranquil—magnolias, streaming epiphytes, and palmettos, looked so foreign, that when I came to what in Devonshire would be called a 'gully,' in this usually flat country, and saw a stump covered with one of the English feather mosses (*Hypnum proliferum*), I was quite surprised. In a clearing, upon my return towards this little town of seven years' existence, I met an old negro, sitting upon his bullock-cart. We had a long conversation: he asked about England, and seemed anxious to talk of the condition of his race, and their prospects in Liberia; he was by far the most intelligent negro I ever met with. He told me he had worked for himself at odd times, and had accumulated enough to buy his own freedom; he purposes doing this, and going to Liberia, he and his wife, with the view of guiding and improving his fellow blacks. He thinks the slaves unfit for freedom in the mass; that only those who have been raised for a generation or two among the whites can be induced to work; and that some few, who like himself have got improved habits, may go back to do good in Africa. Old Dick would not have stopped the slave trade: 'No, ma'am; bring them away to make them better.' Mr. G——, an excellent Episcopalian missionary and clergyman here, who was, educated in the North, is of the same opinion. No one can live long in this country without being convinced of the want of real information, and the injudicious tendency of *Uncle Tom*. He says such books, however popular and ingenious, are false in fact, and therefore bad in principle; and I have already seen enough fully to concur in that conclusion. Untruth will never promote Christianity; and those who sincerely desire to advance the cause of the negro should remain for some months in the Southern States of America; not with the view of strengthening their own prejudices, but single-minded, and with a simple intention to seek, and to accept, such information as really may enable them to understand what will benefit their fellow-creatures. I spent yesterday in visiting every quarry and opening which might enable me to comprehend the geological features of this neighbourhood. Chalk and flint and greensand abound; and I can hear of no other formations within any reasonable distance. I found strong evidence of the up-heaving by volcanic action—fossils plentiful; but I found no gryphites, scaphites, or nautili.

This morning, we return as far as the Orange Springs, for I shall not again be inveigled into a fifteen hours' journey through the sand barrens.

Palatka, February 25.—Our stage did not leave Ocala before eleven o'clock. It was delayed by the non-arrival of the mail from Tampa, a place a hundred miles to the south-west. A crow in this country makes a noise just like the bark of a dog. The deer, which are still frequently shot, are of small size; their horns have never more than five or six points; their weight from eighty to one hundred and sixty pounds. There are panthers measuring twelve feet from the nose to the tip of the tail, which occasionally carry off cows and oxen. A large one destroyed some pigs close to Palatka. Several gentlemen pursued the animal. It took refuge in a large swampy hummock; the hunters then sent their dogs to get the beast out, but of thirteen only eight ever appeared again, and it was concluded that the other five were killed by the panther. Unless alarmed, or wounded, they have never been known to attack a man. After a tedious journey, we reached Orange Springs by seven in the evening. I got a carriage very early, and went to breakfast with Mr. and Mrs. L——, who 'are roughing it in the Bush.' They gave me excellent bread and butter, which was a treat after the hot rolls and buckwheat cakes most usually met with in America. I saw the sulphur springs and lakes, which may have once been volcanic sinks, and got back to Mr. Dickenson's boarding house in time for the departing stage. The weather proved wet, and our journey back to Palatka dreary.

February 26.—I saw a bone here last night seven feet long and three inches wide, wavy in form, and apparently recent. Some one suggested that it might have belonged to a sea-cow. It did not resemble the rib of a whale, though it might belong to the head of a large one. I sketched the form, not being able to guess what creature had ever owned it. As the Walatka steamer makes a trip of thirty-two miles up the North Creek, one of the branches of this 'river of lakes' (a translation of the Indian name of Walatka, the St. John), I took the Charleston boat as far as Jacksonville, and went on board that for Savannah at night. Jacksonville is, to my fancy, the prettiest town between Brunswick and Palatka. There is a large hotel; and in consequence of a destructive fire last year, good brick houses and shops are rising up. In one of the sandy alleys at the back of the place, I found some lumps of porphyritic rock, much to my surprise, for I could not believe they belonged to this modern land. After some inquiry, I found they had been brought here as ballast. I went into a store, where I bought alligator's teeth, limes, and a nice little map of Florida. Professor Baird, of Washington, gave me a note of introduction to Dr. Baldwin; but unfortunately the doctor was away from home, so I did not succeed in getting some botanical information I hoped for. Mrs. Baldwin was very obliging: she gave me a fine specimen of coral from Key West. This name is a corruption of the Indian-Spanish words, 'Chicao hueso, Key of Bones.' We shall touch there in our way from Charleston to Cuba. After making a sketch at Jacksonville, I got on board the *Walatka* before sunset, and after a successful though cold voyage of two nights and one day, we reached Savannah by seven o'clock in the morning of February 28th. My friends, Miss T—— and Mr. and Mrs. H——, received us very hospitably. Miss T—— took me a drive to call upon Dr. Turner, my fellow sufferer in the *Seminole* accident, who took such charge of me as far as Hopeton. I was delighted to visit his cottage, where I found him very busy gardening, and I learned a new and ingenious method of cultivating strawberries. He almost promises to meet me at Chittanoge, if I will make my way into Tennessee from New Orleans. I will try. Before seven o'clock Mr. H—— took me on board the *Calhoun*. The night was bright, but very cold, and an adverse wind and rough sea prevented the steamer from reaching Charleston before six o'clock next morning. Mr. and Mrs. H—— expected me to breakfast; and after three successive nights spent on board three steamers, without taking off my clothes, the prospect of three quiet days in their comfortable house was very consoling. My chalk fossils and pretty ferns excite an interest among some of my friends here. Professor Gibbs spent some time in looking over these acquisitions, and Mrs. H—— promises to plant, and watch over all the living plants this next summer, and then she will forward them to meet me at Boston next September, when I hope my Ward's case will transport them safely to England. But the weather continues extremely cold—I am assured quite unusually so for this part of the world: it is quite as bitter as our coldest March. I often think of the poor troops, for it seems this long severe winter has extended to Europe as well as America. It has been a great disappointment to find no letters here: not one line have I received from England of later date than the 9th of January, and this is the 3rd of March; but I trust mails are awaiting us at Cuba. We are a month later in going to that island than I expected; so I have little doubt but Mr. Crampton has forwarded letters there. Yesterday I spent some hours gardening with Mrs. H——. I have endeavoured to reconcile the pretty fern from Scott's Springs near Ocala, to grow away from its chalky locality, by scraping lime off the wall; but it is so fairy-like and fragile in appearance, I fear it is of a tender, fanciful nature; and the sheltered arched cave and dripping stalactite of Florida is very unlike any home I can find for it. However, I have plenty of specimens in my press, and if the plants die I must be content with their lifeless forms. We embark to-morrow morning in the *Isabel* for Cuba—another three days' voyage; but there will be a fine moon, and at last I hope to leave winter behind me. There seems little hope of getting away from it until we reach a tropical climate. Every one here is shivering and complaining of such unusual cold—for, of course, Southern dwellings are ill prepared to combat it—and the poor trees and shrubs look unhappy under this northern treatment. I have sent boxes of seeds and plants to Dorsetshire; of course, the weather is also unfavourable for their travels, and I fear it may render them of little value; but still it is no use to keep seeds through another season. The mail goes to-day. I shall like to know when my packet reaches home.

Yours affectionately,

A. M. M.

Charleston, March 3, 1855.

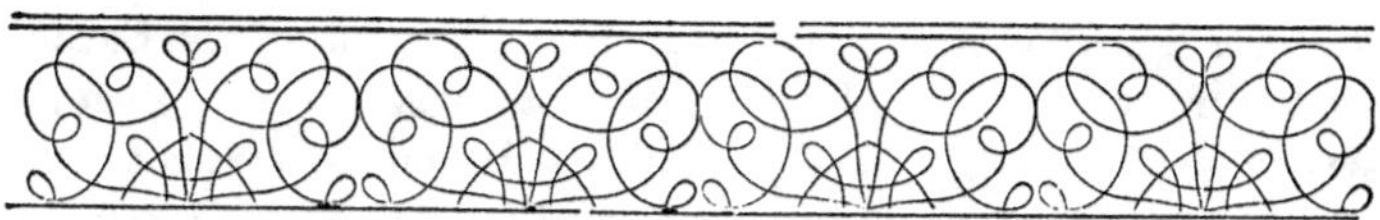

LETTER XX.

On Board the Isabel,
Between Key West and Cuba,
March 7, 1855.

My dear Friends,—

In spite of the rocking of this steamer, I can write this morning; and I want to tell you some things, which may be shoved out of my memory by the excitement and novelty of Cuban scenes. The day before leaving Charleston, I spent some time at the Museum, where Mr. Holmes, the curator, thinks that my brown Florida flints, although they strike fire, are not analogous with the black flints in England. As I found no scaphites, or nautiluses, and no real terebratulæ, Mr. Holmes thinks my chalk is of the same date as the cretaceous formations of Carolina and Alabama. I have not seen them, so I cannot judge; but with the exception of whatever paleontological differences there may be (of which I am not learned enough to judge), Florida chalk and Dorset chalk are twin sisters: yet it requires exact knowledge to distinguish old red sandstone from the new red by the general appearance of either; so I suppose there is some resemblance between these chalky sisters, and that new chalk and old chalk are difficult to distinguish: but this matter must be settled by a wiser geologist than I pretend to be. I have heard of the genuine sea-serpent at last! You know I always advocated the reality of such a reptile—partly founded upon its admission into the Scandinavian Mythology, in which every symbol was borrowed from Nature. Last spring, when Captain Peat, of the steamer

William Seabrook, was going up an island porti on of the Savannah River, he, as well as his crew and passengers, saw a gigantic serpent just before the vessel; it quickly disappeared; a notice of the circumstance was inserted in a local newspaper, and treated with the usual incredulity. Captain Rollins of this ship says, he, like the rest of the world, disbelieved the report; but the next day, during the passage of this steamer to Savannah, on approaching the bar of St. Helens, he was called by his look-out man to see 'the biggest log that ever was.' On looking through his telescope, he clearly saw that the object in question was no tree, but a monster as long as the *Isabel* herself, in rapid motion; as he watched it, it reared its snake-like body and head high out of the water as the funnel of the steamer, looked about for an instant, and then plunged down, leaving a swirling eddy where it had shown itself. No reasonable person acquainted with the calm seaman-like character of Captain Rollins, will suspect him of either exaggeration or error in describing a fact; but this, I believe, is the first time that the sea-serpent has been supposed to be seen or heard of in southern latitudes: it is probably a denizen of the deep seas, which rarely and accidentally gets into shallower water; and if it is an uncommon creature, I think the argument that no bone or skeleton has ever been found, cannot stand against such strong evidence as we have of its existence: there *may* be some weight or property in the skeleton which prevents any part of it from rising to the surface out of the sea caves where it usually lives and dies.

I was fortunate in finding my old friend G. P—— embarking in the *Isabel* at the same time as myself: his society and aid will make not only my voyage, but my residence in Cuba much more agreeable; for as his physician has ordered him to counterbalance the effects of an unusually severe winter by a visit South, he, like myself, has no other objects but information and amusement; so I hope to benefit by his assistance as well as his company. The voyage of three days and three nights from Charleston was very pleasant; we had calm weather, and a splendid moon; and although upon running a few hundred miles between the Gulf Stream and the coral reefs and islands south of Florida, there was sufficient motion to affect all the extremely sensitive of our party, neither R—— nor I were ill for a moment.

Two small Government vessels, with surveyors, were occupied in raising beacons at intervals along the reefs. Upon one of them I saw an erection quite novel to me; a residence and lighthouse, built upon an apparently transparent iron framework, about forty feet in height, so that the waves of the sea pass through the foundation instead of undermining it; a retired naval master lives with his family in charge of this useful, but alarmingly fragile-looking establishment. He has a small yacht, in which he or some of his household occasionally visit the mainland, and I believe they reside in their airy dwelling without apprehension, although a few years ago, when every house on Key West was inundated during the most violent storm ever known, a lighthouse built upon the most southern point of the United States territory, on a very small island in the sea, was washed away with all its residents.

The captain told me that when about a mile from the Florida coast, he sometimes could distinguish bears walking about on shore, and he pointed out a small island in the chain which extends from the mainland down to Key West, which a few years ago was inhabited by a settler and his family. The Indians came forty miles in canoes, attacked the place, and murdered every individual except the wife and daughters of the master, who crept in among some sand and lumber under a small wharf. After making themselves too drunk to look after these, the Indians left the island, so that a few days afterwards the women were rescued unhurt. Now, the United States troops have enclosed the savages within a certain district, where they can do no injury, and eventually they will be got off after the other tribes, westward. It was with regret that I found it beyond midnight before we reached Key West; as the steamer only stayed half an hour, while she landed a few passengers and some goods, I could only go for a few minutes on shore; and my first introduction to cocoa-nut trees was by moonlight. However, we were lucky to have a moon. I picked up a few stones that I might see what the land was made of, and afterwards remained on deck till two o'clock, so as to see the fine revolving light of a house about nine miles out at sea. I was on deck as soon as the Cuban land could be distinguished, and we had a charming run down to the island—flying fish among the waves, and the elegant man-of-war birds sailing about over our heads. In general outline, the island is straighter and less mountainous than I expected; it did not look more elevated than the cliffs of Brighton, in some places white and chalky in appearance. But nothing can be more picturesque than the Moro, and the entrance into a beautiful and extensive harbour. At a distance the hill upon which the Cabanos fortress stands has a resemblance to what is called the Look-out at Weymouth; but, as you near it, it has a much more rugged appearance, and it is as if rent and cloven by volcanic action. A Moorish-looking battery, or wall, standing upon each fragment, it looks a very strong place. I must not sketch here without special permission from the Capitan-Generale. I never saw any harbour filled by a more interesting assemblage of ships. English men-of war (my heart jumped at the sight of that flag), a very fine Spanish steamer, the *Princeton*, a handsome American, and many of their schooners which are so specially airy and graceful. By-the-by, at Key West, I saw a Governmental United States schooner with three masts, which was to me a new kind of craft. A boat, containing a messenger from Madame Almy's boarding-house, took us on shore towards the bright, gay, Spanish-looking town. We were detained for half an hour in a cool, clean building, with iron railings on one side, through which peeped Spanish and negro and mulatto eyes, eager to seek employment in carrying baggage for strangers. Mr. P—— and I walked up to the hotel. From the descriptions I have read of Spain and Italy, I should suppose its appearance and our reception such as I should expect at Seville or Cordova. A fine English-looking coach, with gaudy hammercloth, had its domicile on the ground-floor. It belongs to the mistress of the mansion, who occupies it during her evening drive on the Pasco. She speaks English, being Anglo-American born, and Cuban by marriage. Ladylike in manner and deportment, she takes her post in the society of her house, and manages the concern with the assistance of a housekeeper. The rooms are comfortable, and the table is well served. The interior laid out in open galleries, and high rooms with painted cornices and ceilings, have the look and arrangement (I imagine) of an old Spanish palace. In the evening, Mr. P—— took me a drive in a volante round the town and its environs. After all I had heard of the peculiarities of the habits, dress, and social customs of the Cubans, still I was surprised; for it appears to me that Havana is more Spanish, more Moorish, more unlike Europe, and resembling more what I fancy Spain might have been in the time of Charles V. than anything my imagination conceived. The wheels of the volantes were higher and more eccentric. The negro drivers, in their costume and jack-boots, surpassed the old French postilions. The ladies, in full-dress evening gowns, *decolletées*, short-sleeved, and *coiffées*, as if for a London evening party. The houses flat-roofed, many-coloured, and Moorish-looking; the trees generally new to me, and the flowers strange; the horses, with their plaited tails tucked up on one side, stiff and inelegant; negro soldiers in straw hats, and mulatto women in gay turbans; all this, added to unknown tongues, and a splendid southern sky, mystified me, and made me feel dreamy, as I had never felt before; and yet I have looked at some accounts of Cuba, and read *Cuba as It Is.* I wonder whether anybody ever did acquire clear ideas of distant countries and strange manners by reading, or by hearing of them.

There are many more African-looking negroes here than in the Southern States of America. Perhaps the Anti-Slavery movement, although mistaken in its objects, may have providentially intended to raise and educate an improved negro race without fresh importation, for the purpose of ultimately civilizing and Christianizing Africa. I don't think that negroes from Cuba would be likely to regenerate or improve their race. I believe, on good authority, that the free blacks here are profligate and irreligious; and they look far less happy than their brethren in servitude.

February, 29.—I spent the greater part of the morning bargaining for some articles of attire. Shopping here is conducted quite after a Turkish fashion; you are expected to bargain, and consider, and discuss for an hour, before you conclude a purchase. Ladies seldom go into a shop; the best part of its contents are brought to their residences, or displayed in the volantes in which they drive to the shop-door; and three times the price intended to be taken is often asked in the first place; then the buyer offers three times less than she intends to give, and at last, after many objections and remonstrances on both sides, the bargain is struck —a sad waste of time and profanation of truth; but it is useless to rebel against Spanish custom. Before breakfast, G. P—— took me out walking by the harbour to the market, where the brilliant-coloured fish and the strange-looking fruits were very interesting. I was surprised to see great pholases (one of the boring shell-fish) as an article of food, and numerous other bivalves which did not look tempting. We afterwards visited the garden in front of the Capitan-Generale's palace. There were fine palm trees, which at first I mistook for dates. I am quite puzzled by the trees here, as they are so strange; for, though we may be well acquainted with tropical flowers in our hot-houses, the larger products are of course less known to us; and as yet I have found no one here who can give me botanical information. The Spaniards are accused of eradicating trees as much as possible; and certainly I do not see anything like groves around Havana—only avenues, and occasional rows of palms. Mrs. Crauford, the Consul's lady, will have a pic-nic to-morrow in the most shady garden known here, because it is a deserted residence.

March 10.—Last night I went to Mrs. Crauford's reception, in one of the most beautiful houses I have yet seen here. It was built by a wealthy gentleman, and as he is for the present residing with his wife at Paris, he has let his house to the British Consul. The entrance (like that of the most of the palaces here) is a high, Moorish-looking hall, with a *porte cochère;* from this springs a fine, geometrically-built stone staircaise, leading first to a music-gallery; besides other rooms, a splendid drawing-room and anteroom, the one with an ornamental marble floor, the other *en parquet*, of a pattern elaborately worked in various woods; Pompeian ceilings; a beautifully ornamented dressing-room, and a bedroom beyond—*recherchées*, and in good taste. I was introduced to all our naval officers, as well as to the Americans in harbour. I drove there and back in a volante *al fresco;* although in an evening dress, it was perfectly warm and pleasant. The interior of the houses, with their spacious windows, entrances open to view and well lighted, looked gay and cheerful, as we went—returning at half-past ten, I was not quite without apprehension, as I was told robberies were frequent at that hour; however, we safely arrived at our hotel in the street of the Inquisitor. In my room everything which passes out of doors can be distinguished, and the noise and chattering is unceasing. Last night I was amused to hear an English sailor trying to comprehend a Spanish companion; it seemed evident the latter had given Jack Tar a dog, but Jack was complaining it did not understand English. The Spaniard said something in reply, and then Jack rolled down the street vociferating 'Venga Cane—venga Cane!' In the morning, I heard an American gentleman declaring that something he was asked to do would be 'as much trouble as taking charge of a lady.' I rose early, and while sitting writing near the large open window of my room, in the highest of these low houses (it has a stone balcony, with a strong iron grating upon the external edge, closed at the top, so that nothing can ever fall out), I suddenly saw a tall broom, like those used by housemaids for lofty halls in England, swaying about within my grating; in a moment it swept off a little flower-pot, and dashed it to atoms in the street below. I rushed to see the cause of this invasion, and there stood a tall soldier, looking first at the fragments and then at me, with an expression of grief on his countenance that was undoubted; so I looked as benignant as I could, but this flower-pot contained a very rare, if not new fern, I had discovered near Ocala; and all the way from Florida, I have brought it on my lap, with some pains and trouble, in hopes of taking it, growing, across the Atlantic; but it would probably have perished, sooner or later, and perhaps sudden death was better than a lingering one. This exterior dusting must be necessary here, where almost all the windows and balconies are coved by iron gratings: they give rather a prison-like look to the houses, but as the windows and entrances are each from twenty to thirty feet high, extending from the roofs to the ground, or within three feet of it, having only lattices within, and no glass, so much light is admitted that there is no gloom. Any of the houses in this town might be used as a fortress, they are so strong and massive.

We had a very pleasant pic-nic party yesterday, given by Mrs. Crauford, in what is called by custom the Bishop's Garden—or 'Quinta del Obispo'—but it belongs to the Conde de Penalver; he having built a residence in Havana, does not make use of his pretty villa. The house is a ruin, and the garden neglected; but this last circumstance makes it more interesting in a botanical point of view, as plants are to be found there which, under ordinary circumstances, would have been destroyed; I found many treasures, some of them valuable seeds. Immediately after my return home, Mr. Crauford came to take me to the Capitan-Generale's. His palace is eastern-looking, like all the edifices here. Upon going into the reception-room, I saw about twelve chairs on each side opposite one another across the room, a space of three or four yards between—one row for gentleman visitors, and the other for ladies. Madame de Concha soon came in alone, dressed simply in morning costume; after a little, the Capitan-Generale followed, and I was glad of his arrival, as I could not speak Spanish, nor Madame French, so the Consul was obliged to act as interpreter between us. The Capitan-Generale is a quiet-mannered, gentlemanly person; he sat down by me, and we conversed for some time in French, he obligingly promising the necessary permits for travelling here and sketching—saying 'Nous ne sommes pas des tyrans ici!' He assured me of his anxiety for the success of England in the present war, but expressed doubts of the result; and he imagines the struggle will be a long one. The Spaniards do not believe the English understand fighting, which is odd enough when the battles of the Spanish campaigns of Napoleon must be fresh in their recollection. While the Capitan-Generale was talking with me, several gentlemen entered and placed themselves on the chairs opposite, after mutual bows; and when I thought our visit long enough, I made my courtesy, and we departed. Mons. and Madame de Concha were, for a short time, in England—I believe as exiles. Madame is sister to the Duquesa de la Vittoria. When I came back to the Hotel, Governor and Mrs. Fish came to see me; they have just returned from an expedition into the interior. I am afraid I shall not have completed my little tour here in time to embark with them in the next passage of the *Black Warrior*, for New Orleans. While I am writing, I see two mulatto women with cups in their hands, standing at the great, wide, coach-house looking door opposite; they are sharing their breakfast with a negro; and now two or three more come to gossip with them. This is the way all of black race like to eat; they never willingly sit down to a regular meal—they prefer carrying their food about, and taking it at irregular hours. Nothing eatable is safe from their depredations, and this not from hunger, for they are always plentifully fed, but from their monkey-like habits. Mrs. Almy tells me no one unaccustomed can judge of the annoyance it is to be served by negroes, and that she shall bless the day when she is enabled to return, perhaps to England, where she will no longer be tormented by slave labour. I believe this to be the general feeling of masters and mistresses in the southern countries. For their sakes, I wish I could have hopes that rice, cotton, and sugar may, some of these days, be generally cultivated by free labour! I firmly believe the boon will be greater to the whites than to the blacks themselves; but I fear blacks alone (in the long run) can endure work under a tropical sun.

The Coolies are a miserable race; they perform less work, but are the slaves of slaves—it remains to be seen whether they can long endure. I do not think people in England have any idea of the idleness which characterizes the black people. Unless forced to exertion they will lounge about for hours, aimless and unoccupied yet they rise with the sun. For three hours this morning, since I got up, these women have been lolloping and gossiping in my sight, and there they will be until they find the heat too great for this kind of enjoyment. Whether they have masters or mistresses I cannot tell; but the house is large, and apparently well furnished; and yet these people are idling there from morning till night, unless the sun drives them in occasionally. One hardly ever sees a bonnet worn here, and I am beginning to do without, by means of a cap and a black veil—to avoid being stared at. The first day I thought the omission impossible, but general custom soon reconciles one; and yesterday I went in an open volante, a league into the country, in such a dress as in England I should only wear in the evening, with a black veil added.

The volantes are a singular choice for the prevailing vehicles in such narrow streets. They are so long and so wide that it is impossible to turn; so one set go down one street and up the the next. Of course if a horse falls, the two wheels only are very awkward, but they say the poor beast generally lies still, and you have time to escape. Sometimes one carriage or cart stops the way, and there you must sit in patience as long as it may please these inert people to dawdle; although the least energy would make way, they never think it worth while to be in a hurry.

Matanzas, March 14.—At last I am really sensible of being in a tropical climate! I have slept in a room with an open window (as large as our house doors), on a thin sacking couch without mattrass, pillows as hard as bricks, only a thin muslin coverlet, protected by a mosquito-net; and after sleeping soundly from nine o'clock till three, I am writing by candle-light, stars shining outside; the moon will be in abeyance till we cross the sea to New Orleans, having fully done her duty during our last voyage. Last night I remained from sunset upon a kind of piazza at the top of this house, to watch for the 'Southern Cross.' I saw it rise rather to the east of south; it then seemed to leave gradually westward, before it sank in the horizon, about in a line with Orion, which was gloriously bright almost over our heads. The Great Bear appears to me topsy-turvy, and becomes quite a secondary constellation here, and the Cross is only dimly seen, because we are not far enough within the Tropics to catch more than a glimpse of it. The two upper stars look fine: the two side ones more distant from each other than I expected; the lowest faint, and not quite in a straight line with the upper ones. The British Consul, Mr. Da Costa, was very polite in coming immediately; and he remained and aided me to discover the Cross. The master is a Spaniard of the old country, who speaks French readily and a little English, besides Spanish. Upon our first arrival there was a long *parler* carried on in several languages by the party from Havana, which consisted of R—— and me, three American gentlemen, all old acquaintances of mine, one Englishman who crossed with us in the *Isabel*, and who was introduced to me by Mr. Molyneux, at Savannah, a Cuban, and a Spaniard. It was difficult to apportion the sleeping-rooms opening out upon an interior but external gallery, so that no one might interfere with another, and the poor signor was almost in a fever before that arrangement was complete. My little nest has a fine view to the west. I bribed an ancient black with one eye to wipe the floors for me, and for R——, next room, with fresh water, which cooled them considerably; and we are now well lodged, without a creeping thing of any kind among us.

This is a very pretty town; the sea runs into a deep bay, filled by ships of many nations, come to be laden with sugar; it is a cleaner place than Havana, and the blacks and mulattos less numerous. I did not leave the house last evening, but occupied myself in making a sketch of the bay from hence. We left Havana by the six o'clock train the day before yesterday; reached Guines by nine; went to see a cave in a chalky hill three miles from the village—a fatiguing and difficult expedition, but I found numerous flowers known in our gardens and hot-houses; among them the pretty Asclepias tuberosa, Ipomœas of all colours and sizes, a lilac, a scilla, a solamena, and other things new to me, and the whole country was dotted over by cocoa-nut trees. That neighbourhood has little other foliage, although during our journey by rail I saw fine mango and other trees—among them a palmetto as tall as the Chamærops of Florida; it looks something like the same species. We passed many haciendas, the plantations belonging to which were in high cultivation, great herds of cattle and many horses feeding about them; and there were tall chimneys indicating steam-engines for crushing sugar.

On Sunday last, we went to the service on board the *Vestal*, commanded by Captain Thompson, then moored in the harbour of Havana; the *Buzzard* steamer left a day or two before, and the *Argus* will remain, while the *Vestal* is expected at this place. It is curious to hear the watchmen belonging to the towns in Cuba. They sing out the hours and the state of the weather in a stentorian tone, always preceding their announcement by a shrill and prolonged whistle. I observe that their voices are tuned nearly to the same intervals, though of course one is rather more musical than another. A thick fog obscures the view this morning—it was the same yesterday; it indicates that the day will be a hot one. Yesterday the thermometer stood at 86°, unusually high for this month, but I do not find the heat so oppressive as when at 80° in England.

Matanzas is situated in an almost circular basin, formed by low hills of a nearly even height, except when broken by a chasm through which flows the River Yamorri—to the north-west. The houses, like those of Havana, are almost all low, having usually not more than one, or at most two storeys, some of them with flat roofs, and others heavily tiled by circular shaped tiles, as if rows of chimney-pots were strung together, and laid half a foot apart. In a garden just below my window I see a magnificent Oleander, and a fine yellow Bignonia (*stans?*), in full bloom. I heard an amusing anecdote with reference to botanical ignorance; as a lady had heard the name of Hedysarum gyrans, next day she gravely informed a gentleman, 'that plant is the harum scarum gatherum.' So little attention is paid to natural history here, that I can get no assistance as to the botanical names of either trees, flowers, or shrubs, and as many of the former are yet without bloom, it is difficult to make them out even with the assistance of Loudon; it is the same with out-of-the-way fruits—one is a *pappy* and another is a *mammy*, and so on; but the local terms do not help one the least.

Mr. Da Costa, the Consul, was so obliging as to take us an interesting drive last evening up heights to the north-east, from whence I was able to sketch the Pau of Matanza, and a fine valley beneath, dotted in all directions with cocoa-nut trees, but I observed few trees of any other kind. By a road impracticable for any other vehicle than a volante, with its giant wheels, we reached a villa and plantation belonging to one of the proprietors here. The foliage all round appeared so strange; Tree Euphorbias, Shrubby Cactus, immense Cannas, and thickets of Coffee, Bananas, &c. For the first time I saw cocoa-nuts; some were gathered, and I drank some of the juice which looked like clear water, and tasted nearly the same, with a slight *soupçon* of sugar. I was quite surprised to see a green nut (placed with a hole in it over a tumbler) pouring forth such a bright, innocent-looking liquid. I supposed it would always have a milky hue. The nuts enlarge by degrees; but it was a long time before I could find out which of the palms was the true cocoa-nut tree. Some said this was, and others doubted, and said it was a tree resemblsng the one that produces the nut, whereas, there is only that single cocoa that I have yet seen here. There are tall Arecas and Palmettos, which are probably the same as those of Florida; and there is the Date (*Phœnix*), and the Sago Palm, and Bactris, but two kinds of cocoas I have not yet seen here. At this plantation of Mr. Jinks's I for the first time saw sugar crushing. It was, in this instance, not done by steam, but by horses and mules, negro boys sitting as postilions, laughing and shouting, and the whole affair having such a wild, unearthly look, though it seemed a case of enjoyment to all except the poor beasts concerned in this kind of merry-go-round, that I could fancy the employment might have been selected by Dante for one of the punishments of his *Inferno*. The driver, who received us and showed us every hospitality, was a handsome, good-humoured, intelligent-looking Cuban creole. At Guines, where I saw a large plantation, all the sugar was distilling for rum, a spirit which bears a high price at this moment, and is therefore more profitable than sugar. Coolies were employed there as well as negroes, but they do not seem equally fitted for labour, and are more to be pitied than the negro slaves, for their masters are indifferent about their comfort. The sun set as a more magnificent globe of fire than I had ever before seen it. There was just enough twilight when we left the plantation for me to watch that we went safely down a long and steep white chalky descent into the valley below; and I regretted that afterwards I could see nothing of the beauties of our drive, excepting fire-flies, which sparkled among the aloes, and yuccas, and coffee bushes, as we proceeded along a track, which, if the Consul and the other gentleman on horseback had not assured me was free from danger, I should have thought could hardly have been safely traversed; but with the exception of every now and then sinking in ruts, and passing over rocks, large enough to have overset an English vehicle, we had no difficulties, and the negro postilion and his two little white horses, appeared quite at their ease. We passed by two haciendas, in our road to the pass through the Yamorri River makes its way to the town, and into the sea beyond. The name 'Yamorri' is by tradition derived from the dying exclamation of a native warrior who fell into the stream. It does not seem very deep. Another river flows along the opposite side of this place, and there is also the Cardinas a short distance down the coast to the south, but I believe none of them are navigable. I have lost time here in looking about, owing to the early mornings having been thick and foggy ever since we came, an unusual circumstance. It is too hot to stir in the middle of the day, and the evenings are very short, so that I shall accomplish less here in four days than I should do in two elsewhere.

Matanzas, March 16.—I saw some nice plants in small gardens yesterday. The Copaiba is a very pretty tree, and I hope to get a bulb of a gigantic lily, some Crinum or Amaryllis, which they tell me has a purple and white flower. A Ceanothus-looking shrub has here the name of tree mignonette from its fragrance. I went in a volante to draw from the Yamorri Pass. There are caves in the cretaceous rocks above, one of which is so extensive that it is believed to pass under the whole of the town of Matanzas. Looking up from below, I saw some stalactitic pillars supporting rocks above. I sketched one of them. In some places here the rocks look as if they had all been submitted to the action of fire, and this more completely than in Florida; for in these I see no organic remains. I think they must all have been burnt up, while at Ocala they seem only to have been warmed up. I suppose Cuba to be older land than the most southern part of the United States, although from Havana to Matanzas, I see only cretaceous formations—but coal is found not very distant from Havana, and the hundreds of miles farther south allow space enough for anything. This morning I am going to a plantation a few miles down the coast, south; to-morrow we return to Havana, and I shall have one more week there before crossing over to New Orleans.

Your affectionate

A. M. M.

LETTER XXI.

MATANZAS, CUBA,
March 17, 1855.

MY DEAR FRIENDS,—

I hope the letter which I sent off yesterday will leave Havana by this day's mail; it is impossible to be certain that all I write reaches you, but I generally send packets by the best opportunities. I have not always time to read over my communications, and never to copy them, so I shall be sorry if any are lost, as they will be such a refreshment to my memory at home. After closing my letters yesterday morning, I set off in a volante very early, and had a beautiful drive by the sea shore to a plantation called ——, the residence of Monsieur ——. The finest view I have yet seen of Matanzas is from a point about a mile out of the town, along the southern coast. Mr. J—— was so obliging as to accompany me part of the way on horseback; and as I soon got out of the carriage to gather flowers and pick up shells, I was quickly attracted by the nature of the rocks, which here border a sandy beach: there were fossil corals, and organisms in great variety, close to the sea. On a hill beyond, I found innumerable shells; bullas nearly as perfect as the recent ones on the shore below; then evident marks of volcanic action; then chalk resembling that at Ocala, with occasional fossil remains; higher up still, but not distant more than a few hundred yards, I saw a coarse kind of white freestone, which negro workmen were quarrying out in large blocks for building materials; then the road became exactly like the bed of a former river, although still rising a hill; it was little else but boulders and water-worn stones, which in England would have been considered impracticable for a carriage; but neither the calecero, his little thin white horses, nor the volante, made any objection to jumbling over them; the high, strong wheels mounted up and leaped down, without damage; and I could only hold tight, and wonder how horses and vehicle kept together. Before we reached the plantation, the soil was a rich iron-sand, just like that at Abbotsbury. M. —— told me that this soil had produced twenty crops of sugar-cane in succession without artificial aid. As usual, I met with a kind and hospitable reception; a broad avenue of Palms and Orange trees led up to the house; a black nurse was in a verandah, with the one little boy of two years, and Madame —— immediately came out and took me into a comfortable drawing-room, opening at once from the front. The verandah was nearly covered by the eatable passion-flower (*Passiflora grandilla*), and M. ——, who was for some time in England, must have had English gardens and groves in his mind, while planting the trees of his own country, instead of imitating the Spanish fashion of underrating them. The refreshing verdure of our lawns is beyond attainment within the Tropics, but he has selected trees and shrubs having reference to ornament as well as use; with oranges and pomeganates, and fruits, the names of which I have still to learn, he has associated a loquat, *Mespilus* (or *Eisobotria Japonica*), with the elegant foliage of the palm and bamboo, and the pretty weeping fir (which I never saw before, but suppose to be a *Cryptomeria*), making the middle distance unusual in appearance, and I tried, rather unsuccessfully, to sketch it. M. —— ordered a volante, and took me to a forest about a mile from his house, where I saw all kinds of novelties—among them a Heliotrope smelling like Jasmine, and a prickly shrub with a holly-shaped leaf, and flower resembling a Dryandra, only I never heard of one of that family, except as Australians. To avoid being knocked down by a large herd of horses and oxen, who were eagerly galloping down to the River Coheinva, a fine stream, when we reached it, M. —— placed me upon a bank, where the wild scene below could be witnessed without inconvenience. All the animals plunging and swimming about, while negro boys, looking just like bronze statues, leaped now on a horse, sometimes from a horse to an ox, and then into the water; or diving down, they made their appearance unexpectedly in the very midst of the beasts. I was not inclined to descend from my elevation till the whole assemblage, having drunk and bathed to their satisfaction, galloped off.

This river is wide and deep enough to float a seventy-four, and, as there is very little bar at the mouth, under any other kind of government it would be made navigable. It is impossible to visit Cuba without being struck by the fact that its resources are undeveloped, and its improvement prevented by mismanagement. My sympathy cannot but go with the Cubans, who are anxious for some improvement, although some political prisoners are likely to be put out of the way by strangulation for evincing an impatient spirit under the iron despotism by which they are ruled. My compassionate feelings are roused, so with every inclination for the support of authority, I cannot but wish that Europe may aid, instead of opposing, the ultimate freedom of this fine island—fine, at least, as to natural productions, but in great part rendered unproductive by the tyranny and ignorance of man. I observe many indications of Spanish cruelty, particularly towards animals. Slaves are pretty well treated, because their well-being is a matter of dollars in the pockets of their masters; but one sees chickens tied up alive by their legs in the markets, and one hears of bull-fights and cock-fights attended even by women. These things exemplify the character of a people, and show how backward their civilization is. I spent the day with my pleasant hosts, and M. —— was so good as to accompany me back to Matanzas after dark, although he thus exposed himself to a double night journey over the rocky track, which I can hardly call a road: however, we jumbled safely back, and I went immediately to Mr. Russel J——, as Mrs. J—— had been anxious about my safe return. Mr. J—— promises to forward my collection of this day at once to England, for it alone will fill a box, with shells, fossils, plants, and seeds. I found some difficulty in tearing myself away from such an interesting locality, where I have not seen half I should like to see. Not very far from the pass of the Yamorri, I understand there is still an Indian sacrificial altar. None of the aboriginal race are now left on the island: they have faded away before the more intelligent white men, and perhaps it may be, in the course of Providence, that Anglo-Saxon energy is one of these days to supersede Creole inertness and Spanish cruelty.

March 17.—I went by railroad back to Havana, and this time I tried to settle the controversy which has been waging in my mind between the two palms most common here. It is evident that the real cocoa-nut has a less smooth bark and a more plumose, falling foliage than that tree with the smooth white stem and stiffer leaves, most common all about the country; the latter bears a smaller nut, with which pigs are fed, instead of the true cocoa-nut; and a gentleman I met last night says the former is called here the Royal Palm, and that it is not a cocoa at all. I shall find out its botanical designation at last. I suspect it is what I first supposed, an Areca (Betel-nut).

There is much of the red iron-sand all the way to Havana. We arrived in time for dinner, but in such a ferruginous state that it required considerable patience to wash ourselves clean. Before sunset I took advantage of the pass I have received for drawing, and Mr. P—— took me up to the Fort El Principe, from which there is a view over Havana. Upon showing the order, signed by the Capitan-Generale, and assuring the Commandant that I only wished to sketch '*la perspectiva*,' and not the fortifications, we were permitted to enter.

Sunday, *March* 18.—We went to the service on board the *Argus* steamer, commanded by Captain Purvis. The English and Austrian Consuls, with Mrs. Crauford and Mrs. Scharkenberg, Mr. and Mrs. Backhouse, &c. &c., were also on board; and the captain provided us with a plentiful lunch. The sailors sang the Hundredth Psalm; and they also chanted part of the service guided by an harmonicon. We visited the engine-room and machinery, store-closet, &c. &c., which were beautifully kept. The *Vestal* is gone upon a cruise. I have been told a dreadful fact, confirmatory of the blood and murder which are caused by our unfortunate perseverance in keeping an Anti-Slavery squadron on the coast of Africa. One of our captains having been capsized in his gig, within the bar of a river, his only hope of safety was to swim to shore, near a barracouta, where he expected to lose his life in another manner. The people belonging to it, however, succoured him, and received him with kindness; but, before returning to his ship, the slave merchant requested his company to a distant building. Upon opening the door he was struck with horror at the sight of five hundred blacks with their throats cut. 'Do not look reproachfully at *me*,' exclaimed the man; 'this is *your* doing, not mine. I would willingly have avoided such a massacre, but you prevented me from getting the slaves off. I could neither feed nor provide for them; and self-preservation obliged us to dispose of them as you see.' The Consul here, and Mr. Backhouse, son of Mr. Backhouse, formerly of the Foreign Office, are the only people I have met with among either diplomatists or clergy, who support Abolitionist notions. Mr. Backhouse informed me that the reason it is unnecessary to fasten doors and windows on the plantations is, that the negroes are all safely locked in their respective dwellings at night. Now, I have ascertained that this is not so, though of course Mr. Backhouse believed it; and moreover, it would be absurd; because any one who is acquainted with the nature of negro houses must be aware they are so slight that the inhabitants can get out anywhere; and that, therefore, it would be useless to make a show of locking doors. In the cities the laws do not permit slaves to be out after nine o'clock at night without a permit; but even this regulation is not always enforced. In the evening I went to the Cortuna Valdez, a shady walk by the side of the harbour, and took a sketch from thence.

Havana, March 20.—Yesterday the heat was so intense I did not go out till late. This morning Mr. P—— accompanied me in the barge of the *Argos*, to visit the Cabanos, a very strong fortress, behind the Moro. It was once taken by Lord Albemarle, and England had possession of Havana for two years. At that time the English soldiers made use of one of the churches for Protestant service, which so desecrated it in the eyes of the bigoted Spaniards, that it has never been applied to sacred purposes from that time to this. In mounting towards the fortress, I found many interesting plants—some of them new to me. One of the pretty blue Commelinas usual in our gardens is here indigenous; Ipomœas, and Melias, and Bignonias, intermixed with Cactuses, are all over the banks, and fruits of different kinds grow within the walls. The Governor (who must, I suppose, be a Spanish General) was very gentlemanly and polite; much more so than the Commandant of El Principe, who consented to our admission with reluctance, I imagined, as if some degree of suspicion crossed his mind: and one cannot wonder that in these filibustering times everything here is carefully guarded. This fortress (the Cabanos) is of immense extent, much larger than the Citadel of Quatre; and at present it is occupied by a large body of troops. It took us so long to go over it that I put off visiting the Moro till to-morrow.

After dinner Mr. P—— took me a drive round the suburbs of Havana; two other American gentlemen, acquaintances from Baltimore, accompanied us in another volante; these carriages had two horses each, one ridden by a black postilion (with his tall jack-boots, and embroidered swallow-tailed, short-waisted jacket), cantered in the old French fashion by the side, but a few paces before the horse in the shafts. Our boy was a true negro of the ourang-outang class, with a projecting muzzle and falling-away chin; he was so surly and obstinate, that at last Mr. P—— got out and borrowed a cane from the other vehicle. We observed intelligent glances passing between the two drivers, and ours immediately improved in civility; the hint was sufficient, but no verbal argument would have had the smallest effect. We passed by the fortress called the Altares, on the hill below which fifty Filibusterers, who were taken prisoners from boats in an attempted invasion of the Island two or three years ago, were shot. The execution of ten out of the number would have been less cruel, and probably better policy; but is impossible to deny the right of the Cuban government to execute foreigners landing on their territory for hostile purposes; at this moment there are political prisoners under condemnation, whose death may be justifiable, Estampes, &c.

We returned to the city by a ferry across the harbour, and in the evening I attended a reception at the palace. The Capitan-Generale does not appear to be more than forty-five; his manner has a tinge of melancholy, and his position, however distinguished, must be in many respects arduous and painful. How far he is obliged to act harshly it is difficult to judge. He introduced me to General, or rather Admiral Castanos, who commands in the port, and who speaks English with a good pronunciation, although he informed me it was chiefly acquired from books.

After my return home, the American commander of the *Princeton* steamer came in. He mentioned having lately visited Jamaica, after an interval of ten years since he was there before, and that he was both surprised and shocked at the rapid deterioration of the island. He says the blacks are fast sinking into a state of gross vice and immorality; and even when they agree to work upon the plantations, they steal half of the crops to be gathered in, and sell it in the most barefaced way. Ladies cannot venture out without danger of insult; and he considers our West Indian Islands are on the road to ultimate ruin. This is the opinion of every observer I have met with lately who has been among them—people of different professions and of various shades of politics—but all in agreement upon that one point, and a sad and dreary agreement it is!

Yesterday, the boat of the *Argus*, commanded by Mr. Elton, took Mr. P—— and me to the Moro. Upon landing beneath it, I found the beach strewed with various specimens of corallines, some of them so perfect they look as if fresh. The situation of this fortress is fine, though commanded by that we visited yesterday. I saw the windows of dungeons, where it gave me a pang to know political prisoners are confined; and there is a general opinion that an execution will take place to-morrow, perhaps that of Pinto. People well informed believe there is no credible evidence against Ramon Pinto; but he is a man of talent as well as character, and the Castilian party are exasperated against him, so that there is reason to believe the Capitan-Generale will not refuse a confirmation of the sentence of death; but with three of our men-of-war here, besides Americans, and considering the protection we have afforded to the government, could not our Consul-General object to such a tragedy being performed? Surely it is sufficient to confiscate his estates, and sentence that noble though unfortunate man to banishment, instead of garotting him!

I believe fifty of the subordinate offenders are to be transported to the Manillas. It is sufficient to live for one fortnight under the rule of a despotism to be made sensible of the blessing of constitutional government. Here all is doubt and suspicion. This unhappy Pinto has a wife and seven or eight children, and he is said to be clever, brave, and well-intentioned: perhaps right in principle, though mistaken in the choice of means and the selection of time: but I am assured that against him there is no accusation as to rebellion, but one of intended assassination of Concha, which is incredible.

Upon entering the cutter again, we rowed a short distance out, for me to make a short sketch of the Moro from the sea, and I returned to the Calton Hotel by ten o'clock. After dinner, Mr. P—— and I took a long drive round the suburbs of the city, and it was dark before we returned. We passed through Guanobacova—a place famous for cock-fighting. There, I am told, hardly a house is without its fighting cocks. After our return, I went to take leave at the Palace, where my reception has been always obliging and polite.

Areco oleacea is the palm which has given me so much trouble here. At last I have made up my mind it is no cocoa. This was my first idea; but the difference of opinion and the total ignorance about vegetation here led me to doubt my own correctness. Only yesterday, Monsieur Sauralle, a gentleman who has paid some attention to trees, assured me this palm, which he designated *Oresodoxa Regia*, was not to be found in London; yet it is there as Areca. I have had this morning my first introduction to a scorpion. I saw something in a little basket, standing close to the dressing-table, which I mistook for a fossil. I touched it with an exclamation, when a maid (fortunately not black) saw what it was, caught up the basket, and carried it at once to a man a few yards from my door, who killed the creature instantly. A negro woman would have laughed and stared, and have allowed it to sting me, before she would have remembered that a scorpion is an ugly customer. This is the first venomous thing I have met with in America, and it is the only one dangerous in Cuba; not so bad either, I am assured, as the same creature in other localities, for its bite seldom proves mortal here. There are some snakes to be found in the island, but none venomous. By-the-bye, yesterday a lady from Louisiana told me that a snake there (she could not say if it was a rattlesnake) milks the cows, and that it has the power of charming a cow once milked, back to the same spot, where she will call the reptile as if it was her calf. A red appearance in the milk left behind shows what has occurred; but there is no danger to the life of the cow, and by being carefully shut up away from her snake milker, the mischief is repaired.

Havana, March 23.—No *Crescent City* has come in to-day, though the *Isabel*, from Charleston, the *Philadelphia*, from New York, and the *Diver*, British steamer, have all arrived; we shall therefore be detained over to-night. There is a whisper that another political sufferer will be brought to the scaffold immediately. I have not heard particulars of that case; but every fact which can be discovered confirms me in the suspicion that the death of Pinto was a murder—not an act of political justice. His last communication to a friend was his assurance, as a man of honour, that he died guiltless of those things for which his judges had condemned him. Five thousand people attended Pinto's execution; solemnly and apparently mournfully, they witnessed his firm and calm submission to the garotte, after having been refused the death of a soldier. This act must bring misery upon the heads of those who have caused it.

I am told the British Consul had not sufficient diplomatic rank to warrant a protest from him. So while England is carrying on a crusade against the interests of the sugar planters, and which really injures and deteriorates the black race, it is abetting murder and tyranny over the whites; and because this island bears the name of a colony (although of much more importance than Mexico), Englishmen have been imprisoned and ruined without redress; and if a British subject dies here, there is no minister capable of protecting his property, or of saving his widow and family from an arbitrary interference with their rights. We have only power to do mischief, without making our influence felt for the advantage of our own people. This Government is, in fact, a Viceroyship. Havana (particularly at this moment) is a situation of great importance, and yet the British Government have no strong and powerful representative. Here I feel so mortified at the poor figure England makes, that I quite long to get away from the place. I am packing up a box of fossils and recent corallines collected on these shores for the London Museum of Practical Geology; except by the weight of the former, they are in such a perfect condition, that they would hardly be distinguished from fresh specimens. I cannot gain information where the older formations commence, but there is good coal on the island. I have picked up serpentine upon its shores, and I am told that there is granite somewhere towards the south. I have not seen more than sixty miles out of the seven hundred, to which length Cuba extends.

Military uniforms are visible in every direction, and fortresses bristle all round this city, yet there is no such thing as public confidence, or a sense of general security. Poor Cuba! from the little I have seen, I can hardly hope that the future will be free from bloodshed. No simple arrangement of sale and payment will settle her destinies, or give her prosperity. If individuals in this state of existence have to pass through a discipline of trial, so it appears that nations must gain freedom through suffering.

The day before yesterday was stormy, with thunder and lightning, fit accompaniments for that morning's work; so I was fortunate in not embarking upon a troubled sea, which may be less rough for our passage if we are to go on board this afternoon.

Crescent City, March 25.—By half-past ten o'clock yesterday morning we got on board, being obliged to come two miles across the harbour in an open boat, because there is a regulation obliging the American steamers to coal at an inconvenient place; and though this vessel would have been able to come in last night, because she arrived after sunset the authorities obliged her to wait at the entrance till after the sun rose again, on pain of being fired at. Once, a captain, being ordered to moor himself alongside of a convict ship, refused to take that situation, and put out again to sea till the morning.

The present Government of Cuba is permitting acts which tend to excite indignation and pugnacity in the United States. It is reported that some authorities have insulted and seized upon a Consul, and that a Spanish man-of-war has fired into an American ship, and that the Capitan-Generale has neither offered redress nor apology. Havana is a tempting prize, and the Spanish Government affording a fair pretext, who can wonder that there are filibustering expeditions? Passing out of the harbour, a gentleman pointed out the spot where Ramon Pinto was executed. He described the scene as follows:—No very apparent show of military force, but the scaffold was erected in an open place, between a large barrack and the small fort opposite the Cabanos, from whence troops could have been drawn if necessary. We concluded the prisoner must have been moved from his dungeon in the night or early in the morning. When all was prepared, he was brought out from the barracks, dressed in white, with a black cross upon his cap; his companions, only the executioner and one priest; a band playing the Dead March. He had only to walk about two hundred yards; he simply declared his innocence of the crimes attributed to him, and then, after seating himself in the chair of death, he gave the signal; the garotte was applied, and, without any apparent struggle, life soon became extinct: for a while, I know not how long, the body was left to be gazed at; that sight perhaps made five hundred Pintos where there was one before, and raised a detestation of General Concha and his myrmidons which will probably cause the extinction of the Spanish rule in America, and bring down retribution upon the chief who now exercises it. Perhaps I have dwelt too long upon this terrible occurrence; and writing as I have done at odd moments it is possible I may have repeated facts, but there has been no time to read back; you have the feelings and the impressions as they arose, and at such a moment it has been impossible to write coolly or free from painful excitement. Thank God, I have now left that bloody shore.

We have a large vessel and fine calm weather; our captain says it will take three days to reach the bar of the Mississippi River; I fear we shall enter it in the dark. The only peculiarity I have observed in this part of the Gulf of Mexico during our present voyage is the colour of the sea, which is unlike anything I have remarked elsewhere: it is neither green nor sky-blue, but precisely the tint of a sapphire—which the captain tells me is its usual appearance; this colour does not seem to be affected by either clouds or sky, for though we have had a calm voyage so far, it has by no means been cloudless, and I write on the third day of our passage to New Orleans at a distance of six hundred miles from Cuba. On board, I have been reading Mrs. Stowe's *Sunny Memoirs:* it contains some pretty and true descriptions of scenes and facts in Scotland and England, and yet I cannot but regret that she did not meditate more deeply upon her own axiom, that—'The power of fictitious writing, for good as well as evil, is a thing which ought to be most seriously reflected on,'—and not ignorantly used. Had Mrs. Stowe lived for some months among the institutions and the people which, in *Uncle Tom*, she thoughtlessly, perhaps not intentionally vilified, she would have used, not misused her undoubted talents; and as it is, she ought to have blushed at the fulsome flattery which called her novel '*The genuine application of the sacred Word of God to the several branches of her subject.*'—Dr. M'Neile's Address, April 11th, 1853.

I did not say much about the aspect of Slavery in Cuba, because my opportunities for observing it were few. In a certain sense the white population there are slaves, and of course the state of the blacks is modified by that circumstance; from what I heard, too, the social morality of the Cubans is at a very low ebb, their religious principles wretched, and the prevalence of immorality and irreligion will act and react upon the blacks as well as the whites; so I do not believe Cuba to be a country where Slavery, as a system, can be fairly studied. We expect to reach the mouth of the Mississippi to-night: if there is no fog our captain will cross the bar; but one hundred miles of the river must be traversed before our vessel reaches New Orleans, and I shall write no more till we get there.

St. Charles Hotel, New Orleans, March 29.—We reached this place before three o'clock yesterday; but owing to the tide swinging the *Crescent City* round just as she came up to her moorings, there was no landing till after four o'clock. I did not undress the night before, for our *Seminole* accident has made my nerves rather touchy at night; and though we were off the Mississippi before eleven, the captain was obliged to fire a gun three times, and at last dispatched a boat before he could get a pilot on board. The mouth of this river, and its channel for the first hundred miles, is narrow and poor compared with the Walaki, the St. Lawrence, or the beautiful Ottawa; I am told it is wider higher up: as yet I have seen nothing on its low muddy banks but some thriving plantations fringed with neat negro dwellings. Till we arrived I did not know our steamer was named from the shape of the city, which is built upon the crescent form of the shore. I never saw such a fleet of steamers as line its wharves, no, not even at London or Liverpool: perhaps this is owing to their being all moored together; but there is more shipping here than I have observed in any of the other ports except New York and Boston. The place, though flat, is handsome and apparently well-built; but although it has been for so many years attached to the United States, and the Creole population has not now a majority, yet they are an influential ingredient, and give the tone to manners and customs; so that New Orleans has more of a Southern air than even Charleston or Savannah.

Yours affectionately,

A. M. M.

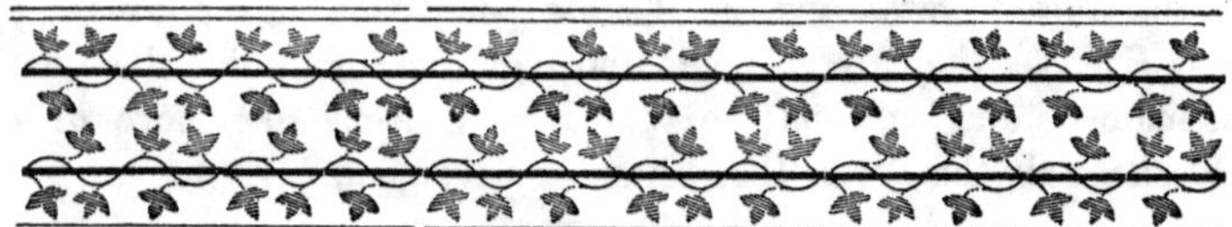

LETTER XXII.

NEW ORLEANS, *March* 31, 1855.

MY DEAR FRIENDS,—

I left the St. Charles Hotel yesterday. Mr. Robert G——, brother to my Virginian friend, called to bring me to his pleasant and comfortable house, and in what may be called the 'West end' of New Orleans. I find myself established, and quite at home, with every luxury and attention that a traveller can require. The weather is still as fresh and cold as an ordinary dreary March with us, though more roses are in bloom than we could find so early in the year in England. Several loquat trees (*Eisobotria Japonica*) placed round the garden are only just beginning to ripen their delicious fruit, with its golden, or rather apricot-coloured hue; in most seasons before April, peas and strawberries are plentiful, but they are not yet to be had. My ideas are rather puzzled about seasons: after the dog days in Cuba, I feel as if this ought to be autumn, not spring; but I have no doubt that an interval of colder weather wll be salutary to our constitutions before we pass the approaching summer in the Northern States. Instead of growing thin during my travels, I was beginning to fear that, on my return to England, I should make my appearance in too portly a style; but three weeks at Havana have obviated that fear. In my room here it is pleasant to have a four-post bed, which brings English customs to mind. I never saw anything but French bedsteads in the North. No curtains are required; a full and wide mosquito-net, without opening, and which is put back during the day, and looks like a transparent bonnet-box over the pillows, is drawn forward at night, and protects me completely from the invasion of insects. This is a better contrivance than those at Cuba, where I found a persevering mosquito would often succeed in establishing itself within the curtains. The wood of which the bedstead is made looks like a kind of walnut; the top has a heavy projecting eave—this, I am told, is advantageous, as it gives room for the iron rod underneath upon which the mosquito-net is hung. While I am writing a black woman enters: they walk in and out of your room, just as the fancy takes them, without knocking; and the door must be locked if one does not wish to be intruded on. The negroes are curious, and like to come and ask questions, and see what you are at; so 'Emily' inquires if I will let her make the bed while I am in the room; being as well inclined for a little talk as herself, I agree. She tells me the coloured people are well content and happy; that she was 'raised in Virginny,' and came here from Richmond; that masters and mistresses about are very tender of their people; that she has got her husband and three children, babies almost, the youngest an infant, then in the house; she does odd jobs after dinner, but she says that on the plantations it is not often the people work after dinner (she is munching something all this while); they have usually task-work, which can be quickly done if they choose; that the black population don't like bacon—'they likes to have fresh meat three times a day, and what they likes beside.' She seemed utterly astonished when I told her that the English working-people could seldom get meat at all, and that they had not as much firing as they chose, &c. &c. 'Lord bless you, missus, that would never do at all here: why, some of the coloured ones have got a'most as much jewellery as their missuses; they gets their own way tolerable somehow; and they very often desires to be sold when they be affronted.' 'Emily' thought that in England slaves would have it all their own way entirely; and this is the idea that darkies have of freedom: plenty to eat and drink, finery to their heart's content

—no work. Here they despise the free negroes. One woman was offered her freedom in my hearing: she took the offer as an insult, and said, 'I know what the free niggers are, missus: they are the meanest niggers as ever was; I hopes never to be a free nigger, missus.' A slave quarrelling with another black, after calling him names, at last sums up as the acme of contempt, 'You be a d——d nigger without a master!' This is the consequence of the fact, that free negroes being idle and profligate are generally poor and miserable. A common reproach among them is to say, 'You be's as bad as a free nigger.' I think if any unprejudiced person sees the state of the free black population in Canada, and then makes a tour of a few months in the Southern States, with an open eye and unprejudiced mind, he will come to the conclusion that things are better than names; and that if by a *ukase* he could carry back all the darkies (from ignorance and misrepresentation induced to run away from their masters) he would benefit the blacks, whatever he might do for the whites, who, I believe, would be very much averse to receive these contaminated negroes again, except from motives of duty and compassion.

Mrs. Stowe gives great credit to a young lady who, becoming the heiress of a few slaves, gave them all their freedom. I have heard of a young lady who succeeded to the possession of negroes, and nothing else; by emancipating them she might have gained a fine character from the Abolitionists, and have cast off not only a responsibility, but a heavy expense; instead of which she sought occupation for herself, laboured hard, and earned the means of existence for her poor black dependents, as well as her own living. Which of these two ladies acted the more Christian part? Last night, conversing with a very intelligent gentleman who has travelled in Canada, I remarked that free negroes there were in a much more degraded, suffering, and irreligious state than any slaves I have seen; and that they often reproach the whites with having, by false pretences, inveigled them to their destruction. He said, 'I will tell you a circumstance which occurred relative to that matter. A confidential black, who was treated with the greatest kindness by his master, took it in his head one day to run away, with the idea of establishing himself in Canada. When in that country I accidentally fell in with him, acting as waiter in an hotel: we immediately recognized each other; and, with tears in his eyes, he said, 'Oh, sir! tell of the family; how is this one, how is that?' I answered his inquiries, and then asked how he got on. 'I get on in the season pretty well; I make some money, but very bad in the winter. Oh, sir! beg my dear master for me; beg him to forgive, and take me back again.' And I feel sure that these negroes who are not so far gone in drunkenness and profligacy, as to have lost all self-respect, would generally make the same request; exceptions only prove the rule. My woman on the Detroit River was taken care of by a husband, who, having occupation as a black pilot (an employment for which their strong local perception peculiarly fits them), was the only really contented black I met with; but she lost her children, and may, perhaps, end in being motherless; while in slavery, they would have been healthy. As to the separation of families, I see that great pains are taken to avoid that evil. I believe that it hardly occurs more frequently than in England from other causes: and I imagine a law might be enacted to make it less easy here. So in this case, as in every other social abuse, the governing power should regulate, but not wholly forbid, or the result will be the encouragement of twenty evils where there was one before. I have seen a great many visitors to day; among them some very agreeable people.

April 1.—A dinner-party here included the Bishop and Mrs. P——, Professors Biddell and Linton (the latter from St. Louis), Colonel Seymour, Dr. Smith, &c., &c. I am invited to accompany a party into the State of Mississippi to-morrow or Tuesday, as an expedition, and gladly accept. At nine o'clock Mr. Miltenberger called to take me to the Opera, to see the last two or three acts. I have been little gratified by the operas elsewhere in the States. At New York, Grisi and Mario were wretchedly supported: and the dresses and choruses were so miserable that I was hardly inclined to do more than just look in at the house here; but I was most agreeably surprised. The Italian Opera in London was never better *mis en scène*, though Donizetti was given in French. I think the opera was *La Reine de Chypre.* Although the *prima donna* was neither Grisi nor Sontag, her voice, expression, and acting, were all good; her toilette perfect; indeed, as a whole, I never saw a piece better *costumé;* being close to the stage, the details were made evident to me; and three fine male voices of different kinds, gave effect to the principal characters. I must go again, and know more about this opera than it was in my power to find out last night.

The house, though not large, is well arranged, but after a different plan from any one I ever saw before. I was told that being the last day of Lent, the Creole ladies were not there. This morning the weather is warm, some rain the night before last has softened the air, and I suppose now the summer will come here.

By-the-bye, I got a lady to write down for me the extraordinary and terrific screams of the watchmen at Havana and Matanzas. I must let you have the benefit of them, premising, of course, that the hours vary:—

'Las diez y media y sereno.'
'Las once y nublado.'
'Las doce, y la ciudad està siempre fidelisima.'

As to the last assurance, I think I should not be sorry it should be a doubtful one.

There is a report that the President of the United States has ordered some American men-of-war to go and sink the Spanish frigate which fired into the steamer. I don't much wonder if he has done so; and really I think Europe might be inclined to join with America in bringing the Spaniards to their senses, for as despots, they are quite as bad as the Russians when they dare to show their will, and in cruelty worse. I must tell a story, which will exemplify the mode of government and internal state of Cuba more graphically than anything else I can write.

Not long ago there was a servile *émeute* among the negroes of a plantation; the authorities immediately seized the ringleaders, tortured them with cat-o'-nine-tails, with nails in them, cutting flesh off their backs, inquiring all the time, 'Did so and so instigate you —or, so and so?' The poor blacks at first answered truly, 'No one told us—we did it ourselves.' At last the name of a planter forty miles off was mentioned, and not knowing him, to escape from torture one said, 'Yes, massa—he, massa.' This gentleman was busy on his grounds about three o'clock in the afternoon, when forty soldiers entered, and asked his name; he gave it, and civilly invited them to take some refreshment; but they immediately put a rope round his neck, and proceeded to attach it to one of their horses. He entreated that if they meant to take him prisoner, they would at least allow him to mount one of his own saddle-horses. But no; they actually trotted this man of property and education forty miles, dragging him after them. When they arrived at the place where he was to be confined and examined, eleven other people were selected to stand with him. The negroes were then brought in, and desired to point out Mr. ——. Fortunately for him, being quite unknown to them, they selected the wrong man; but if by any accident they had pitched upon him, his life would have been the forfeit. As soon as his non-complicity was thus ascertained, the negroes were taken out and shot without further ceremony, and Mr. —— was allowed to find his way back to his own home. This is Cuban law and justice. It may be guessed what kind of a chance was afforded to Pinto.

Yesterday, April 1st, was Sunday; Bishop P—— called and took me to his church, where the service was like ours, with the exception only of a few omissions. The interior of the edifice was ornamented with sufficient painted glass to throw a cool light into it without making it obscure, and all the decorations were in good taste. The 1st of April might have been May with us—the temperature just high enough for enjoyment.

April 2.—Mrs. G—— took me to visit a lady in the neighbourhood, in whose garden I found many things new to me, principally shrubs. A capsicum as small as a pea, which looks like something different from what we call bird pepper; and a

12*

privet, which, though the leaves resemble a Chinese privet, I think is hardly the same, as it is quite a timber tree, and very handsome. I gathered many seeds.

I dined with the British Consul, Mr. Muir, and met his mother-in-law, an agreeable old lady, though she is of the Wilberforce and Hannah More school, almost the only person I have met with South who still advocates abolitionist ideas; her son-in-law, a clergyman, and a granddaughter did not agree with her in opinion. I afterwards drank tea with the Bishop and Mrs. P——. One remark of his struck me: he said, that for the sake of the Christian and moral welfare of the Irish emigrants and the African negroes, he would desire to pass a majority of the former through the kitchens, and all the latter through the plantations, of the United States. The Irish paupers are so ultra in their politics, and so saucy in their manners, that they have given rise to the 'Know-nothing' movement, which, however reprehensible in its mode of proceeding, is only a practical illustration of the impossibility of fairly carrying out the idea of equality. These emigrants are, without doubt, as a class, the most disagreeable and overbearing people in the Union. They are specimens of the true democrat when united with ignorance—levelling all above themselves, and insolent to those they fancy beneath them. Bishop P—— walked home with me; no bonnet, and hardly a shawl was required; the evening balmy and pleasant—just perfect in temperature.

Osyka, April 5.—I date from one of those marvellous places in the Bush, which in this part of the world are born, educated, and grown up in the course of a few months. When I landed at Boston, there was not a tree felled where this town is now in existence; yet I am in a comfortable hotel entertaining thirty or forty guests daily at its *table-d'hôte*. This house, the woman said, 'had been built full five months.' The town as yet does not consist of more than fifty houses; but there are two hotels, three or four stores, a good railway station, and everything else looking as if established thirty years, excepting that as yet there is no church, and the stumps of trees are still left in all directions.

But I must begin from the beginning, and tell the adventures which have obliged me to sleep at Osyka, with an uncertainty as to when I am to get back to New Orleans. As I had made two pleasant acquaintances there—Dr. Smith and Dr. Riddell (the latter has bought a house and property eighty-six miles off, in the Mississippi territory, where he means to move his wife and family when the heat sets in)—they invited me to accompany them in an expedition to see a pretty country beyond the pine barrens, which stretch away as far as the State of Mississippi; a railroad has been opened in that direction during the last year. We started yesterday at seven o'clock; at a station about half-way here, one of the points being wrong, the engine ran off and plunged deep into a quagmire; the train was brought-up without damage to any one except a poor boy, who was at that moment oiling the cow-catcher: he imprudently jumped off, and he was so seriously injured that he is since dead. We got out, walked to the station, and in about half an hour another engine was attached to the cars; we reached Osyka by two o'clock, though, at my request, the conductor brought-up the train for a few minutes to get some specimens of a very curious water-plant, something between a Pothos and an Orontium, which Dr. Riddell agrees with me is new: it resembles Loudon's description of Pothos acaulis, having leaves quite destitute of nerves, but the spike is hexandrous, not triandrous.

There was some difficulty in getting a conveyance five miles to the pretty location, which Dr. Riddell promises to call 'Chatawa' (Silver Spring). There is a beautiful spring close to the house, and various mineral springs, containing iron and soda, at a short distance from it. I walked about a mile and a half through the forest, delighted by the brilliant butterflies and flowers. I found old acquaintances in our gardens at every step —Viola cucullata, Sisyrinchium anceps, Verbena Aubletia, Houstonias, Phloxes, Alliums, and Trilliums, a curious Asarum, and a plant with two leaves (*Podophyllum*, May apple), which they tell me produces a fruit so excellent, and so fragrant when ripe, that it can be scented yards away. The people call it May apple.

I shall find out its trivial name, but at present it has only just put forth leaves, and there is no sign of a flower. It is not more than a foot in height, with toothed foliage as large as a cucumber leaf, but smooth, shining, and variegated. At 'Chatawa,' I found a numerous German-Polish family—children of all ages—fathers, mothers, uncles, aunts, nephews, nieces—very hospitable people, who have sold their house to Dr. M——, with the intention of flitting to Osyka, which will soon be a place of consideration. I had a comfortable bed, and all the necessaries of life, though not many of its luxuries; and, after twenty-four hours of enjoyment in a lovely spot, with every promise of increased beauty under better cultivation, I got into a wagon and left the banks of the Tangipahoà River and the mineral springs which surround it, with regret that I could not follow the projected line of the railroad (as yet only complete to Osyka, so called by the first proprietor after an Indian beauty), thirty miles farther to the river Balsalà, where I understand the scenery is still fine; and perhaps I might have done so instead of spending another day and night here, for when we arrived at half-past one o'clock yesterday to take the two o'clock cars, no train had arrived, nor has yet arrived from New Orleans. Either some accident, some damage to the locomotive, or some obstruction, has occurred; and now, at eight o'clock on Thursday the 5th, we are still detained, without being able to guess when we are to have the means of return. Still, I am not bored—there is plenty of interest and amusement; for I find fortification agates and flint fossils in the railway-cutting above, besides the flowers of the pine barrens around, and as long as the cars which were to fetch us have not sunk in some of the swamps we yesterday traversed (when the train danced up and down on the line more than was pleasant, from the boggy nature of the ground), I am content to wait here for twenty-four hours more.

New Orleans, April 6.—The cars came up to Osyka so as to bring us back here by seven o'clock last night. It seems they had other accidents during their return on the 3rd, by running over cattle, till the locomotive jumped into a bog, fortunately breaking its couplings, so that the cars were left on the line, where, of course, the passengers sat up all night. Between damaging engines and killing cows, the economy of leaving railroads without protecting them by fences, in a country where wood is of such easy attainment, appears to me very short-sighted. Thunderstorms began early to-day; they accompanied our journey, and have been pealing and blazing all night. I never saw such lightning; and the torrents of rain are sufficient, I should think, to overflow the Mississippi and swamp New Orleans, situated as it is lower than the river. I cannot understand how this city keeps out of the water. I hear about banks called levées, but Holland must be a joke in comparison to this amphibious place.

April 7.—Yesterday, being Good Friday, was strictly kept here: that is not the case, I believe, in any other State of the Union. The day was gloomy, but not wet; an afternoon rainbow gave promise of fine weather, which is realized this morning, and I hope to see more of the environs of New Orleans than I have done as yet.

April 8.—Another execution at Havana. But however severe and cruel the Cuban policy may be, there seems to have been sufficient proof that Estampes was engaged in a conspiracy against Spanish despotism, and therefore his condemnation stands on different grounds from that of Ramon Pinto.

I visited a widows' asylum, not long opened here, which appears to be one of the best regulated charities I have ever seen. It does not separate mothers from children, but offers a home to both, only premising that the former are to contribute their labour, as washer-women, sempstresses, &c. &c. towards the support of the institution. A few pensioners without families are sheltered and provided for, when incapable of exertion; but the system is one of assistance to those who are willing to work.

Order, cleanliness, and comfort reign throughout the asylum; and an excellent Scotch matron superintends it, under the direction of a committee. The children, from infants of a few days to those able to be employed, are well trained and taught under the eye of their mothers. All the inmates expressed themselves with gratitude ; in some cases respectable aged widows had their private apartment; in others we saw mothers with their own two or three children. Widows without families have a separate eating-room, and live at one side of the house, away from the noise of children.

I heard an amusing story yesterday, exemplifying negro character. A gentleman had ordered one of his black gardeners to widen a ditch, and as he complained of the difficulty of the job, Mr. —— engaged a white labourer to assist him. The two men were left to work on together. After a while the master went to see how the job got on: he found that the Irishman had done three times the work the other had accomplished.

'How is this, Charles?' said Mr. ——; 'you have done very little. See how much more the other labourer has finished.

'Ah, massa, that very true; but white man use to work. You can't 'spect me—a nigger—demean myself like he.'

And it is generally so: the negroes consider themselves as privileged, instead of being degraded by their situation. A black complained that his master did not use him well. 'But how is that; pray do you not get good bread?'—'Yes, massa, pretty good bread.'—'Have you not enough, then? Are you over-tasked? Do you get as much meat as you like?'—'Ay, massa; but then the meat too fat—me don't 'prove fat meat.' When masters or mistresses want change, it is a common occurrence for them to apply to their negroes, who have almost always silver about them.

It is observed that many of the Irish emigrants have the same unfounded notions of their prospects in America, as those entertained by some negroes, of England. An Irishman begging, was offered a job of work; he accepted it, but said he thought it 'very hard.'—'Hard,' said his employer; 'what do you mean? Did you come here and expect to pick up gold in the streets?'—'No, not altogether that, but I thought if I asked for it, it would be given me.'—'But suppose I divided what I have with you—what would happen when that should be gone?'—'Arrah!' said Pat, 'I don't exactly know—but I suppose then we must divide again!

I cannot wonder that this place is unhealthy during the hot season; there are deep gutters and stagnant waters at the sides of almost all the streets. It would be a marvel if yellow fever, or something of the kind, did not prevail. Whether the situation is so low that good drainage is impossible, I cannot say; but I only wonder that the population is not decimated every summer. I should be sorry to take my chance in such a swamp.

On Sunday I attended a church where the singing, though good in its way, reminded me more of a Roman Catholic than a Protestant house of worship; it was not congregational, but operatic.

April 9.—I have been occupied all the morning writing letters to England. The *Illustrated News* of the 10th of March gives an apocryphal report of the 'Dangerous Conspiracy at Cuba,' in which Ramon Pinto is asserted to have announced his intention of assassinating the Capitan-Generale in his box at the opera. This is the authorized version, I suppose; but no person acquainted with the character of Pinto will believe it true. In the first place, even his enemies admit that he was a man of sense, talent, and principle; and those who know the present state of Havana must be well aware that such a plot would have been absurd and silly, as well as wicked. Anonymous and false stories are easily got up and propagated when a man is dead, and cannot refute them; but the time will come for such accusations to recoil upon the inventors.

Certainly the black servants in this country are more petted and humoured than even the domestics of Europe! There is an ingenious kind of diorama of the *Pilgrim's Progress*, now exhibiting here. Six household blacks, belonging to a lady here, were to go and see it. In England three servants would have gone one evening, and three another; but here they preferred to enjoy the sight all together, so the mistress and her daughters undertook every department of household work, even to that of the kitchen, that the black ladies and gentlemen might gratify their wishes. I could write fifty stories of this kind, which prove the kindness and consideration shown towards the race called slaves. The name of 'dark children' would, in nine cases out of ten, be more appropriate. It is the fashion with us to cry up the Spanish system in preference to that of the United States. Whatever the laws may be, I feel sure there is more of oppression and cruelty to be detected in Cuba than in all the other Southern States put together. We must bear in mind that the best laws will not prevent the possibility of their violation; and I sometimes doubt whether more cases of cruelty and over-work, and even starvation, among apprentices and 'maids-of-all-work' in Great Britain might not be discovered, than we could detect in the households and plantations here. The buying and selling operation is certainly very unpleasant and revolting to our ideas, and the whites here dislike it; but it is curious how very little is thought of the matter by the blacks themselves. It is not true that women can be sold away from their children; but slaves often urge their masters and mistresses to sell them for some fancy or freak, and a gentleman to-day had a quarrel with his negroes, because he wanted to set them free. 'It's very hard, master; you have a right to keep us, master;' and at last the majority positively refused to go, even though master offered them a 'fit out' if they would accept their freedom. I believe they are quite right. With all my love of liberty, if I was of the black race, I should much prefer being a slave upon one of the Southern plantations, than any free black man or woman I ever met with in America. So, in now thinking Slavery not so bad an institution, I act up to the maxim of 'doing as I would be done by.' This week I am going to visit plantations in this neighbourhood, but I have now seen so much and thought so much upon the general question, and also of the character of negroes as a race, that I do not think anything I may see in Louisiana, Texas, or Kentucky, can much alter my conclusions. My wish has been to seek after truth; I suppose many will doubt my having attained it, but one thing I know, that it has been sought for by an unprejudiced mind, without reference to any ulterior consequences. No pains or fatigue have deterred me from investigation. I give you the fruits of it—consquences are not my affair.

Last night I went to see the diorama exemplifying the *Pilgrim's Progress*, in the hope that it might make me more worthy than I am of a work which has been one of the most highly valued of all literary productions; but in vain—excepting the Parables, and one or two stories in the *Spectator*, I never could enjoy anything allegorical. A brief allegory is very well —but an allegorical volume! I never could wade through it!

All the houses here, except some in the old town and centre streets, have gardens—not very extensive, generally from a quarter to half an acre; but the soil and climate are such that everything grows luxuriantly. Magnolias, jessamine, roses, oranges, lemons, loquats, and a hundred other things beautiful and good; and then the mocking birds and butterflies, and the pretty little chameleons! For this month it is delightful to be at New Orleans; but one month in the year in this city—that should be all. I would not be a resident here for any temptation that could be offered me. I wonder whether the Mississippi will ever descend from its trough and make an excursion to Lake Pontchartrain? It has wandered about here and there in its time, and it is a marvel to me how this same river now keeps up above the surrounding country. It brings down so much clay from above, that when the water runs over, it makes a kind of boundary for itself at the edge, and this, with the help of artificial *levées*, makes the great stream stay in its course. But I am disappointed to find it so ugly and muddy; they say this is all the fault of the Missouri, which darkens and spoils the complexion of the Mississippi after their union.

Thursday, April 12.—Yesterday I went to a wedding. Like all others I have attended, the ceremony (episcopal) took place in a room; otherwise it was very pleasing. The bride and bridegroom remained for lunch, but no toasts were given. The ladies all sat down, waited on by the gentlemen, and when we left the room the gentlemen took possession of the table. After dinner, I walked to call on the Bishop and on Mrs. Polk. Visits in these countries are usually paid in the evening, to avoid the heat of the sun. It was the same in Cuba.

Yesterday, a clergyman who has been long in the employment of the Colonization Society for establishing free negroes in Africa (the Bishop presides over the one here), called to make his report. His views accord with those I have advocated. He is convinced that there has been too hasty emancipation, and that the Liberian plan has been much injured by a want of discrimination in the choice of the blacks sent out there. He told us a mulatto from Louisiana was anxious to keep his people under the same control which benefits them here, to avoid throwing them into the contamination of Liberian society; but the charter of freedom in that Colony is so strict, that his only resource was to get far enough to be out of the reach of mischief, and to bind his people by the apprenticeship law, which, though good as far as it goes, does not tend as much either to the happiness or the ultimate good of the negro as the slavery system well administered. When this is the opinion of Ministers of the Gospel, and of Bishops, not themselves slaveholders, is it reasonable of the abolitionist theorizers in England and America to fancy that their opinion and their conclusions are the only true and scriptural ones?

On Sunday next, I find that a steamer sails for Texas. Upon good advice, my plan is to land at Galveston, across a large land-locked bay, and up a bayou to Houston, where we can procure a stage to a Texas Washington; from thence I can reach the capital, Austin, on the Colorado River, a place which, though bordering upon inaccessible forests, I am told has great beauty of scenery in its neighbourhood. I wish to avoid wild Indians and poisonous snakes, so I must not attempt to penetrate inland; it is said that from Austin we must come down somewhere between the two rivers La Bara and Colorado, to Matagorda Bay, where a steamer will be attained to bring us back here, touching at Galveston. The voyages must be about two days and nights each way. You will think me adventurous to undertake this; but these new countries are so interesting to a person fond of Natural History and fine scenery, that one makes up one's mind to undergo some inconvenience and difficulty for the great pleasure with which the journey is repaid. Then there is the stimulant of an only opportunity! The idea that I never again can hope to have another opportunity for transatlantic tours, makes me willing to undergo a great deal,—and on the whole, I think Southern scenery will be better worth my while than the Falls of St. Anthony, or even Lake Superior. I walked this morning from the St. Charles Hotel to the cottage, and found Professor Riddell returned from Chatawa. We looked at specimens of Orontium aquaticum, and decided our Osyka specimens are not the same Orontium as that. I then went to see Mr. L——, who promises to take me to his plantation to-morrow.

New Orleans, April 14.—We missed the train yesterday by two minutes, owing to the ferry-boat which crosses the river to the station being too late; but Mr. L——, being a director of that railroad, got us into a baggage truck of a succeeding train, in which, comfortably seated on boxes, we reached our destination. Mr. L—— carried a bag of sugar-plums for the little negroes. We saw more than fifty under ten years of age on the two plantations. The black people seemed to consider Mr. L—— more in the light of their father than their master, their black hands held out to him and Mrs. F——, without either doubt or fear, and at every corner some darky was to be met, with a request or an inquiry. We returned in the evening, after apleasant and satisfactory day, having visited two sugar estates, at a distance of from twenty to twenty-five miles from New Orleans on the Mississippi.

On board the Steamer Louisiana, bound for Texas, April 15.—Yesterday was a busy day. Before nine in the morning Mr. D—— took me a drive to dig up some roots of a pretty Iris (*Hexagona*), which I had seen flowering in one of the canals which surround the city. These canals, half natural and half artificial, are communications between the river and the lakes at the back of the city: they are called Bayous. At one o'clock I went to the apartments of some ladies in the St. Charles Hotel, from whence the British Consul accompanied us to the stand on the course, from whence we saw a race between two celebrated horses, Lexington and Leconte. A few days before, the former won a match against time, by going four miles in seven minutes and twenty seconds; he now beat his antagonist with such ease the first four-mile heat, that the owner of Leconte requested leave to withdraw his horse, and the people were disappointed of the expected second heat. I was glad, being quite content that the fine animals should be excused further contest. Though I have often been at English races, I never before saw a horse more graceful, or more beautifully formed, with such apparent gentleness and good temper, and yet with such an air of conscious superiority as this Lexington: he ran like a deer, without either effort or straining, and his firm, elastic, reaching step in walking, gave one confidence that it would hardly be possible for any other horse to match him. Yet he has four very white feet, which hitherto has been considered a bad sign; his colour a bright dark-bay, with white star on his forehead; not a very small head, but with ears well-placed; a fine large tail; not bony-looking, but I was told his backbone is remarkably large; fifteen hands three inches high; one eye full and wild, but the right eye less convex; nostrils large; jawbone uncommonly wide; shoulder strong and very oblique; he has not a long back or long legs, but his action is quite beautiful, so powerful, free and elastic, as if movement was no trouble to him. Thus, I have written you a rather groomish history. I don't know that I ever took so much pains to describe a horse before, but really this one was worth the pains. The ground was much crowded; it is a two-mile course—no, by-the-bye, the horses went three times round to make up their four miles. The situation between the New Orleans Cemeteries and Lake Pontchartrain; near, and upon the course, are some fine live oaks ornamented by the drooping Tillandsia. In the evening I went to the Opera, where I saw many Creole beauties; but the opera was a new one, which I did not admire as much as *La Reine de Chypre*. This morning at eight o'clock. Mr. G—— took me on board the Galveston steamer, *Louisiana*. The river was calm, but very muddy; it is about as wide here as the Thames at Greenwich. The town and shipping looked gay under a brilliant morning sun. I meant to send this letter from New Orleans, but forgot to do so, and now I shall try to get it off from Texas.

Yours affectionately,
A. M. M.

Extracted from an English Letter, by permission.

March, 1855.

To me much has happened, within the last few months, showing manhood and womanhood. This expedition of nurses—this woman's crusade in the service of the sufferers by war and pestilence; Florence Nightingale entreated rather than requested by the government to take the command; in one week the necessary preparations were made—Protestants, Catholics, Sectarians, all forgot their *isms*, and verified the story in *Evenings at Home*. Look at the consequences, independently of the direct object. A woman is called upon by the public to take a lead in the humane department of war, amidst difficulties and dangers which it has hitherto been thought indelicate for a woman to encounter, yet she is of the true feminine type—of a caste accustomed to the luxuries and refinements of life, not blighted by misfortune, in the vigour of youth, not exalted by party influences, for she belongs to no party. The truth has done it. Perhaps the two finest instances of heroism in the British campaign are these—the death of Sir William Young when giving the precious draught to a wounded Russian, receiving in return a mortal shot; the absolute lonelinesss of Dr. Thomson, left with hundreds of the dead and dying, and certatn to be visited by Cossacks, fulfilling his ministry, escaping then, to die a few days after of cholera; and what can surpass the exploit of the more fortunate Lieutenant Maxse, riding through a tract of country occupied by the Russians, to carry in his own breast (for writing was not safe) orders from Lord Raglan to the fleet? And the poet has mingled his breath with the cannon's roar and the last pulsation of the soldier's heart: a soldier from the ranks was heard by one near him on the battle-field, to utter with his last breath—'Footprints on the sands of time;' the soldier was from Brighton, and the writer of the account did not know the words to be Longfellow's: he had heard them quoted in a sermon of Robertson's.

ON THE DEATH OF NICHOLAS.

He fell like a column which, firm at its base,
Was unshaken a moment before,
No vestige of crumbling decay marked the place
Where it stood—the wide world looking o'er.

'Twas not for the hand of a mortal to dare
The red bolt of vengeance to grasp;
He seiz'd it unshrinking—he vow'd not to spare,
But fatal fire burn'd in that grasp.

For Power is a Nemesis, sent to destroy
The will that submits not to law:
Once more 'tis revealed! Oh, profane not with joy
What nations should witness with awe!

March, 1855.

ADDRESS TO AMERICANS OF THE UNITED STATES,

ON THEIR REPORTED WANT OF SYMPATHY.

'Am I my brother's keeper?' says the New World to the Old;
It cannot be, it cannot be! your hearts have grown so cold
That ye can hear, without one pang, the dirge across the wave
For England's bravest sons who find on Eastern shores a grave.

Has every drop of Saxon blood been chased from out your veins?
Are not *our* ancient glories *yours*, although ye scorned our chains?
Ev'n then ye proved one ancestry, a kindred bond of yore,
With those bold men of Runnymede who Freedom's charter bore.

Oh! by that name—by every field *our* noble fathers won,
Ere yet your fearless bark of faith had sought the Western sun,
Disown not now the common cause—betray it not to might,
Nor dare to raise a neutral flag when Wrong contends with Right.

A. I. N. B.

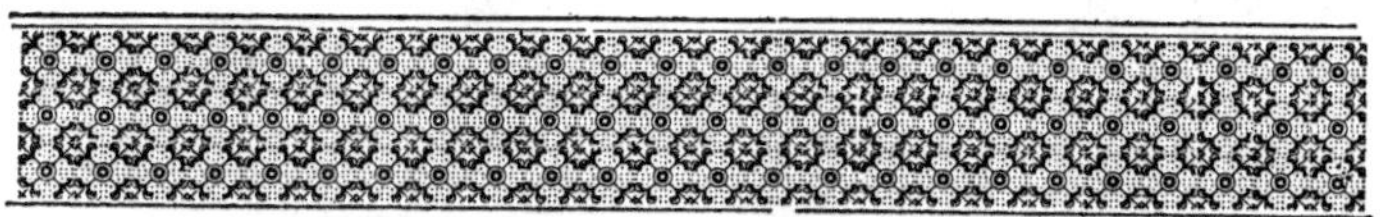

LETTER XXIII.

New Orleans.
April 6, 1855.

My dear Friends,—

At last your letters dated January have reached me; probably more will come by a steamer which I see has arrived at Boston: it is well that a treble or a double set did not come at once. Only now I am made aware, for the first time, of ——'s resignation of the editorship she volunteered. I don't think I should ever have thought of the publication if she had not proposed it, but I could not write to her what I did not see or think. I am sorry, and think she had better have trusted to my endeavour to tell the truth, which, if it is not the truth, can never hurt any cause: but the subject in question is too serious a matter to be blinked for the sake of any individual friendship or individual interest, and at any cost I must sacrifice the opinions and impressions of friends to my own honest convictions. I might hesitate or doubt, if I trusted only or wholly to my own unaided judgments and perceptions; but when these are justified by the opinions of nearly all the people who appear to me in other respects the best and wisest on this side the Atlantic—for though authority may not be much, evidence is a great deal, and I feel supported and encouraged by a hope that I may at any rate do something to counteract the evils which in my judgment have arisen out of mistaken and superficial inquiries—Northern clergymen in Florida, Scotch ministers in the North, and bishops with dioceses each as large as all England; men devoted to religion, charity, and learning—self-sacrificers, fearless, incorruptible; men who have never quailed or hesitated in the most difficult and awful paths of duty, when cholera lay on their right hand and yellow fever on their left; Bishops of Georgia and of Louisiana—Elliott, the nurse, the consoler, the comforter—walking calmly about among the pestilential corpses of thousands of his fellow-citizens—can such a man as this be blinded by interest or prejudice to say that apparent slavery is in most cases real freedom to the black man, and a severe trial of responsibility only to the white? I cannot help fearing that we have been running a tilt against civilization and the best interests of religion, whilst in our ignorance we have fancied ourselves the champions of Christendom? Some of my friends in the North say it is the abolitionists only who have sympathized with England during her late sorrows. I am glad they have felt sympathy; but I find sympathy also among the people we have ill-used and vilified, and that is even more touching and precious than the kindly feeling of those whose mistakes we haved petted and encouraged. I am afraid what I am writing will not please any of you; but do not fancy I have been hoodwinked and cheated into an advocacy of Southern institutions, when, wholly unknown and unsuspected, I have seen with my own eyes, and heard with my own ears. Of course I cannot write half the evidence I have collected; evils I do not deny; and where are they not to be found?

It is now as cold here as Christmas, and as cold as November. Many thanks for the *Multum in Parvo.* —— does not say if she undertakes the editorship which —— repudiates: if not, it must wait till I get back. I do not wish to wear out ——'s eyes or patience, but, to avoid a bad return for the hospitalities shown me, I have mentioned here the intended publication, a strong interest in the matter has been expressed, and I am assured by my American friends that they will not complain of my abusing them *a little*, because they believe that I shall not do so spitefully, which is certainly true: but I would not 'marry a slaveholder,' as —— recommends, depend upon it, if I could; a situation which involves such a trial of patience and philanthropy would be quite beyond me. I think I should turn savage myself if I was bound to be served for the rest of my life by darkies; only their childishness could induce me to bear with them. You should hear R—— illustrate the comforts of negro servants! and in my private opinion no earthly power can ever wash the blackamoor white, morally or physically; though it is possible, by great pains and perseverance, to advance them to *piebaldism*. I dare say I provoke you by repeating the same things over and over again: it is so difficult to remember what I have written.

I am going to stay for a while with the brother and sister of my American acquaintance in London: her gratitude has been so unbounded, that I believe it is that which has made me popular in the United States; we met at New York, and I hope we may meet again before I return home. I think of staying here until the weather improves: it is too cold to think of stirring yet; but I intend by-and-bye to get a peep at Tennessee and the Mammoth Cavern. This is a short letter, but it shall go by the next post.

Yours affectionately,

A. M. M.

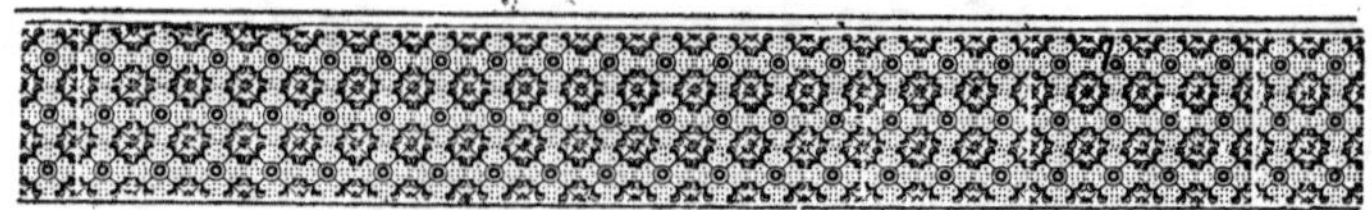

LETTER XXIV.

GALVESTON, TEXAS, U. S.,
April 17, 1855.

MY DEAR FRIENDS,—

I ought to have sent my last packet from New Orleans, instead of which, owing to hurry, I have brought it here, from whence I am afraid its despatch will be more distant and less secure. After a passage of thirty-six hours we arrived here last night. Although the weather was very fine, there was a swell of the waves, which made the majority of the passengers unhappy. R—— says she was worse than in crossing the Atlantic. I was not positively ill, but rather uncomfortable yesterday; and as I hear of a mail route from Austin, the capital of this State, *vià* Natchitoches and the Red River, I mean to return to New Orleans that way; we shall then only have three or four miles of a river steamer instead of the sea-voyage. But it has only been by falling in with a gentleman living in that territory that I have ascertained the possibility of a land journey. I was told even by Texas residents at New Orleans that there were no conveyances; but arrangements in these new countries are so rapid that circumstances one year ago may have been all changed in the last few months. As yet I have only looked out of the window of the Tremont Hotel. This seems a clean, flat, sandy place; the houses irregularly built, and all of plank, but comfortable-looking, as these wooden houses are, unless they are set on a blaze. There are many savage tribes to the north-east of this State, but the theatre of the present war between the United States and the Indians is one thousand miles off. Beyond Austin there are Comanches, Pawnees, Kesways, Cherokees, and Creeks, and towards Missouri, the Osages; but the Choctaws, which tribe borders upon the Red River and the settled lands, are the gentlest and most civilized of all these nations; so, while the other tribes are in a way to become extinct, the Choctaws keep up their numbers. They boast that they have never embrued their hands in the blood of any white man. They have comfortable houses and a settled polity—sheriffs, &c. &c.; and there is an idea of some day admitting them as a State into the Union. I saw one of them attending the educational convention at Washington in European dress, and looking like a gentleman. I should like to visit that people. On board the *Louisiana* I conversed with a military man who has been through great part of Florida. From him I learned that the river which runs up by Appalachicola is for some distance like a gulf; he does not know if it is lost in the swamps by Alligator Swamp towards the Altamaha and Savannah rivers, but that is probably the case; and after seeing the narrow channels which divide some of the islands south of Florida, it is easy to believe that it also was once separated from the mainland.

The distance from hence to New Orleans by sea is about four hundred miles. Galveston is an island. I have just returned from a drive along some fine sands which extend for miles upon the flat shore, where there must be excellent bathing. The population of the town appears to be a mixture of Germans, Dutch, French, English, and Americans. Almost all the tradespeople I spoke to were of the first-mentioned nation. I was surprised to see such a number of hairdressers in proportion to the size of the place: there are three within a stone's-throw of our hotel,—'Hyppolite and Batiste,' from Paris! where hair is 'instantly dyed,' and wigs, toupets, and fronts are well made, &c., &c. Artificial proceedings for outward adornment which are now little practised in France and England, appear to have emigrated to this side the Atlantic.

Washington, Texas, April 19.—We left Galveston in the

Houston steamer at four o'clock, to go fifty miles up the bay and forty miles up the bayou to Houston. These bayous are very curious. I observed one of them at New Orleans, but not having ascended it in a boat, I was not fully, aware what odd sea-ditches they are. They must be peculiar to this coast—I never heard of them elsewhere—and I imagine their navigation is one of the most singular in the world. It was a bright starlight night when we ascended that which leads from Galveston Bay inland. I sat upon the prow of the vessel, with another lady, from eight o'clock till midnight, too much interested to think of either fatigue or damp. Our steamer, near two hundred feet long, was navigated the whole way through a channel hardly more than eighty feet wide, though deep enough to float a man-of-war. Negroes holding braziers of blazing pine-wood, stood on each side the vessel, illuminating our passage, the foliage and even the beautiful flowers so near that we could almost gather them as we floated by; a small bell was ringing every instant, to direct our engineers; one moment the larboard paddle, then the starboard, was stopped or set in motion, or the wheels were altogether standing still, while we swung round the narrow corners of this tortuous channnel; the silence of the bordering forests broken alone by the sobs of our high-pressure engine, which is less expensive in construction, and enables a vessel to draw less water than a low pressure. Now and then a night bird, or frog croaking with a voice like that of a watchman's rattle, accompanied the bells and the escape valve. But human voices were awed into silence during our solemn progress, which seemed to me to belong neither to the sea nor the earth—it was, indeed, a kind of amphibious proceeding. A downward steamer once passed us: I was glad we did not meet at one of the narrowest places, for there, I believe, they sometimes edge by one another, absolutely touching; but this navigation, however extraordinary, is considered peculiarly safe. The depth of water being so great and so still, it is difficult to understand how these bayous have been formed. They are deep trenches running up into the interior—Nature's canals—no streams come in at the termination, and the water is always salt or brackish. In two or three hours after our arrival at Houston, we were obliged to get into the mail for this place; so, coming in the dark and setting out before daylight, I know little of Houston. It is said to be pretty, but must be flat, for soon after leaving it we entered upon prairies which extended for fifty miles; fine grass and beautiful flowers, fertile though sandy plains. Once or twice, when we stopped to water the horses, I got out for a few minutes, and while the rest of the party dined, I rushed back to gather what I could; but it was very tantalizing to me to pass all kinds of new plants without being able to possess myself of them. In the few opportunities afforded me, I got about twenty: one or two of genera, and the others of species, either unknown or little known in our gardens.

It was ten o'clock last night before we reached Washington: the driver declared we must start again at three this morning, so I rebelled, and have let the mail proceed to Austn without us. I must give up that capital, however picturesque the scenery may be and content myself with visiting General Samuel Houston, at Independence, twelve miles farther than this place, and then turn back towards the Red River. It is useless to run through a greater extent of country without pausing long enough to see it; and we must be back at New Orleans by the end of the month. The route here from the sea-shore is very thinly peopled—no towns, no villages; and only an occasional settlement here and there, mostly Dutch. After leaving the prairies we came to a very pretty district, resembling English park scenery; fine scattered trees and woods with the brightest and most luxuriant verdure I have seen in America. At times the oaks and the sand reminded me of Kent; but these oaks are not the same species as ours, yet are the Texans fine trees. The dwarf 'Black Jack' is abundant all about. We passed the Brazo River in a ferry-boat, left for the convenience of the public, without a ferryman. It was large enough to admit the coach and four horses, with the passengers, who got out, and a rope guided the whole across a quiet narrow river. During our passage the planet Venus appeared to hang like a diamond upon one of the horns of a young moon. They remained for a while in close proximity, but I do not believe they ever quite performed an eclipse. I think the planet appeared for some time in conjunction, hanging like a diamond on one of the moon's horns, which afterwards passed above, or Venus went below, whichever it might be. A fancy crossed my mind that this was a good omen, beautifully emblematic of the Star of Christianity, touching and rising over the Mahometan Crescent; but I was obliged to get into the carriage, and I could not then see the finale; both had set before we reached Washington. As we came along, one of the gentleman passengers, at my request, caught a singular little reptile for me, which is here called the horned frog, but it has a tail, and is not more like a frog than the gelsemine is like jessamine. I shall try to reconcile it to live and become my fellow-traveller.

Since I wrote the above, I have been spending two days at a small town called Independence, and there a boy gave me another of these creatures, which will be a companion to the first; and I hope to get them safely to England, an offering to Mr. Owen. Yesterday they both eloped from a tin box; so as nothing in the shape of a cage could be procured, I went to a store, bought a large metal sieve, and persuaded a carpenter to let it into a circular piece of wood, grandly enough made of the cedar, which is used for common purposes in this country: the carpenter's shop was perfumed by its shavings. The sieve, with the sand at the bottom, is an airy and pleasant abode for my prisoners; and I can watch their evolutions without difficulty; they seem gentle, harmless little things, and being crustaceous, and not slippery-feeling, I have no objection to them. Their appearance is most antediluvian, with their fringes and horns, and birdy-expression of countenance.

I spent two pleasant days at Independence, where I boarded R—— and myself in the clean, though simple abode of a Mr. and Mrs. Holmes; he is building a house, in which he means to receive boarders and travellers. In the meanwhile (although Mrs. Holmes was occupied with an infant only a fortnight old) he gave up his own parlour—a canvas and boarded room, covered by a nice clean mat with a door opening at once upon the high road; a couch for my bed, and muslin curtains—half crimson, half white—across the windows. This room was quite free from the odour of tobacco, and very neat.

I called upon Mrs. Houston, and found that the General is absent at Huntsville; but I was invited to take tea, and I spent the greater part of my time with Mrs. Houston and her pleasant family-party; she was so kind as to lend me an excellent horse, by which means I saw much of the neighbourhood; and this morning I rode twelve miles across the Awah River and swamp, to seek for a fossilized forest and for flowers. A gentleman accompanied me who was an excellent backwoodsman and guide. We crossed the swamp and river, which would have been impassable during a less dry season; and before long we saw a wolf, and a singular bird, called a water-turkey; it has a head and form resembling that bird, but it has also web feet, and such a power of remaining under water that it will dive for ten minutes at a time. We soon came to the petrified forest, which is said to be ten miles in extent. I found fine specimens of fossil-wood, whole trunks of trees, and large branches. The weight of a bullock-wagon passing along a track, had crushed one of these fossil trees, and I gathered up some specimens. All these stone trunks lie prostrate. Further on, three mocassin snakes lay basking upon some mud in the channel of a small river, below our path; they looked venomous, though inert; and I felt glad to be fairly out of their way. A pretty small pair of deer's horns had been dropped near a bush, and I persuaded my guide to pick them up, but he having no great liking for unnecessary trouble, hung them upon a tree, with an assurance that we must pass the same way in returning; but he forgot this, and returned a mile to the right, so I lost them after all. Though the weather was sultry, and our ride tiring for the horses, they would not touch water at any of the lesser streams we crossed because (Mr. D——— said) wild beasts, such as panthers, wolves, and bears, had drunk there. We saw the tracks of such animals, but there is no danger of meeting them, as they take care to get out of your way. The only beings who crossed our path during this long ride were a gentlemanly-looking boy, about twelve years old, accompanied by two negroes, all on horseback; they were seeking horses which had strayed in the forest. We went as far as some ancient Indian mounds; and I found Phlox Drummondi, indigenous, upon a small sandy prairie; in colour a dark ruby, very beautiful; each plant was a small annual, not more than half a foot high, yet I conclude it is the original of all ours. We got back safely to Independence by three o'clock, having been on horseback since five in the morning, but I had been too well amused to think about fatigue.

Huntsville, April 22.—This is a pretty scattered town. We left Independence yesterday evening, slept at Washington, and came on in the mail at three o'clock this morning. The Brazo was again to be crossed in a ferry-boat. A mile from thence one of the horses became ill, but after laying down almost immovable for a quarter of an hour, he got up and went twelve miles without any apparent difficulty. About half way we met General Houston on horseback, attended by his negro groom. Nearly all the country between Washington and this place is fine rich prairie land, interspersed with picturesque oaks; it resembles Somersetshire, Kent, and Windsor Forest by turns; the grass abundant, and beautifully green. We saw some deer; and, at one place in the water again, two of those poisonous mocassin snakes; I also heard of bears and panthers, and of a black snake, a kind of boa, ten feet long, which moves with great rapidity, and throws itself upon deer and cattle, and has been known (though rarely) to follow and attack people. We reached this place just before sunset. At a small log-house, in a lonely situation, a ladylike woman and her child, a girl about ten years old, got into the carriage. We were surprised to learn that, in the abscence of her son of seventeen, for college attendance, this lady lived entirely alone with her daughter; she had learned to fire off a gun, in case of emergency, but she confesses that the alarm and uneasinees consequent upon her lonely life is more than she can bear much longer. The roads here are by no means bad; we had a very comfortable coach, well-horsed, and well-driven, and there is really no difficulty whatever, except fatigue, in traversing this part of the country.

Crocket, Texas, April 24.—We left Huntsville by half-past six yesterday morning, and arrived here by moonlight early in the evening. With the exception of scenery at Trinity River (which we crossed, as usual, in a large ferry boat), the drive to-day (through deep sand, and in swampy places upon shifting corduroy roads) was monotonous and uninteresting: we had three companions in the mail, rough-looking, but courteous, well-informed men; all of them Texan agriculturists; one had served in Florida in the Seminole war, and had lived much among the Indians: another, a bright-looking young man, was returning to his farm and a father eighty years old, after two years' wandering upon the frontier line of Mexico, hunting and shooting. He had been among companions who could not persuade him to accompany them to California; but he said a wild life had great charms for him, and that he should find it difficult to settle down at home. He thinks Texas the finest State in the Union, as it is the largest in point of extent; and that railroads and more people are all it wants. We passed many cotton plantations during our journey to-day, and large numbers of cattle, apparently of the Holderness or the Durham breed. Dairies are little thought about; it is cultivating beef, and oxen for draught, which is the object, not milk, cream, or butter. One hardly ever sees cream in America—never in this State. Upon arriving at an hotel, or rather tavern, in Texas, one is shown into a room where the mistress (usually very young) acknowledges the arrival of visitors, and offers a chair; but it would be quite beneath her dignity to go with you to your room, or even to see that you have necessary comforts; she 'will desire the servants to attend.' After a while a negro girl, or perhaps two or three, will show you a bed-chamber, and hang about to watch you and your packages; and it is usually necessary to scold or speak sharply before they will bestir themselves to 'fix the chamber;' and if you are not careful to put your things out of the reach of curiosity, a bevy will assemble as soon as your back is turned, to amuse themselves with your cap, bonnet, or perhaps your combs and brushes. The 'lady' sits at the head of the table at tea or supper, but it seems quite an offence if you suppose she knows anything about the bill, or even respecting modes of travelling or distances: to any such inquiries she will say that 'You must ask at the office,' or 'Inquire of Mr. So-and-so—she knows nothing of such things.' So, though the blacks make good servants if they are strictly disciplined and well watched, yet at these hotels they are careless and troublesome beyond measure. Twice during this tour, when the night departure of the mails allowed passengers but an hour or two of rest, I was just asleep, when a black woman would come screaming at the doors waking me, saying she wanted to come in to 'find the blacking-brush which is left under your bed, missus,' or to 'look for a quilt,' probably to use as a table-cloth, or it may be only an excuse to gain entrance. I positively refuse to let them in, but then I am completely aroused, and there is small chance of sleep afterwards.

April 27.—On board the *Rapid* steamer, Red River, Alexandria.—After our long fatiguing journey, we are fortunate in getting accommodation in this comfortable steamer, which will take us down the Red River to the Mississippi, and so back to New Orleans.

Alexandria, Monday morning.—I go back to say that we arrived at this place by moonlight, after four days and nights' hard travelling, but in coaches so good and so well appointed that, although the roads were very rough and dusty, we had no cause to be frightened, except in passing the loose plank bridges, most of them with no pretence of a rail to prevent vehicles and horses from going over the sides; but we were assured that accidents are of rare occurrence, and these coaches have such fine horses, and such admirable drivers, that I never travelled at night with such confidence as through the wild forests and natural roads of Texas. As yet there is no other road-making than cutting down trees actually in the way, the stumps of which are often left a foot high, to be shunned by the driver and horses, who learn from experience how to avoid them even in the dark.

After Crocket, we left the more open country; but all the way to Huntsville the soil is a red sand, with rolling hills covered by rich forests, but the timber is not so thickly set as to be drawn up without leaves or branches; and we only occasionally passed through a pine barren. Natchitoches is a very pretty town; the houses with nice gardens, and the drive through open woods, containing a great variety of trees, for some miles along a raised terrace, from which one sees a fine hilly country in every direction, is very interesting, until you come to that which my fellow-travellers informed me was the most beautiful twenty miles of all, and then I was rather disappointed to find that its beauty consisted only in rich land, and fertile cotton, sugar, and maize fields.

Upon reaching a bayou which falls into the Red River, we drove along the shore of its muddy slow stream—at present so low from the long drought, that it is like a great ugly ditch, with snake fences and acres of red flat fields on our left. I thought of the American who considered Salisbury Plain the most lovely district in England. Part of the former picturesque tract is dotted by cotton plantations and comfortable-looking abodes. We saw occasionally gangs of people at work in the fields, under a driver, but all seemed contented and merry. I pitied the overseer, who sat idle upon his horse, and thought I should prefer being one of the labourers. The black women generally dislike being taken as house-servants; they prefer the work and the more general society of the fields. We saw two mocassin snakes in the water—one large snake, which is only accused of eating up chickens, and another big enough to be a boa.

Several rivers were crossed during the day: Angelina, Black River, and Bayou Sabine. This would be a very favourable path for emigrants into Texas, as a hilly country is less liable to fevers, and the people would be more easily acclimated. A Mr. Hall, at New Orleans, is spoken of as an excellent adviser for new settlers. Such adventurers should arrive before December, come straight up the Red River from the Mississippi as far as Alexandria, from whence they would easily reach a favourable locality. A party of thirty emigrants, who could purchase about three hundred acres of ready cleared land for about 60*l.*, and divide it among them, would have a much better chance of immediate comfort and prosperity than any one individual taking the whole quantity; and if there is a carpenter among them, he would be the most successful of all. I should much prefer settling in Texas to any other part of the Union I have seen, unless it was the Highlands of Virginia. There is certainly more chance of fevers in the South; but if people come in the early part of the winter, and are not imprudent, they will be tolerably safe. Game abounds here, and fish in all the streams.

I have at last ascertained what is meant by the Chinquapin— a nut which has been frequently mentioned, but till now I could never fit any tree to the name. It looks like a chestnut of a small delicate kind. I have discovered that it is the Castanea pumila. In a rich prairie, some miles beyond Independence, beyond the district called Atewa, I found a beautiful Phlox, of a rich velvety crimson. It may be that one described in Darby's *Botany of the Southern States* as 'pilosa,' or the original Drummondi, but I should call it crimson, not purple. It appears to be confined to the locality above named. I have not seen or heard of it anywhere else. A few miles south of Independence, a beautiful bright sky-blue Ixia-looking flower, unlike any Sisyrinchium I ever saw, though I think it must be one. Texas can hardly yet have been thoroughly botanized, so that it is not impossible for me to fall in with new plants. I brought the two little Crustaceans on my lap all the way from Washington. They appear in good health, and tolerably well content with their sieve. I think that they must be examples in the reptile creation (as the family of Alligator Gars are among the fishes) of forms which are generally by-gone. They occasionally accept a fly as food, and I am told they will eat ants and ant-eggs, but, like tortoises, they seem very independent of meals, and quite as well content without as with them. Fear does not appear to seem a trait in their character. They do not try to escape from my hands, or to suffer from being taken hold of. Their little horns and bony excrescences are, I suppose, considered sufficient defence. They are the gentlest and least aggressive creatures I ever met with.

We are hospitably sheltered on board the *Rapid*, but she has engagements which will detain her here till to-morrow morning, so I must be content in the meanwhile to make acquaintance with mocking-birds, 'whip-poor-wills,' alligators and fireflies, all of which abound on the Red River; and I have also found one or two more flowers new to me, by walking on shore this afternoon. On the shore, too, I saw trails of snakes across a sandy path. One must have been very large; but as we kept the road we were not afraid, for these reptiles generally get out of the way of intruders.

April 28.—We began moving down the Red River, towards the Mississippi. The two days before, our steamer was occupied taking in freight—cotton, sugar, and molasses—and a large portion was put into a barge attached to the *Rapid*, to prevent her drawing too much water in passing a shallow. When that was accomplished, the additional cargo was shipped, and the barge left behind. Alligators were plentiful along the shore to-day; pretty white cranes and occasional water-turkeys accompanied our passage. A gentleman on board described a bird he had shot in the neighbourhood of Red River, which must resemble the Apteryx from Australia, to be seen in the Regent's Park Zoological Gardens, except that it is smaller.

Before the junction with the Mississippi, the Red River opens out into what is called Old River, because it is believed to be an ancient bed of the Mississippi. We have now got into the main channel of the latter stream; but its shores have not yet become flat and uninteresting, for we are still in the rolling country of red sand, from which the Red River derives its appellation and muddy complexion.

April 30.—Just arrived by five o'clock at New Orleans, after a quiet and pleasant voyage. Nothing remarkable yesterday, except the town of Baton Rouge, which is prettily situated on the banks of the river. It boasts of the State-house and a fort, and is considered the capital of Louisiana. I observe that the local governments generally hold their sittings at those places which in point of size are third-rate. There is a certain jealousy of influence of large cities, which prevents them from being selected for legislative meetings. The Mississippi banks are much prettier about a hundred miles above New Orleans, where the chalky formation, which follows the alluvial, and precedes the red sandstone rocks in all the Southern States and in Cuba, begins to rise above flat plantations of cotton, maize, and sugar.

After leaving the Red Banks, I saw no more alligators, though I believe they are occasionally to be found below. We have been fortunate in a bright moon, which has almost turned night into day. I have seen no fossils either before or after the red sand in Texas or Louisiana, but I daresay there may be some, as I have before found plenty of nummulites, echini, pectens, &c. I suppose all these formations are what the geologists call Eocene. I should like to speak of new chalk as distinguished from old chalk, for it seems pretty clear that they are made much after the same fashion, only the chalk of England is an elder brother, and has black flints and different fossils from the younger one, whose flints are brown; but I suppose this proposition is very ungeological. A gentleman here has given me specimens found in sinking the Artesian well in New Orleans; and though it has been sunk nearly two hundred feet, still it produces only sea-sand, and broken or unbroken shells. The Mississippi appears to have travelled about a good deal in his time, and I should not wonder if some day he should take a fancy to join Lake Pontchartrain, and perhaps he may move across the city of New Orleans. I have seldom time to read over what I write, and therefore my letters may contain repetitions; if so, you must excuse them. All I saw of Slavery in Texas confirms previous conclusions. Workmen are so much wanted in that fine country, that it would seem impossible to abolish slave-labour, at any rate for many years to come: perhaps some Africans might be benefited and improved by being brought there. The old settled States are naturally unwilling to be troubled with fresh importations; but I think Texan agriculturists might be willing to take charge of them. It seems to me that kind and good people I have known do not yet understand the real bearings of this Slavery question. I daresay in former times there were more abuses than at present: it is the slaveholders who come from the North who prove the least patient and most severe masters; so I suppose abolitionists judge by what they know of them: of course there are much stronger ties of affection between masters and servants who have been born and bred together, than between those whose immediate tie has been only a pecuniary one. I must copy a letter which has been lent to me by a gentleman here, in answer to some inquiries addressed to sisters by cousins in London, after the perusal of Mrs. Stowe's novel.

It is well written, and embodies the opinions and feelings of the great mass of masters and mistresses in the Slave States of America.

'My dear Cousins,—

'We render justice to the benevolent and philanthropic notions which have led you to write to us in deprecation of Slavery; and though our lot, like the Patriarchs of old, is cast in a land of bond and free, we believe we may venture to assure you, that our human feelings and Christian sympathies have not been weakened or put aside. We must, however, express our surprise that you, and your sober-minded, cool-judging country people, should have allowed yourselves to have been so much excited by a work of fiction, however skilfully wrought out, and that you should have been led to regard it as a true picture of negro life in America. We have never either seen or heard of any such scenes as are depicted in the romance you refer to. How can we believe that such black saints and white demons have ever had existence, except in the excited imagination of the authoress of *Uncle Tom?* Slave-trading and slave-dealers are regarded with as much disgust here as with you, and as to the rupture of the marriage tie, to which you allude, it is the result (when it occasionally happens) of misfortune to the owner, or of crime in the slave; and in your country, separations of families are caused in a similar way. It is the exception, not the rule. We have read of such things in England, as men selling their wives in a public market, with halters about their necks; but surely it would not be just to charge such revolting practices upon the English nation. So far as we have had an opportunity of judging, there is much less, rather than more, misery and distress among our slaves than among your labourers: they are generally well-treated, happy, and content; and certainly self-interest, if no other motive, must induce their owners to treat them well. Religion is cultivated among them, and in our Sunday-schools classes of black children under a white teacher are common. In fact, one of us offered once to take such a class; but the superintendent deemed her services more useful to the class she then had under instruction. Indeed, our sympathies are much more frequently and painfully excited by the misery we witness among the poor, ignorant, destitute emigrants who come to our shores from Europe; many of them (it is said) shipped off by Union Workhouses to avoid the expense of their maintenance.

'You must bear in mind, dear Cousins, that this Institution of Slavery was left to us by our fathers, and that England introduced it. One of the grievances charged upon her in the first Draft of the Declaration of Independence was this very institution; and Great Britain only followed (after many years) the early act of our Government prohibiting the Slave-trade. At the period of the Revolution, Slavery prevailed in nearly all the States of the Union: in a few years it was abolished by seven of them, and but for the ill-judged agitation of the North, it would ere this have been done away with in Maryland, Virginia, and Kentucky; and in view of these facts, may not the subject of emancipation be safely trusted to the moral feelings and intelligence of those whose business and duty it is to deal with it? The evil (if evil it is) is so engrafted upon our social system, that to get rid of it without producing greater evil, which would affect the servant even more than the master, the cure must be worked out cautiously and gradually.

'Emancipation is not always a boon, even to the robust and able slave; but it would be a curse to the aged and infirm, and to the helpless children. At the cost of twenty millions sterling you have brought ruin and ultimate desolation upon your West Indian Colonies: they stand as a warning rather than an example to our country. We are under the guidance and protection of Divine Providence; and the way in which, by his infinite power and goodness, great ends are attained, is generally beyond our finite comprehension;—for ourselves, we are willing to believe that this apparent evil of Slavery is a means conducive to a great and merciful end. Compare the Christianized and civilized American negro, with the brutal, idolatrous, polygamist African nations, and you will find the former advanced far above the latter in the scale of humanity.

'Our countrymen are civilizing and Christianizing three or four millions of negroes, who will eventually return to Africa to civilize and Christianize the whole negro race. Is not this a great and good result, and will not the end sanctify the means?'

The letter further dwells upon the mischief which is done by an ill-judging interference, and concludes by reminding us that we have social evils of our own to attend to and to cure.

New Orleans, May 1.—I returned here to breakfast yesterday; and in the evening Mr. and Mrs. G—— took me to see the garden belonging to a railroad station at six miles' distance. There I saw a very pretty Peruvian shrub, with lilac flowers, which the Irish gardener called 'Darbyana integrifolia.' I cannot say if the name is a legitimate one, because he appeared very hap-hazard in his nomenclature; and as there are few people to interfere with it, I suspect he sometimes invents an appellation when he is doubtful about one. Roses, Oleanders, and Honeysuckles bloom here with a brilliancy and in an abundance beyond anything I ever beheld in Europe; and last night the fireflies, sparkling in every direction as we returned home, were very pretty. They are brighter than our glow-worm; but as their wings are opaque, they shine only in flying, and their flights are so transient, that they appear and vanish just like sparks, but the light resembles the light from diamonds rather than sparks of fire. I am told they are still more numerous after rain; but the mosquitoes increase also—therefore I should not wish to double the number of either.

There have been some serious burglaries and robberies lately in New Orleans. A black man entered a house not far from this a few nights ago; being disturbed, he attempted to leap from the window; a gentleman within seized his hand, and tried to detain him in a hanging position, until assistance came. With the arm left at liberty, the robber drew out a revolver and shot his captor, who was obliged to let him go. The wounded man is recovering, but a bullet in his face is yet unextracted.

Although this robber was a black man, the police in England and France being now so well organized, it is believed that many of the more desperate characters have taken refuge in the United States; either this, or the want of a strong detective force, has caused a great increase of criminal acts in America.

On Thursday, the 4th, I propose to leave this place for Mobile; then to proceed, *viâ* the Tensaw River, by Montgomery and Atlanta, to see the Stone Mountain of Georgia, and Chatanooga, in my way to Nashville and the Mammoth Cave.

Great anxiety is expressed here for rain; the drought has now been of long continuance, for the single day's rain which accompanied a thunderstorm on the 4th seems to have been very partial, and almost confined to New Orleans. The cotton growers begin to despair, and all the crops are suffering so much, that a famine is predicted if relief does not come soon; and, as the houses here look to their great tuns or cisterns of rainwater for their principal supply, the absence of wet weather is a great distress to New Orleans; besides which, steamers also are delayed or stopped by want of water in rivers tributary to the Mississippi.

May 2.—There was a total eclipse of the moon last night, finer than anything of the kind I ever saw before. The obscuration began from the southern limb soon after eight o'clock, and the moon was not bright again till midnight; for one hour and forty-eight minutes she looked like a dark orange, much smaller than usual; but she was visible throughout, except after she began to brighten up again, when a few clouds passed over, and rendered her invisible for a short time. The wise and anxious hope for rain after this event. My horned frogs (for so I must call them till a better name is provided) excite great interest; although they are not entirely unknown to people here, nobody can say whether any living specimens have been sent to England. I wished to show them to Dr. Riddell, but he is gone up to Chatawa with his family, and he is not likely to return till after my departure. A heavy shower of rain has fallen this afternoon, and it is hoped that more will follow. An opportunity occurring, I shall close this letter, and probably not forward another packet till I reach Cincinnati or Indianapolis.

Yours affectionately,

A. M. M.

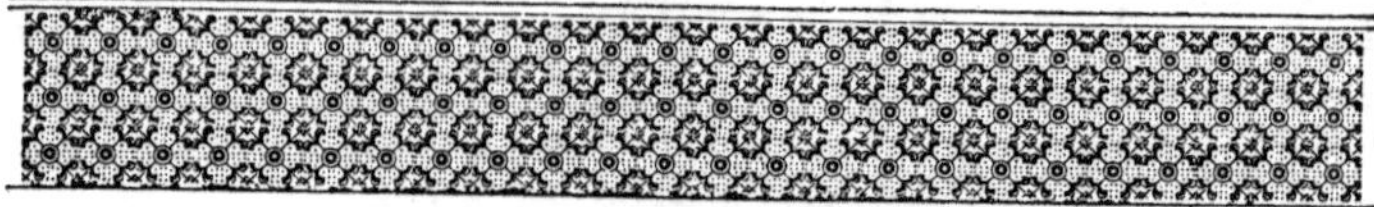

LETTER XXV.

ATLANTA, ALABAMA, U. S.,
May 7, 1855.

MY DEAR FRIENDS,—

After five days' hard travelling, we got here this evening—I should say five days and three nights; for with the exception of one night's rest at Mobile, and one (till five this morning) at Montgomery, since leaving New Orleans, on Thursday last, we have never paused an hour anywhere. Night-work is the only serious obstacle to journeying in America: it is very fatiguing, and where there is a pretty country to pass through, very disappointing to strangers; both in Texas and Alabama this evil at present is incorrigible; because, through wide districts, there are no places to pause at, and the mail being the only means of conveyance, of course it cannot be detained for any one. I might have attempted to get up the Alabama River from Mobile, but the water being low, there was considerable risk of grounding for some days upon sandbanks; besides which, I see more of the country and of the vegetation by coach-travelling; and although it is often very tantalizing to pass by trees, and shrubs, and flowers, either new or rare, without being able to get at them, still it is something to observe the botanical features of a district; and by taking every opportunity, during a change of horses or a stop for meals, I have secured several interesting specimens, and sometimes get a sketch. From New Orleans a steamer brought us in about fourteen hours to Mobile: that town is prettily situated along the bay; it seems a pleasant place of residence, with a hotel (Battle House), the best managed I have met with in the United States; for usually, with a great deal of show, these places are conducted upon so little system, and with so little real comfort, that I much prefer European inns to the most gorgeous American hotels; and in point of expense, the latter equal, if they do not exceed, the former. Government-street in Mobile is also the handsomest street I have seen anywhere: it consists of detached houses with gardens; some have the usual fault in this country of being whitened to a dazzling and unnatural whiteness; but a custom-house is in process of erection, with granite of a soft grey colour, and it seems likely to be an example of good architecture, as well as of pleasing tint. An agreeable family (to whom I was introduced by my friend Mr. W——, of Baltimore) made me profit as much as possible by the few hours I was able to stay at Mobile: they chose a pretty drive, and I was enabled to visit the first interesting nursery-garden I have met with; there I saw Cactus triangularis, with hanging roots. I was told that a gentleman at Cincinnati had the best collection of cacti.* Next day, Saturday, a steamer received us on board, and leaving Mobile Bay, we went up the river Tensaw, a stream beautiful as the Altamaha, and bordered by woods far exceeding those of Georgia: live oaks, catalpas, magnolias (as large as elms), just come into blow; the macrophylla with its flower still sweeter and more splendid than the grandiflora, melias, gleditzchias, cedars, sweet and black gum-trees, &c., with huge alligators occasionally basking beneath these verdant shores, and elegant birds flying above them.

At Stockport we found two roomy four-horse coaches waiting for passengers: five gentlemen, R——, and I took possession of one intended to hold nine inside, which would have been close packing; so we were fortunate in not being quite as much cramped as we might have been. Nearly the whole two hundred miles to this place is deep sand, varying from white to red; at first,

* Since destroyed by fire.

through pine barrens like those of Florida, only covering a rolling country instead of a flat one; but within fifty miles of Montgomery the forest becomes as various, and as rich, and as hilly, as that of the eastern part of Texas, and much resembling it in character and in soil—a red iron-sand. At one of the little post-houses I got a nodule of iron ore, which they said was plentiful in the neighbourhood. By midnight we arrived at Montgomery, a clean-looking, gas-lit town, of which I could not see a great deal, for it was necessary to be in the railroad cars by six the next morning. A short distance from Montgomery the line was bordered on each side by hedges of Cherokee roses, vivid evergreens with single white blossoms, and the foliage so thick that it is said not even a snake can get through it: then we went by the prettiest scenery of all—passing the rivers Coosa and Tallapoosa, and near the spot where General Jackson fought his 'Battle of the Horseshoe' with the Cherokees and Choctaws. One of my poor little horny, crusty reptiles is dead, in spite of all the care I could bestow upon him. I fear the other will not survive the long journey in prospect; perhaps it would be better that these creatures should travel at the usual season of their torpidity; now, the sun makes them too much inclined for an active life, and they evidently think it necessary to eat flies, whereas, in the winter season, that would not be requisite.

To-morrow, I am going some miles out of my route to see what is called the Stone Mountain of Georgia. Atlanta (so spelled here) is a town about eight years old, though there was a settlement and two or three houses as much as fifteen years ago. During my last passage in the steamer from Mobile, a black woman came and sat down by me in the stern of the vessel. From what we hear in England, I imagined negroes were kept at a distance. That is the case in the Northern States, but in the South they are at your elbow everywhere, and always seek conversation. This was an old nurse, an aunty, or mammy, as they are sometimes called (all ancient women of the darky kind here are addressed as aunties). She was very communicative, told me she had a young mistress in Texas (sisters have sometimes a common property in slaves left by their parents); that she was very fond of this master and mistress, and she ran on as follows—'But there 'tis hard to be divided from t'other; but then people must have their 'flictions in this world. When I was a young girl, there, I used sometimes to fancy 'twould be a fine thing to be free; but, there, I don't now think 'twould be mighty fine at all; there, I have everything I want in the wide world, 'cept jewellery, and that I don't want at all now, and, there (some of the coloured people have such a lot of jewellery you can't think); I say, Cissy, now (addressing one of her charges) don't go for to tumble over there; now if you gets into the water, we sha'n't have you a bit more, and then your poor old aunty will die of it—that she will—and won't see her no more. I say, missus, I don't let master keep my children up o' nights as some of their papas and mammas do: I says, 'Master, it sha'n't be, it sha'n't—it isn't fit for they little ones as ought to be in their beds;' and so my children have got colours in their faces, that they does.' I asked her what she thought of slaves being free here: her reply was, 'I say, missus, it does 'em no good, nor any one else. If people has a fancy to make 'em free, send 'em to Africa, the place they comed from, I say. Why, missus, these free niggers are half their time bad niggers; and they does insult they niggers as keeps to their own masters and mistresses, and are mighty better and happier too, and that makes 'em mad to see. It is not right, missus, by the 'spectable slaves to have them there free niggers, with their jewellery, and their flowers, and their 'bacco, and their drink, idling about saucy and idle, it gives the dark people a bad 'kracter; and I say, missus, it isn't right. Send 'em away, I say, and then they may go and sit in the sun and do nothing, just as the half of them do.' So she ran on in a stream of talk, all much to the same purpose. One question to set these people off is generally enough to have the benefit of all their thoughts; but it is better to keep one's own opinions in the background, for they are so imitative, they will often reflect you if they can. The day before yesterday, I heard of an intelligent negro just freed by his master, after thirty-six years' good service. He was fifteen when brought over, remembered his native tongue, and intends to return to Africa. He strongly expresses his gratitude for having been brought over to America, and says, 'Master, don't you let white masters and mistresses hurt the Slavery Institution. I say, Master, it be *Good* Almighty's school for the coloured people it be, that He have made. Why, Massa, what would such a man as me have been without the slave merchant? How should me have got a bit of education as me have? And now go and try to give a bit to the race out there, who would a bring us over? I say, Master, we should ha' been worse than slaves, but for the Slavery Institution that brought us here to know how to work, and to hear about the good Almighty, and to know about what we should never have known in our own country. No, Massa, don't hurt the Slave Institution.' What would Mrs. Stowe say to this Uncle Tom? for he is the nearest to Uncle Tom of any negro I have heard of, and he will make a capital African missionary.

Chattanooga, May 9.—The day before yesterday I went sixteen miles on the Augusta railroad to see the 'Stone Mountain,' which was in all respects more singular and curious than I expected. There is a comfortable little hotel in the small village called from the hill 'Stone Mountain.' * Mr. Clarke, the intelligent master, was so obliging as to drive me himself in a little wagon to that side from which the most interesting view is to be obtained. You must imagine an enormous granite bolster laid upon a deep valley, coming as straight as the side of a house down eleven hundred feet, then rounded towards the top five hundred feet more, smooth, and without vegetation, excepting at one spot towards the western summit, where numbers of grey eagles are to be seen. Granite pillars a quarter of a mile long could be hewn from its perpendicular sides. It is said to be legitimate granite, with brilliant brownish-looking mica in it; but I have got specimens for geologists to decide upon. It is externally a dark grey colour. I crossed a small stream to the foot of the precipice. I know none, not even the Martenswald of the

* Burned to the ground the night after I was there.

Tyrol, so gigantic—I should think that eagles alone could surmount it. A plummet, with the rope eleven hundred feet in length, has been dropped in a straight line from above the spot I stood upon, which resembled a beautiful English rock garden, bounded by fine trees, with thickets of Kalmia latifola in full bloom on one side, the mountain wall on the other. After passing a stream and rising an eminence in a wood full of scarlet and pink Azaleas, I came to acres of tabular granite, from whence I attempted a sketch of the gigantic stony pillar before me. A photograph might give a true picture, but any pencil must be incompetent. I found Asplenium alpinum in fissures at the base of the precipice, but no other vegetation. The flowering shrubs are plentiful around, but I saw few smaller plants in blow; and my guide told me the earlier months in spring are most favourable here for such things. He was the first American I have met with (except Botanical Professors) who takes an interest in flowers. He gathered a large bouquet of Azaleas, Kalmias, Vaccinniums, &c., and thanked me for having been the means of bringing him to the rock garden, which he had never visited before when the Kalmias were in bloom; though he had a great pleasure (he said) in wandering alone about the mountain; 'but then I could never have persuaded my ladies to come to such a place as this.' We had to scramble across a stream and over the rocks, certainly; but I would have walked barefoot through the waters rather than have missed the scene. I do not wonder that American ladies in the mass look dispirited and 'sick' (the word generally used in the United States for ill), they take so little exercise, and lose the best enjoyments of life in their neglect of natural beauty for artificial pleasures; and no wonder they are victims of consumption and *ennui*. I returned to the hotel for dinner and an hour's rest, then took a young negro boy for my guide, and walked half way up the mountain, so as to sketch it from near the eagle's 'cairn' (as it would be called in Scotland). The descent was hot and fatiguing, but I got back in good time for the half-past four o'clock train, and our obliging landlord went to Atlanta by the same cars, and took great charge of me.

He expressed a strong wish to visit England, and it would give me pleasure to pay him any attention there in return for a kindness and courtesy not by any means common among the masters and mistresses of hotels in America, who generally consider it rather derogatory to show personal civility to their customers.

May 9.—By a quarter-past four in the morning we left the Atlanta, and travelled here through a fine country, only settled within the last twenty years. All the stations are small villages. I find Chattanooga a pretty scattered town on the banks of the Tennessee River, within five miles of 'Look-out Mountain.' In twenty years more it will acquire the population, as well as the name of a city, here given by anticipation. I procured a carriage at half-past two o'clock, to convey me to the top of 'Look-out.' I ascended by a beautiful drive through rocks and wood. I walked up some particularly steep places, and added two pretty new flowers to my collection—a crimson Lychnis and a pale lilac Geranium; but through all this country flowers are scarce. I see only shrubs—junipers, cedars, &c.—which excite my wishes in going along by the cars.

Upon reaching what is called 'the Point,' a view of Chattanooga and Tennessee River, flowing through mighty forests, was very fine. This hill is a strong contrast to the Stone Mountain; not so unique in any way, but still fine. Sandstone rocks were heaped upon one another like some of those at our Tunbridge Wells, though this formation must be much older; and I saw some conglomerate of quartz and sand. After making a sketch, my very young coachman (a boy not more than fifteen) drove his two spirited horses with great tact and caution down the rough descent.

We passed two or three slight summer residences, built by gentlemen of Chattanooga, as cool resorts for their families in the hot season, and there is also an hotel on the mountain. I reached the town again happily before sunset, without any accident or difficulty, though I had no one with me but my young driver. Being tired, I went to rest, and slept for nine hours at once, to make up for lost time.

Nashville, May 11.—It was dark when we reached this place, at half-past ten last night, so I missed the last thirty miles of scenery; but certainly the previous one hundred and twenty we passed through is a most beautiful district. I never knew any territory belonging to the old red sandstone that was not beautiful. The neighbouring kingdoms of limestone and granite may be more majestic, but then they have sometimes an aspect of sternness and desolation never worn by the red sandstone. Here are all the beauties of Braemar and Ross-shire, and the Odenwald, watered by a river almost equalling the Rhine in breadth, volume, and colour, to which must be added the rich and varied foliage of the south. This is what may be seen for more than a hundred miles between Nashville and Chattanooga. We passed viaducts over ravines, in which some fortunate settlers had established their log abodes in situations the most enviable; and here there are no snakes and no malaria to take off from other advantages. I would willingly live in Tennessee.

I am up early, and before going to breakfast, or being distracted by thoughts derived from another fresh locality, I must give you the benefit of past observations; and I want to remark as one of them, that the Americans must not be depended on for information as to facts regarding their own country, particularly not for any facts of natural science. They are not sufficiently aware of the importance of such things, and their love of practical jokes is strong. I might instance the *Floating Island in Lake Solitude*, which never had any existence but in the imagination of its inventors; and I will tell you one story as exemplifying this Transatlantic habit. An old lady, who possessed more botanical curiosity than is commonly met with among ladies in this country, requested a sailor nephew, about to visit South America, to bring her a Mexican Cactus plant. Captain —— forgot his aunt's wish while in that country; ashamed to confess his delinquency, and not being able to resist the temptation to have his joke at her expense, he procured a flower-pot, buried in it a large rat all but the tail (which he tied in gardener-like fashion to a stick), and wrote on a neat tally the name, 'Cactus *Rattailiense*.' When he presented this, the old lady exclaimed, 'What a queer plant! why is it called Rattailiense?'

'Don't you see, my dear Aunt, it bears a strong resemblance to the tail of a rat?'

'Well,' said she, 'that is very odd; and it certainly smells something like a rat too.'

The captain went off to sea again before his fraud was discovered, and trusted to the effect of time and absence to procure his forgiveness.

I have heard some curious anecdotes of Achille Murat, who lived for some years in Florida. He was considered a man of talent, but eccentric. After the present restoration of his family, some one said, 'Perhaps in due time we may again see you an exile in this country.'

'No,' said he, 'never. Now they have again accepted us in France, we shall cut their throats, or they must cut ours.'

Having once made a few thousand dollars by a speculation, he presented his wife with a magnificent tea-service, at a time when she could hardly provide necessaries; and this was owing to his strong faith in the 'Future' of his race. After his return to France, when he had arranged an expensive establishment, a person to whom he owed seven thousand dollars applied for repayment, which Achille said was impossible.

'I thought,' said his creditor, 'that living as you do now, you could find no difficulty.'

'Why,' answered the Prince, 'it is true I have sufficient to keep up my situation, but I have not enough to pay my debts.'

I believe, however, he has since liquidated them.

Since Louis Napoleon became Emperor, he has presented a complete set of the 'H. B.' caricatures to the library at Albany, New York State.

I think these stories are genuine; but I have seldom given credence to second-hand information. I should only have believed Captain Rollin's own account of his sea-serpent, and if that calm observant sailor has fallen into the fashion of this country of imposing falsely-strung yarns upon strangers, I must give up all confidence in the veracity of American informants.

Three Forks, Kentucky.—After a fatiguing journey (nine inside passengers in the mail coach) we reached this place at eleven o'clock last night, setting off at five in the morning; and it is rather an unpleasant consideration, that after visiting the Mammoth Cave, seven miles from hence, we must take the mail again to-morrow night, and proceed on towards Louisville at the same hour we disembarked from that conveyance here. These inevitable night journeys are what I dislike most in American travel. I have fallen in with a gentleman and lady who are shortly going to England. They are so obliging as to take charge of this packet; I shall therefore put off telling you what I think of the Mammoth Cave till my next letter, and only add that I found Nashville a pleasant town. It is watered by the Cumberland, a river which floats steamers, but it is much inferior to the Tennessee both in size and colour. A very handsome State-house, or Capitol, is nearly completed at Nashville. Well situated upon a hill, it is the best architectural building for its purpose I have yet seen in the States. The style is Ionic: eight pillars support the pediment, upon each of the four sides, and the lantern above the roof is ornamented by octagonal slabs to match. This lantern being unfinished, one cannot perfectly imagine its general effect; but, judging from the good taste evinced by the architect, Mr. Strickland, (an Englishman, I understand,) in his plan, it is probable that the completion of this building will be worthy of its commencement. Its material is the beautifully coloured grey limestone of Kentucky. I had the pleasure of making acquaintance with Mrs. Polk, widow of President Polk, whose burial-place and monument are in the garden upon one side of her residence. It is a handsome but simple erection, bearing an inscription worthy of the man whose life and death it records; and I sympathized with feelings which do not shrink from the sight of the last memorials of valued friends who have preceded us. I had not time to see much of the neighbourhood of Nashville, but I met a few agreeable people there; and could have made a pretty sketch from the Suspension Bridge, if the departure of the mail on alternate days only had not prevented me from staying a few hours longer. In haste,

Your affectionate

A. M. M.

THREE FORKS, KENTUCKY,
May 13, 1855.

LETTER XXVI.

MAMMOTH CAVE,
May 14, 1855.

MY DEAR FRIENDS,—

The Mammoth Cave is not the wonder I expected. Perhaps my expectations were raised too high, and so, as is sometimes the case, I do not fairly appreciate what has been considered secondary only to the Falls of Niagara; but, in my opinion, the Stone Mountain of Georgia is a greater marvel of nature than the caves of Kentucky.

Underground rivers are by no means rare: they are very numerous in Florida; and the Mammoth Cave is evidently the deserted bed of ancient streams. In some places it resembles gigantic drains, of which one of the most curious features is the regular, smooth, plastered-looking roof and sides. I have seen no elegant stalactite pillars like those of the Adelberg Cave in Carniola. The caverns here are heavy-looking, dark and dismal; but there are some gigantic pits and domes, frightful from their height and depth. The stalactite altar, in what is called the Gothic Chapel, and a comfortable arm-chair of the same material, were the most interesting things I saw. There are casts of fossils on the walls of what is here called oolitic rock, a fine emericite in one place. I see also at the hotel fossil wood of the coal formations, which were procured about seven miles off, but not from any of the Caves. On the whole, I was more interested by plants at the mouth of the cavern than by our five miles' walk within;

and to-morrow I shall probably ramble above ground, instead of beneath it. I found Podophyllum peltatum in flower for the first time; a singularly pretty, one-flowering, bluish-grey Aster,* and other novelties.

Several people came with us in a stage-coach from Three Forks, and it is to convey us back to-morrow afternoon, in time to rest before the mail takes us on.

Three Forks, or 'Bells' (as I find they call this place, to which we returned this afternoon, May 14th). Instead of the coach taking us on, as promised at Nashville (where they persuaded me to pay for the whole distance to Louisville), it arrived here loaded, and we are detained till passengers may happen to be scarce. This is the kind of treatment travellers are subjected to. It is impossible to place any dependence upon the assurances of agents; when they have got your money, they will, without compunction, leave you in the lurch. The lady and gentleman who have taken their passage to England for the 23rd are in the same predicament, and are of course still more inconvenienced. Instead of underground investigations this morning, I botanized in the woods above the Mammoth Cave, and found many interesting plants, particularly a pretty dwarf Iris, quite new to me; Phacelia fimbriata, with ivy-shaped leaves, and fine specimens of Botrychium Virginicum, and other ferns in fruit. I walked as far as Green River, and made a sketch there: it is well named, for the waters look solidly green. This river falls into the Ohio, and by going down it, and then up the Cumberland, there is a water communication with Nashville; but now the rivers are so low this is not practicable. All the party, excepting myself, entered the Cave this morning at eight o'clock, and did not emerge again till six in the afternoon. They admired some of the caverns much more than those we saw yesterday, and tell me that the imitations of flowers and forms of various kinds in the snowy gypsum are very beautiful; but the expedition was tedious and

* I suppose this to be 'Aster grandiflorus,' though Darby's *Botany* says that plant flowers in October, and that it is two or three feet, this is not one foot, high.

fatiguing, and I do not repent my decision against it. No eyeless fish were to be procured—the water was too low; though they are the great curiosity of the place. The preserved specimens I have seen have rudiments or marks where eyes should be, and I suppose that the organ has perished in process of time, from want of use, many generations one after another having existed and died in the dark. I have seen two species, a kind of perch and a crayfish.* Stephen, the guide who accompanied us, is a mulatto of great intelligence: he is at present a slave, but is to have his freedom next year, and then goes to Liberia with his wife and family (he would not wish to be free in this country); and it is to be feared that when beyond control, a certain propensity for strong waters will be his destruction. His appearance is that of a good-looking Spaniard; he is considered much the best guide, and he has not only acquired a perfect knowledge of the locality of the Cave, but also some degree of scientific acquaintance with its geological and chemical productions: besides which, he seems to have read and studied the history of other places of the same nature, as far as he has been able to procure books.

I am inclined to believe that nearly all the district was tunneled or undermined by water, which the lapse of ages has dried up, or drained off by numerous rivers. The caverns I saw in Cuba were probably owing to rather different circumstances, in which volcanic action played a larger part. The Cueva del Candela was an extensive opening above the plain in the side of a hill, whereas these Kentucky Caves are all below the surrounding country.

Six o'clock, May 15.—I have been awakened by the singing of the mocking-birds in a small orchard close to the English-looking garden here: there is a tame one in a cage downstairs, who sings unceasingly, and I suppose he attracts all the birds of the neighbourhood: at night their song resembles our nightingale; this morning it is exactly like that of canaries. Although my wanderings in the woods yesterday lasted some hours, I did

* I have now got the latter.

not feel apprehensive of snakes: one of the guides told me before I set out, that although there are rattlesnakes, and some other kinds occasionally here, yet, in his opinion, the popular fear of them is much greater than necessary: that they always get out of your way if possible, and he has himself often walked over them, without danger; they never wound unless driven to it in self-defence. There are many pigs, too, in the woods above the Mammoth Cave, and they are perfect snake scavengers, eating up all they can rout out or fall in with. I saw the tail of something darting into a hole, but could not be sure whether it was snake or lizard; besides this, I caught sight of no animal but a frog with large eyes. After I had been out five hours, one of the negroes came to look after me, and I was glad to make over my flower-press for him to carry back; I had a sketch-book, a bamboo stick, and a tin case (none of the smallest); and these often obliged me to go twice over the same ground, because I could not carry them all at once; and yet it was a much greater enjoyment to be without an attendant who would have hurried me, and look bored, if he did not express himself so. The negroes, too, watch your every motion with such eager curiosity, and will hardly let you stir without their help. My friend was very loth to go; he tried to persuade me that it might rain, or blow some of the trees down upon me; but I said I was not afraid, and that if it rained very hard, he might bring out an umbrella to a spring near, to which I meant to find my way; so at last he left me to my own inventions, and no difficulties occurred. I returned to the hotel by half-past three o'clock. Immediately after the Cave hunters came back, we were summoned to get into the coach; for the road being bad, we had to walk up and down some of the hills, and to arrive again at our starting-place before dusk. After tea there, we went to rest, preparatory to our expected night journey, and we were packed and ready, when we were told it was impossible we could be taken on; so we were obliged to reconcile ourselves to twenty-four hours' pause. Next morning, I was agreeably surprised to find my Anglo-American friend, Miss G—— had arrived with a party to proceed to the Cave, so that my detention enabled us to meet. My Hortus Siccus also will benefit much by the time I was able to bestow upon it, and a walk in the forest surrounding this place was the means of my adding a singular fern to my collection; excepting that fern, I did not find much that I had not already put into my press at the Mammoth Cave; a brilliant orange Coreopsis, probably one of those we already have in our gardens, is common in these woods, which are sprinkled all about with rocks, but none of large dimensions.

Louisville, *May*, 17.—At ten o'clock the night before last we got into a crammed coach at Three Forks; nine inside, two of whom were negro women; also a black baby—and such a frightful specimen of black nature as one of these slave women was!—her mouth just like a catfish; and then so sulky mannered and unaccommodating; she took her own share of the room, and added to it as much as she could possibly steal from her neighbours. Talk of white freedom! why I never saw women of the white classes in England as independent and assuming in manner as some of these darkies. I can imagine what they must be in the West Indies, since we have given them free scope there!

Yesterday afternoon the rain poured down in torrents, a great boon to this parched country, though it did not make our tedious journey more pleasant; the way to Louisville was through open woods and fields and glades, which would have been English in character, if the everlasting and ugly snake fences had not kept us constantly in mind of America. We ferried over the Salt River just at its junction with the Ohio, having before travelled along one of its beautiful shores, and then we passed through Elizabethville, and Nolinn's Creek; so called from a hunter of the name of Linn. In the early times of the settlement his party having lost their companion in the forests, separated to seek him, and having given their rendezvous at this spot, each man as they came in called out *No Linn;* this was the origin of the name. Louisville is a large city on the banks of the Ohio; it has no very attractive features, and as we must proceed by rail to Cincinnati at eight o'clock this morning, I shall not have time to see much here. There is a heavy ugly Court-house, in an unfinished dilapidated-looking state, and the streets are ill-paved; I understand the population mounts up to fifty thousand, and this hotel was so crowded, that if it had not been for my accommodating English friends who gave up a room they had engaged, we should have been obliged to seek beds elsewhere.

Cincinnati, May 17.—We crossed the Ohio River this morning by a ferry-boat at eight o'clock, to start from the railway station, which has the most roomy and comfortable cars I have yet met with in America. We reached this place, one hundred and twenty miles from Louisville, by three o'clock, passing by a series of picturesque low-wooded hills, which are called the Knobs of Ohio. President Harrison's tomb is on one of these elevations, near a pretty town named Aurora. Kentucky is on the opposite side of the river. We are now in Ohio, which bears the appellation of the Buckeye State. Nearly every State and each chief city has what may be called a local designation, and some of these are extremely appropriate: I will give you a list of those I have ascertained:—

New York, Empire State . .	Empire City.
Massachusetts, Bay State . .	Bay City.
Philadelphia, Key State . .	Quaker City.
Kentucky, Corncracker State .	Pittsburg, Smoky City.
Indiana, 'Hoosier'* State . .	Cleveland, Forest City.
Illinois, Sucker State . . .	Wheeling, Bridge City.
Virginia, Old Dominion . .	Cincinnati, Queen City.
South Carolina, Palmetto State .	Saint Louis, Mound City.
Missouri, Wolverine State . .	Louisville, Falls City.
California, Gold State . .	Galena, Garden City.
Georgia, Rice State . . .	Memphis, Bluff City.
Louisiana, French State . .	New Orleans, Crescent City.
Florida, Shell State . . .	Indianapolis, Railroad City.

May 18.—Soon after reaching Cincinnati yesterday afternoon, I set off in the hope of seeing Mr. Longworth's Cacti; but, unfortunately, the green-house, with everything in it, was destroyed by

* Madame Pfeiffer mistook Governor Wright, when she gave, from his authority, another derivation for the word 'Hoosier.' It originated in a

fire, about three years ago; and it is an exemplification of Transatlantic indifference to such things, that a loss of the finest collection of Cacti in the United States, and perhaps in the world, does not appear to have been known except to those immediately concerned. I found nothing very new in the glass houses belonging to Mr. Longworth; but in one of them the Victoria Regia was in flower; and there is an intelligent young Scotchman as gardener. Mr. Longworth's residence, though in the town, is large; and within the grounds, on either side, he has erected other handsome houses, for two sons-in-law. Mr. Longworth was away from home, but Mr. Anderson, who married one of his daughters, was so obliging as to show me the first works of Power—one a charming ideal bust, entitled *Genevra*, and the other a bust of his patron, considered very good; it reminded me of Seneca.

The agriculturists were blessed by much rain yesterday. We are now come far enough north to feel a change of climate; and an advantage to me will be the getting away from a species of tick, which was the torment of my Southern walks. The insect is as large as that, which in England is rarely named to ears polite, though here it is the usual designation of every creeping thing. This tick is so insidious in its approaches, that you are not made sensible of having one upon you till it has fastened itself tightly into your skin. After botanizing in the neighbourhood of the Mammoth Cave, I felt tormented during our night journey to Louisville; and upon arriving there, R—— extracted twenty-five of the little wretches; they are very tenacious of life; and, if the head is left behind, greater irritation ensues; but the suffering to me has not been greater than that caused by the sting of a mosquito. These and cactus spines are two great hindrances to botanical researches in the Southern States.

Cincinnati is handsomer and more attractive than Louisville, and worthy of its distinctive name, 'Queen City.' Geologically, the formations which surround it are singular. I believe they

settler's exclaiming 'Huzza,' upon gaining the victory over a marauding party from a neighbouring State.

belong to the Devonian group, or rather the Lower Silurian; but there is limestone resembling in colour and appearance (though not in fossils) what is called 'forest marble' in England; it lies in flat strata about a foot, or half a foot in thickness, alternating with clay; and, in some places, I observed both indurated together into a striped rock, dark and light grey. I have got a few specimens, with fossils, Trilobites, Orthises, &c.; and very large Trilobites are found here.

Mr. Mitchell, the astronomer, took me up to his Observatory, situated upon a commanding elevation overlooking the town and winding Ohio. This will one day be a gigantic city; already her population amounts to two hundred thousand. The emporium of the Western States, Cincinnati is both commercial and manufacturing. Her citizens have built, and are building, palaces; and, if the first settlers could but have imagined the future of the great capital they were founding, instead of rooting up and burning down the trees on the numerous heights, and then partitioning them out in small lots for building, they would have preserved them, or some of them, in their forest attire, in public parks and gardens for their city, which, by this time, must have been the Queen of the States, in beauty of scenery as well as in situation. Professor Mitchell tried to explain his wonderful astronomical instruments to my unmechanical comprehension. I can only see that he has made great discoveries. By means of a galvanic battery, he produces an electric spark each second, in the interior of a clock, by which he works his whole observing machinery above. Through this agent he has superseded the old transit-glass; and the exact situation of stars is instantaneously jotted down by a mere finger-touch from the observer, upon a connecting rod. I do not know whether this is a clear explanation, for though I understand the commencement and conclusion of the operation, I have not sufficient knowledge to trace it through all its mysterious doings. The Professor himself drove me up and down some of the terrific hills of this precipice town; he and his pretty little horses and light high-wheeled carriage seemed so used to the business, that I did not insist upon jumping out, otherwise I should have been very unwilling to have been driven by the very edge of descents which it makes me now giddy to think of. A mizzling rain forced us to give up a proposed drive into the surrounding country; and I was obliged to be content with cursory views of the principal streets; after which Mr. Mitchell took me to his house to drink tea and spend the evening with Mrs. Mitchell and his family.

Saturday, May 19.—This afternoon I go on by rail to Indianapolis. I have now taken leave of the Southern States, but I must make some more remarks upon the Slavery question. Louisville and Cincinnati are places in which, I believe, Mrs. Stowe once resided; and I quote an opinion she advances in her last work which proves her entire ignorance of negro constitution and habits. She asserts that Canada is the best locality 'to develope the energies of the black race.' Before saying this, it would have been well if she had studied the condition of the free negroes in Canada. The very climate itself is utterly unsuited to them. Mrs. Stowe quotes, as mistaken and absurd, the sensible remarks in Boswell's *Life of Johnson* respecting negro slavery, which I must re-quote as wise and true: 'To abolish a status which in all ages God has sanctioned and man has continued, would not only be robbing a numerous class of our fellow-subjects, but it would be extreme cruelty to the African savages, a portion of whom it saves from worse bondage in their own country, and introduces into a much happier state of life; especially when their passage to the West Indies and their treatment there is humanely regulated. To abolish the trade would be to shut the gates of mercy on mankind.' And I must add this: the opinions I have heard from intelligent slaves coincide with those here quoted. Because some slave-manacles were seen by Clarkson in a Liverpool shop, he decided at once upon the inhumanity of slavery—so says Mrs. Stowe. Tyrannical men and women in Great Britain have actually starved apprentices to death—is apprenticeship therefore murder? I trust no Englishwoman can be found willing to bring such an accusation against her people. Let us imagine two brothers in this country engaged in trade:

one buys a plantation, with two hundred negroes, to raise cotton, on the Mississippi—the other sets up a mill to spin cotton, at Cincinnati. Trade is bad with the elder: he must raise or buy corn and clothes to feed and clothe his labourers. Trade is tight with the other: he dismisses his work-people, who may starve or perish, and there is no law which can make him responsible for their sufferings. I will conclude this subject with one more anecdote, for the truth of which I can vouch. A Southern lady and gentleman brought a mulatto slave to Cincinnati, who there fell in with some abolitionists, and was imbued with a feeling of discontent. Her master and mistress observing this, proceeded to New York, where they told the girl that they did not wish to retain a servant against her will, and giving her twenty dollars, they added, 'Take this money and your freedom.' The girl took it, and went out. She entered a theatre, and was told 'she must go to the entrance for coloured people.' In a church she is ordered to sit with the blacks. Trying for a place in an omnibus, the driver says it is no place for her. She hurried back to her mistress to return the money, and entreated she might be taken or sent back to that South 'where black people are free.'

Indianapolis, May 19.—We reached Indianapolis soon after the evening closed in. As hours are early in this part of the world, I determined to go to an hotel for the night, so as not to intrude on my friends at an inconvenient time. This was acquiesced in by Governor Wright, who visited me soon after my arrival.

May 20.—The Governor came early, and took me to his house. At half-past ten o'clock we went to the Episcopal church, where the duty was admirably done by a Mr. Talbot, originally from Kentucky, who preached a sermon, good in matter as in manner. Dinner was at one o'clock, and at two I accompanied the Governor to visit two large Sunday-schools, belonging to different denominations. There are about fifteen in this town. They have each a superintendent; and young men and women of the various churches in the place give them assistance. In England we might take example by the wisdom here which limits Sunday-school attendance to one hour, and leaves the place and period of Divine worship to be regulated by the parents. If the teaching at school is not such as to induce the children to go willingly to church, a forced going will not benefit their religious feelings; and too often the fatigued, bored appearance of Sabbath-school children in our churches, is a sad commentary upon the want of judgment evinced by the British public in this matter. The Sunday is kept at Indianapolis with Presbyterian strictness. No trains start, letters do not go, nor are they received, so that a father, mother, husband, or wife may be in extremity, and have no means of communicating their farewells or last wishes if Sunday intervenes. Surely this is making man subordinate to the Sabbath—not the Sabbath to man. I have been amused at a story told me of an inhabitant of this place. The Millenarian doctrine has been rife here; all through America fanatics have lately spread an idea that sublunary matters were to close yesterday, May 19. A man not usually inclined to intemperate habits, called at a store as the day waned, and requested a mug of porter to support his spirits through the expected catastrophe. Time wore on—still the elements looked calm. 'It wont be over yet awhile; I must have another glass. 'Tis very depressing to have to wait so long; give me some drink.' This continued till the poor frightened soul became dead drunk; and he was much surprised next morning to find the world going on much as usual—with the exception of his aching head.

May 21.—Governor Wright invited me to accompany him in a morning walk at sunrise—four o'clock. I had some letters to write previously, but by five we perambulated parts of the town, which is peculiarly laid out; the Court, or rather Government-house being in the centre (and it is said also the centre of the Union; but that can only be a temporary centre, for this place lies eastward of the middle of the continent); and all the streets converging towards it.

I occupied this morning in arranging my dried specimens of plants, which occasionally require attention. We dined at one o'clock, and Mrs. Wright, at present an invalid, was sufficiently recovered to join us at table. After dinner I was happy to see Judge Maclean, whom I knew at Washington; he is come to hold a court; and Governor Powell, of Kentucky, is also expected to-morrow. The Governor took Mr. Maclean and me a drive to see the Asylums for the Deaf and Dumb, and for the Blind of this State. They are both fine institutions, paid for by the people through special taxes, imposed for the purpose, and paid ungrudgingly. They have sufficient ground attached for out-of-door occupations and exercise. The deaf and dumb make shoes and bonnets, farm, &c., so as to acquire a knowledge which enables them to gain their future livelihood: and the girls are taught to be sempstresses, washerwomen, cooks, &c. Such charities should always be situated in the country; town life cuts off the most necessary and advantageous means of training the inmates to healthful and useful pursuits.

From the cupola of the Asylum for the Blind the view is wide. These extensive plains of the West extend one thousand miles in the direction of Canada, and as far towards the Rocky Mountains. There is one height or bluff about fifteen miles off, which I must go and look at. Indiana produces freestone, coal, and iron. The Wabash about sixty miles from hence, is the most considerable river. Before we left the asylum, some of the blind pupils sang quartettes and duets, accompanied by one of their number on the piano. They sang in tune and with good taste.

I have heard much of Democracy and Equality since I came to the United States, and I have seen more evidences of Aristocracy and Despotism than it has before been my fortune to meet with. The 'Know-nothings,' and the 'Abolitionists,' and the 'Mormonites' are, in my opinion, consequent upon the mammonite, extravagant pretensions and habits which are really fashionable among Pseudo-Republicans. Two hundred thousand starving Irish have come to this country, and in their ignorance they assume the airs of that equality which they have been induced to believe is really belonging to American society. They endeavour to reduce to practice the sentiment so popular here—but no—that will never do. Ladies don't like their helps to say they 'choose to sit in the parlour, or they won't help them at all, for equality is the rule here.' Mrs. So-and-so of the 'Codfish' Aristocracy doesn't like to have Lady Anything to take precedence of her; but Betty choosing to play at equality is quite another thing! Now at Indianapolis I have found something like consistency, for the first time since I came this side the Atlantic. I do not assert there is equality, for the simple reason that it is not in nature; and (as Lord Tavistock once so well said), 'the love of liberty is virtue, but the love of equality is pride;' but here, the Governor of the State is a man of small income; his salary is only fifteen hundred dollars: he has really put aside money-making, and his son, an amiable young man, instead of wasting his time in rioting and drunkenness (which, alas! is too much the case with the sons of the 'Aristocracy' in the United States), keeps a store to make his own fortune, and, as he nobly said yesterday, to provide for that father who has disdained to sacrifice his country to himself. Governor Wright did not think it a degradation to carry a basket when I accompanied him to the market this morning, and his whole demeanour is that of a consistent Republican. I do not care what a man's political creed may be (though I much prefer the monarchical principles of old England), but I do admire consistency; and I consider the 'Know-nothing' movement as a consequence of uncertain principles.

May 22.—This day Governor Powell of Kentucky came on a visit here. He was in Canada two years since, and he spoke with admiration of Lord Elgin, and of his manner of conducting the affairs of that Colony. The heat has suddenly become intense; to my feelings as hot as any day we had in Cuba. At last I conclude that winter has really given up our company, after returning to it so frequently, that I feel as if I had passed three winters and three summers in America.

May 23.—I went at five o'clock this morning to the Eastern market-place, where I first saw squirrels sold like rabbits for the table ready skinned. When dressed, they are exactly like young chickens. I believe it is the grey squirrel. This evening the

Governor had what is now in the States universally called a *levée;* after the same fashion as the President's receptions. Governors of individual States occasionally open their doors to all the citizens who choose to attend, and it is considered a compliment to stranger guests like the Governor of Kentucky and myself, that the attendance should be good; so the rooms here were filled. The Governor and his lady do not receive their visitors, but we all went into the room after they had assembled. No refreshments are expected on these occasions, but every one shakes hands upon being introduced. The assemblage was very respectable and orderly; it concluded about eleven o'clock, having begun at nine.

May 24.—I went to see a Devonshire man and his wife, who have a vineyard: they have been settled here twenty years, and are natives of Dartmouth; they look back to the old country with regret, and think they might have done as well there as here; though they have a cottage with an acre of ground their own property, and a married son and daughter doing well, but poor people. Their youngest boy is an inmate of the Indiana Lunatic Asylum. Mrs. N—— was brought up in the family of the lady who nursed the Duchess of Gloucester, and remembers helping to make a cradle for the Princess Amelia. She was much delighted to find that I knew Miss A——. We spoke much of England; I told her she was now adopted by this country, and that with her family here, it was wrong to hanker so much after that of her birth.

Mr. N—— buries his vines in the ground, as soon as the wood has hardened, during the cold months of the year. I wonder whether this plan would make the vine more prolific in the open air with us.

Mrs. Wright gave an evening party of invited acquaintances; a great many agreeable people from this and the adjoining State. One lady sang some of Moore's Melodies very sweetly; but, as yet, music is not much cultivated in America; either the ladies do not devote sufficient attention to it, or there are not good masters. This is almost the first time I have heard an American sing with taste and expression. This party did not conclude before midnight.

I have spoken of the Stone Mountain to gentlemen, engineers, professors, and military men; but the gigantic precipice, and the curious geological facts of that elevation seem quite unknown to any of them; as yet they do not appear to have attracted the notice of scientific men. I imagine that the tabular masses spread upon the rising ground on the opposite side of the valley beneath the precipitous wall, must be the *débris* of that part of the mountain which fell away upon the upheavement of the mass in an almost fluid state—at least this is the idea suggested by its appearance. I hope some one more able to understand it than I am, will visit the place, and decide how far my supposition is probable.

I am told the thermometer stood at ninety-two degrees in the shade the day before yesterday, and the weather continues very hot, but there is now rather more air. Last night a naval gentleman told me that part of an iron fastening belonging to a ship had been found half embedded in a mass of iron, which had been supposed an aerolite, lying on a prairie in this country. From this fact a very modern origin for the locality is deduced, because it is concluded that a mass of the kind in question must originally have been left by an iceberg. I mention this as it was named to me, without pretending to decide upon the truth of the matter.

Thursday Mrs. Wright gave an invited reception, with a standing supper. All went off well, and I saw the principal people of Indianapolis. Next morning I drove with a young lady to see what are called the Bluffs of the White River, sixteen miles, distance. I was surprised to find that the road there was by no means what we should call a *plain*, it was rather a series of continued low elevations, and many short but steep hills mark the road. It passes through a pretty country, bordered by farms, and watered by small streams, making their way to the White River, which attended our drive within a short distance. 'The Bluff' proved to be a rather higher hill than others, overlooking the river, and thickly timbered, but without a rock of any kind. I found the large leaved blood-wort, the may apple, and a pretty red columbine, growing plentifully in soil formed by the dead leaves of a thousand autumns. The inmates of a pretty farm near at hand gave us hospitality and a share of their dinner, while our coachman acted as guide, and entered into my botanical researches with great interest. We made our way over the hill down to the river bank, where we saw the laborious but useless works for the formation of a canal, entered into by the State at an out lay of hundreds of thousands of dollars just before railways were put into action, and abandoned in consequence. The small town of Waverley is situated a mile beyond the hill we came to visit. Our drive home was a chilly one. The thermometer has again descended below 50°. These sudden changes from intense heat to cold are much greater than those we have in England.

Saturday and Sunday were very cold, with slight showers. It is supposed much rain has fallen in other parts of the State; a most acceptable conclusion of the long drought, which has excited much alarm for the fate of the crops. There are two well conducted newspapers in this town, but they fall into the same error (which is almost general in the press through the States), that of attacking the institutions and the character of the Parent State, in a tone both virulent and unjust; and this, I am sorry to say, is not so much the practice of native Americans as of editors born in England; even those whose parents look back with love and veneration to the country they have left; and, in one instance, though their son is a powerful, a moral, and usually a conscientious writer, yet is his pen dipped in the gall of bitterness whenever it approaches subjects which touch upon Great Britain. He forgets, or in his ignorance he does not know, when echoing vulgar abuse of the Old Land and the English aristocracy, that, as a whole, they give an example of energy in action, and simplicity in manner, which might well be copied here. British distinctions are not derived solely from mammon, therefore mammon is not the sole god of their idolatry. Individuals are not valued and judged in England (as is too generally the case in America) by the satin they may have upon their backs, or the dollars that chink in their pockets; but each individual, in fact, is appreciated according to his intrinsic qualities. Those who know the old country best will admit that the influence attached to respective grades of society is lost by those whose habits are unworthy; while, on the other side, men like Hugh Miller, and others who could be pointed out, are not precluded from the highest distinctions if they earn them. Yet such paragraphs as these have been going the round of the United States' papers:—'The meanest aristocracy is that of birth; it ignores intellect, energy, courage, and good deeds; it demoralizes Government, defeats armies, and disgraces manhood. If there were no aristocracy of birth in England, great men would have risen from the ranks to lead the British army in triumph', &c., &c., &c. Do these Democrats not know that the English people have no wish to see their army, like that of France, the chief aristocracy of the land? I should be sorry if the time came when the sword alone should be permitted to hew its way to the principal distinctions of England. Now, a man may rise more easily in the law, the church, the literary, or even the artistic path, than in that of the soldier. Let our young men of fortune still buy their commissions, and place themselves under strict discipline, and then occasionally, by succession, a poor man derives the benefit; but never let the brave aspiring English peasant know that his strong arm and great heart are the means by which he may most easily acquire a marshal's *bâton*, a ducal coronet, for then a military despotism may one of these days supplant the freest Constitution in the world. The press of the United States is fond of calling names: 'British Flunkeyism,' 'Mock Emperor,' 'Mock Representation.' Americans have chosen their forms of Government—the best, probably, for a young rising people. Let them be content with their own, without abusing that of their mother land; but there are signs in the horizon which foretell that their Government may not stand the test of centuries. I copy from American papers, that 'Judge C——, for several years occupying the position of Associate-Judge, and having held other offices of honor and profit as an old and influential citizen of Harding County, has been arrested for counterfeiting!' And these prohibitory liquor-laws, which the local legislatures have been so busy in enacting! What would be thought in England of legislators who now drink more liquor 'than was drank by that legislature who passed the prohibitory law.'

The Temperance Legislature of New York, while on a visit to that city, got on a 'drunken spree, and broke up in a row!' Of course, in these remarks I am not alluding to the intelligent and really distinguished men of America,—men who have crossed the Atlantic, and made themselves acquainted with English institutions and English manners. No people are more fond of titles than Americans when they can get hold of them. 'Generals' and 'Judges' and 'Colonels' are plentiful as blackberries. Mere boys assume these appellations often without much claim to them; and every member of Congress expects to be addressed in society as 'Honourable.' Our members of Parliament are satisfied to be so designated in the House itself, but do not claim the title out of doors. Yet, I should be sorry to hear even a suspicion attached to the name of any individual belonging to our legislative bodies, of such gross derelictions from duty and honesty as are not uncommon among the 'Honourable' members of the United States Congress.

Washington is a very sink of corruption. Those who know the place cannot deny that a large proportion of the gentlemen (and ladies, too,) assembled there at one period of the year are open to bribery, and that Bills to put the *almighty dollars* into certain pockets, have been got through by the aid of establishments open to certain people, liberally supplied with liquors and gaming tables, and that when people have lost money, purses have been at their disposal, of course with the understanding that their votes went in the right direction. Can anything of political profligacy be raked out of the faults of the old country to match this? or can the worst inventions of the English press equal the assertion, that John Bull publicly rejoiced over the death of the Czar, and that the British are a 'nation of brutes?' No individual or people can claim the merit of perfectibility, and I should not point out the blots in the American escutcheon if they were not inclined to be too busy in falsely bespattering those of their neighbours.

An electric despatch invites me to attend the wedding of two young friends at Albany, and particular circumstances make this invitation imperative. So for the present, at any rate, I must give up my intended visit to the Prairies of Ohio and Illinois. By taking the early train to-morrow, I can reach New York State in time, and allow for a few hours' visit to Dr. Kirtland, at Cleveland who has been ill, and cannot meet me as he proposed to do. I close this packet here, and let it go by the first opportunity.

Yours affectionately,

A. M. M.

Indianapolis, *May* 27.

P.S.—This rambling epistle is hastily sent off, and I will write again from Albany.

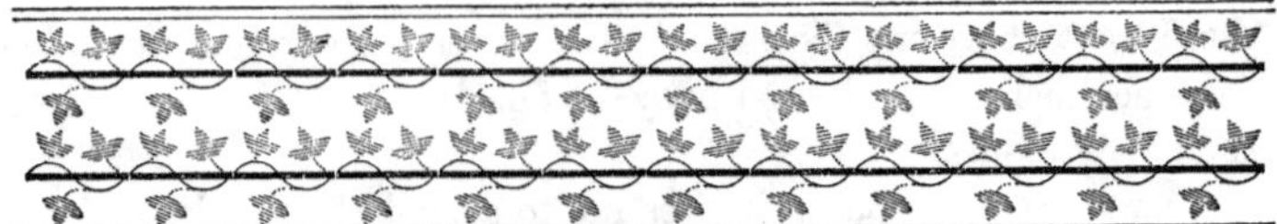

LETTER XXVII.

ALBANY, *May* 13, 1855.

MY DEAR FRIENDS,—

I left Indianapolis early on Monday last, slept at Cleveland, and spent a few hours with Dr. Kirtland at Rock Point, which hours I cut off the time necessary for my journey by travelling all night. I hope this will be my last night's work during the remainder of my stay in America, for it is a very disagreeable business. The wedding of my young American friends will take place to-morrow, and then I shall be able to decide whether there is any chance of my being able to accomplish the tours in the Adirondack and the Prairies which were planned last year.

May 31.—While at breakfast yesterday morning, I received an invitation from the two Bishops of Pennsylvania and New York to accompany them to the consecration of a new church at Troy. Miss P—— was so obliging as to come for me. We followed a beautiful line of railway for about an hour. In the society of two of the most distinguished and excellent men in the United States, I enjoyed this drive. The little Gothic church is almost perfect in style and taste, and although strictly architectural externally, as well as internally, it is original in design. Every seat was occupied, and a finer sermon than that preached by the Bishop of Pennsylvania, for such an occasion, I never heard—equally good in matter as in manner. There were several clergy who took part in the service. We had the *Hundredth Psalm* congregationally sung, and the *Halleluja Chorus* well played; if a theatrical kind of anthem had not been inserted between them, the music would have been as satisfactory as the other arrangements, excepting that the service was rather too long. We afterwards lunched at the house of Mr. and Mrs. T——, and did not get back to Albany till six in the afternoon. The wedding ceremony, which took place about nine o'clock the same evening, was performed by the Bishop of Pennsylvania, in the presence of a large party. This is the fifth marriage I have attended in America. I cannot resist a kind proposal of the Bishop's, that I should accompany him and Mrs. Potter through a visitation tour in some of the most beautiful parts of his diocese. I shall join them in Philadelphia the 6th instant. Whether the Adirondack and the Prairies will also be comprised, I cannot yet tell. Letters await me at New York. I have had so few from home these last three months that I am very anxious. I was roused by a great noise made by men in the house at three o'clock this morning. Americans do not seem to have the least idea of considering the comfort or the slumbers of other travellers in an hotel, if it please them to make an uproar during the night. I heard corks drawing, and as the Maine law has been introduced into Albany since Mr. Seymour's government, I suppose that day abstinence is made up for by night jollity.

Albany, June 4.—I have been resting and preparing for a fresh start the 6th. I shall leave R—— with friends here, and be quite independent of all but my episcopal guides, for Bishop Potter has engaged to give me over to the care of his brother of New York, somewhere on the borders of Lake Champlain, the last week of this month. I wish to see Ticonderoga, where my mother's father, General Grant, took the 42d Highlanders (a regiment he first raised) into battle eight hundred strong and came out two hundred!—a Balaclava in its way. The sermon of the Scotch previously is worth recording: 'My lads, I hae nae time for lang preachments, a' I hae to say is, nae cowards gae to Heaven; and if ye dinna kill them they'll kill you.' I visited Dr. and Mrs. H——'s pretty cottage, and dined with Mr. and

Mrs. Hall, the evening before I left Albany to join the Bishop and Mrs. Potter at Philadelphia.

June 6.—I set out at five o'clock in the morning, and reached New York about half-past nine. I remained at the St. Nicholas hotel till six in the evening, and saw there Governor Seymour and Sir Charles Grey, who soon returns to England. By the mail train, after a disagreeable journey, owing to tipsy rowdies being in the same cars, I reached the Pier House, Philadelphia, at half-past nine o'clock. This town looks to much greater advantage, now the trees which border the streets are in leaf. After walking about all the morning, weather damp and showery, so violent a thunder-storm came on in the afternoon, rain pouring down in spouts, and from one house the water falling from the rough tiles in so heavy a cascade, that it seemed as if a river had suddenly burst from the skies. I never saw rain in Europe like this.

June 8.—Mr. S—— was so obliging as to take me to the Kensington end of Philadelphia to call upon Mrs. R——, a Quaker lady, to whom I was introduced at Washington, but she was on a tour in Kentucky. In this quarter of the town I saw a simple monument, erected on the spot where William Penn made his compact with the Indians. 'The only treaty ever made without oaths, and the only one which was never violated.'

The local Government have purchased ground to make an open square here. We afterwards visited Mr. Girard's College for the nurture and education of boys, without reference to the religious persuasions of their parents. I understand the children are religiously and morally brought up, but a particular clause in the will forbids the entrance of any clergyman into the building. It is a fine erection; the pediment supports gigantic Corinthian columns, the roof being entirely marble; such was the weight, that rows of parallel brick arches were erected, a few feet only apart from the supports. I went to the top. It is made for eternity, and is a magnificent specimen of architectural skill. Inmates may be received from New Orleans as well as Philadelphia, because the former was the first port to which the founder had a venture; his trade was principally with China, and it was in Philadelphia his fortune (the whole of which is devoted to this College) was made. He left directions in an elaborate will, that all articles of household furniture, and even his wearing apparel, should be preserved; the latter, books, china, &c., are in glass cases. If the same funds had been left for educational purposes, there would have been less glorification of the founder, but greater results.

Afterwards I went to the Museum, where there is one of the finest ornithological collections in the world, fossils, and a most curious collection of shells, upon which an elaborate work, entitled *Types of Mankind*, was founded. I understand the book is written in a scoffing and offensive style, attacking the Bible under the influence of strong prejudice; but that it contains valuable facts: a habit among religious people of making the truth of the sacred Scriptures to depend upon their own narrow views, has but too frequently arrayed the discoveries of science, and the visible works of the Creator, in opposition to that written word with which (properly understood) they never have been, and never can be, otherwise than in accordance.

At the Reading Station I joined the Bishop and Mrs. P——, with their party of travellers; in all seven; among them a lady and gentleman with whom I dined at Baltimore. The railroad crosses and recrosses the river Schuylkill, a pretty course, until we arrived at the hotel at Mount Carbon, near Pottsville, a picturesque situation. I was out at six o'clock next morning to put a recollection into my sketch-book; after breakfast we all went on delightful railway excursions in a small car belouging to the directors, up to the first coal mines of this mining country, through which the Bishop is making his visitation. Nothing could be more interesting than its geological features, particularly to a person but little acquainted with the history of coal. It lies very near the surface in extensive basins—an anthracite of the most brilliant exterior, which, after being created, has apparently (for the purpose of rendering it more accessible) been heaved up and dislocated by the protrusion from beneath of conglomerate rocks thrown up in strata, sometimes perfectly vertical. This operation has been repeated over and over again through the district we are visiting, with overwhelming evidence of design.

In the shale above, we found the usual carboniferous fossils, and below red sandstone. All this goes on through Pottsville, Tuscarora, Tamaqua, and to Summit, one of the highest situations, where we slept the second night. From thence, early on Sunday morning, we whirled down an inclined plane by gravity alone, about nine miles, in a little open car, to Mauch Chunk (*fat bear* in the Indian language), a place set deep among the hills by the rapid dashing Lehigh, reminding me of Schalenbad, near Frankfort, in Germany, but much more beautiful. Instead of wood slides down the mountain, here the locomotives rise up, dragging long trains of coal waggons on ascents a mile and a half long, with a rise of fifteen hundred feet. We mounted the highest, and descended by curves and gravity a distance of sixteen miles. I was ashamed to shrink from the excursion; but I must confess that terror and anxiety mastered enjoyment with me, the whole proceeding was so novel and terrific. Long practice must be necessary to convince a mind of its security. I heard Bishop Potter catechise the children in church, concisely, but most effectively; and after morning service, and an excellent sermon, he confirmed a lady and gentleman of mature age. Baptisms and confirmations of grown up people are common in this country. The episcopal church is increasing rapidly, and at this place (Scranton), from which I now write, where the English and Welsh miners are numerous, I am told the people evince great attachment to it. The general affection for their bishop, and his worthiness, must tend much to strengthen this feeling.

We remained two days a Wilkesbarre, a town on the Susquehanna River, in the Valley of Wyoming; coal-fields surrounding it in every direction, and, as at Manchester, descending planes of railroads carrying off the produce on one side, water carriage taking it away the other, and the neighbourhood so beautiful that volumes of sketches might be made here. We visited a valley about two miles distant, where coal excavations, now deserted by the Baltimore company, resemble the openings of Egyptian tombs, and the entrances going straight into the mountain, are like vast halls supported by massive pillars of coal. I think there are more English settled in these mining districts of Pennsylvania than in any part of the United States I have visited—more born English, I mean. I have before seen hordes of Irish, but English sparely scattered; here the Irish are in the minority. Those I have talked with say they are physically comfortable, and they do not dislike their new country; but they still prefer the old one—they do not think that practically there is more liberty here than in England; and an old soldier told me, in his opinion, the men in authority here 'are not as fitting for to bear rule as them with us.'

We are now at Scranton; here iron is plentiful, and found in juxtaposition with the coal. The railway bars are manufactured and laid down at once, transmuted from the surrounding rocks, and made the means of conveying their own treasures! It has been said 'an undevout astronomer is mad;' surely here one is made to say 'an undevout geologist must be insane!'

I am in hopes this ugly name of Scranton may be changed to that of Lackawanna, the Indian appellation for a lovely valley, which terminates the coal region on this side. I am now (June 16th) writing from a town called Montrose, situated in the northern part of Pennsylvania; it is a very elevated situation. We rose a hill for some distance. The railway had conducted us about forty miles from Scranton; our way followed the course of a deep glen, much resembling Glen Tilt, in Blair Athol, and we are hospitably received at the house of a gentleman here.

Montrose, June 17.—After Morning Service the Bishop's duties took us to the house of a gentleman and lady, near Springfield; and I do not think I was ever more interested by any religious services than there. A country church, which probably accommodated from two to three hundred people, was filled to overflowing by a respectable looking congregation, of which the majority were men. After an excellent sermon, touching upon the dangers, particularly imminent in thriving communities, of the prevalence of a mammonite covetous spirit, the Bishop gave a short and simple explanation of the reasons which make confirmation a rite of the episcopal communion, preparatory to the reception of seven candidates; one a venerable looking old man, and the other six considerably past youth. The whole congregation remained as witnesses, wrapt in mute attention; the ceremony was strikingly impressive. That cartoon of *Paul preaching at Athens*, was vividly brought to my mind by the massive figure and countenance of the Bishop of Pennsylvania, earnest, eloquent, self-forgetting; every eye turned upon him with an expression of love and veneration which could hardly have been exceeded in Apostolic days. Here, too, were early converts; here, too, might be doubters and cavillers to whom the scene was new; but I felt sure that on this occasion many a sheep was gathered into one fold under one shepherd; and by a shepherd, too, who would watch over his increasing flock with wisdom as well as tenderness. He is now received under a roof not professedly attached to his church; but the hearts are with him, whether the external profession of its inmates may be his or not.

A visit to this district is extremely refreshing as a counterpoise to the more worldly, ostentations, selfih communities of commercial places. Here simplicity of manners, quietude of dress, and friendliness of feeling, are united with refinement and culture; it is under such circumstances that the American character is seen to advantage. Agriculture predominates, and trade is subordinate; the influence of the former is certainly more salutary; and when farming and gardening are pursued as a relaxation by men engaged in commercial life, I have remarked their beneficial influence upon character. A fine view of part of the Alleghany chain of mountains is obtained from this place; and there is an interesting little farm belonging to our hosts, which supplies the best butter and cream I have tasted in the United States; and what is more, the butter is churned by the willing co-operation of animals I never before saw industriously occupied. A small circular treadmill turns a wheel, attached to a kind of piston, which falls into the churn; a ewe and her lambs are engaged in walking up-hill, towards a small hole in the wall of the shed which shelters the machine. A little salt and some meal placed in the hole is at once an incentive, and a reward of exertion; and the old and young sheep appear most contentedly employed, while a dairy-woman is spared labour. She at times stops the machinery to rest the animals, who always seem willing to walk on again after a few minutes. As the movement depends upon weight, a sheep is more useful than a dog for this avocation; besides which the latter is less plodding and not so benefited by clambering; and the fattening of the mutton while her work goes on, is a proof it agrees with her. I have ordered one of these machines, and hope it will be a useful present to an English dairy.

We returned to Montrose the evening of the 18th, as the Bishop was engaged to lecture there upon the 'Character of Washington,' in aid of the funds for building a parsonage house. His confirmation next day was at a place named Pike, and he allowed me to accompany him to see the Wiolusing (valley of peace). More appropriate and beautiful Indian names have been retained hereabouts than is common in America. The Susquehanna (winding river) twists about so as almost to encircle the country we have been traversing. We left Montrose early on the 21st, and went by New Milford to Great Bend; wooded hills and vales are diversified by lakes and streams the whole way to Owego (or Auwega, the Indian name), from which place I now write; the Susquehanna again flowing opposite our hotel, as it did a hundred miles off at Wilkesbarre. To-morrow we proceed to Towanda.

June 26.—Another pretty place on the Susquehanna. We have again followed that river from Great Bend. The valley from Waverley here is exceedingly fine, much resembling that of the Inn in Bavaria; but the carriage-road follows the edge of a precipice nearly the whole way, and it is so narrow, that once when we met a small wagon, the horses were taken off, and the vehicle backed some distance before we could pass. On Sunday last I saw a young lady, of mature age, baptized; the baptismal font (as is usual in America) was within the communion-rails, between the reading-desk and pulpit; and to those who consider symbolisms

15*

secondary to other considerations, this is pleasing and convenient, as the recipient kneels down at the rails. In the evening the Bishop confirmed the persons also chiefly beyond youth; and in the afternoon he had a Service, principally for children.

27th.—Mr. W—— took charge of the rest of the party during a glorious drive of twenty miles across the mountains, while the Bishop and Mrs. P—— went off to another point for some distant duty. We did not meet them again till we had slept at the pretty town of Elmira, where Mrs. W—— and I took a pleasant and beautiful walk to one of numerous hills which surround the place, and there we saw a brilliant sunset. Here the formation is sand-stone, rich in fossils. The River Chemung flows through Elmira. We retired early and were up again by four o'clock. The Bishop met us at a station near C——, and we were driven to Wellsborough by a gentleman who came with his carriage. There several hospitable houses were opened to the party, but we at last concentrated it at Mr. C——'s, which was sufficiently large to receive us all, and to bestow every luxury and comfort.

At first I was taken charge of most kindly by another family, and I felt almost open to the charge of ingratitude when I left them, at the instance of our guide and governor, to rejoin the rest of our travelling party; but the son of those I deserted still undertook to aid my sketching and botanical propensities. In a distant ramble he procured me some yellow water lilies, the large leaves of which were more dark and shining than ours (*Nuphar advena*, or Spatter dock). They ornament the small creeks about here. Gray mentions the plant as most common in shallow waters. We found it blooming only at a depth of three or four feet, and sometimes the flowers were to be observed quite under; perhaps this was in consequence of a late sudden rise in the streams. Linnæa borealis was plentiful, carpeting a forest of gigantic white pines; and in the meadows I found Aster graminifolius.

Within thirty or forty miles of this place, Rosa Lake gives rise to three streams, which flow north, east, and south. One empties itself into the St. Lawrence; another into the Chesapeake, and a third into the Gulf of Mexico; so that these mountains must indeed be the Highlands of the United States.

On Thursday, the 28th of June, we left Wellsborough, after entering the cars sixteen miles off. We journeyed to Batavia, passing by Bath and the medicinal springs of Avon. On the 29th, the rest of the party left me to proceed to Niagara, and I went alone forty miles by railroad to Canandaigua, where I again find myself the guest of Mr. and Mrs. G—— with whom I stayed some days last October.

On Monday, July 2nd, I hope to reach Utica, where R—— is awaiting me, with the Governor and Mrs. Seymour. The weather is now intensely hot: for three days the thermometer has ranged above ninety degrees in the shade. Very active locomotion must be given up till after August, and I shall take this time for making quiet visits among friends in New York and New England States; first seeing Trenton Falls, where I hope once more to meet the Bishop of Pennsylvania and his party. We were together three such pleasant weeks! I feel sure that not one unkind thought, or even one careless word cast a shadow over the enjoyment of a single individual among the seven who thus journeyed together; and yet I have heard it said that travelling in company is one of the most severe tests to which temper and friendship can be subjected. I do not subscribe to that opinion. Change of scene is in itself a healthy kind of excitement, and therefore it is likely to make people good-humoured, and more accommodating than usual. I should be sorry to pin my faith upon the every-day kindness of a cross traveller.

The country between Batavia and Canandaigua is less attractive than that we have lately seen. We came through part of the Genesee Valley the day before yesterday, which is very fine. Twenty years ago that was the boundary of civilization; now it is in the midst of towns and settlements. Anglo-Saxon energy, with a dash of German determination and Irish quickness, is flying over this immense continent almost as fast as the stream of electricity pervades and connects its most remote localities. Talk of American nationality! as if America is not an epitome of the world; and surely the inhabitants of America may well be proud of their cosmopolitanism, instead of fostering a narrow sectional spirit. They may succeed in transferring the blood of all nationalities into a pure New World stream, if it be only healthfully taken charge of, with the sole exception of one dark current, with which they are entrusted for purification, not amalgamation—for education, not adoption. I forgot to say that my intention of joining Bishop Horatio Potter was given up, or rather he has given me up. His brother concludes that Church affairs drew him another way; and I have had quite sufficient to fill up my time without attempting Ticonderoga at present.

Utica, July 3.—Yesterday I accomplished, without much difficulty, a solitary journey here. More numerous packages (occupied by stones and flowers, &c.) than were quite convenient for an individual to undertake, during the necessary change of cars at Syracuse, exercised care and patience; but I brought them all safe, and I have now rejoined R——. My English letters have been delivered at New York—a disappointment, as I hoped to find them here; but the electric telegraph will bring them quickly, and in the meanwhile I find some interesting American correspondence, particularly a letter from Bishop Elliott, in answer to an inquiry of mine as to whether Miss Bremer had not misunderstood his opinion upon slavery. I am not forbidden to quote from his reply, and I therefore extract freely from the conclusion. He first explains that he had only agreed with Miss Bremer in combating some extreme opinions. It is too important not to be made use of.

The Bishop then says:—

'Is is well for Christians and philanthropists to consider whether, by their inteference with this institution, they may not be checking and impeding a work which is manifestly providential. For nearly a hundred years the English and American Churches have been striving to civilize and Christianize Western Africa, and with what result? Around Sierra Leone, and in the neighbourhood of Cape Palmas, a few natives have been made Christians, and some nations have been partially civilized; but what a small number in comparison with the thousands, nay, I may say millions, who have learned the way to Heaven, and who have been made to know their Saviour through the means of African slavery! At this very moment there are from three to four millions of Africans, educating for earth and for Heaven in the so vilified Southern States—educating in a thousand ways of which the world knows nothing—educating in our nurseries, in our chambers, in our parlours, in our workshops, and in our fields, as well as in our churches; learning the very best lessons for a semi-barbarous people—lessons of self-control, of obedience, of perseverance, of adaption of means to ends; learning, above all, where their weakness lies, and how they may acquire strength for the battle of life. These considerations satisfy me with their condition, and assure me that it is the best relation they can, for the present, be made to occupy. As a race, they are steadily improving. So far from the institution being guilty of degrading the negro, and keeping him in degradation, it has elevated him in the scale of being much above his nature and race, and it is continuing to do so. Place an imported African (of whom a few still remain) side by side with one of the third or fourth generation, and the difference is so marked that they look almost like distinct races—not only in mind and knowledge, but in physical structure.

'That monkey face, the result of an excessively obtuse facial angle, has become, without any admixture of blood, almost as human as that we are accustomed to see in the white race, and it has a facial angle as distinctly a right angle as that which belongs to the Caucasian family. The thick lips have become thin—the dull eye is beaming with cunning, if not with intelligence; the understanding is acute and ingenious. Their knowledge, when they have been instructed by missionaries or by owners, is respectable. A man has been made out of a barbarian, an intelligent and useful labourer out of an ignorant savage—a Christian and a child of God, out of a heathen; and this is called degrading the African race, by holding them in slavery! Such language is only of a piece with that miserably false sentimentalism which is pervading the world—such sentimentalism as thinks it cruel that a child should be disciplined or a criminal punished; which looks so tenderly upon the means as quite to overlook the great end those means may be working out. God's ways are not discordant with this way of Slavery. He who sees everything in its true aspect, with whom a thousand years is as one day—in whose sight the light affliction of this life, which is but for a moment, is far outweighed by the glory which is to follow—cares very little for the present means through which His will is working. What is it that a man should be a slave, if through that means he may become a Christian? What is it that one, or even ten generations should be slaves, if, through that arrangement, a race be training for future glory and self-dependence? What are the sufferings (putting them at the worst) which the inhumanity and self-interest, and the restraints of law can inflict for a few generations, when compared with the blessings which may thus be wrought out for countless nations inhabiting a continent? What is to be the course and what the end of this relation, God only knows. My feeling just now is, that I would defend it against all interference, just as I should defend my children from any one who would tempt them to an improper independence; just as I should defend any relation of life which man was attempting to break or to violate, ere the purpose of God in it had been worked out.'

And these are the opinions of Bishop Elliott, of Georgia, the man who remained nursing and consoling the sick and the dying, and burying the dead, when Savannah was decimated by yellow fever, and when thousands were falling victims around him! After this, who will dare, with a self-laudatory philanthropy, stand up and contrast his own abolitionism with the patient, practical doings of a conscientious slave-owner? Unhappily, it has of late years been too common among well-intentioned weak Christians to set up a stock of philanthropy at the expense of others. Let all do the work at their own doors, and the work of God in the world will be well done. If each man will reform himself, human nature will be effectually mended. But, as theory is easier than practice, so it is more common to look after the mote in our brother's eye than to take the beam out of our own.

As a commentary upon the Slavery question, I add two articles taken from newspapers—one, the account of a negro wedding, the other descriptive of a negro funeral. I must also mention that, in conversing with the free blacks, I rarely find them contented with their situation. An intelligent well-looking black carried my things from an hotel at Batavia to the train. I inquired if he liked the country ?—'Pretty well, missus, but——' There is always a 'but' from the lips of a Northern black—rarely expressed in the South, where it is generally, 'Mighty fond of master or missus; black people well to do, not often too much work, missus;' 'Many has got plenty of jewelry, missus;' 'We get our own way tolerable, missus,' &c., &c.

STAUNTON, *June* 24, 1855.

A SLAVE WEDDING IN OLD VIRGINIA—THE INVITATIONS—NEGRO ARISTOCRACY, &c., &c.

I send you herewith the originals of three invitations to a negro wedding, which is to take place on the 27th, at Richmond. The envelopes are in the best style of De La Rue and Co., open-work embossed, and of the finest texture. They enclose an embossed card, inscribed thus :—

MR. and MRS. TAYLOR will be pleased to see you on Wednesday Evening, June 27th, at 8½ o'clock.

MARIA JOHNSON.
ADAM HAWKINS.

Richmond.

The superscription is as follows :—'Mr. Charles Jackson and lady, present;' the second is to 'Mr. Henry Cassie and lady, present;' and the third to 'Mrs. Jane Hawkins.' The notes are written in a neat, Italian handwriting, and tied with white satin ribbon, *à la mode de Paris.*

These invitations were all received by members of my family. Mrs. Hawkins is my cook; Mrs. Jackson my Laundress; Mrs. Cassie my *fille de chambre.* They are all slaves, and their husbands are also slaves, owned by some of my neighbours. The happy bridegroom is related to my coloured family. They will doubtless have a happy time of it, and I commend to Greeley the case of these 'oppressed children of Africa.' I am sorry that every abolitionist in the land should not have an opportunity to see one such Virginia wedding.

VALLEY.

A LARGE NEGRO FUNERAL.

A coloured man named Samuel Betterson, an ordained deacon of the 3d Coloured Baptist Church, was buried yesterday afternoon. A very large number of his friends followed him to his grave. We noticed in the procession, three uniformed fire companies, and another joined them on the South Common. The Porter's Association, of which he was a member, turned out, and wore black scarfs, with white rosettes. We also noticed in the procession, two or three Female Benevolent Associations, distinguished by suitable dresses. A spectator counted thirty-five carriages, well filled, besides a number of other conveyances, and many on horseback, following the hearse. It is estimated that between two thousand and two thousand five hundred coloured persons were in the procession.

The mother of the Rev. John Cox, the coloured pastor of the 3d Baptist Church, was also buried yesterday afternoon. About fifty carriages, containing her relations and friends, followed her remains to the grave.

John Guerrard, a coloured fireman, and a member of engine No. 5, was also buried yesterday afternoon. The members of his company, in uniform, and a large number of his friends, in carriages and on horseback, followed him to the grave.

We will add, for the information of our northern friends, that the funeral processions above noticed were perfectly quiet and orderly, and that every thing connected with them was conducted with the utmost decorum and propriety.

July 4.—I am now again with Mr. and Mrs. Seymour. Utica is a pleasant town; the Valley of the Mohawk, in which it is situated, is highly cultivated. Mrs. J. Seymour took me last evening to one of the low surrounding hills, and I thought the view resembled those from some of our Gloucestershire elevations. We went to see the pretty rural cemetery, and sat down upon a boulder of granite, once considered the sacred stone of the Indians. It was brought from a distance of thirty miles to save it from destruction, and room was left around the little mound where it was placed for the interment of any of the red people who might wish to be buried near it. Many of them attended the consecration of the cemetery, but not one has ever availed himself of the privilege of interment there, partly because the tribes have almost all gone West; and any individuals who may still linger in the Oneida land are too poor to incur the expense of distant funerals.

Here there is an American nursery gardener really fond of flowers—the first time I have met with a native of the United States with that taste powerful enough to induce him to devote himself to their cultivation. All the nursery men I have made acquaintance with before have been English, Scotch, or Irish, and none of them found sufficient encouragement to be much devoted to their pursuit. This, the Anniversary of American Independence, is a day of noisy rejoicing, taken advantage of by boys and men for a Saturnalia of squibs and crackers, which are not only unceasingly exploding to-day, but have been unpleasantly active ever since I arrived, on Monday. It is more alarming for horses and for petticoats than even our celebration of Guy Fawkes. In the afternoon, Mr. and Mrs. Seymour are to take me to the residence of their brother-in-law, forty miles off, at Cazenovia, which I understand is a beautiful locality, and one abounding in fossils.

Cazenovia, July 5.—We went thirty-five miles by cars, a few miles in a stage, and at Chittenango Mr. L—— met us with his carriage. Chittenango means, 'the river flowing north;' Chenango, 'the water going south.' From Chittenango there is a gradual rise of eight miles to Cazenovia. Limestone caps the hills: as you advance, scarlet berried elders appear accompanying it; and by the sides of the valley I found Psoralea Onobryches, the scarlet maple, and a beautiful rose-coloured Calystegia, so different in tint and character from Sepium, I can think it only a variety. We stopped on our way to see a pretty fall of the Chittenango. I expected to find Cazenovia a wild, rocky, mountainous lake, the settlement built of log-houses, and buried in pine-woods. I find a calm water, something like Wenham Pond, about four miles long, with an ornamented regular little town, and Mr. L.'s house overlooking the water—a solid, brick, English-like residence. It is all pretty, but quite in a different style from that my imagination had pictured. The situation is as high as the Lake of Geneva. We took an interesting drive yesterday to see one of the sulphur sinks, or green ponds, twelve miles' distance, and on the way there were extended views in every direction. One fine prospect took in the whole length of Lake Oneida, twenty miles; and in that direction it seemed possible to see almost to Canada. Valleys between these limestone ridges are believed to be the work of denudation, and such circular ponds as those we saw yesterday have been possibly caused by the melting of salt formations, which Mr. L—— thinks may have been carried off to enrich the salt-pans of Syracuse. The fossils of this district are very interesting and new to me: I never before saw such gigantic Trilobites—they are almost as large as the cast of one shown to me at Cincinnati.

At last I have seen a humming-bird; and, foolishly enough, I was surprised by its humming. I thought the name was owing to their resemblance to a bee on the wing, but they hum louder than any bee; and the one I saw sat a long time on a sprig, and seemed to be drying his little self in the sun, after the wet in the morning; if disturbed, it only flew to a post near the tree upon which we first observed it, and then went back again. I did not see him feed; yet I understand he is seldom to be seen but on the wing feeding. Yesterday, Mr. L—— pointed out the king-bird, a little unarmed bird, which, by activity and perseverance, asserts a sovereignty over the feathered tribe, and chases even hawks away from a field. I observed him banishing a crow six times as large as himself: he follows incessantly, and torments until his subject flies off. Here I have been shown some curious nests. It seems the cow-bird in this country is as indolent a mother as our cuckoo: she lays an egg in the nests of other birds, and leaves it to take its chance in a strange family. A species of linnet is wise enough to find out the liberty taken at her expense: in one instance she inserted another nest above the intruded egg, so as to leave it unhatched; in another, the linnet contrived to sink the cow-bird's progeny below her own eggs. The oriole will appropriate any silk or worsted put in her way, and I am to have a very pretty nest interlaced with scarlet wool; and the fine line of a fishing rod, with the hook attached, has also been turned in with other materials. The yellow linnet is a very showy little bird. I have seen here also a milk-white woodpecker, with black wings and neck. What is here called a robin is more like one of our thrushes, with a faint tinge of red on his breast. It may be remarked in this neighbourhood, elevated as it is, that a large quantity of drift has at some time been brought here from Canada. Large boulders and rolled pebbles of granite and gneiss form part of it; and as these increase in size and quantity going northward, their progress and direction can be traced. In a forest near the 'Green Pond,' for the first time I found what is called the walking fern (*Camptosorus rhizophyllus*).

Friday, July 6.—We set off to see a pretty waterfall about eight miles from Cazenovia, and as I sketched from long grass in a down-pour of rain, I got thoroughly wet; but the interest of the place kept me warm, and no mischief happened from the drive back in wet things. In the afternoon we were rowed upon the lake very pleasantly by a little girl under twelve years of age.

July 7th.—I returned with Mr. and Mrs. Seymour to Utica, in our way to Trenton Falls, where we met three of my fellow-tourists in Pennsylvania; but the Bishop and Mrs. Potter had been obliged to go off in another direction.

July 8th.—This is the most charming and rural hotel I have seen in America; it is situated almost in a dense hemlock spruce forest, and has a garden quite English in style and neatness; and the rooms, brightly clean and comfortable, are decorated with prints and drawings chosen with artistic taste. The present landlord married a daughter of the first possessor of this property twenty years ago, and is now the owner. Everything about it is in accordance with the beauty and magnificence of its natural scenery: no forced ornaments or glaring paint jars upon the feelings or hurts the eye. Here is a kind of mesmeric influence which impresses the heart unconsciously: a sincere worshipper of nature is at once assured that one of her most lovely shrines cannot be desecrated by an adoration of Mammon's golden idol. Mr. Moore is worthy of Trenton both by taste and education. This name Trenton was formerly Oldenbarneveld: one regrets it, although originating from the Hollanders, not the Indian, whose appropriate appellation was 'Kangahoora' (leaping waters), and he called the river Kanatá (Amber River), equally descriptive; for at some places the falls resemble liquid amber, and occasionally the tumbling stream appears to have an edging of gold. The Governor and Mrs. Seymour first took me to see it from the Forest-walk, where the chasm below resembled that of the Tilt at Blair Athol, only filled by a wider, larger river, and by a succession of higher falls.

After dinner Mr. Moore took us a long walk, over wall and fence, to see a railroad in process of formation, by the aid of a very powerful and ingenious machine, worked by steam. The ground it is excavating is a hill of sand; an immense scoop, with a kind of trap-door behind, pokes in and fills itself, and then turns quietly and majestically round alone to the wagon at one side; the scoop then opens and at once deposits half a load, while people above push down the undermined ground; at this rate a mountain rapidly vanishes. I am no mechanic, but there is a simple grandeur in these evolutions which touched me considerably. I have always felt that even railroads have their poetry, and if I were a rhymer, this grand, solemn workman would set me rhyming.

In our way back Mr. Moore was so obliging as to accede to my wish that he would take me into a forest swamp, to see the mocassin flower growing; as we had to go down a steep woody hill, guided by a man living near, the rest of the party, excepting one young man, deserted. I was fully repaid for a rather difficult scramble by finding numbers of the beautiful pink Cypripedium spectabile (I should not call it purple) and Lilium Canadense by its side. The latter I have occasionally seen by the edges of railroads, but I never before gathered it. The pretty little white anemone-like-looking Dalibarda repens was also in flower all over the adjoining banks.

Next morning Mr. Moore took charge of us during a walk to all the falls along the edge of the torrent; without his experienced guidance I should have been afraid to undertake this, but as the water was high enough for beauty, and not too high for safety, it was very enjoyable. I sketched the three principal cataracts. It will not do to compare them with Niagara—it is an entirely different kind of thing; but certainly after Niagara I should prefer visiting Trenton to any other water scenery in America. Some of the party were obliged to leave us at one o'clock; but Mrs. Seymour and I delayed our departure till five, and remained out till near three.

Within the spray of one of the falls I discovered a small fern (some species of *Pteris*) not described by Gray, and I cannot help hoping it is altogether new to botanists. It is about the size of an Asplenium Ruta Muraria, but a bright green, and the fronds soft, not shining, and not crisp, like the Pteris crispa. We returned to Utica in the evening, and yesterday Governor Seymour came with me to Albany. I now write again from the Congress Hotel, and to-morrow it is my plan to go over to visit Mrs. Edwards, at Lenox, Mass. I understand it is a pretty place among the Berkshire hills; from thence I shall go on to spend a month among my Boston friends, and there I shall have enough to do to unpack and arrange the numerous boxes of stones, shells, and plants, I have at different times forwarded to Mr. Long's care.

Yours affectionately,

A. M. M.

Albany, July 11.

P. S.—In coming from Utica yesterday we almost followed the course of the Mohawk River, and came through several places which still retain the Indian names—Canajoharie (the 'boiling-pot') from a spring which resembles a small whirlpool, and Schenectady ('the end of the pine plain').

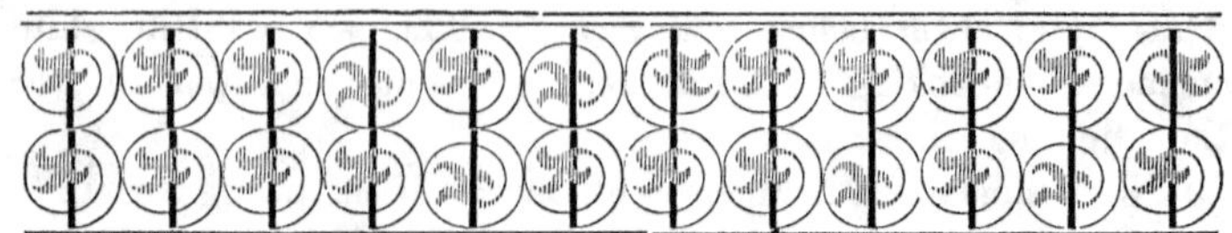

LETTER XXVIII.

LENOX, BERKSHIRE HILLS, MASSACHUSETTS,
July 13, 1855.

MY DEAR FRIENDS,—

This place differs from all those I have before seen in the United States. A cottage belonging to my hosts is situated on an eminence, nearly in the centre of an extensive valley; yet the surrounding country is hardly a vale. It is a depression made up of numberless unequal hills, and bounded by higher irregular ones, with fine mountains showing north and south, at a distance of about twenty-five or thirty miles. Saddleback to the north, emulates Loch na Garr, near Balmoral, in form; Washington southwards is its twin mountain, though apparently less grand. About a mile in front of the house there are small lakes, bordered and half hid by woods and broken ground. At present no offices or interfering plantations shut out the panorama, and its effect upon the windows and lawn is almost perfect—rather Scotch than Swiss in character; but, as seen from the house, it is a view which embraces a wider and more varied extent than any I know elsewhere as a home prospect. Although many have one side from which a still greater expanse of hills, valleys, and lakes may be seen, I am not acquainted with any other spot which has such views on every side. Mrs. and Miss Catharine Sedgwick live near Lenox. One evening we drank tea with them, and met Mr. and Mrs. R. P. James. Mrs. Fanny Kemble has a cottage near.

Authors and poets seem to congregate around this, the 'Lake District' of the United States.

Through Miss Sedgwick I got some Indian names of places—names that are now fast fading out of memory; but she has rescued these from the talk of an Indian woman, and they are worth preservation. A river, now called Housatonic, flows below Lenox. This is a corruption of 'Awastonook' (over the mountains). The Indians so called it when they came from the Hudson. There is a spot called now Elizabeth Lot (Elizabeth is 'Auchweemée,' the name of a berry). That place was also 'Nanwodtamá' (middle of the town). In the pronunciation, the first syllable, *Auch*, should be spoken gutturally. Kinkerpot, a small lake near, has not so euphonious a sound as usual; it was 'Kinkapotamia' (where a mare was drawn out of the water). A beautiful meadow, where maple trees grow, bore the name 'Hackpeehink' (the nation's sugar place). *A* should be uttered long as in *far;* the *ch* gutturally; *u* with a long sound, as in *full.* 'Hackpeehuckchoo' (the rising mountain), and Scott's Lake between Lenox and Lee, was 'Natchovtashmuch' (cutting bulrushes). 'The rattlesnake mountain,' 'Taheecannach,' but that word signifies *heart*, and it was for some reason associated with the affection then borne by the Indians towards the white race. 'Cachcawalchook,' one of the mountains near Stockbridge, means 'crossing the mountains.' 'Massmasschaick,' a 'fish's nest,' is now Monument Mountain. The tribe of Indians who came to these parts from the North River was called 'Mahéecannéek.' 'Choo,' or 'Chook,' means mountain. 'Queecheeochook,' 'mountain river.' 'Pahquinapack-kuch,' 'dark water.' 'Pangqueseek,' the name of a marsh near this place. 'Washcuing' and 'Washenée' are now the Salisbury Lakes.

I was taken to visit a Shaker village, which, perhaps, from the beauty of its situation, appeared less gloomy than the establishment I saw last year near Albany. But, after all, these places are little better than open mad houses. The inhabitants generally look ill and depressed. One pretty rosy little girl about thirteen attracted our notice. She looked quite out of place, but fortunately, as Shakers are not bound by vows, she may be freed some of these days—and inmates often do grow tired of such a cold formal life, and make off. One woman, not long ago, left this village, and engaged herself in one of the most noisy factories she could find. I suppose the contrast was agreeable. Another day I went to see what is called the Ice Valley, near Stockbridge. Heaps of massive rocks are thrown one upon another in a narrow gorge, to which the sun never penetrates; and in some deep holes winter snows accumulate, and remain unthawed through the hottest summers. Rambling about and sketching have occupied my time during a pleasant ten days passed among the Berkshire hills, so journalizing has been at a standstill.

Cambridge, near Boston, July 23.—I am now with Dr. and Mrs. Gray, at the Botanic Garden. We came by Springfield, through which town the Connecticut flows, a fine river. The path of the railroad goes through a mountainous district the first fifty miles.

July 24.—I went to the cottage of my friend, Mr. F——, at Brookline; and I was surprised to find it rurally situated, among woods and hills, equi-distant from the villages of Brighton and Brookline, instead of being in a flat uninteresting country.

July 28.—I took the railroad five miles to Boston, and saw Captain Judkins, who this time has brought in the *Canada*, instead of Captain Stone. Captain Judkins was sent with troops for the Crimea, in the *Arabia*, but he got the fever and was invalided home; Captain Stone replaced him; and on Captain Judkins's recovery, he took charge of the *Canada* till the large new steamer, *Persia*, just launched, is ready for sea. I have engaged my old berth for the last week in October, as that time is considered favourable for making the voyage home. In one of the papers I see that a Creole, at Havana, has been thrown into prison on suspicion of possessing a likeness of Ramon Pinto. Yesterday I heard another anecdote, illustrative of slavery and the negro character. My informant, who was lately travelling in Virginia, was at Sulphur Springs. The master of the hotel had a clever active black waiter, but he was a 'bad boy.' After some particular act of misconduct, the master called up his slave:

'You are a hopeless rascal, Horace; I will have nothing more to do with you. Here are some dollars and your papers of freedom; go off into Kentucky, and never let me see you again.'

'Can't possible, massa; won't go, massa.'

'Won't! but you must! you are quite able to take care of yourself.'

'Sha'n't, massa. Fac is, can't no way 'gree with them free niggers.'

And Horace remained; his owner might flog, but it is hardly possible for him to shake off a servant determined not to go; selling is the only way. But respectable slaveowners are very adverse to this mode of 'proceeding; and it is not easy to get rid of a troublesome negro.' In some respects the masters are the slaves of their servants, who often dictate instead of obeying. I here repeat, what probably my friends in England will be slow in believing, that, in the mass, Southern slaveowners are conscientiously fulfilling their trying and painful duties; and that I have seen more of comfort, cheerfulness, contentment, and religious principle among negroes of the Southern States, than among any other working population of the same amount, either here, or in England. In the Northern States the whites have great physical and mental advantages; but there is an absence of true contentment among them, and a prevalence of insanity sad to contemplate. I suppose the restlessness consequent upon a new country and Republican institutions does not tend to real self-happiness. I must positively assert, that the countenances and manner of Americans as a nation, do not express contentment. That there may be heart-rending abuses in the South I do not deny, though I have not witnessed them; but what is there which is not liable to abuse? I could tell of heart-rending abuses in the North. 'Offences will come, but woe unto them by whom they come.' No one can doubt that the change of the education and improvement of a black population, through slavery, is a trying and arduous responsibility—a task for which pecuniary advantages are a poor compensation, and one which is not often repaid by either pecuniary or moral profit; and there are dangerous and awful temptations accompanying it; but are not temptations God's discipline for life? We cannot suppose they will ever be removed; but we must take care they 'bring forth fruit in due season.' Personally, with all my love of freedom, I would much prefer to be a slave in the South (not in Cuba), than one of those pariahs, called free negroes in the North.

I am now with an abolitionist friend, who, like most abolitionists, has never visited the South. We can therefore sympathize only in a wish to see those States free where black labour can be superseded by white—and this for the sake of the white race rather than the black. I cannot praise those Southerners who keep their slaves, all the while maintaining that Slavery is a dark spot, to be washed off the first convenient opportunity. Such slaveowners are sinning against conscience; they must believe in slavery as one of the means by which it pleases the Most High to discipline the white and the black for higher things; or they must at any cost repudiate Slavery altogether. Had the civilized world united to regulate instead of attempting to abolish, each black, as he gained sufficient knowledge, habits of forethought, and industry, might by law have been given the right to purchase his own freedom at a certain age, and such negroes would have gone back to Christianize and civilize Africa. But the futile endeavour to abolish, instead of to regulate, has resulted in injury instead of benefit to the black race; just as the Maine Law punishes the use, rather than the abuse, of spirituous liquors. At one house, the house too of a great abolitionist and promoter of the Maine Law, I met with 'tipsy-cake,' and saw it liberally bestowed even upon children! So we may eat drink, but we must not drink drink! Is not this humbug?

August 6.—We have been paying a very agreeable visit at the house of that good Mr. Forbes, who headed a petition to his Government, and commanded ships which brought out American contributions of food to the starving Irish. This was indeed a brotherly act—a grateful acknowledgment of the 'one ancestry' which now and ever should be a bond of affection between our lands; and I trust whatever family jars and misunderstandings may have arisen in past times to separate parent and children, the 'war hatchet' is now for ever sunk in those unfathomable ocean depths by which England and American are at once divided and united.

Milton has a charming vicinity, fine trees, hedges, and even roads, bordered by hedges, from which hang lovely draperies of sinnax and vines, English in outline if not in detail. The village is on high ground, and has every here and there extensive views, with the sea, and Boston, and Boston Harbour—particularly from the granite quarries towards the blue hills. I spent a whole morning there, with an American friend who sympathized in the pleasures of sketching. Rattlesnakes are not uncommon, but that reptile is fortunately timid, and rarely stings; even the women and children who are scattered about 'berrying'—that is, gathering the berries of a productive huckleberry (*Vaccinium* or *Galyussacia resinosa*). Men find thick leather boots or gaiters quite sufficient protection, for rattlesnakes never strike high.

We passed one pleasant day on the sandy sea shore above Nantasket River—a pic-nic party; and there I saw, as last year at Newport, young ladies and gentlemen dancing among the waves, as it is a convenient place for bathing. Mr. Forbes went into the water and experimented upon his travelling-bag, life preserver—which he thought effectual enough, but then the sea was very calm. Many vessels dotted the offing. A sandy bay extends five miles in one direction, whilst the other side is indented by rocky inlets, Cape Anne clearly visible in the distance. Among other plants, I found for the first time Lycopodium rupestre.

Brookline, August 10.—Before my return here, I spent a morning at the Botanic Garden, Cambridge, with Dr. and Mrs. Gray, to meet Miss Morris, a botanical lady from Philadelphia; we called at the house of Professor Agassiz, but he was deeply engaged in 'embryological researches,' at Nahant. From Brookline I went to the Beverley shore, to spend a few days with Mr. and Mrs. L——, under whose hospitable roof I met with my first welcome this side of the Atlantic, and I wrote about their pretty place last year.

Providence, August 18.—I came here on the 14th, for the meeting of the American Scientific Association, that I might see the wise men of the West assembled together. I am in the pleasant and even luxurious abode of Mr. and Mrs. M. B. Ives, who sent me a kind invitation through Mr. President Wayland.

August 15.—We attended the morning session; that day there were no separate sections. Professor Lomax (after the Chairman, Dr. Torry, had opened the meeting) read a paper upon the temperature of planetary bodies, and of the space through which they travel. This subject raised an animated and interesting discussion, which was carried on by Agassiz, Henry, Bache, Pierce, Rogers, &c. &c. The question about a lunar atmosphere seems still doubtful; one astronomer present adduced proofs that signs of twilight were evident, which would speak to the fact of an atmosphere for the moon. (I forgot to mention that I passed a delightful day with Professor and Mrs. Agassiz at Nahant, and he was generous enough to admit the value, and be pleased with the fossils I brought from Ocala and the Silver Spring, in the middle of Florida, and he also said that the existence of cretaceous tertiary formations there had not before been ascertained.) During the discussion of Professor Lomax's papers, a pretty general agreement appeared to be arrived at; that the question of temperature must be so dependent upon whatever internal heat the several planetary bodies may preserve or evolve, that any calculation with regard to their distances from the sun, cannot give certainty about their individual temperature. But Agassiz expressed a decided opinion, that if there are animal organisms inhabiting the planets, they must be constituted in a manner entirely different from terrestrial creatures; and if (as I think Whewell remarks) the laws of fluids, of light and of motion, are similar in the earth and the other bodies, then it seems a fair deduction that as yet there has been no creation of life in worlds incapable of supporting such life as we know of. Professor Bache, Director of the General Coast Survey, showed that the commonly received notion of the existence of one great tidal wave, is a mistake. He stated, that although something is known as to the direction of tidal waves in the Atlantic, very little or nothing has yet been ascertained respecting those of the Pacific. President Wayland had an evening reception, which everybody attended; it was a very pleasant party.

During the morning session of August 16th, Bache gave an account of a great earthquake wave on the western coast of the Pacific. Professor Brockleby read a paper upon remarkable frozen wells near Owego, which have ice during the hottest summers. Agassiz, as usual, charmed and informed every one by his lucid statement of some zoological facts, and Mr. Blake gave us a new and interesting notice upon the geology of California.

In the evening there was an assembly at Mr. Allen's, where I was introduced to Miss Maria Mitchell, the American Mrs. Somerville; she is as simple and unassuming in manner as our great *astronomess.*

Friday.—Professor Hall explained much about graptolites that was new to me; he used a lady's parasol to exemplify the form of some of these polypi, and Agassiz following, made some of his lively, instructive remarks, in which he amused the audience by calling the parasol 'this tool;' he showed that some of the associated polypi are probably higher in the scale of organization than single individuals. A terrific gunpowder explosion, which occurred at Wilmington some short time ago, by the blowing up of three wagons (which, though under a regulation of separate departure, had contrived to travel in company), afforded opportunity for another lively discussion, which explained some of the curious phenomena observed to result from that explosion; and a debate (also conversational), upon Professor Bache's account of the co-tidal lines upon the Pacific coast, exemplified how naturally each branch of science dove-tails into all. To the zoologists these tides offer reasons, which partly explain the geographical distribution of fishes. To the mathematician they read or resolve problems;—whilst they also aid and confirm the observations of geology, and thus it was shown how the cultivation of each science elucidates every other branch of knowledge. As to the mathematical and optical sections. they were beyond my comprehension, and I therefore avoided them as much as possible; but in doing so, I missed hearing Mr. Jones's observations on the Zodiacal Light, which I am told were deeply interesting. From two hundred and fifty careful observations, he decides it to be of the same nature as the ring of Saturn; but another great astronomer asserted that Saturn's ring is gradually approaching the body of the planet, and that within eighty years they must meet. I do not understand how these two discoveries are to be reconciled. During the section of Natural History this morning, Professor Agassiz showed by a clear chain of argument and deduction, that the newly discovered jaw of a species of shark brought from carboniferous formations in Western America (I think from Wisconsin), belongs to the sword-fish division of that family. Professor Henry made a useful practical statement, respecting the best mode of testing building materials; he mentioned that blocks of stone coated (or rather divided from each other) by plates of tin, support double the weight borne by those which have lead between them, because the latter substance gives way to pressure much more easily than tin. Mr. Blake continued his observations upon the geology of California, and the mountainous ridges along the western coast, and Professor Hitchcock exhibited curious drawings from the foot impressions of a most extraordinay four-toed, two-legged kind of frog, which must have been larger than the largest elephant we know of. I cannot feel sure that I have discovered the pith of what I have been listening to these last three days, in this hasty sketch, but perhaps it may enable you to judge that a great deal of information was elicited, and that the subjects brought forward were by no means dry even to unscientific hearers. Saturday evening I went to a party at Professor Caswell's; and yesterday I visited the President and Mrs. Wayland.

Last night a gentleman of high reputation in the legal profession told me that the free black people die out so rapidly, that, although himself a man only in middle age, he remembers when almost every servant in the town was black or coloured, yet now few of that race are left. His general views upon the subject of slavery were in perfect accordance with those observation has led me to adopt; and he thinks that, notwithstanding the eagerness and activity of the anti-slavery party, even in the North, a majority of the calm and unprejudiced minds would coincide in these opinions; and that many former abolitionists are adopting them. Dr. Adams, who distinguished himself on the anti-slavery side, after a visit to the South of sufficient investigation, has published a pamphlet recanting former opinions. Judge Wayne, also, confirms my observations respecting the strongly aristocratic feeling which prevails among the slaves. They consider it is losing caste to connect themselves by marriage with the people who may belong to masters of their own race, or even with those of inferior 'Buckras;' and he has known many instances of respectable and educated blacks (of individuals who have heen elevated, not degraded, by slave institutions) who have positively refused offers of freedom; saying they did not want to leave a country the laws of which they understood, to go to one, where, perhaps, they may find themselves uncomfortable, and that among whites it was far more respectable for them to have a master. This I am inclined to believe is the opinion of the best informed and most superior among the black men—of course there will be exceptions; but it is the giddy and profligate negro, as a general rule, who seeks freedom by running away. This subject is so frequently a topic of conversation, that, as long as I remain in America, it will turn up in every-day remarks.

Monday, August 21, was occupied by papers and discussions upon various subjects. Mr. Lawrence gave a lecture on minerals of the Wheatley lead mines, and the method of analyzing sulphates, arsenates, and molybdates of lead. The Rev. Mr. Brooks stated a large number of facts, showing the fatal results which have followed from the marriages of blood relations. This brought up Agassiz upon races—his observations were very curious and striking. Then we had Mr. Blake's notes upon the mammoth Red-wood trees (*Sequoias*) of Calaveros county, California; that tree named by Lindley, 'Wellingtonia,' is also a sequoia, Dr. Torry says. Mr. Blake gave me a specimen of this wood, which, washed over with a sponge dipped in a solution of soda, immediately became so dark as to be almost ebony like. That evening an assembly was held by the Mayor of Providence. Mr. Brown and I leave for New York this morning, the 21st; and as Agassiz and many others of the scientific body, consider it their duty to attend the funeral of Mr. Abbott Lawrence in the Auburn Cemetery to-morrow, the meeting must be nearly at an end. Professor Bache and others offered their tribute of gratitude yesterday in eulogiums upon Mr. Lawrence, who was so great a benefactor to science that the sincere regrets of that body are united to those of all other classes upon his death.

New York, August 23.—I got to the St. Nicholas Hotel after a pretty but dusty journey from Providence. General Scott will accompany me to West Point. He is the commander-in-chief of the American army—an old soldier, six feet five inches in height, who, although he still suffers from wounds received in warring with his old country brethren, does not belie his Scotch descent either in appearance or feeling. I have taken rooms at the New York Hotel for the 27th, to be near the place where the Educational Convention will assemble,—the same Convention I attended at Washington, and the next assembling of which I then promised to visit.

West Point, August 25.—This, indeed, is the finest locality possible for a military school, and it appears to bestow such an education as, with some variation, might be a model of early training. Five years is the usual term, and seventeen, or at earliest fifteen, the age of admission. During my travels in the United States, whenever I have fallen in with a young man who struck me as superior in information, and even in manner, I usually found he had been a Cadet at West Point. It is situated in a beautiful highland district upon the banks of the North River. At present the summer vacation is still unconcluded, and the Cadets who do not take advantage of it are encamped in tents, on what is called 'The Plain,' and subject to complete military rule. Last night we went to evening parade. There was a bright moon in unison with a glowing sunset as we left the ground; it was altogether one of the prettiest and most cheerful scenes I have witnessed in America, where one great lack is the absence of athletic games and merry out-of-door amusements for the people. The puritanical leaven has, I suppose, checked everything like games, and this may be one reason for the depression and melancholy which prevail through the general population. There appears to be no reasonable medium between rowdyism and gloom; and so even fires are taken advantage of by the young men and boys to get at something like a 'lark.' I am going on to the Catskill Mountains to-morrow.

Mountain House, Catskill, August 27.—This hotel, hung like a bird's nest two thousand five hundred feet above the North River, at the distance of thirteen miles, is placed on a beautiful spot, just where a sunrise can be seen to most advantage; and I am so fortunate as to have a room, the windows of which look the right way; but unfortunately the sun rose concealed this morning—still it was fine to see the clouds chasing each other across the moss below. I heard a lady in the open gallery asking in sober earnest, 'Is the sun going to rise this morning?' He was certainly up, though not visible; and the valley was soon also entirely concealed. I went out by six o'clock, and had a pleasant scramble on one of the mountains above till heavy rain came on; but before seven it poured. We came up the river from West Point yesterday in a steamer going over to Albany. I was surprised to find the distance fifty miles—charming scenery all the way: in some places the Hudson is as wide as Windermere Lake, and I could have believed myself there; and sometimes this river may be compared to the Rhine; but it more frequently resembles a chain of lakes. There is a good carriage road all the way to this place; though the ascent is very steep, we mounted it in four-horse coaches. I walked with some acquaintances the last three miles, and came through the scene of Rip van Winkle's adventures. How the materials for building this great Palace of the Hills were ever dragged up, I cannot imagine. It was a noble thought to plant it here, where thousands, if not millions, of human beings will, in the course of time, find enjoyment, and may regain that health and those spirits which have perhaps been lost in the turmoil below. Fresh cool air may always be found here, I am told, even during the hottest summer; and one feels as if beyond, as well as above, sublunary things. There is no church within reach, but being Sunday morning, service was read by a minister in the house.

After dinner, I walked with some friends to see the highest waterfall I ever heard of, called 'Cuatskill,' which is, I suppose, the same as Catskill. The word 'skill' or 'gill' originates in a Dutch name; and Clove (as they here call a pass beyond) I have little doubt, has its origin in 'Kloof.' The 'Cuatskill' pours down its stream two hundred feet into a deep rocky dell. It is a much higher fall than the Staubach, in Switzerland, and the surrounding scenery is as picturesque, though without the high Swiss mountains. The water makes another leap of eighty feet a little farther on.

Monday morning, I again went out before sunrise, and again no sun was visible. At six o'clock, the clergyman, Mr. W——, accompanied me to see fine masses of conglomerate rock upon the Southern Mountain beyond our hotel, and at seven we took our departure through a deep pass, resembling some of those in our Highlands of Scotland. By a circuitous route, the plain below our hotel was reached, and the house was seen upon the edge of the precipice above us. A ferry-boat made its passage from the small town of Catskill across the North River, to meet the cars from Albany, which conveyed our party to New York.

August 28.—I attended the Educational Convention, where an excellent farewell address was delivered by Bache, the retiring President. He dwelt forcibly upon the great existing necessity for universities—not mere buildings of stone, or schools for youth—but assemblages of learned men—cosmopolitan institutions; places where men not learned may become so; places where real talent may be fostered, and where scientific information can be found by all who earnestly and diligently seek it,—centres from which all knowledge, theological, mathematical, historical, scientific, &c. &c., may radiate to the remotest corners of this vast country, and imbue the hearts and minds of the great American people with something which shall direct and balance the influence of the *almighty dollar*. The Bishop of Pennsylvania joined the evening exercise, when a paper was read by Professor Tappan, of Michigan, on the 'Relation of Common Schools and Colleges.'

Wednesday, August 29.—An excellent lecture was given by the Rev. E. B. Huntingdon, principal of the public school, Stamford, Connecticut, on 'Mental and Physical Activity.' In the evening the Rev. F. B. Huntingdon, Professor of Moral Philosophy at Cambridge University, made a most original and striking address on 'Unconscious Tuition;' fine in language, attractive in delivery, and very practical in matter, although permeated throughout by poetical feeling. He touched even upon the ill effects of the want of refined habits, and the absence of gentlemanly bearing, in those who instruct, and forcibly pointed out how ugly tricks and coarse manners corrupt and debase the young placed under their influence. He said—'The teacher who sits in his chair with feet placed higher than his head, who munches apples and nuts like a monkey, and even sends forth American saliva—like a member of Congress! in all these acts is unconsciously losing the respect of his pupils, and exercising an evil influence over their character.' How true it is, that the most eloquent and accomplished orator has little permanent influence when we feel, perhaps without being able to explain, the effects of a screw loose in his moral character; perhaps there is selfishness, an absence of honesty, a seeking for applause, a something we know not what—we have never been told; but unconsciously, while we admire the talents of the orator, we refuse him our sympathy. Unconsciously his character tells upon our minds—he is no thorough man, and we feel it.

Thursday, August 30.—After attending the Educational Meeting in the morning, I spent the rest of the day with a party of friends on Staten Island. It reminds me of the Isle of Wight, but New York and North River, with their innumerable bays and creeks and islands, form a more varied and beautiful scene than the Southampton River, and the coast of Hampshire. It requires half an hour to cross over by steam; the island itself is picturesque, and well-wooded: there is a particularly pretty view from a villa belonging to Mr. Cunard. Staaten is sixteen miles in length. I have at last found, in one of the State reports from Texas, some mention of 'horned frogs' (*Phrysonomas*), there are two or three species to be found in Texas and Mexico; mine was Phrysonoma cornuta. The Phrysonomas are true saurians; their bodies, instead of being smooth like frogs and toads, are covered with scales; they never hop or leap as batrachians, but run very fast like spiders. Their upper spines are as large as miniature horns of a gazelle. (I saw at Providence a little stuffed deer from Japan, not much larger than a kitten, and with horns hardly more considerable than those of a Phrysonoma.) They are singular creatures, and give one the idea of being stragglers left behind by one of the extinct races; the surface of their bodies is covered with scales, and there is a double abdominal row, quite prickly.

August 31.—The *Canada* has brought favourable news from England, which I am inclined to believe will be received with satisfaction by the best minds in the United States, for Russo tendencies lie merely on the surface. Some of my friends went away early, and I only attended the Convention to hear Professor Barnard, of the Mississippi University, upon the improvements that may be introduced into American colleges.

During my stay in New York, I have taken one trip of fifty miles down what is called the East River. It is rather a narrow arm of the sea, extending above a hundred miles, forming Long Island: it passes with a rapid current through the narrow passage called Hellgate, where once an English ship was wrecked. The river is there divided by Randall Island, which I last year visited with Governor Seymour to see all the penitentiaries and charitable institutions.

September 3*rd*.—I spent some time in the Astor Library, where I looked over some of Agassiz' publications, and the beautiful Zoological work of Dana. In the evening a friend took me to see Rachel's first American appearance as *Camille*. Seventeen years ago,

I witnessed her London *débût* in the same character. I think her experience, and a longer cultivation of art, do not improve upon the first and natural expression of genius. She is more cultivated, but she cannot touch the heart now as she touched the hearts in the year 1838. She was well received by a crowded house, and the little *Comédie* of *Les Droits de l' Homme*, by Premanoy, was well acted; three sisters of Rachel's performing all the female characters.

September 4th.—I visited the remains of the American Crystal Palace to see part of a Californian mammoth tree (Red-wood), described by Mr. Blake at Providence. The grandeur and singularity of this trunk surpassed my expectations, the trees must appear as much larger than cedars, as cedars exceed hawthorns in size. Some articles still remain in this Crystal Palace, which is now the property of Barnum; the building itself, though so much smaller than Paxton's, is less simple in ornament, and loses in effect from being too elaborate. I intend to proceed to-morrow in the direction of Lake George and Ticonderoga: in that neighbourhood I am to be joined by Governor Seymour, who promises to guide me through part of the Adirondack, that Highland district of New York State, still a wild forest, although it is as extensive as the whole State of Massachusetts. It is principally frequented by sportsmen for the sake of the game and fish, which have been as yet but little disturbed. When we were at Ogdensburgh we almost touched that territory, which is partly bounded by the St. Lawrence. The streets of New York are much shaded in some places by Ailanthus glandulosa, and as most of them are now flowering, or producing their key-like tassels, they look very pretty. I have not detected the disagreeable odour which they are accused of emitting, nor have I heard of any poisonous influence from them, but perhaps something of that kind may be discovered later in the season. This letter shall be sent from here by post now; perhaps the beauties of Lake George may induce me to begin another.

Yours affectionately,

A. M. M.

LETTER XXIX.

SARATOGA, N. Y.,
September 5, 1855.

MY DEAR FRIENDS,—

I did not imagine that my next letter would date from this place, but imperative circumstances determined that it should be so. We left New York by six o'clock this morning, under the supposition that we were to reach Lake George before night; but though we were at Troy at eleven, all calculation was thrown out by information that no train could take us on till six; we were not told that by going back to Albany, another line might forward us sooner; this one had been impeded by an incendiary, who had fired a railroad-bridge, about twenty miles from this place. Having once before visited Troy and made acquaintances there, I walked into the town. All the families I knew were still away on summer tours, a custom nearly universal here in cities; people having usually no country places, take to the country at large. However, I was so fortunate as to find some friends accidentally at Troy, who afforded me shelter, a warm bath, and some dinner, and kindly walked back with me to the station at the hour of departure. Precisely at six, the train left Troy, but the one hour (usually time enough for reaching Saratoga) was lengthened into three; for at the river, which was to be crossed, passengers, luggage, and all, had to be transferred into a large ferry-boat; and it was necessary to carry weighty boxes up the steep bank of our railway track on the opposite side—a slow process. So we had two hours of travel after dark; and I at once determined to sleep at the United States' Hotel, at Saratoga. Spiteful mischief is too often perpetrated on the railroad tracks. Last year a train of cars, upon which I went in the night from Niagara to Canandaigua, was thrown off by the abstraction of a few feet of rail; and the other day several lives were sacrificed by the same thing having been done. I have heard lately of two other bridges having been intentionally set on fire; and these fiendish acts are rarely followed by detection. What can be too bad for wretches who thus unmercifully destroy unoffending people, out of some feeling of individual spite! But we may be sure that fear and remorse will ultimately persecute and haunt such men, until they yearn to end their miserable lives by that rope they may for the present escape.

Saratoga, Tuesday morning.—It is as well that I have been obliged to stop at this place, so much spoken of, though watering-places afford small attraction to me. Upon getting up this morning, however, I can see nothing from windows looking in two directions, but one maple tree imprisoned in a small court; and young maples, set as thick as pines, edging angular walks, and dotting some green and well-shaven turf, in a square enclosed on three sides by this hotel. The air feels cold and October-like. I think thermometers range more widely and vary more suddenly than in England: one very cold day succeeds an intensely hot one; and then, perhaps, we have two hot ones again; and the nights are usually cold at this time of the year; sometimes even frosty. I already see a brilliant colouring of foliage, which shows the leaves have been touched by frost.

Lake George, September 6.—I left Saratoga by the early train; one hour's morning walk being enough to give me some idea of a place which is a ruralized Baden-Baden, or Homburg, or Schwalbad, or any other *bad*—I dare say a pleasant resort for people who seek only fresh air and disagreeable water, and numberless acquaintances. It resembles German baths, with rather less gambling, more dancing, and more dressing; and I was delighted to get away from such annoyances, to this charming lake, and to find myself in an hotel quite homelike. A coach brought us the last fourteen miles; we came by Glen's Falls, where the water rushes finely, in spite of lumber and saw-mills, down a descent of seventy or eighty feet; then we passed a place called 'Bloody Pond,' the battle of Lake George having been fought near, in 1755. You may remember, this engagement was between Sir W. Johnson, aided by Hendrick, the Mohawk chief, and the French general Dieskau, with his Canadian Indians. Now we are among the very scenes depicted in *The Last of the Mohicans.* Cooper calls this lovely lake, Horican (Transparent Water); I believe he confessed it was a supposititious Indian name; but I cannot find out any other given to it by the Aborigines. The French appellation was St. Sacrament; that of the English, Lake George; and both historical and local associations now confirm it.

I am at an original hotel, called a Lake House; much pleasanter and less staring than a new place, built in a beautiful situation at the southern end, 'The William Henry Hotel.' Here I do not feel as if I was at a place of public resort, though the house contains a large number of guests. It has easy access to the water from a lawn, for bathing, fishing, or boating, and bowling and billiards may be enjoyed by those who wish for them. I find pleasant families here who do not make gay attire and good dinners the first objects of life. Horican (Transparent Water), that was a characteristic name! Lake George unites the beauties of Loch Lomond, Windermere, and Wenham 'Pond;' and is as beautiful as any lake I know, excepting that its mountains, though fine, are not so rugged as some of our Highlands. It is wide enough, without the shores being too distant from each other; the water has, in many places, a depth of one hundred and twenty feet. It empties itself into Lake Champlain, near Ticonderoga; so called from Checonderoga, an Iroquois word, signifying 'sounding waters,' on account of the noise made by the water rushing from Lake George. *The Last of the Mohicans* has made this neighbourhood doubly interesting. Yesterday we had a gay and touching celebration of the hundredth anniversary of the victory gained by the British and Americans over the French, in September, 1755. My own maternal grandfather led his Highland regiment during the conflict of those days; and this commemoration was one which enlisted my sympathies. Gentlemen and ladies walked in two separate processions to the church, where, after a short prayer Dr. Van Renssalaer gave a detailed historical account of the events of 1755, and the years succeeding. After firing off cannon, there was a beautiful array of boats, decorated with flags; most of them had only one lady in the stern; mine carried the English ensign. Mrs. Potter had the Scotch thistle. English and French flags waved in union on this occasion, and the band played *God save the Queen*, with other airs. There were about twenty-four boats marshalled in line upon the lake, or sweeping along in succession, at the command of a Commodore. The scene was very gay upon the beautiful waters; and, when night came on, the darkness was illuminated by a liberal display of rockets and Roman candles. A subscription was proposed for raising a monument on the old battle-field to the heroes who fell there, particularly the gallant Indian chief, Hendrick; and I hope the object will be accomplished.

September 10.—I went with a party in a steamer twenty miles up the lake to Ticonderoga, which is a small town on the Lake George side of the fort. There are still ditches and fortifications which mark the battle-field. Sixteen hundred British were killed in that engagement.* The fort is situated on a peninsula, which runs into Lake Champlain: it is a beautiful site, commanded by a mountain which has been named Defiance. The rest of our party went to dine at an hotel near, but I remained for two or three hours, sketching and wandering about the fortifications, which are very extensive. This is the only interesting ruin I have seen in America.

September 12.—Yesterday, in my way here, I stopped for an hour or two at the hotel to wait for a steamer. The landlord took so great an interest in a sketch of the fort, which I made from a window in his house, that he would not hear of my paying

* The French entangled them among the branches of felled trees, so that their forces were scattered and destroyed.

either for my own dinner or R——'s; the only repayment he would accept was a hasty copy of my drawing.

At Westport I was fortunate in finding Mr. H. L——, who drove me up to see his pretty cottage, situated upon a rock which commands a splendid view. While I was absent this morning, Governor Seymour arrived with his niece, and he has gone on to Elizabeth Town, to make necessary arrangements for our camping out of town in the Adirondack. We are to join him at an early hour to-morrow morning. Weather promises to be favourable, and the black fly has vanished, so that we have every prospect of enjoying our gipsy expedition.

September 12.—We started before six o'clock, and joined Mr. Seymour at Elizabeth Town. We met Professor Baird, who is staying there, and Mr. H——, one of our *compagnons de voyage.* We set off after making backwood arrangements, and selecting kettles and pans. Tea, biscuits, lemons, portable soup, and arrow-root went into small space; these, with trout and venison, will feed us nobly for a week. Branches of the hemlock spruce with waterproof coverings, duvets, blankets, and air-cushions will form our couches; and our Governor carries a tent in case of wet weather. We reached the Saranac Lake about an hour after dark, conveyed by buck-boards and wagons—much too civilized a mode of proceeding; but we go on in boats or on foot, and hope to travel more than a hundred miles with packs on our backs and staffs in our hands—this will be delightful! On our way yesterday, we passed through fine passes and grand mountains. I made one sketch in which Tahawas 'the cloud splitter,' was included. We thought ourselves unhappy at sleeping in the little Saranac hotel last night, though it was three in a room, constructed of rough boards and laths; still this will be the last time for some days we shall have any other canopy than heaven, and the small tent which is to be carried with us. Our drive from Elizabeth Town to this place was about thirty-two miles; the road rough, but practicable by walking up the steepest parts. In our way we picked a variety of wild fruits, blackberries, huckleberries, cherries, and above all, a little red plum, which though rather hard and acid, I thought would make a good pudding at our first camp in the woods; so I got enough for that purpose. It was quite dark for an hour before we reached Baker's—the name by which this last house of reception on the Saranac River is known. We had no other difficulty, however, than making our way once nearly into a shed, instead of following the road, and after backing out, our proposed resting-place was soon reached.

While the party were putting up, I parted with R——, and sent her back in the carriage to embark again in the steamboat to Westport. She will go round by Utica to Canandaigua, to give Mrs. Seymour a report of us so far; and I shall pick her up again at the latter place, where she will remain with our hospitable friends, Mr. and Mrs. G——. Miss M—— and Mr. S—— walked on a mile or two to the lake side, and left Mr. H—— and one guide to accompany me, after I had made a sketch of the place and surrounding mountains from a hill above. On the edge of Saranac Lake we found a small house, three boats, and various articles prepared for forest expeditions. One boat was set apart for two dogs, guns, and baggage, taken care of by one Jamie M'Cleland, who had enough of Scotch recollections to induce him to look with a pleased expression at one of my name.

Mr. Moody, the head guide, rowed the boat, in which I had a comfortable seat of cloaks and cushions, with the Governor. Miss M——, his niece, and Mr. H——, were conducted by a fine youth of nineteen, who goes by the name of 'Prince Albert,' and it is believed he was so christened at two years old, though he looked shy and annoyed when asked about it, and said he believed it was '*Pliny* Albert.' The weather was perfect, as we rowed along the beautiful Saranac Lake. For the first time I saw the Loon, and heard it utter its wild cry, more resembling a mocking laugh than anything else. I could have fancied it saying, 'You intruders, you—you will have enough of me before you have done.' A fine eagle next soared over our heads, and ravens also.

We floated on water as smooth as glass, passing by lovely islands and fine rocks, until we came to the first rapid, an inlet into the next lake, where we disembarked, that the men might carry and push through their boats. I sketched during this operation, while Mr. S—— mended the slight terminal pole of his fishing-rod, which an accident had broken; then we proceeded to a small 'round lake,' prettily set among the mountains, but very shallow, the rushes and Lilypods growing plentifully over it. Now we had a portage. Each man carried a boat on his head, and we loaded ourselves with as much as we could carry. M—— and I filled my Scotch plaid with baskets and bundles, and we bore it between us. The distance was short, but it was above an hour before we were again afloat in the Upper Saranac, at the end of which our first encampment was to be made. Upon landing, we chose a pretty spot; the guides hastily built up a great log fire. I gathered up some brush and fir-cones to help the blaze, and we broke off small branches (or 'feathers') of the hemlock spruce, which makes the sweetest and best foundation for an Alpine couch in this country—sweeter than, if not so pretty as our heather. Over this the Governor spread a thin oilskin. My air-cushions were the most valuable; we puffed them up, and with these, my leather bag as a bolster, large plaids and felt coverings, and Mary M——'s black and scarlet shawl as a curtain of division, we, two ladies, and two gentlemen, slept soundly, after making a hearty supper off trout and potatoes. I had provided a dozen lemons, aware that when no milk can be had, the juice is an excellent addition to tea, and this plan was unanimously approved. To our guides the idea was quite new; and, as all forest fare is common pot-luck, they were quite pleased. 'It isn't bad,'—'Right fine, I'll assure you;' but the first sentence implies almost as high praise as 'It won't hurt you;' and that is the *acme*. I concocted my pudding with the wild-plums, deprived of their stones, biscuit, brown sugar, a little butter, and some water; but, as some hours' stewing was necessary, this dish was not produced before our breakfast. One of the boats was turned upside down for a table; our candlesticks, a large potato placed upon a tin pail inverted. The guides bivouacked close around the little tent. About half-past two o'clock, according to a common habit in the forests, we all roused up for half-an-hour, replenished the fire, and I removed my stew to a little fire of its own, that it might not get quite stewed away before morning. We then again composed ourselves to sleep again, and had comfortable naps till daylight. During the night I heard a horrible noise once or twice, and, imagining it might be the howl of a wolf, I called to Moody, who assured me it was nothing but a screech-owl. At five o'clock began preparations for breakfast—frying pork, broiling trout and potatoes, and water for the kettle of tea; at last, trout were broiled in the same pan with the pork gravy, an excellent dish. We two ladies went down to the lake to make our toilet, and balanced ourselves in one of the empty boats, to use tooth-brushes, &c. While the rest of the party were packing up, and preparing to undertake the portage to Story Creek, I made a sketch before the tent was struck, and caught one of the men in the act of carrying the boat, with his head concealed underneath, like some nondescript shell-fish.

Before we started, the gentlemen hung a small mirror of M——'s on a tree, and very composedly shaved themselves. The guides took the boats upon their heads, and after two returns they transported all the baggage the rest of the party could not carry through two miles of difficult portage. Then we reached the Otter's Creek and Raquette River, where at last, at the junction of the streams, there was such good fishing, that a long pause ensued. The trout were large and plentiful. The Governor caught several, weighing from two to three pounds. Mr. H—— lost two of his best; one owing to his young boatman, and the other owing to his own hurry in pulling up his prize. I landed to sketch the scenery, and was so much absorbed as to leave my parasol in a bush. We rowed back half a mile for its recovery; however, Mr. Moody took this trouble without a murmur, and Mr. S—— having extremely enjoyed his sport, I believe he was rather pleased to take another look at that pleasant locality. We did not again join the other boats until our arrival at the next rapids, where we were obliged to resign ourselves to another tedious portage; but the row down Raquette River had been delightful—it flows through a deep forest of maples, pines, and tamarisks; the crimson tints of autumn blending with dark and orange foliage, tiny seedling red maples dotting the rocks and the bogs; the cardinal flower, blue gentian, and lilac asters occasionally showing themselves; but through this whole region, the autumnal flora has not a great deal of variety. I gathered some berries of a Rhamnus, saw very large leaved willows and species of Vaccinium (one very good indeed); the scarlet berries of Cannas Canadensis everywhere enlivened the forest; and there were also the white Partridge berry, bright trillium seeds, and the large and small wintergreen, Gaubtheria procumbens.

Now and then the starry flowers of Houstonias lingered on the ground, and raspberries and low blackberries refreshed us on our way—these, with the exception of white and yellow Nymphæs, called by the people 'Lilypods,' were all I saw of flowers or seeds. Deer feed much on these lilypods early in the season, and as they come down to the rivers and lakes in search of their tender shoots, they fall an easy prey at that period; but now they feed upon higher ground, so dogs are sent off who hunt out a single one, and chase him down to any part of the lakes, where they are loosed; there they keep him in the water, and by their baying call their masters to finish the chase. Our gentlemen were not successful in shooting any, because, owing to the long distance we had to travel through this wilderness (about one hundred and fifty miles), the mornings could not be spared for hunting; and although two attempts were made by despatching the hounds in the afternoon, they did not bring their game back until too dark for even the accustomed to get a shot. Maple and birch are considered the best wood with which to build a fire: the common distinguishing phrase is 'hard and soft wood.' Hard is applied to deciduous trees, soft to the pines and evergreens. 'How finely the soft and hard trees are mixed on that mountain,' said one of our party.

Upon landing below the Raquette Falls, we had a mile and a half of difficult portage: the signs of a trail were at times hardly visible; gigantic timber felled by storms, or by time, crossed the obscure path, sometimes every twenty yards; deep bogs, and slippery rocks impeded it, and we had often to retrace our steps, or seek a blazed tree before we could find our way; each individual of the party straggled on as he or she could, with their loads. When Mr. S—— had conveyed his to the edge of the river above the Falls, he kindly returned to relieve me of whatever basket or bundle I had been able to carry; and so we all at last reached our intended camping place, a beautiful spot. Our tent was soon pitched, a bright fire in front of it wast lit, just at the edge of the water, and another blaze for cooking, made near to our boat-table. The largest trout were boiled, the smaller ones broiled, with excellent potatoes, for our supper; tea-lemonade our beverage. As an awakening amusement for an hour afterwards, we played a game of whist, with a not very white pack of cards, procured from one of the guides; and then after arranging our couch as before, we slept very soundly till after one o'clock, when the fires were made up, and then we slept again till morning; not a sound disturbed the forest, except that of the rippling waters at our feet; but when we awoke at six, a gentle rain pattered upon the surrounding trees. However, it was no more than 'the pride of the morning,' just enough to make us more sensible of the blessing of fine weather. M. M—— selected a sheltered rocky nook, a little way back for our dressing-room; there we bathed, and adjusted our toilet with brushes, combs, tooth-brushes, a luxury of towels, and even a tiny mirror hung upon the lowest branch of a fine hemlock spruce; this smartening up of the individual woman marked our Sunday morning, for no Sabbath-day's rest can be set apart for travellers in the Bush, who must get to their journey's end by a certain day, or go without the common necessaries of existence. We came forth again arrayed in cleanliness: its opposite is at times picturesque, but certainly not comfortable. On the whole, I was impressed by the tidy habits of our three guides; they omitted no opportunity for using the fresh pure water to wash away impurities, either on their hands or upon our culinary matters, and never left cup or platter in a soiled state, if they could help it.

Before our starting, the Governor rowed me over to the opposite shore for a sketch of our resting-place. A few miles further up the Raquette River some of our party saw the track of a wolf, and we heard the partridge drum: this noise is caused by the wing of that bird, which in plumage is like ours, but in size it comes nearer to our pheasant. Wild-ducks appeared numerous, but they kept at a distance. Now again we got sight of distant mountains; of late, the forests and swamps have been low and flat. The approach to Long Lake is so thickly covered with lilypods, rushes, and other water-plants, that it seemed as if we were making our way across watery meadows. When we reached the lake itself, the wind blew freshly, and our boatmen had to row eighteen miles against it and the wavelets which arose. Occasional settlements dot the shores: a boy of ten years old paddled his little boat towards us, and when we asked him if many people lived there, he answered, 'There is the baby, and a few more.' Evidently, that baby was the individual of most importance. We again saw wild-ducks, an eagle, a gull, and a loon; and at one spot (a rare sight in this wilderness) two small wagons were waiting to be transported across the lake.

A Mr. and Mrs. Carey, with a family of young children, possessing cows and horses, and a house in the background, lived just behind the rocky knoll where we decided upon forming our encampment—under some tall pine-trees: they supplied us with excellent milk and bread and butter, an unaccustomed luxury, and also with some straw for our beds. Mrs. Carey, a pleasing young woman, visited us with a present of blackberries after supper. The 'Owl's Head' was a prominent mountain beyond, and a young crescent moon arose not far above it. In the morning we had some fine rain; but with the aid of my large umbrella, I did not miss a sketch of our camp: and the palmetto fly-flapper I had brought all the way from Mobile proved of great use in frightening away mosquitoes. Alas! I afterwards lost it during one of the portages. Here it was decided to leave one boat. Mr. Carey was to convey the chief guide with a second one in a wagon, a cross-cut through the woods; and we all packed into the remaining boat, as there was some probable difficulty in getting through rapids and portages. The guns and dogs having both been conveyed to the land carriage, whole flights of ducks passed fearlessly within shot, as if they had by some means become aware of their security. After two or three portages, fatiguing and difficult enough, the men determined to attempt pushing the boat through the last rapid. Now touching one rock, now fast upon another, the water rushing by, I did not think the adventure a pleasant one; at last we came to a dead lock. Jamie M'Cleland proposed that Governor Seymour and Mr. H—— should jump upon a rock, water-surrounded as it was, and by so lightening the boat, we were with difficulty floated up to a landing: here we quickly heard Moody's whoop, and he came up with a partridge he had killed during his progress by land: and soon the whole party was again mustered, for our gentlemen had waded on shore from their rock and thus rejoined us. This day we saw the track of a moose-deer on the edge of a stream; plenty of tracks and signs of smaller deer: one or two solitary cranes, and a bald-headed eagle. It was muddy walking; we were thoroughly bespattered, but Jamie endeavoured to console us by the assurance that he had 'seen women looking much worse.'

In these forests, the variety of funguses is beyond description; some, just like beautiful white coral. Many were, in form and substance, quite different from any drawings or models I have seen; the colours scarlet, orange, pink, pure white, black, drab, and rose; and bunches of that odd monotropa, the Indian pipe, constantly fringed our path. It seems to me that there is something nourishing in the air of these Alpine forests: I never felt very hungry, although our meals were far apart, and usually very light in substance. As we rowed down the Raquette Lake, I observed a yellow sunset, with heaped-up clouds to the south, and a suspicion crossed my mind that stormy weather was brewing. At a rough clearing, our guides pulled up. A shanty belonging to a Mr. Beech was not a great way off, and, oddly enough, there was another clearing on the opposite shore of the lake, owned by a Mr. Wood.

Our tent was pitched on a cleared spot, near where a famous eagle once had his eyrie upon a tall pine; both pine and eagle are gone—the latter died, and the former was blown down. Some dried venison was procured, and a neighbour provided milk. We composed ourselves to rest, and slept till midnight; then growling thunder, vivid lightning, and pouring rain disturbed our slumbers. A wet morning followed, and any intention of striking our tent was abandoned. It was a violent storm—probably an equinoctial gale. We had only to be patient and enduring, with the conviction that 'Time and the hours run through the roughest day.'

In the afternoon the weather cleared, and we went by the lake to visit Mr. and Mrs. Beech, while the gentlemen and the guides went off hunting. But their dogs did not immediately find, and again, it was too dark to shoot a deer which was hunted down to the water. The ladies returned to our tent, and as I had a reserved provision of arrowroot, I determined to make a large kettleful, flavoured with lemons and molasses, adding to it a portion of Malaga, and putting in biscuits. This made a comforting warm mess for the cold and tired hunters upon their return.

After the violent rain of last night and to-day, we found our hemlock spruce beds rather damp, although the guides had turned the tent so as to face a large fire, and accommodate it to a change of wind. In spite of all the wet, however, no colds were caught, and early on the 20th of September we embarked again on the lake in high spirits. The guides had stowed themselves under one of the boats during the night, which perhaps sheltered them even more completely than our tent did us.

During this last pause in our wanderings, we could not help being struck by the wild, careless, picturesque appearance inside that tent. Seated upon the floor, where we were taking our meals, with pans of tea, and plates of tin, air-cushions, and variously coloured plaids and felts scattered around; sketch-books and presses, books and maps; a large tin case, containing our store of grocery, a huge basket full of biscuits, a hammer ensconced among bunches of berries; tallow candles, under protection from the damp, towels, hats, bonnets, and other articles of attire impartially scattered; accidentally bestowed touches of scarlet and blue upon the interior, lit up as it was by the warm glow of a blazing wood fire—this would have formed a picture for Gerard Dow.

I forgot to say we ate Mr. Moody's partridge for breakfast, and it proved excellent. I did not omit to sketch this encampment before we left it. As we rowed up the Raquette Lake, a slight snow-storm overtook us, but it was soon over. Even during that early morning, with its fog and snow, the lake was beautiful, with numerous bays and islands, and blue mountains rising in the distance. We passed through a narrow channel for some way, then disembarked for a portage to the eighth lake of the Eckford chain; for eight lakes of differing magnitude are strung upon the Moose River, and we were to pass through all. We now found a sandy beach which before had been rocky. The cheerful little crossbill hopped fearlessly around us, and wild-ducks flew away. After rowing across the eighth, another portage brought us to the seventh lake. There was some difficulty in pushing the boats over a sandy bar at its entrance from the narrow stream we had just traversed. The seventh lake is quite encircled by hills. We observed a tempting rocky promontory, and as the sun was getting low, we decided upon landing upon a pretty sheltered beach behind it.

Our tent was pitched behind a gigantic fallen tree, against which the fire was made: it served as a convenient table for our cooking operations, as well as a good back for the blaze. I made a can of excellent portable soup, a provision we had before tried with success; but now I added a little arrowroot, an onion, potatoes, two or three spoonsful of sweet wine, and several biscuits. It was generally agreed that this mixture 'would not hurt anybody;' indeed it might anywhere have been considered an excellent soup.

I found a quarter of a pound of portable soup, or a quarter of a pound of arrowroot necessary to make the quantity sufficient for seven hungry bodies. Although I brought these things with me from England more than a year ago, they were in good preservation; and I recommend London portable soup to all travellers in the Bush, and advise them also to add lemons and a good store of sugar, brown and white, to their other preparations. We had a bright moon this evening. Some hunters and fishers were upon the lake, and from the latter our people procured trout, and all enjoyed this camp particularly, even though no deer were attained. We had a misty morning, but the mountain tops soon peered out. We again embarked, and passed from one lake into others, sometimes by such narrow outlets that there was a difficulty in finding them, until at the last our boatmen rowed twice a considerable distance before a swampy-looking egress was discovered: this led us into a pretty winding creek, and another short portage brought us below the falls of the Moose River into its rapid stream. Here we had only one boat. The Governor (for our other gentlemen had been obliged to leave us before we entered the chain of lakes) walked on to make some arrangements at Arnold's Farm, and we two ladies, in charge of Mr. Moody and M'Cleland, had a pleasant row, seeing many canvas-back ducks before us in the river. The former shot one, which I have no doubt would have been very good for dinner, but we never had any time or opportunity for trying the experiment. Mr. Seymour remained to make arrangements with the guides, while his niece and I walked on to Arnold's Farm. There we found Mrs. Arnold and six daughters. These girls, aged from twelve to twenty, were placed in a row against one wall of the shanty, with looks so expressive of astonishment, that I felt puzzled to account for their manner, till their mother informed us they had never before seen any other woman than herself! I could not elicit a word from them; but, at last, when I begged for a little milk, the eldest went and brought me a glass. I then remembered that we had met a single hunter rowing himself in a skiff on the Moose River, who called out, 'Where on the 'arth do they women come from?' And our after-experience fully explained why ladies are rare birds in that locality. At this place we expected to find horses, but owing to our twenty-four hours' detention on Raquette Lake, they had been sent off to bring up some gentlemen from Brown's Tract; pedestrianism was therefore our only resource. Jamie M'Cleland came up from the river, and explained that unless we made some further progress this evening, we should not be able to get through the forest during daylight to-morrow, and delay was of importance, so we decided upon trudging on as far as possible. Jamie took the tent on his back, and Mr. Seymour and the other guides were to follow as soon as they could select positive necessaries from our baggage. Mrs. Arnold was furious—she did all but try to detain us by force—declared we could not get on, and that she should soon see us back again; but necessity has no law: we felt the importance of determination, and we had become too experienced gipsies to fear camping out. For one mile we had a pleasant path, then commenced the series of bog-holes which, with few and short intervals, were to be scrambled through for sixteen miles. The worst was, that as night closed in, we could not find a dry spot upon which to pitch our tent. At last we sent Jamie on, and he brought us the news that, at a short distance he had found a little knoll above the bogs.

Dark as it was, we reached this spot, without any other mishap than an occasional flounder in the mud; but all the lumber around was soaking wet. No fire could be made till our guide had cut down a tree—for he had not forgotten his axe; and his experienced arm soon felled a birch of considerable size, cut it in logs about two yards long, and so built up a fire, which we assisted in lighting, by breaking off dry brush from the surrounding bush. Jamie worked hard; and before Mr. Seymour and the other guides joined us with exclamations of astonishment how we had ever got through the places which had nearly swamped them, the tent was raised, hemlock branches gathered, and a good fire blazed all ready for cooking operations. The young moon occasionally peeped through the foliage above our heads; but it was too thick for much light to be visible. Our only misfortune at that moment was the sufferings of poor young Prince Albert, who lay upon the ground agonized and quite useless. We gave him what comfort we could; and I administered camphor, which soothed the pain, and enabled him to get asleep. Our head guide told me he knew the value of that substance in most cases of slight illness; and that he seldom went into the forest unprovided with some of it.

Before daylight next morning we again aroused ourselves. Fortunately sufficient portable soup and arrowroot was still left to make a good warm mess for breakfast; and this nourishment is so lasting, that, with the exception of half a biscuit and some water, I got on upon it till we reached our resting place at Bonville, after nine in the evening. At this encampment, we parted from our three guides, who had conducted themselves excellently well through all our difficulties. Jamie, a Canadian, was going back to take his young wife, of nineteen (to whom he had been four years married), to his father's house, near Montreal. 'An' won't she be glad to see me back. I wouldn't change my gal for any gal in the States, or in Canada either.' Jamie is a sober, handy fellow. I feel sure he is a good husband, as he certainly made a thoughtful, intelligent attendant on us two women in the Bush. The Governor fell in with Mr. Wood, of Raquette Lake, at Arnold's, and engaged him to see us safely through the concluding passage of our travels; but, as the only chance of getting assistance to meet us, it was necessary to send him on. Mr. Seymour must always be considered a brave man, for having undertaken alone, to take us that day's walk; but having never passed through this track before, he was happily not fully aware of what he undertook, or he confesses he should have been afraid. The path we had to follow was a road cut through the forest fifty years ago; planks had been laid down and corduroy bridges made; but, as no settlement followed, left to entire neglect, the rotten timbers only made bad worse; and I imagine that it would be impossible to find anywhere a track so difficult to get over as that through which we patiently laboured for ten consecutive hours. Mr. Seymour's patience and good humour never gave way. Putting off the packages on his back, he now extricated one companion, now another, from a boggy 'fix.' I never shall forget the astonishment of Mr. Stephens, of yacht celebrity, when, on horseback with another gentleman and guides, he met us emerging from the Bush! They had four horses; and our *avant-courier*, Mr. Wood, had secured one of them, upon which I mounted; and, although it was not easy to keep my seat upon a man's saddle in getting over such ground, I soon found the benefit of being carried on the last few miles by some other agency than my own feet. Mr. Seymour and his niece walked on; in one mile more we again reached the Moose River, and crossed it in a boat; and another two hours brought us to the clearing, where a small wagon was procured—rough enough, but still a wagon—which took us to a comfortable hotel, at the small town of Bonville, from whence, after a good night's rest, we got on by coach and cars to Utica. A singular and touching circumstance occurred to me in the coach. An old man and a younger one conversed in Welsh. I could not help inquiring what part of Wales they came from, for that tongue awoke in my heart early memories. The old man knew Caermarthen; had been at Abergwilly, and spoke of my father as 'that charity man.' David Owen was quite blind; but that meeting was pleasant to us both. After fifty years, to hear one's father's name spoken of with respect and affection, in this far distant land! There are many Welsh people settled hereabouts. Owen's home was a small village near Trenton Falls. As we passed over a bridge,—

'Now,' he said, 'we are near my home.'

'Not being able to see, how do you know that?'

'Ah! do I not understand the voice of that bridge?' And one or two miles beyond, the old man and I parted, he shaking me by the hand, with his blessing. Three days at Utica were necessary to recruit and repose myself. Now I write from Canandaigua, on the eve of starting for Chicago and St. Louis.

Buffalo, September 27.—We left Canandaigua at ten this morning; but, having reached this place by four, we cannot proceed till half-past nine o'clock. By travelling all night, we may arrive at Chicago to-morrow evening, and be at St. Louis next day.

Chicago, Friday night.—We have travelled four hundred and ninety-two miles since ten o'clock last night; very rapidly and pleasantly to-day, only changing cars at Toledo. The previous night's journey was a crowded one; a great number of the men in the carriages indulged themselves in the habits of the backwoods, which made them very unpleasant neighbours, although their appearance was respectable; and I was glad of a change which gave us another set of fellow-travellers. The country between this place and Cleveland is in a rapid course of settlement. There is not an evergreen of any kind to be seen—neither firs, spruce, nor cedars; the forest consists entirely of 'hard' wood trees, of which there is a great variety—chiefly beech, oak, plane, ash, and poplar. I did not observe much hickory, or any acacias; and, as the timber is not on the whole of great size, I suppose there is less difficulty in making clearings in this district than in some others I have passed through. Numerous towns are starting up—as usual, with names not particularly well selected.

After Toledo, we passed through Hudson, Hillsdale, Jonesville, Coldwater, White Pigeon, &c., &c. On approaching Chicago, the country begins to acquire a prairie character; and I saw such large fields of grain, and so many signs of improved farming, that but for snake-fences, I could have believed myself in some parts of England. A rolling district, dotted by small lakes, prevails about Hillsborough, while for a hundred miles this side Lake Erie the forests are flat and undiversified. In marshy plains, bilious fevers are common. I was told that sleeping in respirators is a certain preventive. I wonder whether this has been tried at Norfolk, where there has been of late such dreadful pestilence. During our journey here, I heard of the Fall of Sebastopol—sad, sad carnage. My anxiety to know the names of those who have last sacrificed themselves for England and duty must, perhaps, remain unappeased for days. Friends and friends' sons still there to be risked—heroes and Cornelias: they will have their reward.

During our mountain expedition I was struck by the one fact which gives American armies an advantage in warfare—the practical rifle skill which backwoods' sport cultivates. Our guides always took off the head of a squirrel with their guns, to avoid (as they said) 'injuring the skin,' so that every American soldier is a good marksman, while many of England's brave peasantry, though willing and ready to fight, hardly know (upon their first enlistment) how to fire off a shot. This morning, I remarked a circumstance which has before attracted my observation travelling in railroad cars. Men in the garb of gentlemen, and who would be indignant at being addressed by any other appellation, were busy helping one another to drams of brandy in the early morning. Quart bottles of spirits extracted from carpet-bags is no uncommon sight. This habit is rather illustrative of that aristocratic law which denies liberty of action to the poor and sick, while it does not trench upon the freedom of the rich and luxurious. Have fanatics who advocate this law ever considered that the same principle might be applied to the 'Tree of the knowledge of good and evil?' Would not these people have preached to the Saviour upon the impropriety of his first miracle, or the dangers of the sacramental wine? About forty miles from Chicago we passed the first prairie town of Joliet. Before entering it there is a cutting through a kind of alluvial conglomerate, formed of gravel, sand, and round water-worn pebbles; and around it there are well cultivated farms, backed by forests; large fields of grain, and numerous herds of cattle. We soon traversed a prairie, and saw wide, wide plains covered with grass and flowers on every side. It is too late for the great beauty of the flowers. Now there are but few in but Asters, Coreopsis, and Solidagos. After Bloomington where we stopped to dine, nothing could be more bleak and dreary than the towns, or rather villages, among them Lincoln, Chatham, Girard; the population squalid and dirty; nothing looking clean but the white painted wooden houses, scattered over the black trod-down prairies; not a fence, not a bush, not a garden. These places appear to me much more desolate than any forest clearings; there you can, at any rate, make large fires to enliven the scene. Our journey was unpleasant: in the day it rained, and every window would have been closed if I had not kept mine open with a parasol before it. At night a rough-looking set of men opened every glass wide. Whatever the mornings may be, almost all nights in America are cold. A superabundance of air in the cars is not often to be complained of; but I have seldom met with any consideration for ladies in this particular. In travelling to Chicago, when I had a small bit of my own window open, a gentleman three seats off came and put it down, with out any request or one word of apology. No room for more in this letter.

Yours affectionately,

A. M. M.

LETTER XXX.

St. Louis, Missouri, U. S.,
October 1, 1855.

My dear Friends,—

It was almost twelve o'clock at night when the *Reindeer* steamer landed R—— and me at this place. The river voyage of twenty-five miles was a most unexpected termination of our long railroad journey from Chicago. It seems this line is just on the point of being opened to a terminus at St. Louis,* and meanwhile a kind of mystery (very commonly thrown around unfinished rail lines) has enveloped the communication between this place and Chicago. I was assured of going through, but the manner and the means were left unexplained, and it was with some surprise that I found myself transferred from an omnibus into a steamboat, instead of a hotel. Upon landing, I determined not to invade my proposed hosts, Dr. and Mrs. P——, at that time of night; so after procuring a carriage, we drove to the Planters' Hotel, where I had the most reasonable charge for a night's lodging and breakfast that I have paid in America: and after breakfast, my friends came and removed us to their own comfortable house. In the afternoon, they drove me to see the Cemetery, and also to visit Mrs. P——'s father and mother, a few miles out of town. Colonel O'F—— has a very singular and interesting place, built on the site of some aboriginal city,

* Since I left America a terrible accident has occurred, by the fall of a bridge.

and upon the summit of one of the ancient mounds. In digging foundations, hundreds of skeletons of a very old type were found; stone hatchets; and, among other relics, one delicately worked small mocassin. The trees which now shade (and so bury the dwelling that but a very small peep of the Mississippi can be obtained from its portico) were, with the exception of one poplar, all planted by Colonel O'F——. He purchased a considerable estate there forty years ago, and has a charming garden, with some of the finest Magnolias macrophylla, pumila, and purpurea I ever saw, excepting in the forests round Mobile: magnificent evergreens, Ilex opaca, Red cedars, and various pinuses; Ipomœa, Quamoclit, and Coccinea, forming bowers six feet high, and rose bushes fifteen in height. I brought away the first ripened seed-vessel of Magnolia macrophylla I ever saw. I think this tree, flowers and fruit, still handsomer than grandiflora; the leaves are larger and finer, although neither so dark, shining, or persistent as those of the grandiflora, and the flowers also are larger, though not so numerous. In the evening, the Botanist, Dr. Engelmann (introduced by a note from Dr. Gray) called, and gave me much information; my pleasant friends Dr. and Mrs. L—— also.

October 2.—Dr. L—— came before nine in the morning, and drove me out to see various parts of the town and environs. I wished to make a sketch or two, but it was difficult to find any spot from whence the Mississippi and the city could be made picturesque, and there would have been no satisfaction in a mere bird's-eye view. At last I drew the great river, with that now small village upon the opposite bank, called Cahokia, a place which was once of importance, but which St. Louis has supplanted and so completely eclipsed, that its name is hardly known beyond its immediate vicinity. I made one more drawing looking back upon St. Louis, taking as foreground one of the most picturesque and singular limekilns I ever saw; it is so rare to find a picturesque bit of building in America, even a limekiln. My pleasant kind frieud then took me to see Dr. Englemann, where, upon a small lead at the back of his little town house (which was trellised by a Catawba vine, in full bearing), is to be seen the most rare and curious collection of Yucas and Cacti, cultivated this side of the Atlantic; most of them from Mexico. The Doctor kindly gave me a little box of seedlings, which I hope to import safely into England. These objects of interest delayed my return to Dr. and Mrs. P—— until after their dinner hour. I was easily forgiven; but they and some friends were waiting. We spent the evening with Dr. and Mrs. L——. Although I was obliged to be on board the steamer at six, I did not go to rest till two o'clock in the morning.

Chicago, October 3.—A beautiful day; and as Lake Michigan is the only path by which I can hope to attain Mackinaw and the Sault St. Marie, after reaching Milwaukie by railroad, fine weather is of great importance; but the elements have been unceasingly good-natured to me: ever since I left the shores of England, rain or sunshine has always come at the right time for my particular objects, and if this good fortune will only continue till the second week in November, and see me well across the Atlantic again, I shall have the greatest reason to be thankful.

Now I must go back to my leaving St. Louis yesterday morning. After performing every other act of hospitality and kindness possible, Dr. and Mrs. P—— and Dr. L—— were up at five; the two gentlemen accompanied me to the *Reindeer* steamer, and remained till the starting-bell rung. At St. Louis I have left a valuable and valued friend, even if in this phase of existence I meet him no more. We steamed away from the first forest of only funnels I ever beheld. At New Orleans there was also an immense assemblage of steamers, but there I saw also sailing-vessels, boats, masts: at St. Louis no boats but steamers; no sails, no masts. It was a striking object for contemplation, not a picturesque one certainly—still full of meaning. Some of the names, too, were suggestive—Reothuk, Shenandoah, Monongahela—Indian sounds, poetical and characteristic, and appropriate to the waters of the Mississippi and the Missouri, which fall in about twenty miles above St. Louis. We saw the junction of these streams, and saw, too, how the heavy molten waters of the Missouri contaminate the purity of the Upper Mississippi. For a short distance that bright blue river keeps apart from his uninviting comrade, but he cannot long avoid contact; his azure robes are first spotted, then soiled, and at last they are miserably and hopelessly discoloured and embrowned, and they must roll on hundreds of miles, and pass New Orleans a muddy compound, until they are purified, but lost in the sapphire waves of the Mexican Gulf.

We reached Alton about nine o'clock: it is a pretty place, which I did not see in the dark on Saturday; the last forty miles, too, of that journey was through a rather fine country, not prairie, but woody. Before leaving the *Reindeer* steamer, I had some conversation with a sensible lady from Chicago, who regretted the way in which the great majority of American young women are sacrificing health to vanity. She agrees that it is not so much climate as bad management which crowds the cemetary with early victims. An idea has gone forth that fragility is interesting, and young ladies almost cultivate ill-health! She told me that, standing at her own door one morning, she observed three girls between twelve and fourteen passing to school; it was damp weather: these children were lightly and showily attired, with thin silk slippers to set off their feet to advantage—instead of good substantial boots. These kind of absurdities are common in the United States. I have found out a reason why ladies travelling alone must be extravagantly dressed; without that precaution they meet with no attention and little civility,—decidedly much less than in any other country. So here it is not as *women* but as *ladies*, they are to be cared for!—and this in Democratic America!

I saw flocks of prairie birds, both going and coming; and I was told that they are a kind of grouse, generally called 'prairie chickens.' If they were roasted as we roast game in England, they would be very good: I have only tasted them broiled, so as to be dry and hard. There was nothing which struck my fancy, in the manner of expression, as peculiar in prairie life. I no longer hear the singular affirmation 'Yes, sirree,' or 'No, sirree,' which was made use of among the Adirondack Mountains, to express something very positive.

October 3, *Milwaukie.*—I am brought to a stand-still. We arrived at Chicago too late for the Mackinaw steamer of yesterday. I was told that by taking the cars here early this morning, we should get a lake conveyance; but, on reaching this place, not only my hope of a steamer till Friday is vain, but owing to what is called a State fair, it has been with the greatest difficulty that I have procured a tiny bed-room in a secondary hotel. The town, though scattered and extensive, is crammed to overflowing. I am glad to observe that in these parts the taste of the settlers induces them to preserve the Indian names. We passed to-day by several places, such as Waakeyau, Shenosha, &c.; near the last-mentioned town I observed a beautiful Gentian, growing in dry places by the side of the track. I do not know one exactly like it; the colour was as brilliant as Bavarica, but several inches taller.

The site of Milwaukie upon Lake Michigan is supposed to have been once covered by its waters, and fresh-water shells are found in the elevations behind the city.

On Saturday morning I may reach Mackinaw, in the steamer *Niagara*, but the delay I have met with puts an end to all hope of my reaching Lake Superior, as Saint Marie is too distant, and I must follow the Collingwood line from Lake Michigan across Lake Huron, then to Toronto by land, and by Lake Ontario to Oswego, so as to reach Utica on Monday.

Thursday, October 4.—Yesterday afternoon I set forth upon a voyage of discovery, to find out a spot from which I might take a sketch of the city. Making my way over a bridge to higher ground, it was evident that the present site of Milwaukie was once covered by water; below some bluffs, a mile and a half from the present lake, there is a most distinct beach, and shells are found just beyond. The town authorities are going to great expense to cut through and level these bluffs, which, left as they are, would diversify and ornament their town. This levelling process will puzzle future geologists. I think the water here tastes of iron. By-the-bye, I quite forgot to mention the wonderful Iron Mountain of Missouri, situated in St. Francis County, about eighty miles south-west or south of St. Louis: it rises to a height two hundred and sixty feet above the surrounding country, and there is said to be many million tons of ore above the surface! It is known as specular oxide, and yields from sixty to seventy per cent. of pure iron. There is also the Pilot Knob, Shepherd's Mountain, and other valuable deposits in Madison County, on the line of the Iron Mountain Railroad. These deposits vary in their character and produce; and yield iron adapted to various purposes. There are immense works and forges erected in Franklin County. About fifty miles west of St. Louis are large iron works, and in various other localities along the Mississippi; abundance of iron is found also at that place on the Macamaco, where iron has been manufactured for some years past. The South-west branch of the Pacific Railroad passes through extensive deposits of minerals—iron, copper, lead, and coal sufficient to work all the mines on the line; indeed, it is believed the metalliferous region of Missouri covers an area of near thirteen millions of acres: it also extends into Arkansas and the Indian territory; that country is said to be all magnesian limestone, rich in lead. It surprises me to hear that the Iron Mountain is thickly timbered: I should have expected it to be devoid of trees of any size. I made my sketch this morning, from a house belonging to Mr. G——, which stands upon an isolated bluff, the earth having been so cut away all around it as to leave the buildings above in a doubtful state of security. Mr. G—— told me they are seeking compensation for the injury done to their property, as it will be impossible for them to remain on it another year. I walked up to look at the fair, but as there was a great number of people, I was afraid to encounter so large a crowd, and kept aloof; at the same time I did not see one instance of intoxication or disorder: the visitants were generally well attired, good-humoured, and quietly amusing themselves. In short, this State fair of Milwaukie was a very creditable specimen of the conduct and civilization of the citizens of Wisconsin.

This afternoon closes in with a wetting fog. I hope it does not intend to be so thick to-morrow as to drive me back to

Chicago; for I will not embark on the lake and take the Collingwood line, unless the weather promises well, though I shall regret to return again *viâ* Toledo and Buffalo.

Milwaukie, October 5.—At nine this morning I am told the *Niagara* has arrived; and after a storm last night the weather is fine.

On board the Niagara Steamer, October 6.—According to the usual fashion in this country of furnishing false information, after giving up my rooms and going down, bag and baggage, to the wharf, the only vessel there was a steamer going back to Chicago. Fortunately, at the steam agency office, I had fallen in with the principal agent for the Collingwood line, to whom I feel indebted for a civility and attention I should not have received from his subordinates. He got my things safely taken care of before he was obliged to embark for Chicago, and did all in his power to facilitate my passage in the *Niagara* whenever she might arrive; but six hours of tiresome waiting on that wharf, in very uncivilized company, ensued. At last, in despair, I went up to the office, with the idea of changing my ticket for the railroad. Evidently there was a great demur about allowing this. I had been unwise enough, upon the faith of the *Niagara's* supposed arrival, to pay for my tickets through to Oswego. I recommend travellers in America never to take tickets in advance, beyond the first office, as, if anything occurs to make a change of route necessary, they must bear in mind that *re*fund is a very bad fund. However, just as I had secured a carriage to remove my things from the wharf to the railroad, with a determination to go off, and take my chance of ultimate justice, the steamer was announced to be in sight, and upon her reaching the dock we found that bad weather had delayed her departure from Chicago until eight in the morning, although a telegraphic message shown to me at the office stated she had left that port at one hour after midnight. Of course, if such had been the case, her delay of seven hours after the usual time gave reasonable cause for anxiety. Captain Miller was very obliging, and I immediately procured a comfortable berth, where I could rest after so many hours of suspense and anxiety.

Of course, this detention puts Lake Superior and St. Marie out of the question. The doubt is, whether I can even attain Utica by the day I am engaged to be there. If we reach Toronto too late, we may miss the steamer to Oswego, and be again delayed some hours. The lake is not very smooth: it still retains some agitation from the storm of Thursday, and I see many people suffering from sickness; however, it was well to be on shore during the bad weather. So far my delay was a fortunate one. Last night I suffered from an illustration of the want of thought and consideration for others, which appears to me to make itself more evident among the population, particularly of the young generation, in America than in Europe. Being much fatigued, I retired early, and the same thing was the case with a majority of passengers; but there was a piano in the saloon, close to my berth. After ten o'clock at night, a young girl sat down to perform—not harmonious music, for such a disturbance might have been forgiven; but she perseveringly amused herself by striking the instrument in a style so utterly discordant, that, after a while of patient endurance, I opened my door, and inquired whether it was right at that time of night to keep the passengers from sleeping? She repeated my words with an air of ludicrous impertinence, and, though she paused for a little while, before long the annoyance was continued, if not by her, by others, without the smallest excuse or apology! Thus do the rising generation here mistake rudeness for Republicanism, and selfishness for independence; but we must not be too hard upon them. As this great and growing nation advances in life and experience, it will advance also in civilization and true Christian politeness; Rowdyism will cease to be considered manliness, or extravagance gentility. Noble American spirits are setting an example, correcting these errors. A few more years, and their influence will permeate and pervade the length and breadth of American society. As yet, that society is but roughed out—not polished: the polishing will follow in due time.

Already in Boston I have remarked that simplicity and comfort are advancing beyond ostentation; dress and furniture there evince more attention to suitability than to mere show. In every other part of the United States, with the exception of Mr. G——'s, of Canandaigua, and one or two other houses, magnificent curtains, expensive carpets, and fine mirrors, are more abounding than in England; but useful tables, writing materials, and other little comforts we consider imperative, are wanting. That singular fashion—which is almost general—of making the drawing-room and parlours so obscure, that the inmates might as well live in cellars, is one reason why necessaries for employment are scarce. Tables would be almost useless where no one can see to write or draw. I have been told it is the heat of this climate which makes people thus darken their rooms; but they have a long winter, and sunshine is as carefully excluded in cold weather as in hot; besides, I never heard that in Italy there is such an intense love of obscurity. It has happened that I have opened a blind in some of the hotels; and the chambermaid, upon entering, rushed to close it with an air of as much alarm as if the sun was shining in to the injury of some valuable picture.

This morning we have had some negro music; two darkies singing duets, accompanying themselves with a guitar and violin. Their voices good, and (like those of most of the negroes) in perfect tune. One song had a chorus imitative of barking dogs, which amused the younger passengers extremely. By eight at night we reached Mackinaw—that island, with a fort once known as Michilimackinac, a name I had so often heard in my childhood from an old friend, whose husband served in the early American conflicts between the English and French, that I wished much to see the place which owned it, but it was too dark for much observation; I could only tell that a fort is still in existence, and there is a large pointed rock, like a sugar-loaf. The town is small, with a population of about two thousand. A steamer lay alongside the wharf; she proved to be the *Lady Elgin*, the very boat in which, if it had not been for false information, we should have embarked on Tuesday night, at Chicago. That apparent disappointment has proved an advantage, for she was disabled in the next day's storm; and we escaped both fright and danger, while we should not have been advanced one mile on our voyage.

Toronto, October 8.—We arrived at Collingwood by seven o'clock this morning, after a tedious and anxious passage from Mackinaw—anxiety for others more than for ourselves. As the *Lady Elgin* was not considered in a safe position at that place, and had no means there of repairing her damages, our captain decided upon taking her in tow. The following night and day proved rough; and, if the heaving of the vessel had caused the towing lines to give way, it would have been impossible for the *Niagara* to have afforded more assistance. What an awful consideration that such an accident would have obliged us to leave the unfortunate *Lady Elgin* and her passengers to their fate; which (as she was quite helpless) would probably have been a watery grave. It was a great relief when once we passed Lake Huron and the lower end of the Georgian Bay, for then apprehension was over.

During this voyage we saw the Manitoolia Islands, and Fox and Duck Islands; of course I abandoned all notion of Sault St. Marie and Lake Superior. The cars received us upon landing at Collingwood; and passing by Lake Simcoe, I was glad, after travelling ninety miles before breakfast, to reach this place by eleven o'clock. At nine in the evening we must embark upon Lake Ontario, in the *Canada* steamer for Oswego. I shall be glad when my last voyage upon these inland seas is happily accomplished. Again we were subjected to false information, although I sent down to the agent who had charge of the baggage (which was checked through to Oswego) to ask for the steamer belonging to the Collingwood line. R—— was informed that our passage must be made in the *Canada*.

'Are you sure that is the Collingwood line?' she asked; and was answered, 'Oh, it is all one.' Yet, when we showed our tickets upon going on board the steamer, we were informed that they were useless, and that our passage must be again paid for; besides which, we then found that our baggage had been previously sent at five o'clock by the *Mayflower;* so there was the inconvenience of its absence added to additional expense. Our night voyage across Lake Ontario was a quiet and safe one; the

Canada is a fine large steamer. We reached Oswego by eight o'clock, and if it had not been for unexpected delays in attaining the landing wharf, we should have been in time for the nine o'clock train to Syracuse; but as it was we had to wait, with as much patience as we might, until half-past eleven.

By three o'clock I reached Utica, to find a never-failing cordial reception from my friends there. In the course of the afternoon Mrs. Seymour took me to see Colonel Jowett's fine collection of Silurian fossils; there I found very curious and unique specimens of the early crustaceans, a great variety of Trilobites, and some things I never before heard of; the most singular were found at Niagara and Trenton. Colonel Jowett was so obliging as to offer me some duplicates, which I shall like much to have. At night I took leave of Governor and Mrs. Seymour, and parted from them with a deep and grateful sense of the untiring and affectionate kindness they have evinced towards me during the past year. The early train for Albany started at five o'clock in the morning, and I reached Awastanook, near Lenox, sufficiently early for a pleasant drive in the afternoon.

Thursday, October 10.—Mr. D—— went with me in search of a white rose I saw blowing last July upon Rattlesnake Mountain, as the season is now favourable for taking up suckers. We were successful in finding an abundant crop, and I am rather in hopes that this Awastanook rose will prove a novelty to the botanical world.

Thursday afternoon, and all Friday, the rain poured down in torrents; I thought myself fortunate in being comfortably housed, and that this storm did not catch us on Lake Ontario.

Saturday.—The morning, though cloudy, was only wet underfoot; a carriage was ordered, and I drove with one of my friends, to fulfil a promise I had made to an occupant of the farm from which I had made a sketch of Lenox and the surrounding country, that she should see the drawing. We found with her two intelligent young women; daughters I conclude. The premises resembled a comfortable English farm; a large spinning-wheel was in use in the parlour. I observed maps, and other indications of education, with a certain degree of refinement; and all the inmates evinced an intense and delighted interest in my sketch; they expressed the most lively gratitude for being allowed to see it, and eagerly pointed out every familiar tree and cottage. In return, I learned the Indian name of that pretty lake, on the borders of which Hawthorne wrote his *Seven Gables*—*Mackinaw*,—'*the Mountain Mirror*;' what an improvement upon that un-euphonious appellation of Stockbridge Pond!

Monday, October 16.—This morning at nine o'clock I must take leave of Awastanook forever. Thankful for my enjoyment of its lovely scenery, and convinced, too, that this spot will ever remain impressed upon my memory, as a 'Mountain Mirror,' which to me has reflected only truth and beauty.

Boston, October 16.—Although I came by railroad from the Berkshire Hills last summer, I was yesterday still more strongly impressed by the beautiful country it passes through; perhaps the late rains have embrowned and deepened the rapid torrents and numerous lakes of that Highland district; while crimson and golden tints added brilliancy to forests which are at all times varied in foliage. I could only regret that almost all the houses and farms are so very white and uniform in appearance; I did once see a sky-blue stable, and occasionally a red barn, and such colours were quite a relief to the monotony. How subdued and quiet the grey stone buildings of England will look, after the almost universal white paint of American erections.

I find myself again under that friendly roof which sheltered me first, and promises to shelter me last on this side of the Atlantic; as I shall embark on the 24th, upon my homeward voyage, this will probably be the conclusion of my letters. Before closing them, I must once more return to the subject of Slavery: in the first place, to extract a few observations from a letter written by a gentleman of known experience and ability; and then to answer an accusation made against me by some Northern friends, who affirm that I have not spent sufficient time among slaves and slaveholders to judge fairly. My correspondent says:—'The phenomenon of African Slavery, as it is sometimes called, is in truth no phenomenon at all. Where is the country, or the period of history, wherein slavery did not exist in some shape or the other? Slavery has always existed, and will continue, as long as there is a disparity in the intellect and energy of men. I do not enter into the question of the Unity of Races, which is supposed to be derived from Bible authority: it will be sufficient to assert that this race, known as African, is inferior to the Caucasian. As a people, the blacks are sensual and stupid, lazy, improvident, and vicious; unless under guidance, they have no idea of cherishing those virtues which elevate our common nature; they have an alacrity for sinking—nothing more. In their own country they are either savages or slaves. There is at this time, and there have been for long periods, a large number of free coloured people in the slaveholding and non-slaveholding States of the Union; but even constant attrition against Yankee sharpness and shrewdness, has failed to elicit one scintillation of talent or genius from this race. When they pass from bondage, it is only to swell the volume of insignificance or vice which has characterized their past history. But besides this, I would remark that we should reflect upon the fact of Slavery, more than upon the manner of its regulation. The Virginian negro, who is held by law as a slave, is really little more a slave than the man who works in the mines and manufactories of England. The first is held in subjection by a well-devised system of police, the other by a necessity stronger than any police. It is no answer to say that the Englishman can, if he chooses, leave his employer; that power only exists in theory, as the penalty for severing his bonds is *starvation*. His real master is Capital—which, being in its nature greedy, grasping, and selfish, it doles out to human labour the smallest possible amount which will sustain life, and keep the working machine in due order. There are three millions of slaves in the United States, and they constitute the only black people who are progressing in civilization and Christianity—who are orderly, quiet, contented, and industrious. They are well fed, well clad, and in physical comforts will compare advantageously with the same number of operatives in any part of Europe.

'The only favourable results yet marked out for the African race are due to the American system of slavery; and until experience shall have demonstrated that some other policy will result in greater blessings to the negro, I cannot but regard efforts to abolish the present state of things as thoughtless and unwise, if not unjust and inhuman.'

So much for the opinion of a good man who has long studied the question here. My visit to the South may not have enabled me to ferret out and investigate all the evils there may be to discover there, and it would be absurd to ignore the possible existence of cruel masters and ill-used slaves; but I saw nothing, and heard very little, which would substantiate accusations; yet early rising and active habits gave me opportunities of using my eyes and ears, in the fields and the forests, and in places where not many travellers would be suspected. The varied aspects of New York, and Paris, and London, are dwelt upon and described every day, and yet how few writers think it necessary to seek out and reprobate the slave-holders of those cities. Now I hear it said—'Bad things may be done in free countries, but they are not done legally.'

The *abuses* of slavery are no less illegal; and let us confess, and acknowledge repentantly, how cruelly England, or rather English law, did first neglect, and then persecute children, human beings born, and perhaps nurtured in crime, through the indolence and negligence of society. Then, because of the very weakness and ignorance thus induced and fastened upon these helpless ones, have they not been incarcerated in prisons? denied those very occupations and exercises positively necessary for the moral, intellectual, and physical improvement of growing creatures? and when at last the consequences of such treatment became evidenced by an increase of vicious propensities, the poor outcasts, if not legally murdered according to ancient law, have at any rate been whipped and tormented until their hands were raised against every man, as those of every man have been against them!

Of late years the British people have opened their eyes, and they have been looking into, and endeavouring to remedy, such evils; and surely every nation has work enough to do at home; and if each will only put aside distant, and perhaps ignorant philanthropy, until they have done their own immediate business, the world will be in a fair way to be mended; and those crimes and sorrows which affect the white race quite as heavily and pitiably as Slave Institutions press upon the black, will rapidly become ameliorated and consoled.

In the meanwhile, if the observations in these letters jar against commonly-received and long-cherished opinions and principles, I am sorry to differ. Let it be remembered that every case has two sides. Hitherto, of Slavery one side only has been made prominent. It will be admitted by most intelligent thinkers, that open discussion is useful; and if I have drawn mistaken conclusions, they must ultimately rectify themselves. I am not conscious of being imbued with a spirit of partisanship; and I trust nothing I have said will arouse feelings of bitterness, or in any degree wound that kind spirit, through and by which alone this subject should be approached.

These letters were hastily written, sent off by post uncopied, and generally uncorrected. They ask for indulgence; but, as I have always believed that the fresh impressions of any commonly intelligent observer must have some degree of interest, so I make no further apology for this publication; and I shall only add one or two more suggestions with regard to Slavery. If that indigenous earth-nut, from which such a quantity of oil is, or can be, expressed, were to meet with sufficient encouragement upon the African coasts, and if the Blockading Squadron were exchanged for merchant-ships to carry away the produce, the traffic in slaves would gradually be given up for a more remunerative occupation, and it would be one which might absorb all the surplus black labor. Commercial remedies are the only certain and legitimate slavery preventives. By using them, we should save white lives as well as black lives, and white money as well as black interests; and if the slaveholders in the South American

States can be induced to co-operate with us in the Christianizing and civilizing of Africa by a law which may enable all those black slaves who, showing sufficient economy and forethought to save money for self-purchase, are willing to buy themselves, on condition of going to Africa, much good can be accomplished. It is my belief, you may as well attempt to improve the morals, and add to the happiness of idiots, by turning them out of asylums, as to imagine you can benefit the 'darkies' by abolitionism.

Yours affectionately,

A. M. M.

If any wishes should be expressed for the publication of a series of SKETCHES which would illustrate these volumes, Messrs. WILLIS of Henrietta Street, Covent Garden, have authority to receive applications concerning it.

December, 1855.

THE END.

www.ingramcontent.com/pod-product-compliance
Lightning Source LLC
LaVergne TN
LVHW020105110826
845151LV00001B/64

* 9 7 8 1 4 2 5 5 4 4 0 0 3 *